Banking on the Future

Banking on the Future

THE FALL AND RISE OF CENTRAL BANKING

Howard Davies

David Green

PRINCETON UNIVERSITY PRESS

PRINCETON AND OXFORD

Published by Princeton University Press,
41 William Street, Princeton, New Jersey 08540

In the United Kingdom: Princeton University Press,
6 Oxford Street, Woodstock, Oxfordshire OX20 1TW

Library of Congress Cataloging-in-Publication Data

Davies, H. (Howard), 1951–
    Banking on the future : the fall and rise of central banking /
    Howard Davies, David Green.
        p. cm.
    Includes bibliographical references and index.
    ISBN 978-0-691-13864-0 (alk. paper)
    1. Banks and banking, Central. 2. Monetary policy. I. Green,
    David, 1946– II. Title.
HG1811.D38 2010
332.1'1–dc22   2009053367

A catalogue record for this book is available from the British Library

This book has been composed in Lucida using TEX

Typeset and copyedited by T&T Productions Ltd, London

Printed on acid-free paper ∞

press.princeton.edu

Printed in the United States of America

10 9 8 7 6 5 4 3 2

Contents

Preface

We were prompted to write this book by the realization during the winter of 2007–8 that major shifts were suddenly afoot in the world of central banking. After an extended period in which central banks appeared to be capable of doing no wrong, the objectives, and even the roles, of central bankers were being abruptly questioned, as were the tools they had at their disposal and the way they used them. What really was the purpose of a central bank? Had central banks somehow lost their way and forgotten what they were there for? Were long-dormant functions being rediscovered? As we continued to write during 2008 and 2009, such questions became more and more acute.

This is not an academic textbook about the economics of monetary policy, nor is it a detailed historical account of the evolution of the role of the central bank. Still less is it a technical guide to the nuts and bolts of central bank operations and activities.

Rather, it seeks to set recent events in the context of the wider perspective—asking what central banks are for, why their role is critical to the functioning of market economies, how they can best go about fulfilling that role, and whether recent experience and historic perspective point to the need for further reappraisal and reform. We particularly look at the wider political and institutional framework in which they operate.

In setting the wider scene in which the crisis unfolded, we became conscious that the recent and unprecedented wholesale disruption that struck the financial system was in fact foreseen, or at least foreshadowed, by some serious observers, both within central banks themselves and in academia. It is disappointing to note that much of this thinking, whether on asset price bubbles or the procyclicality of capital requirements under the second revision of the Basel capital accord, was largely ignored by practitioners at the time. We hope that this volume, which integrates a review of academic writing with the perspective of current central bankers, will help bridge that important gap.

We also draw on our own direct experiences, whether during the time when we were practicing central bankers ourselves or when we were working alongside the central bank in a separate financial regulatory organization. Inevitably, what we write is colored by that experience.

We would particularly like to thank our former central banking colleagues, Clive Briault, Alastair Clark, Andrew Crockett, Michael Foot, Charles Goodhart, Lionel Price, David Strachan, Philip Turner, Geoffrey Wood, and Paul Wright, each of whom reviewed earlier drafts in full or in part and frequently contributed fresh insights. Staff at the Bank for International Settlements were especially helpful and gave us access to their work. We are grateful to Rosa Lastra for a number of detailed suggestions as well as for the wealth of fundamental material to be found in her own writings. We are also indebted to the many central bank governors and other senior officials, past and present, to whom we talked as we assembled our own thoughts. They were generous with their time, even during what was a fraught period.

At the London School of Economics Nick Vivyan was an invaluable guide to the academic literature. Clare Taylor Gold, Rachel Gibson, Emily-Jane McDonald, and Sally Goiricelaya all worked hard to ensure that a final text saw the light of day. Richard Baggaley at Princeton University Press was encouraging throughout and we are grateful to Sam Clark of T&T Productions Ltd, our copy editor, who pressed us tirelessly to ensure that our sentences really worked and our references too. Susannah Haan also provided helpful comments.

Lastly, we need to note that the views expressed here are entirely our own and not those of any of the organizations with which we are or have been associated.

The final revisions to this manuscript were undertaken in August 2009 and the reader will need to bear this in mind in the ever-evolving world of central banking.

Abbreviations

AIG	American International Group
BCCI	Bank of Credit and Commerce International
BIS	Bank for International Settlements
CGFS	Committee on the Global Financial System
CHAPS	Clearing House Automated Payment System
CPI	Consumer Price Index
CPSS	Committee on Payment and Settlement Systems
CSRC	China Securities Regulatory Commission
DMO	Debt Management Office
ECB	European Central Bank
EMC	Emerging Market Country
EMU	Economic and Monetary Union
ERM	Exchange Rate Mechanism
ESCB	European System of Central Banks
ESRC	European Systemic Risk Council
EU	European Union
FOMC	Federal Open Market Committee
FSA	Financial Services Authority
FSB	Financial Stability Board
FSF	Financial Stability Forum
FSI	Financial Soundness Indicator
FSR	Financial Stability Review
IFI	International Financial Institution
IMF	International Monetary Fund
IOSCO	International Organization of Securities Commissions
IT	Inflation Targeting
Libor	London Interbank Offered Rate
LOLR	Lender of Last Resort
MENA	Middle East and North Africa
MOU	Memorandum of Understanding

MPC	Monetary Policy Committee
NCB	National Central Bank
NPLs	Nonperforming Loans
OECD	Organisation for Economic Co-operation and Development
PBOC	People's Bank of China
RBA	Reserve Bank of Australia
RBI	Reserve Bank of India
RPI	Retail Price Index
RPIX	Retail Price Inflation (excluding housing)
SDR	Special Drawing Right
SEC	Securities and Exchange Commission (U.S.)
SGP	Stability and Growth Pact (EU)
T2S	Target 2 Securities
UAE	United Arab Emirates
WTO	World Trade Organization

Banking on the Future

Introduction

The global credit crisis that began in the summer of 2007 threw a large rock into the calm waters of central banking. Though many commentators, and indeed some central bankers themselves, had for some time been drawing attention to the risks posed for financial stability by global imbalances, surging credit, and liquidity, and narrowing risk spreads, when the crisis hit in August 2007 the speed and severity came as a surprise, not least to central bankers.

The proximate causes of the crisis lay in securitizations based on the subprime mortgage market in the United States, but the first serious signs of a major liquidity problem in the banking system were observed in Europe. On 9 August BNP Paribas froze three funds it managed, blaming "a complete evaporation of liquidity in certain market segments of the U.S. securitisation market." On the same day the ECB launched emergency operations to boost liquidity and injected almost €100 billion into the market, in an attempt to bring down overnight lending rates. The operation was successful, up to a point, but did not prevent the subsequent collapse of IKB in Germany, the first of several European bank failures.

In London, the first major casualty was Northern Rock, a mortgage bank heavily reliant on short-term wholesale funding. The Bank of England initially declined to provide emergency liquidity support to facilitate the sale of the bank to another, larger institution. Lloyds TSB (as it then was) was reported to be ready to take on the bank on condition that the Bank guaranteed funding for a period. But the Bank did eventually provide upward of £30 billion in funding, the disclosure of which led to the first bank run in the United Kingdom for over 150 years and eventually, after an undignified attempt by the government to sell it to Richard Branson, the airline entrepreneur, to the nationalization of Northern Rock.

In the United States, the Federal Reserve cut rates sharply, expanded its own liquidity operations, and broadened the range of collateral it was prepared to accept. In spite of these efforts, by March of 2008 the Federal Reserve Bank of New York was obliged to engineer a rescue of Bear Stearns through a heavily discounted sale to J.P. Morgan, and furthermore to open the discount window to the investment banks, a move which it had long resisted.

Through the summer of 2008 more and more institutions came under pressure. In Benelux, Fortis failed. In the United Kingdom, Alliance & Leicester was rescued by Santander, while Bradford & Bingley was dismembered, leaving the government holding the mortgage book. In the United States, other banks emerged as needing public support, notably Washington Mutual, Wachovia, and Indymac. Then, in mid September, the crisis entered a new and more dramatic phase. The insurance group AIG was expensively rescued, but in the same week Lehman Brothers was allowed to go to the wall, precipitating generalized panic across global financial markets. The U.K. and U.S. governments, followed by others, took direct stakes in systemically significant institutions, including the major investment banks, which changed status to become bank holding companies with Federal Reserve support. By the spring of 2009 the British government owned majority stakes in both the Royal Bank of Scotland and a new entity created by the merger of Lloyds TSB and Halifax Bank of Scotland. Monetary policy was further relaxed over the winter of 2008–9, with interest rates approaching zero in many developed countries. Once zero, or close to it, had been reached, further reductions in the policy rate were no longer an option and central banks resorted to "quantitative" (or "credit") easing: buying commercial or government securities directly, increasing the supply of base money.

As the crisis rolled on, leaving wreckage in its wake in the financial markets and pushing Western economies into recession, questions were inevitably asked about who was responsible for the debacle. The major financial institutions themselves were, of course, the prime suspects. It was argued that their incentive structures had led them to take excessive risks, and that their boards and senior management did not understand the characteristics of the complex instruments to which they were increasingly exposed. The whole credit risk transfer business, ostensibly designed to allow risks to be held by those best able to bear them, appeared to have, instead, left risks with those least able to understand them. There seemed to have been a dislocation between the financial and the real economies, with the nominal values of the derivative instruments, in which the losses were concentrated, parting company from the value of the underlying assets. In these markets business had been increasingly concentrated on creating large risk exposures purely between financial firms, rather than between them and their customers. By 2007 the nominal value of the credit default swap market was over $40 trillion. It was argued that the "originate to distribute model" was fundamentally broken, and that hedge funds—always available to play the role of stage villain—had acted as destabilizing players. They were widely accused of engineering the collapse of Bear Stearns, for example.

Ratings agencies had connived in the fast expansion of the market, earning fees for rating each new securitization. Some ostensibly AAA-rated securities traded at a fraction of their face values. The credibility of the agencies was severely damaged, and many critics pointed to fundamental conflicts of interest at the heart of the agencies' business models. Monoline insurers, whose backing had allowed securitizations to achieve AAA status, collapsed into the arms of the public authorities.

Regulators were also seen as part of the problem: too slow-moving to understand what was happening on their watch and powerless, or even unwilling, to control it. Prudential regulators, whether in central banks or outside them, had overseen banking systems that were undercapitalized when the crisis struck. The capital requirements imposed on banks proved in many cases to be wholly inadequate to absorb the losses incurred, and perhaps, through magnifying procyclical effects, added fuel to the flames of the asset price bubble that preceded the crash. Backward-looking capital requirements tended to fall as asset prices rose. The absence of effective oversight of the creation of credit through the derivative markets was argued to be a further weakness. Regulatory arbitrage had created a shadow banking system, and a proliferation of off-balance-sheet "structured investment vehicles," which regulators had largely ignored. A comprehensive global overhaul of the practices and structures of financial regulation was launched, with parallel reviews in the United States, the EU, and many individual countries.

Politicians, too, were in the firing line, especially in the United States, where pressure on the government-sponsored enterprises Fannie Mae and Freddie Mac to support lending to poorer families was a powerful impulse behind the expansion of the subprime mortgage market. Even private citizens could not escape blame. The collapse of personal savings, especially in English-speaking countries (though the Spaniards have acquired honorary Anglo-Saxon status in this context), and the associated credit-fueled consumption and house price bubbles were factors underlying the boom and subsequent bust.

It was not long before the role of the central banks themselves began to be seriously questioned. How could they have allowed such huge financial imbalances to build up without reacting? Were they, too, asleep at the wheel? Or, as one central banker himself put it, how was it that the radar was not connected to the missile defenses? In retrospect it is easy to see that risk spreads had reached unsustainably low levels and that an explosion of liquidity and credit had fueled dramatic asset price appreciation, especially in the property markets. Consumption growth was further stimulated by the "release" of equity from property. Yet through this period central banks, and especially the Federal Reserve, had maintained low interest rates, focusing attention narrowly on the behavior of consumer prices.

Steve Roach, the former chief economist of Morgan Stanley, argued that the central banks themselves bore the prime responsibility for the crisis.[1] "Central banks," he said, "have failed to provide a stable underpinning to world financial markets and to an increasingly asset dependent global economy ... the current financial crisis is a wake up call for modern day central banking ... the art and science of central banking is in desperate need of a major overhaul—before it's too late." John Taylor,[2] author of a celebrated rule for monetary policy making, similarly placed most of the blame on monetary policymakers: "there is an interaction between the monetary excesses and the risk-taking excesses."

Less outspoken critics advanced similar arguments. Was there not a fundamental problem with the way central banks' objectives had been specified, with a narrow focus on consumer prices? Even if it may be unrealistic to expect central banks to prevent all financial bubbles and head off all prospective crises, they could nonetheless "lean against the wind" of emerging imbalances and bubbles. Economists at the Bank for International Settlements, the central banks' own central bank, had been arguing as much for some years. In an important paper published in January 2006, Bill White, then chief economist of the BIS, maintained that, while central banks had been successful in the recent past in delivering low variability of both consumer price inflation and output, numerous financial and other imbalances had emerged and, should these imbalances revert to the mean, there could in future be significant effects on output growth. He asked whether monetary and regulatory policies should give more attention to avoiding the emergence of imbalances in the first place. Others argued that the central banks had in fact been misled by low reported consumer price inflation, which had been artificially held down by the emergence of China and India on the global banking certainly became "interesting" again, in the sense of the over-worked Chinese curse. In late 2008 the Bank slashed rates by 100 basis points, then by another 150, in short order, which many saw as recognition that it had fallen behind the curve.

But, while it was accepted that some kind of overhaul of practice and procedure was required, there was no easy consensus on what such an overhaul might entail. Was there a need for more coordination of central bank policies with those of other authorities? Should central banks become less powerful and be made more subject to political control, or be given more tools to achieve financial stability? Had the trend of removing central banks from direct supervisory responsibilities gone too far? Should that trend, indeed, be reversed? Did the crisis reveal a need for different types of expertise within central banks—particularly more market-related skills?

In this book we explore these arguments and offer answers to these and other questions. We argue that a new approach to central banking is indeed required in response to the crisis, and sketch out what we see as its key features. In part, this involves central banks returning to their roots in financial markets: forward to the past, perhaps.

To answer the questions, we need, first, to explore the ways in which central banks have evolved in the last two decades, in both developed and developing economies. So we begin, in chapter 1, by reviewing the core functions of central banking, and the global landscape of central banks today.

In chapter 2 we describe the monetary policy challenge, and assess how central banks have performed in recent years, especially in the context of the credit crisis. Chapter 3 discusses the second main focus of activity, in relation to financial stability, including a discussion of the appropriate role for central banks in financial supervision.

Chapter 4 reviews the way central banks provide liquidity to the markets, which has changed radically in the credit crisis, their role as overseer of the payment system, and the part they play in government debt management.

In chapter 5 we explore two of the more controversial questions that have emerged as a result of the crisis: the extent to which central banks should take account of the risks posed by asset price bubbles in setting monetary policy, and the role they should play in determining capital ratios for commercial banks.

Chapter 6 examines the structure, status, governance, and accountability of the major central banks today.

Chapter 7 discusses the particular circumstances of the European Central Bank, and the further reforms needed to make the Eurosystem function effectively, while chapter 8 looks at the development of central banking in emerging markets, including the special case of Islamic finance.

Chapter 9 explores the efficiency of central banks and their cost-effectiveness, a sadly neglected area. Chapter 10 assesses the way central banks cooperate internationally, and the role of the Bank for International Settlements. Chapter 11 reviews the culture and "psyche" of central banks. What kinds of people run them? Has the "central banker as hero" model gone too far? Is there an ideal profile for a governor?

Finally, chapter 12 pulls together the recommendations we make in the earlier chapters and sets out an agenda for change.

What Is Central Banking and Why Is It Important?

Societies become so used to the availability of stable currency, the ability to make payments both domestically and internationally, and the existence of banks and other financial institutions through which to save and borrow that it is easy to forget that each of these is a purely social construct, fundamentally based on trust, albeit bolstered by legislation. Occasionally, unpleasant reminders resurface abruptly that the financial system is fundamentally fragile. It is rare, fortunately, that currencies lose their value so fast that they cease to function—something that we have recently seen in Zimbabwe and that happened in Germany in the 1930s—or that other payment mechanisms break down so that goods and services can only be traded through barter. That tends to happen only in wartime, as in Afghanistan in the recent past or, briefly, when Iraq invaded Kuwait in 1991 and no one knew who controlled the Kuwaiti central bank.

It is more common for individual banks or other financial firms to fail. Banking is itself a fragile business because a bank depends on the confidence of its depositors that it will be able to repay their deposits whenever they want them, even though it has lent them out at longer terms to borrowers. The maturity transformation that banks carry out is in that sense a confidence trick.

All developed economic activity is dependent on this fragile financial infrastructure, which requires its numerous constituent players to play their parts as expected: the provider of currency must avoid issuing it at such a pace that it is devalued; those making payments must deliver them to the intended recipient; savings should be made available to sustain investment and loans provided to sustain business activity, house purchase, or consumer spending.

Society looks to central banks to try to prevent these inherent fragilities crystallizing or, if they do, to mitigate their repercussions. The instruments at their disposal are quite limited and, in a sense, not very sophisticated. Their main tool is their own balance sheet, as it is by acquiring and selling assets and liabilities, borrowing and lending, that they can seek to influence prices and interest rates in other markets. The effectiveness of these actions is far from guaranteed—indeed the central bank's own balance sheet may well be constrained—and is dependent on the wider economic climate in which they are operating. So the use of the balance sheet has to be supplemented by suasion or guidance to the markets and to economic agents generally. Indeed it may be as much through persuasion as through economic action that a central bank achieves its aims. The combination of the two determines whether what the central bank does makes any difference at all, given that its armory of tools is essentially very limited. Changes in its balance sheet may be backed up by an array of other controls, for which it may be responsible, on the behavior of economic agents. These may be capital or exchange controls, or controls on bank behavior, such as quantitative or price controls. But in open markets such controls are of limited value in the long term.

Because the economic environment changes constantly, the way the tools are used evolves. Political priorities change over time, sometimes quite markedly and rapidly, with switches, even within a single country, from ensuring credit is available to favored economic sectors to restraining inflation, and then, perhaps, to maintaining a particular exchange rate.

Almost all countries now boast an institution called a central bank. Central banking was not always so widespread, nor were its advantages so widely acknowledged. In the United States, there were two unsuccessful attempts to establish a "central" bank, in both cases called the Bank of the United States, before the Federal Reserve System was set up in 1913. There was a strong strand of thinking in the United States at the time in favor of "free banking," and a fully competitive banking system, without the intermediation of a state-owned or state-backed institution at its center. Indeed, arguments about the merits of free banking still rumble on in some academic and political circles.[1]

Advocates of free banking argue that private monetary systems have in the past been stable and successful, and that a competitive banking system is less susceptible to bank runs, while the existence of central banks has allowed political interference in the banking system, which has had the effect of altering incentive structures and which has created instability. These arguments have not, however, persuaded many governments. The balance of evidence appears to show that free banking leads, instead, to systemic instability.[2] So while arguments continue about the sources of financial instability and, while even before the financial melt-down of 2007–9, the incidence of banking crises remained surprisingly high,[3] both the academic and the political debates now focus more on the appropriate functions and responsibilities of the central bank rather than on whether it should exist at all.

But what exactly do we mean by a central bank? The answer is not straightforward. Indeed the definition of the functions that are appro-priate for a central bank has changed considerably through time. As the BIS Central Bank Governance Group points out, in the past central banks "have been understood more in terms of their functions than their objectives."[4]

Historians of monetary institutions tend to date the introduction of central banking to the foundation of the Swedish Riksbank in 1668 or to the foundation of the Bank of England in 1694. But, as Capie et al. point out, at that time there was no developed concept of central banking. The Bank of England was founded as a private bank to finance a war. Not until Henry Thornton wrote his *An Enquiry into the Nature and Effects of Paper Credit in the United Kingdom* in 1802[5] was any theory of cen-tral banking as we would recognize it today articulated. Others argue that the modern-day notion of central banking should be dated from the 1844 Act, which effectively gave the Bank of England a monopoly on the issue of banknotes, or even from 1870 when the Bank first accepted the function of lender of last resort. The other main European central banks took on these responsibilities in the last decades of the nineteenth cen-tury. Nevertheless, Thornton's enquiry into "paper credit" points to the fact that central banks are seen to address the fundamental problem that financial intermediation is based purely on trust documented in paper or, now, in electronic form. If that trust breaks down, payments cannot be made and savings become worthless. Recent events have provided a very sharp reminder of that risk.

Many central banks, especially the oldest of them, began as private-sector companies; others started as public-sector agencies.[6] The Bank of England is in the former group; the Federal Reserve Board and the European Central Bank are in the latter. The great majority are now state owned, though partial private ownership persists in a few cases. In principle, one can imagine an argument in favor of some private own-ership, especially as a stimulus to efficiency, which, as we shall see, is a neglected area. But as the allocation of profits is typically specified in advance, even in partly private institutions, the case is weaker. Central banks are clearly carrying out public objectives, in whole or in greater part, so the case for state ownership is strong. Almost all of the 162 central banks now in existence are state owned. Private-ownership stakes, where they persist, seem more an accident of history than a deliberate policy objective. (In the United States a mixed model is in operation. The Federal Reserve Board in Washington is state owned, while the regional Federal Reserve Banks are statutory bodies that combine public and private elements, and which have boards selected largely from financial and commercial firms in the district.) Private shareholding can entail risks, too. "Rogue" shareholders may challenge a central bank's actions, as has happened in Belgium. Where the shares are quoted there can be inconsistency between stock exchange reporting requirements and policy-driven restrictions on disclosure. There is no strong case, therefore, for retaining private ownership, and a clear trend toward nationalization. Even governments with a strong ideological commitment to privatization have not carried that enthusiasm into central banking. In some cases, though, functions have been contracted out, or sold. The Bank of England, for example, sold off its note-printing works a few years ago.

In terms of their formal responsibilities we can identify a gradual expansion of the range of functions undertaken by central banks up to the 1980s, and then something of an ebb in the last twenty-five years in terms of the breadth of responsibilities, but certainly not in terms of their overall status and influence. The latter part of the twentieth century was a golden age for central banks. While after the foundation of the Swedish and English central banks at the end of the seventeenth century there was a gap of more than 100 years before France established the third central bank, 118 new institutions were established between 1950 and 2000. Every country with a seat at the United Nations wanted its own central bank, and even some jurisdictions that might not normally be regarded as independent countries, like San Marino, set one up. As we shall see, these institutions gradually became more "independent," though independence carries a multitude of meanings in this context. The growing complexity and diversity of the financial sector in most parts of the world, and the rapid increase in government borrowing and in capital movements, gave central banks more and more to do, whether in the form of overseeing payment systems, undertaking basic banking transactions for the government, handling foreign exchange flows, sometimes managing government borrowing, or supervising banks and other financial institutions.

A significant boost to the number of central banks was given by the collapse of the Soviet Union. Each former Soviet state established its own financial system and concluded that a central bank was required to watch over it. Elsewhere, in the Balkans particularly, other new countries have been created. The most recent additions to the central banking ranks have been in East Timor and Kosovo. But it seems probable that the absolute number of central banks has now peaked, and there have been one or two amalgamations in recent years. In some cases a number of countries that share a currency make do with one central bank, as in the East Caribbean or former French West Africa.

And as the number of institutions grew, so did the number of people employed in them. By the end of the last century—if one includes the People's Bank of China, before it was broken up into its component parts—there were almost 600,000 central bankers in captivity. That number has now fallen back to under 350,000, and the trend is now clearly downward, though by no means everywhere. While there are powerful pressures for staff reductions in, for example, national central banks in the European System of Central Banks, there are other places where staff numbers are growing. The People's Bank, in its reduced form, is expanding again, as are some central banks in more unexpected places like Zimbabwe. But in most OECD countries numbers are falling, though by no means as rapidly as they could be, as we will explain when we examine central banks' commitment to efficiency and productivity, which is not as marked as it should be. We will argue that this is partly because of the absence of competitive forces bearing down on the central banking function. It may also be born of uncertainty about just how much "central banking" is enough.

As we shall show, there is a remarkable range of central bank sizes in relation to the populations they serve. Only part of this remarkable difference can be explained by economies of scale or by different combinations of function.

All central banks, when asked what their responsibilities are, say that they are responsible for monetary policy, although a few acknowledge that they operate in partnership with the government, or that they advise government ministers on interest rates. But in fact there is a great diversity of practice in terms of who makes interest rate decisions. In many cases, especially in emerging markets, it is clear that governments are closely involved, whether through direct participation in interest rate decision-making bodies within the central bank itself, through the exercise of some veto authority, or by marking the governor's card in private. Of course, where the anti-inflation anchor is essentially provided by an exchange rate target, the central bank's discretion in monetary policy,

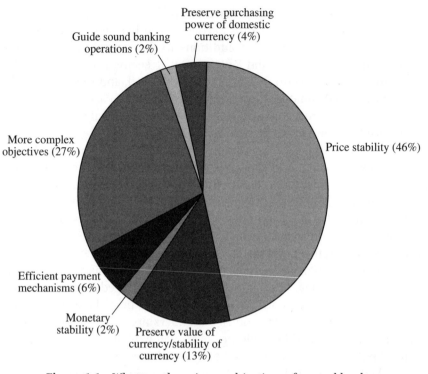

Figure 1.1. What are the primary objectives of central banks.
Source: Swedish Riksbank.

whether setting interest rates or determining the growth of money, is heavily constrained.

In a study of forty-seven central banks, carried out in 2006, researchers from the Swedish Riksbank asked the banks themselves how they perceived their objectives.[7] Around half responded that price stability was their primary objective, but the rest chose a different aim, or combination of aims (figure 1.1). The study also asked banks to set out what, apart from monetary policy, they saw as their objectives. Roughly half considered that they were pursuing aims in relation to the financial system and financial stability. A smaller proportion cited more general economic objectives, in relation to employment or economic activity more generally. The distinction between those banks with a "dual mandate" along Federal Reserve lines, charged with controlling inflation and promoting economic activity, and those with a narrower inflation target type regime seems clear from the analysis, though the implications for the interest rate policy decisions may not be as stark as the data suggest here.

When asked to describe the exchange rate policies within which they operate, central banks give a range of answers. If we exclude the members of the euro area, and the handful of countries (such as Ecuador, El Salvador, and Montenegro) that do not have a domestic currency of their own and which use the dollar or the euro, roughly 40% describe themselves as operating a floating rate regime. In some cases it would be wrong to describe these as "free floats," and the governments undoubtedly intervene, whether directly in foreign exchange markets or in domestic interbank markets, in order to smooth market movements and reduce volatility. These regimes are often described as "dirty floats." So the borderline between floating and managed exchange rates is not as rigid as these distinctions might imply. But twenty-four countries claim that they are managing a floating exchange rate, while sixty-eight say that their rates are pegged, whether to the dollar or the euro or to some basket of currencies reflecting their trade flows. The contents of those baskets may be disclosed or left deliberately opaque, as in the case of Singapore. It is perhaps surprising that almost exactly the same number of countries now claim to be pegged to the euro as claim to be pegged to the dollar. Eight of these countries are members of the West African franc zone, however, which perhaps exaggerates the euro's impact on other exchange rate regimes.

Since the establishment of the European single currency in 1999 a growing number of other countries, whether on the edges of Europe or outside it, have chosen to use the euro as their nominal anchor. The financial crisis has increased the attractiveness of the euro as a stable store of value. The other pegged currencies are mainly linked to the rand in Southern Africa, which exerts a similar gravitational pull on members of the Southern African Development Community. A subset of member countries takes part in a formalized Common Monetary Area.

Another area in which there is considerable diversity of practice is in relation to the central bank's involvement in financial regulation. We shall discuss the pros and cons of such involvement later (in chapter 4). Around 120 central banks have some direct involvement in hands-on supervision, always of banks, and sometimes of other financial institutions as well, though in a few, mainly small countries, they are the regulators of the financial sector as a whole. In around sixty countries the central bank is not directly involved (figure 1.2). (These numbers are somewhat larger than the number of central banks, as they are disaggregated by country, where the supervision arrangements are invariably national, while those for monetary policy are sometimes

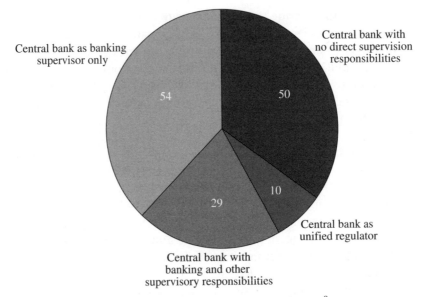

Central bank as banking
supervisor only

Central bank with
no direct supervision
responsibilities

54

50

10

29

Central bank as
unified regulator

Central bank with
banking and other
supervisory responsibilities

Figure 1.2. Central banks in regulation.[8]

pooled between several countries.) But in population terms the ratio is rather different, since banking supervision in China is not carried out by the central bank. A rough breakdown by population suggests that in around 60% of the world central banks supervise banks, while in 40% they do not. In the years leading up to the recent crisis there was a general trend away from central bank involvement in supervision, and in a number of countries, the responsibility was transferred. But it is unlikely that a global consensus on this point will be achieved in the foreseeable future. Indeed the financial crisis has caused a rethink of the optimal role for a central bank in financial stability, and the extent to which that role requires direct involvement in the regulation of individual banks.

There is also little sign of a consensus being reached on the appropriate role for the central bank in consumer protection. When he was governor of the Bank of England, Eddie George liked to say that consumer protection was "not the natural habitat" of the central banker. The ECB has no consumer protection function. Yet at least half of all central banks do play some role in this area. In the United States, the Federal Reserve has been responsible for implementing federal laws on consumer credit. Its performance in that area in the run-up to the crisis has been heavily criticized, and President Obama's reforms envisage a new consumer financial protection regulator to carry out those responsibilities, and more. In

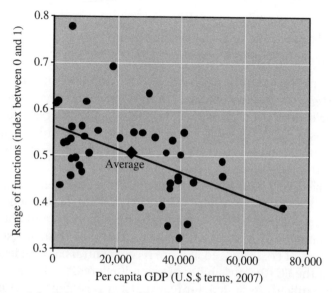

Figure 1.3. Range of central bank functions and per capita GDP.[4]

the United Kingdom, the Conservatives have also proposed a separate consumer protection agency.

In broad terms there is a relationship between the degree of economic development of a country and the range of functions carried out by its central bank (figure 1.3). The BIS plot a relationship between per capita GDP and breadth of functions, drawing on a survey of forty-seven institutions.[4] They posit three main reasons for this relationship:

- In developing countries the central bank may be one of a limited number of sources of financial expertise.
- In those countries the central bank is often used to promote financial-sector development.
- Industrialized countries tend to narrow the range of functions and sharpen the focus of accountability.

So what are the minimum functions of a central bank today, to make it worthy of the name? In 1983 an IMF paper offered what would at the time have appeared to be an uncontroversial list of the functions of a central bank, categorizing them in five areas:[9]

- currency issue and foreign exchange reserve management;
- banker to the government;

17

- banker to commercial banks;
- regulation of the financial system; and
- monetary and credit policy.

Much of this list would now be open to question. Central banks often issue currency in their own name, but by no means everywhere. In some places the central bank manages foreign exchange reserves exclusively, in other cases not at all, while sometimes it manages only a part of the government's foreign exchange portfolio. Where capital controls remain, they are often administered by the central bank.

As for the role of banker to government, while most central banks provide some transactional services to their government, consensus opinion in the recent past has been that the central bank should not manage the government's debt, or be able to lend to the government, except perhaps at times of crisis. Indeed in more recent central banking legislation, notably in the EU, the possibility of extending credit to the government is usually explicitly excluded, for fear that a government under pressure would resort to the printing press. But in 2009 monetizing government debt, once interest rates had descended to zero, became a live policy option once again. The printing presses whirred into action on both sides of the Atlantic.

The central bank does normally act as a banker to the commercial banks, providing payment and settlement services, though the way this is done varies greatly from country to country, and in some cases the central bank's own operational role is modest.

The same is true of financial regulation. Banking supervision began as the credit assessment of the central bank's counterparties, but, as we have seen, it is no longer regarded as axiomatic that the central bank should be the bank supervisor. It may be that in some places, notably the United Kingdom, too rigorous a separation of the central bank from regulation was engineered, to the point where the Bank of England appeared, in 2007, to have lost interest in the financial system, even though it remained the Lender of Last Resort. And in the euro area the central provision of liquidity through the ECB, with solvency support provided by national governments, often working through the national central banks (NCBs), began to look to be an unstable division of responsibilities. We shall have more to say on these points later.

Monetary policy, on the other hand, does typically remain a core central bank function—and one that the bank carries out independently nowadays, rather than as an agent for the ministry of finance, though the setting of objectives, as distinct from the execution of monetary policy, may remain with government. But the traditional credit policy function, whereby quantitative controls on lending were administered by the central bank, has now fallen away in most developed countries. Indeed it may be argued that central banks have paid far too little attention to the growth of credit in recent years. That is an argument we shall cover in much more depth below, where we note the sudden resurgence of interest in the volume and distribution of bank lending.

Rosa Lastra[10] gives a fuller account of what she identifies as nine separate functions and elaborates on their changing nature and importance. The BIS[4] has published a comprehensive taxonomy of no less than twenty separate functions for central banks. It demonstrates the remarkable diversity of practice that obtains between institutions that might appear to be superficially similar in structure and objective.

One convenient formulation of the overall objective of central banking, which cuts through some of the complexity, is provided by Gerry Corrigan, a former president of the New York Federal Reserve Bank:[11]

> The single theme of a contemporary central bank's functions is to provide stability—stability in the purchasing power of the currency of the country and stability in the workings of the financial system of the country, including the payments system.

But Corrigan's objective, which would be widely acknowledged, does not explain what practical responsibilities the central bank needs to exercise in order to provide that stability, which has been spectacularly lacking in the last two years.

In our view the irreducible functions of a central bank, without which the title is not meaningful, are as follows.

- They must have the capacity to supply ultimate settlement assets for the financial system.
- They must have the ability to act as banker to key agents in financial intermediation. Those agents may not exclusively be banks. At times, this banking function may be extensive, involving the provision of liquidity on an enormous scale, and a range of guarantees to different types of financial intermediary.
- They must perform as the institution that implements monetary policy, whether by setting the price of money (through the short-term interest rate) or its quantity (through the supply of reserve assets to the financial system).

There are other responsibilities that it may or may not make sense to add to this irreducible list, depending on the circumstances. The arguments for and against adding these responsibilities should be considered carefully. Many countries now believe that in addition to implementing monetary policy, it is preferable for an independent central bank to determine that policy as well, but there is great debate about what policy determination means in this context, and what independence means. Should the central bank itself define price stability, or is it better that an objective is set by the government and implemented by the central bank? If the bank is independent for monetary policy purposes, should it nonetheless be obliged to exercise that independence with an eye to the overall economic policies of the government? Is there sometimes a case, in an economic crisis, for suspending the prime inflation target in the interests of a looser monetary policy to sustain growth or, more narrowly, to promote the smooth functioning of the financial system? Should the target be undershot if credit is growing too rapidly? We consider these issues further in chapter 3.

It may also be appropriate for the central bank to be the lender of last resort to banks in difficulty, but it is not wholly obvious that that function should be carried out by the central bank rather than by the government itself, though the lender of last resort function must be able to be carried out by an institution that can lend massively and immediately. Conventionally, the lender of last resort role has involved providing liquidity support only against high-quality collateral. In 2008 it became clear in a number of countries that the central bank's liquidity backing was not enough to stabilize threatened institutions whose solvency was in question, and that direct government investment was required. Iceland was a case in point. Furthermore, central banks' balance sheets may not even be big enough to provide liquidity support on the scale required. In principle, the balance sheet can be expanded without limit, but in effect the constraint is the perceived taxing capacity of the government that stands behind the bank, in relation to the financial risk it is assuming.

The BIS Central Bank Governance Group has proposed a framework to assist in analyzing which functions are what they dub "good or bad bedfellows." The screening mechanism to help decide whether functions fit well together involves three considerations:[4]

- "Whether the objectives are compatible (or at least whether any incompatibilities are predictable and controllable)."

- "Whether a single governance structure is suitable for the efficient discharge of all functions."
- "Whether the skill sets and technology required for each function are similar."

These considerations link in turn to the issue of the location of the responsibility for banking supervision. Should the central bank be a hands-on banking supervisor, because of the linkages between the banking system and the transmission mechanism for monetary policy on the one hand and financial stability on the other? Or are there circumstances in which that responsibility may conflict with the monetary policy role? If the responsibility for supervision is located in another institution, should that agency also then be the lender of last resort? Some argue that collocation of both those functions outside the central bank would make sense.[12] Since solvency support must effectively be provided by the government, it is possible to imagine that a supervisor who is separate from the central bank might have access to a finance ministry overdraft to allow it to provide support, though this would further complicate the monetary policy task.

The nature of the central bank role in financial stability is also open to question. If the bank essentially has one tool, the short-term interest rate, can it sensibly be given two potentially conflicting objectives, in the form of price stability on the one hand and financial stability on the other? That conundrum has come to the fore in the last year as central banks have grappled with the credit crisis. Some argue that only if the bank has access to another mechanism, perhaps the ability to vary bank capital ratios for macroeconomic reasons, does this financial stability role make sense. We examine this argument later on.

So, amid all these uncertainties, the definition of central banking is once again in flux. Before 2007 it was arguable that a consensus was developing in favor of a narrow model of central banking: the central bank as monetary policy institute, with a tightly circumscribed range of responsibilities centering on an inflation target, and limited direct involvement in the financial system. That was true in the United Kingdom, certainly. But this "end of history" proved to be a false sunset. Many previously closed issues have been reopened by the financial crisis. It is highly likely that there will be significant changes in the definition in the next few years. We make a series of suggestions for change in this book.

Has the reputation of central banking been affected by the crisis for the long term? It is too early to say, but the historical record tends to suggest that central banks have the capacity to adapt. As Capie et al. point out:

> If the fundamental evolutionary criterion of success is that an organization should reproduce and multiply over the world, and successfully mutate to meet the emerging challenges of time, then central banks have been conspicuously successful.

But they will need to rediscover that evolutionary skill to remain relevant in the very different economic and financial world of the twenty-first century. We go on to consider the direction of change in which they will need to follow.

Monetary Stability

Central banks are active in three areas in which stability has been seen as a desirable goal of public policy. The three areas are interdependent, but they have sometimes been seen as separate in analytical terms, as well as distinct objectives of policy. They may or may not be primarily assigned to the central bank as its special responsibility. Sometimes other agencies in government are, nominally at least, entrusted with the lead role.

The three areas are:

- domestic price stability, or monetary stability;
- external stability, or exchange rate management; and
- stability in the financial system.

These days, few question the virtues of stability in these areas, though, as Rosa Lastra[1] points out, the "stability" concept is a modern phenomenon. When the Federal Reserve was founded in 1913 its role was "to furnish an elastic currency," seemingly a quite different concept, and the pursuit of "stable prices" was only added as a legal objective in the 1970s.

The distinctions above are, to a degree, artificial. This can readily be seen by considering the influence of the exchange rate on domestic prices, or the impact on the financial system of excessive expansion or contraction of credit. Nevertheless, they are often addressed as separate questions, which can sometimes have damaging consequences.

The pursuit of domestic price stability, or monetary stability, is usually the core field of activity for the central bank, even though it may not set the policy objectives. Monetary policy is now rarely entrusted to other agencies. However, external stability in the form of an exchange rate regime, even though it is intimately linked with monetary policy, is quite often the direct responsibility of government, although they may delegate operational decisions and actions to the central bank. Financial stability is a more elusive concept, to which we return later, but it is as often associated with the responsibilities of supervisory agencies as with those of central banks. Nevertheless, failure to achieve any one of the objectives may adversely affect the other two, and trade-offs between them are sometimes inevitable. Certainly, with only one main instrument, the short-term interest rate, a central bank can focus primarily on either domestic stability or the external stability of the currency, but not on both simultaneously. Whether this single tool can or should be used for the purpose of influencing both domestic price stability and financial stability is a more disputed question, as we shall see, but it certainly has an impact on both.

Here we sketch out the historical background to the central bank response to the crisis. The latter precipitated a major rethink of the techniques through which monetary policy is given effect, and whose consequences are likely to be far-reaching. The background is of interest, as a number of the techniques and approaches now being revisited are close cousins of those which have been used in the past and, for a variety of reasons, set aside. What follows should be seen as a rough guide to the main strands of thinking about monetary policy implementation, which have waxed and waned remarkably in recent decades.

DOMESTIC PRICE STABILITY

It is not entirely clear when central banks first consciously started to conduct what is now called "monetary policy," in the sense of taking deliberate action to use their balance sheets to achieve some wider economic purpose, often through setting the short-term interest rate. With the development of markets in government debt and in private debt it became possible to start constructing an interest rate policy through the central bank making loans and taking deposits, or buying and selling securities, with the deliberate aim of influencing interest rates rather than focusing on the value of local currency vis-à-vis foreign currency or gold. As Tucker[2] puts it, "Everything—and I mean everything—about central banking stems from our liabilities being the base money of the economy."

As a general rule, the central bank can only target the price of money, and hence of financial intermediation generally, or its quantity, but not both, except when markets are not free and either prices or quantities are fixed through administered interest rate ceilings or quantitative lending limits. However, it may also use its balance sheet to influence developments in particular markets, at least in the short term.

The aim of targeting either the price or quantity of financial intermediation is to influence the performance of the economy as a whole. Clearly, activity is immensely varied in its components and the same is true of prices, whether of goods, services, or assets. This leaves open a very wide choice of potential objectives, few of which could be expected to be met simultaneously and all of which are subject to influence, and perhaps determination, by forces largely or, even, wholly outside the control of the central bank. Central banks can rough-tune, but not fine-tune, though that is not always the impression they give.

At the same time, despite these huge uncertainties, the cost and availability of finance exercises an all-pervasive influence over economic activity. As a result, much effort has been devoted over time to determining just what the relationship is between money and interest rates, prices and activity. These relationships are inherently unstable, because of changes in domestic economic potential, changes in the behavior of economic agents, and changes in the fiscal structure and in the structure of the financial markets through which monetary policy is transmitted. Central banks are engaged in a constant search to find those relationships that are relatively stable and that provide some reasonable expectation that policy action will produce the desired result.

Over time central banks have changed their minds about the channels through which monetary policy works, sometimes quite radically, and been given changed mandates by others, both as to the objectives (the target variable) and the means to achieve them (the instrument variable). The policy emphasis has sometimes been on final economic objectives such as prices or growth, while at others it has been on intermediate financial targets such as particular interest rates, the growth of financial aggregates, or the level of the exchange rate.

These priorities or targets have changed over time, sometimes because of new analytical insights, whether about the behavior of the economy or the behavior of the financial system, and sometimes because of new political priorities. The absence of empirical certainty of relationships over any extended period means that the conduct of monetary policy can only be the continual exercise of judgment. It is inevitably based on incomplete and imperfect information and can never be an exact science. At the same time, because the cost and availability of finance is so intrinsic to the workings of the economy, and because the exercise of that judgment can have powerful effects on all economic agents, the selection of those who exercise it and their accountability has always been of intense political interest.

25

As a result of the inherent uncertainties about the relationship between the economy and finance, central banks have at different times focused on many different variables: interest rates, with or without ceilings; exchange rates, fixed, floating, and adjustable; growth in commercial bank assets; credit to particular sectors; overall domestic credit expansion; central bank liabilities or the monetary base; commercial bank liabilities; liabilities to particular sectors; various measures of the money supply, defined as liabilities of various different groups of institutions; net sales of government debt; inflation or inflation expectations; and so on. Very often the choice of focus follows from the particular theory of economic behavior that for a period appears most convincing.

To understand developments in the recent past, and current conditions, some history is necessary, not least to illustrate how significant the shifts in view have been over time, both in terms of what monetary policy might be expected to deliver and in terms of the precise tools to be deployed to meet those ends. These views have inevitably been formed as part of wider debates about how the economy works.

For centuries the main decisions that had to be taken about money were about the issue of coinage and paper money by government and about the price of the local currency in relation to foreign currencies or to gold. In their useful review of the development of central banking from the late eighteenth century to the present day, Capie et al.[3] identify 1873 as "the beginning of the period when the gold standard formally became established as the main exchange rate regime for much of the industrial world." Although in war time priority was given to financing the belligerents' deficits, with inflationary consequences, there was a return to the gold standard in the postwar period until both the United Kingdom and the Unites States were forced off it in the depression of the 1930s. After World War II governments were determined not to see a return to the high unemployment of the interwar years. Monetary management became a subsidiary part of overall demand management, the objectives of central banks were extended to include high levels of employment and growth, and, as Capie et al. neatly put it, the "central bank became a junior branch of the Treasury." Anti-inflation policy tended to center on the imposition of credit controls. While almost all credit creation took place through the banking system, controls on bank lending were reasonably effective.

During the 1950s the weaknesses of direct controls on credit began to be better understood. Changes in the structure of intermediation made credit controls decreasingly effective. Increasing international competition in the provision of credit, made easier by improvements in information technology, made domestic credit control difficult, especially if capital flows were not constrained. The development of the euromarkets, especially the Eurodollar market, in the 1960s showed how a parallel credit market could grow quickly outside a currency's home jurisdiction.

By the middle of the twentieth century two broad schools of thought had developed, each of which saw a quite different role for monetary policy or perhaps no role at all. Much of this period was spent in experimenting with these approaches until, in due course, it became clear that neither of them was thought to provide a clear answer. The terms used to describe the two broad approaches are Keynesianism and monetarism. Both terms are loosely used to cover a wide range of variants, and it is not our purpose to discuss these variants in detail since policy has not typically been debated in these terms—though Keynesianism has staged something of a recovery recently. However, it is important to reiterate that monetary policy, like so much else, is prone to wide swings in fashion.

Blinder[4] provides an accessible description of the main streams of Keynesian thinking. A Keynesian believes that aggregate demand is influenced by a host of economic decisions—both public and private—and sometimes behaves erratically. The public decisions include, most prominently, those on monetary and fiscal policy, i.e., government spending and taxation. According to Keynesian theory, changes in aggregate demand, whether anticipated or unanticipated, have a greater short-term impact on real output and employment than they do on prices. Monetary policy moves that people expect in advance can produce real effects on output and employment only if some prices are rigid. But because prices *are* in fact somewhat rigid, fluctuation in any component of spending—consumption, investment, or government expenditure—causes output to fluctuate. If government spending increases, for example, and all other components of spending remain constant, then output will increase. Keynesians believe that prices and, especially, wages respond slowly to changes in supply and demand, resulting in shortages and surpluses, especially of labor. So activist stabilization policies are advocated to reduce the amplitude of the business cycle.

This analysis led to attempts to fine-tune output growth by, say, adjusting government spending, taxes, and the money supply, although it was recognized that there were serious obstacles to success because of the lags between the taking of action and the action having an effect.

27

Despite these difficulties the underlying policy proposition was that the government was both knowledgeable and capable enough to improve on the unfettered operation of the free market against a background belief that unemployment was ultimately a more important problem than inflation. With sufficiently elaborate forecasting machinery, the mix of policies best suited to the circumstances could be selected.

By contrast, monetarists, as a generality, do not see such scope for fine-tuning, which produces variability and uncertainty, and believe inflation to be a greater concern. Monetarism focuses on the supply of money in an economy as the primary means by which the rate of inflation is determined. As Milton Friedman and Anna Schwartz[5] put it, "inflation is always and everywhere a monetary phenomenon." The proposition, usefully summarized by Meltzer[6], is that sustained monetary growth in excess of the growth of output produces inflation; to end inflation or produce deflation, money growth must fall below the growth of output. These effects are linked to the exchange rate. Given certain assumptions, when inflation is expected to be high, interest rates on the open market are high and the foreign exchange value of a currency falls relative to more stable currencies. Sustained inflation induces depreciation, and disinflation will tend to deliver currency appreciation.

The first effects of changes in monetary growth are on output; later the rate of inflation changes. The intuitive attraction of the proposition that inflation is a monetary phenomenon, backed up by some empirical evidence, led to the adoption by a number of governments of money supply targets, rather than interest rate targets, as the focus of policy. This was despite the difficulty of being sure which of several possible measures of money supply needed to be targeted to bring about the desired objective and of having to deal with substantial shifts in the demand for money. Nevertheless, the worldwide surge in inflation from the late 1960s onward meant that solutions were eagerly sought. The benefits of obtaining a strong anchor for policy in the form of stabilizing the growth of the money supply came to achieve widespread acceptance.[7] In the United Kingdom, for instance, in the early 1980s the Thatcher government required the Bank of England to attempt to control the money supply on a monthly basis by buying or selling government debt to offset any potential deviation from target predicted by an elaborate forecast of the flows in demand for money. (The authors were on opposite sides of this uncomfortable, and ultimately fruitless, endeavor: Davies in the Treasury, Green in the Bank of England.) In the end, short-term monetarist forecasts went awry and confidence in the approach was seriously damaged. Repeated changes in the different technical measures of the financial aggregates being targeted, with names such as £M3, M0, and PSL2, to mention but a few, did not help. Sticking to a firm target for money supply also meant losing control of the exchange rate. The consequence was a switch to targeting the exchange rate in the late 1980s, when the chancellor, Nigel Lawson, adopted a policy of "shadowing" the deutsche mark, with ultimately disastrous results.

Increasing uncertainty about whether the targeting of monetary aggregates was the best way to manage monetary policy, as well as concern about the increasing volatility of exchange rates, which was implicitly the result of individual countries targeting monetary aggregates, led to a number of moves toward finding a different anchor for policy.

In Europe governments favored increasingly robust efforts to peg exchange rates between countries, eventually through the exchange rate mechanism (ERM). An attempt by the United Kingdom to hold position in the ERM led to a humiliating ejection in September 1992 (see chapter 7 on Europe). Elsewhere it led to increasing attention on focusing on a final target: inflation itself. This was regardless of the consequences for the exchange rate, and even though very different views were held as to the precise route through which use of the central bank balance sheet ultimately affects the prices of a chosen target basket of goods and services.

Charles Goodhart[8] provides a clear account of the main theories that have underpinned policy, albeit with alarming, but entirely justified, emphasis on the uncertainty surrounding most of the factors considered. He notes that, following the debates that have taken place, between different categories of Keynesian and monetarist economists, there had until very recently been a (historically unusual) degree of agreement about the basic mechanism through which monetary policy had had an effect on the economy more widely. He describes this consensus as follows:

> Because of frictions preventing full, immediate and perfect adjustment of wages and prices to changing economic conditions, wages and prices are sticky. These frictions remain imperfectly understood, but probably result from various forms of transactions and information costs. Anyhow, their existence means that (unexpected) changes in real interest rates have an effect, after some delay (whose length depends on planning, ordering, executing and payment lags), on real expenditures and real output. Thus, the first of the equations in the small consensus model is an IS [investment and savings equilibrium] curve relating current real expenditures to real monetary and other shocks. In practice, in

forecasting models used by central banks this single equation usually becomes disaggregated into multiple equations by type of expenditure. The second main equation in the consensus model is a supply-side, or modified Phillips curve, equation. This relates deviations in inflation, from its previously expected path, to deviations in output from its natural, or equilibrium, level. Thus if output rises above (falls below) its natural level, inflation accelerates (declines). Unlike the IS curve, whose empirical properties have generally proven relatively successful, the supply side curve has been empirically troublesome....

The third equation is a reaction function, whereby the central bank adjusts interest rates in response to deviations of inflation from target and of output from its equilibrium rate.

Goodhart goes on to explain, however, that few of these concepts are straightforward. There are measurement difficulties in estimating real output, so that whether the final published figure is "correct" is uncertain. More seriously, the time path of "natural," or "equilibrium" or "sustainable," output seems to vary in and between countries over time for reasons that are difficult to explain. Much research effort is devoted to trying to measure and understand these changes and to determining how policy might best take account of them.

Another prominent aspect of recent macroeconomic theory has been the emphasis on the importance for the behavior of economic agents of forward-looking, or "rational," expectations, rather than backward-looking expectations. Although the empirical evidence suggests that most people nevertheless tend to extrapolate past experience into future forecasts, it has become widely accepted that a key role for central banks, besides varying the short-term policy rate, is to influence expectations, notably of future price inflation and also of the future path of official policy rates. If inflation expectations can be anchored at a low and stable level, despite disturbances from, say, oil or food price shocks, a change in nominal interest rates will have a more predictable, and perhaps generally larger, effect on real interest rates than it would otherwise. This implies that central banks must not simply take action from time to time but should also indicate their own views about the future path of their own risks by using a wide variety of tools, such as providing forecasts of various kinds, publishing minutes setting out arguments that look forward to future policy choices, or making speeches that do the same. (See chapter 6 for a discussion of central bank communications.) Such skills of effective persuasion are quite a different set from those required for practical management of market operations, but they have to be integrated convincingly with them.

As a result there has been increasing focus on maintaining and underpinning central bank credibility. Paul Tucker, now deputy governor of the Bank of England, identifies the main ingredients of that credibility:[9]

> Being very publicly committed to anchoring medium-term inflation expectations in line with a clear target, above all else. Inflation outturns being, on average, in line with the target. And being seen to be committed to the essentially technical job of professional economic analysis of conjunctural conditions and the underlying structure of the economy. The counterpart to this is being understood to be ready to do whatever is necessary to maintain well-anchored inflation expectations.

He goes on to note that credibility is not to be taken for granted, but "needs to be earned and re-earned, over and over again."

Central bank objectives, whether overt or otherwise, have shifted over time. Over recent years that shift has, at least in the main developed markets, been away from targeting either interest rates or monetary aggregates to targeting inflation itself, with or without subsidiary objectives.

This movement began when the Reserve Bank of New Zealand was given an inflation target as part of a much wider political aim to give each public-sector body a clear, quantified, and simple target to which it could then be held accountable. Thus inflation targeting essentially derived from a political initiative. Nevertheless, it was consistent with the theory that, in the longer term, monetary policy could only affect nominal variables and not real variables, which would instead be affected by nonmonetary real economic factors. At the same time, in the near term the influence on inflation also appears to result from the bringing about of changes to real variables such as output and unemployment. Furthermore, there seem to be long lags before inflation responds to monetary policy, so that driving inflation rapidly back to target, if it has deviated from it, only seems to be possible by enforcing a large change in output, especially if the deviation initially derives from some supply shock. Shocks were normally assumed to originate in the real economy, though recent events suggest that a shock within the financial system itself may produce comparable results.

Central banks are thus left trying to reconcile the primacy given to price stabilization over the medium term with the short-term desirability of avoiding undue disturbance to the path of output growth. Ascribing primacy to the control of inflation and delegating the responsibility to a central bank creates a politically attractive framework for resolving this dilemma because, if the central bank is made independent, any blame

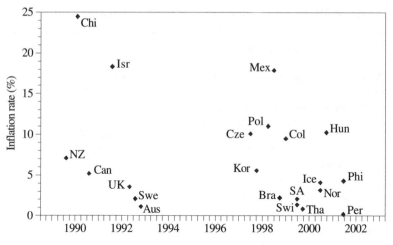

Figure 2.1. The inflation rate at the time of inflation target adoption in twenty-one countries. Source: Bank of Iceland.

for the painful output or employment consequences of fighting inflation is diverted away from government.

Such arrangements, or variants of them, were put in place in many countries from the early 1990s onward, and for a long period of time they looked to be remarkably successful, with an extended period of strong growth and muted inflation—what has come to be called the Great Moderation. In the 1990s twenty-one countries adopted inflation targets, and by 2009 there were twenty-six inflation targets in operation. (Hammond gives a comprehensive account of inflation-targeting regimes.[10].) Some adopted targets at times of high inflation and used them to anchor expectations. Others, like the United Kingdom, used an inflation target to consolidate gains achieved by other means—in the British case through a painful period of membership of the ERM[11] (figure 2.1). For some time, indeed, it seemed that inflation targeting would carry all before it. Ben Bernanke, before he became chairman of the Federal Reserve, was one of its most prominent advocates.[12]

The hallmark of inflation targeting is, as Bernanke and Mishkin explain, the announcement by the government, the central bank, or some combination of the two that price stability is explicitly recognized as the main goal of monetary policy and that, in future, the central bank will strive to hold inflation at or near some numerically specified level. Inflation targets are more often specified as ranges (for example, 1–3%) than as single numbers, and they are typically established for horizons ranging from one to four years. There were, as inflation targeting took root, exceptions to both approaches. Indeed Germany, with the longest overall experience with inflation-focused monetary policy, specified its implicit inflation target as a point and with only a one-year horizon. Initial announcements of inflation targeting generally allow for a gradual transition from the current level of inflation to a desired steady-state level: usually the level deemed consistent with price stability. "Price stability" has never in practice been literally zero inflation, but usually something closer to a 2% annual rate of change in average retail prices. However, as we shall see, the question is now being posed afresh as to how far such major economic choices should be delegated to an unelected, essentially technical body.

Of course, even if inflation targeting is accepted as the policy framework, there are still choices to be made about which inflation rate should be the target, what the time horizon should be, how much variation should be allowed over time, and to what extent account should be taken of other considerations such as activity or unemployment, and how the balance with inflation should then be struck.

In relation to prices, what precisely should be taken into account? Should prices of goods and services like food and energy be excluded because they are subject to supply-driven fluctuations and are intrinsically unsusceptible to short-term control using interest rates? Should housing costs be included and, if so, should this just be rental payments or should account also be taken, in a circular way, of the interest costs of a mortgage or should a factor for the capital cost of a house be included, even though this may fluctuate in a markedly different way from other prices because housing is also seen as an investment asset? Different answers to these questions have been chosen in different countries at different times.

No central bank targets very-short-term inflation, with most looking at one or two years ahead or, in the case of Australia, inflation "through the cycle." This has a bearing on which prices should not be taken into account so that erratic prices that should not affect future inflation, such as food prices, are often excluded.

One possible, indeed obvious, interpretation of the concept of price stability could be stability in the price level itself. In practice, a rate of inflation is almost invariably the target, the reason being that aiming at a price level, even one that changed over time, could be difficult to explain. Unlike when using inflation targets, bygones would not be bygones and a period of undershooting would need to be followed by a period of overshooting, and vice versa. What this would mean is that the near-term target would need to vary according to recent inflation performance and the time horizon chosen for offsetting any overshooting or undershooting. Downward price adjustments could prove costly in output terms. The whole process could be complex and confusing, and would consequently be damaging to credibility. Price stability is therefore usually taken to mean stability in the rate of inflation.

When an inflation target is announced, there is also usually some statement to the effect that control of inflation is the "primary" or "overriding" goal of monetary policy and that the central bank will be held responsible for meeting the inflation target. Sometimes there is no mention of competing goals, as was the case in the Reserve Bank of New Zealand Act in 1989. More often there is reference to subordinate goals, usually relating to growth or employment, or even in general terms to the wider economic objectives of government. In principle, the inflation target is supposed to take precedence in the event of conflict. In practice, central banks always have some room for short-run stabilization objectives, particularly with respect to output and exchange rates. However, as we shall see below, circumstances have arisen where, even though inflation targeting formally remains in place, it becomes subservient, in the face of major financial disruption, to other objectives. The relation between a central bank's price and financial stability objectives (where they have them) has become a contentious issue, as we discuss in chapter 3.

Since targeting inflation directly requires the central bank to forecast the likely path of prices, close attention is typically paid to a variety of indicators that have shown predictive power for inflation in the past. These model-derived forecasts are typically presented in inflation reports, which form a critical part of improved communication with the public about monetary policy and, in particular, the long-run implications of policy actions. However, one ongoing debate concerns how well inflation beyond one year can be forecast.

The adoption of inflation targeting is often linked to changes in the laws or administrative arrangements associated with the central bank. Typically, reforms go in the direction of increased independence for the central bank, particularly in respect of its choice of instrument settings. We discuss this in much greater detail in chapter 7.

One of the consequences of this approach has been an increasingly technocratic focus on the precise numbers involved in either a range of real variables or a particular price index. Enormous effort has gone into determining the possible consequences of differences in real GDP growth of, say, between 0.8% and 0.7% in a given quarter, or whether a price index was rising at an annual rate of 2.1% or 2.2%. Complex judgments about these relationships then feed into decisions about similarly small changes in interest rates, usually of no more than 0.25% in "normal" economic circumstances. (From late 2007 onward, however, there were far larger movements in rates in response to a sharply slowing world economy.)

This concentration on minor deviations in real numbers relates to a desire, which some might consider unrealistic given the many uncertainties about the monetary transmission mechanism, to anchor interest rate decisions in clearly defined and quantifiable factors. Rather like the value-at-risk modeling used by investment banks, such techniques could give a spurious feeling of comfort that the short to medium term can confidently be looked at in this way.

In 2007-8 this approach completely broke down, partly because of unforeseen shocks from commodity prices, but also, more importantly, because the whole structure of financial intermediation changed in ways that meant that these forecasting techniques no longer worked. Central bankers found themselves having to adjust to a new reality and having to move interest rates by 200 rather than 25 basis points for reasons other than changes in the likely impact of real variables on prices.

It is striking that much of the discussion of monetary policy in the last decade and more has said very little about what is happening in the financial system and how that impinges on both inflation and activity. Although in earlier years the focus was on controlling credit or money, the discrediting of the targeting of credit expansion, or of monetary aggregates, as a direct route to price stability seems to have had the consequence that the analysis of the flow of funds in aggregate, and as between sectors, which was a core feature of some central bank analysis some decades ago, almost faded from view. This is not because of lack of awareness of such issues. As long ago as 1986 a G10 Central Bank Study Group led by Sam Cross recognized that[13]

> New instruments may shift the incidence of monetary policy among sectors of the economy in ways that are not predictable. New instruments may concentrate risk in the financial sector, which can make it more vulnerable to large unexpected changes in the macro-economic environment.

These considerations certainly influence the way in which central banks make discretionary changes in monetary policy. As we note below, however, the difficulty of modeling such effects meant that in the event these factors were often ignored or assumed away. Even as recently as 2006 it was possible to read reflections on the conduct of monetary policy by well-respected central bankers that contained no reference whatsoever to the possibility that the behavior of the financial system might have some influence on the economy or vice versa.

Not all central banks turned their focus more or less exclusively on to real economy variables. The Bundesbank continued to emphasize the superiority of money targeting as a means of ensuring both monetary discipline and transparency, though these targets were still driven by inflation goals. Their money targets were designed to be consistent with an inflation target, reduced over time, given projections of the growth of potential output and of possible changes in the velocity of money. At the same time the Bundesbank showed itself to be quite willing to miss its money targets when pursuing them threatened to conflict with the control of inflation.

The ECB effectively continued with a modified version of this system as it devised its own approach to achieving price stability, which the European Treaty allowed it to define itself. The chosen approach has two "pillars"[14] based on two analytical perspectives: first, a prominent role for money, signaled by the announcement of a reference value for monetary growth; and, second, an analysis of a wide range of other economic and financial indicators in order to form a broad assessment of the risks to price stability.

The economic analysis assesses, much as do other central banks, the short-to-medium-term determinants of price developments, focusing on real activity and financial conditions in the economy and looking at, inter alia, developments in overall output, demand, and labor market conditions, a broad range of cost and price indicators, fiscal policy, and the balance of payments for the euro area.

The monetary analysis focuses on a longer-term horizon, because of the observed long-run link between money and prices. It looks at money and credit developments with a view to assessing the implications for future inflation and economic growth. Interestingly, and presciently, when describing the purpose of its monetary analysis, the ECB noted in 2000 that such analysis might help to assess the possible existence and the potential effects of bubbles in financial markets. They went on to say:[14]

> Historically, booms and busts in asset markets have been closely associated with large movements in monetary and, especially, credit

scene, and the arrival in world markets of hundreds of millions of new workers prepared to work at very low rates of pay. The increased savings propensities of Asian economies meant that strong demand growth in the United States was not inflationary.

Former Federal Reserve chairman Alan Greenspan's initial response to this critique was robust. In his view central bankers could not hope to head off asset price bubbles and should not attempt to do so. The most a central bank could do was to mop up efficiently after the event. While the markets continued to power ahead, and confidence in the maestro's ability to keep the music playing remained high, the Greenspan view dominated. But as the scale of the crisis became apparent, more critics emerged. Greenspan himself offered a partial recantation of his earlier view, and by 2009 his reputation had taken a dive.

Other charges were brought as well. Had the central banks failed to keep up with changes in financial markets and grown too distant from them? Sir John Gieve, then the deputy governor of the Bank of England, admitted that "we hadn't kept pace with the extent of globalization."[3] He maintained, too, that the Bank had not had the tools needed to respond to an asset price bubble. That reinforced the argument of those who believed that governments had been wrong to separate central banks from banking supervision.

Neither the European Central Bank nor the Bank of England were themselves direct supervisors of banks. In Japan, too, the Japan Financial Services Agency has the prime responsibility for banking supervision while the Bank of Japan is supposed to oversee only bank liquidity. In the United States, the Federal Reserve has only partial oversight of the banking system and had no direct supervisory relationship with the investment banks at the eye of the storm. Had this partial perspective been a handicap, preventing them from building a full understanding of what was happening to credit? Much of the credit expansion that fueled the boom had taken place outside the regulated banking system.

Furthermore, while central banks everywhere were thought to have a responsibility for something called financial stability, the nature of that responsibility was rarely spelled out, and the tools with which they might promote it were ill-defined, perhaps nonexistent. A large financial stability industry sprang up from the mid 1990s on, producing reviews at a great rate, but it had little measurable impact on policy or on markets. Just as Roach had argued was the case in the monetary arena, was there not a need for a fundamental rethink of the appropriate role of central banks in today's more diverse and global financial markets? In particular, the links between monetary and financial stability looked in need of serious attention, as indeed did the relationship between the real economy and the financial system.

Questions were asked, too, about the effectiveness of coordination between central banks as the crisis hit. Central bankers had long prided themselves on their habits of communication and cooperation with each other. They meet privately every two months at the BIS headquarters in Basel, where, we are told, they talk frankly and openly about monetary and financial developments. These habits of cooperation are far better developed than those between finance ministries, or among other kinds of regulators. But in the summer of 2007 the benefits of this network were not very visible and, despite intensive discussions behind the scenes, it was not until December that the first public signs of a coordinated approach to the provision of liquidity were seen. Even then, it became painfully clear that the techniques they used to assist the market were clumsy and out-of-date. The monetary authorities proved unable to establish the structure of interest rates that they wanted to see, and their money market intervention techniques needed almost constant reengineering.

There was worse to come. Even those who maintained stoutly that the central banks could not be blamed for the genesis of the crisis, and who supported the Greenspan line on crisis resolution, were alarmed to discover that they were ineffective even at the crisis resolution task. Interest rate cuts, even on an unprecedented scale, proved to be inadequate, and even massive injections of liquidity on terms that the central banks would not have considered feasible beforehand failed to rebuild confidence for a long time. During the Greenspan era financial markets had come to believe in the myth of the all-powerful Federal Reserve. It was seen to have feet of clay when the crisis hit.

Perhaps the high water mark of central bank power and influence had been reached. Was the golden age of central banks, a period in which their independence and autonomy had been widely accepted around the world, now over?

What Mervyn King had called the NICE decade—noninflationary and consistently expansionary—came to an end with a crash. Mervyn King himself had come into office claiming the ambition to make monetary policy "boring." By that he meant that interest rate decisions should be as predictable as possible, with deft touches on the tiller from time to time in order to keep inflation within the target range. For a time, he came close to succeeding, but from the middle of 2007 onward central aggregates, and their implications for the economy may depend on the strength of the balance sheet position of the financial sector. This is another reason for the ECB to give a special status within its strategy to the analysis of monetary and credit aggregates and financial intermediaries' balance sheets.

The way in which this analysis is conducted has been frequently refined, but always involves the construction of a wide range of financial aggregates. This analysis serves mainly as a means of cross-checking, from a medium- to long-term perspective, the short- to medium-term indications coming from the economic analysis.

The ECB had some initial difficulty in explaining that the monetary pillar did not represent a "monetary target" or that the economic pillar did not represent an "inflation target." Rather, both together form a framework that organizes the analysis and the presentation of the information relevant for monetary policy making in order to guide decisions that aim to maintain price stability. The ECB always recognized that the weight they continued to put on monetary aggregates set them apart from other central banks. They maintain that the relative lack of disruption from the unwinding of serious credit imbalances in the euro area has in part been attributable to the fact that they had always kept their eye on what was happening in the financial system.

It now seems clearer than ever that the scale of the extension of credit may provide a way of looking more closely at whether unsustainable imbalances between assets and liabilities are arising, whether related to residential and commercial property or to other markets. If credit is rising much faster than nominal activity in general, it may warn of risks in relation to the sustainability of real activity, as well as consequent risks to the stability of financial firms and markets (see chapter 5).

The nature of the links between the activity of financial firms and their clients and real activity is much disputed. It is certainly difficult to measure, and hence to model. That is one reason why many, perhaps most, economists and, in particular, the macromodelers who took over the process of forecasting inflation have for long tended to avoid attempting to model it and why there has been little enthusiasm for targeting categories of financial assets or liabilities.

At the same time, the residential housing crisis in a number of countries, combined in some cases with more general consumer indebtedness problems, has served as a sharp reminder that the behavior of banks and other financial institutions, and of securities markets, has a very direct effect on both activity and prices. It has also profoundly influenced the transmission mechanism of monetary policy in ways that have proved to be intensely disruptive.

These developments have refocused attention on those analysts who identified these risks, monitoring the cumulative build up of unusual and then extreme financial positions. However, while they did warn of the risks of such indebtedness unraveling with disruptive consequences, those economists who were most concerned about asset price bubbles and the mispricing of risk made few monetary policy recommendations in the face of the widespread orthodoxy that interest rates and consumer prices were where central bankers should focus. Their attention centered on regulatory tools designed to constrain the expansion of banks' balance sheets (see chapter 5). The hesitation over using monetary policy tools was linked to a belief that, if consumer price inflation was to remain the prime target, some other instrument was required to tackle excess credit expansion.

Warnings were given, however, in increasingly forceful tones, most notably by the economists Bill White and Claudio Borio at the BIS, that, while substantial economic benefits were associated with reducing inflation from earlier, higher rates, at the same time history also suggested that stability of consumer prices might not be sufficient to ensure macroeconomic stability[15] and that the benefits of focusing solely on maintaining price stability might well have been overestimated. White recalled that Hayek had warned, in his Nobel prize lecture, that economic processes were inherently so complex and volatile that the appearance of structural stability was almost always misleading. White further argued in 2006 that a reappraisal of the conventional approach to monetary policy that then prevailed was necessary because the structure of the global economy had changed remarkably. In particular, he suggested that financial liberalization had increased the likelihood of boom–bust cycles. The integration of big countries into a global economy, combined with the liberalization of markets, appeared to have had material effects on the inflation process and on the transmission mechanism of monetary policy.

White describes the dynamics of the process in the following way. Buoyed by justified optimism about some particular development, credit is extended that drives up related asset prices. This both encourages fixed investment and increases collateral values, and these in turn support yet more credit expansion. With time, and underpinned by an associated increase in output growth, this process leads to increased willingness to take on risks, "irrational exuberance" to use Greenspan's term, which gives yet further impulse to the credit cycle. Earlier experience analyzed in 2001 by Borio et al.[16] suggested that credit spreads, asset prices, internal bank risk ratings, ratings from agencies, and loan loss provisions all demonstrated a tendency to procyclicality. Subsequently, as exaggerated expectations concerning both risk and return are eventually disappointed, the process goes into reverse. As undershoot replaces overshoot, there is a dampening effect on the economy. Frequently, the financial system is itself weakened, which exacerbates the impact.

The orthodoxy of focusing exclusively on retail price inflation is now being challenged as many central bankers come to appreciate just how powerful an effect the accumulation of stocks of debt can have on the economy. In some respects, there has already been an implicit change in behavior. Whereas an excessive expansion of credit was not seen in itself as a reason for tightening, a drop in the supply of credit has been quoted as a reason for easing.

The longer-term implications for inflation targeting remain unclear. Mervyn King continues to argue that "diverting monetary policy from its goal of price stability risks making the economy less stable and the financial system no more so."[17] But elsewhere excessive or insufficient extension of credit is likely to become one of the reasons that will justify deviation from an inflation target, possibly for an extended period of time. So far, no country has dropped inflation targeting in response to misses, regardless of whether the misses are large, unexpected, prolonged, and frequent or small, temporary, and deliberate. Targets are nevertheless missed by substantial margins and for long periods. An IMF study by Roger and Stone suggests that countries targeting stable inflation miss the range about 30% of the time, while countries in the process of disinflation miss their target nearly 60% of the time.[18] Emerging-market countries take longer to disinflate, but their inflation performance under stable inflation targeting is as good as it is in industrial countries. The largest misses often reflect the direct and indirect impacts of exchange rate shocks. Roger and Stone suggest that the resilience of inflation targeting appears to reflect the flexibility of the framework in handling shocks, high standards of transparency and accountability, and, tellingly, a lack of alternative monetary regimes.

OTHER MACROECONOMIC OBJECTIVES

The question of whether a central bank should have other macroeconomic objectives in addition to price stability, whether in the form of a clear inflation target or some more vague formulation, has been addressed in different ways.

The period of immense financial turmoil that started in the summer of 2007, combined with highly volatile commodity prices, has progressively put into question the extent to which it is sufficient for a central bank to focus on achieving a specified inflation outcome over a relatively short horizon. The focus on inflation has not been explicitly abandoned, but many of the actions taken by central banks in different jurisdictions have had other, equally explicit primary motivations, including influencing the availability of credit, the pace of activity, or even simply "confidence."

Rates have been lowered very substantially even when inflation has been above target and sometimes with a less clear indication than usual of when inflation might be expected to get back to target. When this occurred in the United Kingdom in the late fall of 2008 the chancellor of the exchequer, Alistair Darling, issued a reminder that the Bank of England's mandate said nothing about the speed at which inflation should be brought back to target and that the Bank also had an obligation, subject to the objective of maintaining price stability, to support the economic policy of Her Majesty's Government, including its objectives for growth and employment. Subsequently, however, the Bank published an inflation forecast that prefigured the largest expected deflation since inflation targeting had been introduced. Inflation in fact remained above the target range in early 2009, as the Bank cut rates to 0.5% and, in a major regime change, embarked on a policy of "quantitative easing" (the purchase of government securities and other assets from banks and market counterparties), but by that time inflation was expected to undershoot on a two-year view.

As the crisis in the financial system unfolded within the United States, the Federal Reserve reduced rates dramatically without suggesting, at least for a period, that this corresponded to a similar drastic reduction in inflation prospects, thus implicitly confirming that monetary policy had more than one target. Meanwhile, inflation itself, or at least the prospect of it, became quite volatile, with huge swings in commodity prices during 2008 both making stability in inflation quite improbable and making its likely future course quite uncertain. A number of central banks shifted the focus progressively from providing liquidity support to individual banks on the basis of hitherto standard criteria to lending against, and then buying, previously unacceptable assets, including in some cases unsecured lending to the private sector.

This was justified variously as an attempt to keep wholesale markets functioning and to ensure that bank lending to the private sector was sustained. Governments as well as central banks made it clear that an objective of policy was a quantum of bank lending, harking back to much earlier periods during which the focus of official policy was the scale of credit expansion and sometimes the distribution of credit through "window guidance" and other such techniques. Even sectoral distribution became the subject of official interest with, in the United Kingdom for instance, government discussion with the banks about the quantum of lending for small businesses, for house purchase, or for the car industry. In the United States, by contrast, the Federal Reserve and the Treasury said in a joint statement in March 2009 that the Federal Reserve should aim "to improve financial or credit conditions broadly, not to allocate credit to narrowly defined sectors or classes of borrowers."[19] Academic commentators joined in with varying degrees of enthusiasm. Adrian and Shin of Princeton University were among the firmest converts. "There is a case," they argued, "for rehabilitating some role for balance sheet quantities for the conduct of monetary policy."[20] We agree.

The interest in credit was a far cry from the previous overriding focus on narrow adjustment of short-term interest rates. Indeed, over a period of months central banks lost their ability to use market operations to control either the level or, to some extent, the structure of interest rates. The relationship between interest rates and official intervention rates broke down. In the United Kingdom, the early crisis-linked reductions in official rates had little effect on the interest rates that determined the marginal cost of funding for banks and hence, effectively, their ability to reduce their lending rates without further damaging their already prejudiced profitability. In the United States, the Federal Reserve found it was no longer always able to deliver its announced target rate. In effect, the interest rates at which individual banks could fund themselves became a function of confidence in individual names in the interbank market, regardless of the price at which the authorities supplied funds.

Official rates continued to be cut to mitigate the scale of the recession, when it became clear it could not be averted. Central banks found that their actions resulted in the size of their balance sheets increasing at an abrupt and unprecedented rate. The Federal Reserve's balance sheet expanded from around $800 billion to over $3 trillion in a matter of months. Other major central banks found themselves in similar positions. In part this was because the lack of trust between banks started to make the central bank in effect a systematic central counterparty for the private banks, and the central intermediary in the money market. Instead of lending to each other, they managed their liquidity increasingly by borrowing from and lending to the central bank. But it was also because, in order to stop intermediation more generally from collapsing, the central bank was increasingly becoming a major intermediary for the private sector itself. The Federal Reserve began to purchase commercial paper directly and to provide back-up liquidity to money market mutual funds.

At the end of 2008 the Federal Reserve reached the zero bound of interest rates when it announced a target range for the federal funds rate of 0–0.25%. At the same time, it said it would purchase large quantities of agency debt and mortgage-backed securities and was evaluating the potential benefits of purchasing longer-term Treasury securities. The aim was to demonstrate that, even when the interest rate armory was exhausted, the Federal Reserve retained the ability to influence credit conditions and prevent a deflationary spiral, as was experienced in the early 1930s. In effect the changed environment required a different regime.

The circumstances in which a policy of "quantitative easing" might make sense had been set out almost exactly six years before by Governor Ben Bernanke, as he was then, in a speech entitled "Deflation: making sure 'it' doesn't happen here."[21] The speech, when reread in 2009, is both remarkably prescient and blush-making at one and the same time. It is embarrassing because of the confidence with which he asserts that a period of Japanese-style deflation was highly improbable in the United States because "our banking system remains healthy and well-regulated, and firm and household balance sheets are for the most part in good shape." It is prescient in its detailed exploration of the theory and practice of deflation, and the policy instruments that may be used in response. He expressed confidence that "the U.S. central bank, in cooperation with other parts of the government as needed, has sufficient policy instruments to ensure that any deflation that might occur would be both mild and brief."

His argument was that prevention is better than cure and that the Federal Reserve should "use its regulatory and supervisory powers to ensure that the financial system will remain resilient" and should "act more pre-emptively and aggressively than usual in cutting rates" if the fundamentals of the economy suddenly deteriorate. In 2007–8 the Federal Reserve followed that approach more vigorously than the other central banks facing a similar fall-off in demand.

But he maintained that even if preventive action, with aggressive rate cuts, failed fully to affect deflationary pressures, the Federal Reserve was not out of bullets. It would be open to it to expand the scale of its asset purchases and to widen the range of assets it buys, or it could lend directly to the banks at low rates of interest. To influence longer-term rates, once the overnight rate fell to zero, it could announce ceilings for yields on longer-maturity Treasury debt and enforce them by committing to unlimited purchases at prices consistent with those ceilings. In the limit, the Federal Reserve could also buy foreign, as well as domestic, government debt. This menu is frequently, if rather misleadingly, described as the government "resorting to the printing press." In the past, economists have offered more exotic, if less plausible, ways of achieving the same affect. Keynes suggested that the government could fill bottles with money and bury them in mine shafts for determined citizens to recover. Milton Friedman's preference was for the government to drop dollar bills from a helicopter. Increasing money supply in this way would be likely to prevent the prices of goods and services dropping in real terms. Bernanke's reference to this option earned him the nickname "Helicopter Ben."

Do these techniques work in practice as well as they do in theory? The lessons of the Japanese experience—the most relevant recent case study we have—are ambiguous. On the one hand, the Bank of Japan was generally successful in maintaining the quantum of bank balances within its target range, and, in the end (albeit after five years), it was able to move away from a zero interest rate as the price level began to rise. Japan clearly avoided a Depression-style collapse in confidence and activity. On the other hand, bank lending continued to decline after the introduction of the program—though of course it might have been even weaker without it. More worryingly, Federal Reserve researchers conclude that[22]

> While there is little evidence that quantitative easing stimulated overall lending activity, there does appear to be some evidence that it disproportionately supported the weakest Japanese banks [and] may have had the undesirable impact of delaying structural reform.

At the London School of Economics in January 2009 Bernanke sought to distinguish the Federal Reserve's approach in 2008–9 from the earlier Japanese experience, characterizing it as "credit easing," rather than "quantitative easing."[23] The distinction he sought to draw was that

> In a pure QE [quantitative easing] regime, the focus of policy is the quantity of bank reserves, which are liabilities of the central bank.... In contrast the Federal Reserve credit easing approach focuses on the mix of loans and securities that it holds and on how this composition of assets affects credit conditions.

The main reason he cited for the different approach was that credit markets were more dysfunctional in the United States then they had been in Japan in the 1990s.

The switch to quantitative-based action, essentially targeted at growth via credit, even if this was not put in quite those terms, left open the question of what to do about inflation and whether in the United States an explicit inflation target was desirable after all. The immediate motive for this was the hope that a de facto inflation target would help shore up inflation expectations and reduce the risk of deflation, bringing the Federal Reserve closer to the formal targets of the United Kingdom and the ECB. Some economists, such as Mishkin, also felt that a clear inflation target that stabilized general inflation expectations could help in the aftermath of recession, both emphasizing that the Federal Reserve would do what was necessary to prevent deflation and making it less likely that there would be a burst of high inflation, perhaps as a result of the consequences of the efforts to maintain credit.

In March 2009 the Bank of England joined the Federal Reserve in attempting to stimulate money growth directly. They were happy to describe it as quantitative, rather than credit, easing. A little later the ECB also embarked on purchases of covered bonds, which they described as "enhanced credit support." The declared aim was "to encourage banks to maintain and expand their lending to clients."[24] The Bank of England emphasized that "the objective of policy is unchanged ... influencing the quantity of money directly is essentially a different means of reaching the same end."[25] At the time of writing it remains unclear whether the conventional view that central banks are ultimately always able to control the inflation rate over time will prove valid in the face of rapid swings in inflationary pressures. The Bank of England were clear, though, that there had been a switch in focus to operating directly on the supply of money and away from the previous approach of influencing nominal demand by varying the price at which it supplied central bank assets.[26] But, as the new chief economist of the Bank of England Spencer Dale put it in a speech a few days later, "There is also considerable uncertainty over the timing of the impact of the monetary expansion on nominal spending and on the prospects for inflation."[27] That is, of course, precisely the difficulty that had caused the abandonment of previous attempts to target money supply growth. Indeed the scale of the intervention, whose timing was delegated to the Bank by the government, soon became a matter of controversy. The quantities were decided by the Monetary Policy Committee using the procedures followed for interest rate changes, and in August 2009 the governor wanted to intervene on a larger scale but was outvoted.

After these actions by the Federal Reserve and the Bank of England there was widespread concern about the longer-term implications. Surely, it was argued, a monetary boost on this scale would inevitably lead to higher inflation, which would be very attractive to a government that had taken on huge additional debts in the recession and would also help heavily indebted private-sector borrowers to deleverage. Yet this assessment ignored the impact of the institutional changes over the previous decade. Could the Bank of England, within an inflation-target regime, sit back while inflation soared above the range, writing regular letters to the chancellor of the exchequer but otherwise not responding? Yet the alternative, an explicit upward adjustment of the target by the government, looked equally unattractive. The strength of political commitment to low and stable inflation has yet to be tested.

This action by central banks has been undertaken as part of a much wider concerted program by governments to actively seek to manage demand by use of fiscal policy. Another way of looking at the central bank regime change is as one aspect of a reversion to the previously discredited Keynesian approach. In part this has come about simply through a conviction that only government spending could sustain activity, given the sharp contraction in private credit. At the same time an approach focused on aggregate demand through a combination of fiscal and quantitative monetary measures has also received support and is explicitly seen as a return to policies for circumstances for which an inflation-targeting regime may be less well-suited.

One further consequence is the reopening of the debate about the relationship between the government and the central bank in the context of independence. In the United States the ending of the Federal Reserve's obligation to purchase U.S. government debt at fixed interest rates at the time of the U.S. Treasury–Federal Reserve 1951 Accord was seen as laying the foundations for the independent conduct of monetary policy, as indeed were similar provisions elsewhere (notably the Maastricht Treaty establishing the ECB) that were intended to prevent the central bank from monetizing government debt. The prospect of an interest rate of zero, which forces the central bank to monetize government debt if it wants to engage in expansionary operations, has precipitated different reactions. In his 2002 speech Bernanke explicitly referred to the 1951 Accord. His point was that the experience before the Accord showed that a "sufficiently determined" Federal Reserve could peg government bond yields at longer maturities. So, in the United States, the resort to quantitative easing was presented as the exercise of discretion by the Federal Reserve. Some members of the FOMC, however, saw it as the effective end of the Federal Reserve's independence. In the United Kingdom, the fact that the management of government debt remains in the hands of a Treasury agency effectively limits the Bank of England's discretion. The policy announcements surrounding quantitative easing made it clear that the Treasury set the ceiling on purchases, though the Bank was responsible for operational timing. This is clearly a lesser role than setting the short-term interest rate.

So, the events of 2007-9 appear to have set in train, in the United States and the United Kingdom at least, changes to the conceptual framework of monetary policy whose nature and impact are as yet unclear. Although inflation targeting has not been abandoned, the focus of short-term action has been on a combination of seeking to ensure bank liquidity at whatever cost (in line with the traditional central bank role of standing behind viable banks), maintaining or increasing commercial bank lending, lowering rates by whatever amount seems needed to restore confidence, and indeed generally seeking, as part of wider government policy, to expand the central bank's balance sheet by as much as is needed to sustain growth.

New mechanisms have had to be found to give effect to these new approaches to monetary policy. The Federal Reserve has had to be assisted in managing its balance sheet through a special financing mechanism provided by the U.S. Treasury, and new legislation is required to sterilize the effects of lending or securities purchases on bank reserves. Many of the recent changes hark back to earlier approaches that had fallen out of fashion. If inflation targeting is to remain the central framework of policy, these changes will need to be reconciled with that framework. That reconciliation has not yet been undertaken.

The huge increases in government debt and in central bank balance sheets that were implemented in 2009 clearly take risks with inflation over the longer term. They should, absent further shocks, provide a base for some sort of recovery, though the timing is uncertain and the longer-term consequences are highly unpredictable. It must be possible that the risk of making a mistake, and the pressure to ease the fiscal burden of the extra government debt taken on, will cause central banks to delay tightening, especially if the inflation-targeting regime effectively remains so flexible that it provides no effective constraint. Certainly, returning to "normal" conditions after the transformations that have taken place in central bank balance sheets will pose a real challenge for central bank operations. The Federal Reserve has said that, when the condition of credit markets, and the prospects for the economy, warrants it, it will be able to return to its traditional means of policy making: that is, by setting a target for the federal funds rate and by draining liquidity from the system using a variety of market techniques, including reverse repurchase agreements and the sale of the Federal Reserve's holdings of longer-term securities. Chairman Bernanke has declared his confidence that "the extraordinary policy measures we have taken in response to the financial crisis can be withdrawn in a smooth and timely manner as needed, thereby avoiding the risk that policy stimulus could lead to a future rise in inflation."[28]

It is true that, once normality returns, operations that are costly to the commercial banks should be self-reversing. But the route back to familiar territory remains uncharted. The lags in monetary policy are always long, the signs of stronger growth may be picked up late, and the timing problem may have been aggravated by our lack of knowledge about how quantitative policies work.

EXTERNAL STABILITY

The exchange rate occupies a central position in monetary policy, whether as a target, an instrument, or simply an indicator. Latter, then of the Bank of England, presented a useful taxonomy over a decade ago, and it remains relevant today.[29] Even where the exchange rate is not targeted, downward pressure may indicate that monetary policy is relatively loose and upward pressure may suggest tightness. Movements may also signal changes in external competitiveness. In a market economy, with a convertible currency and free capital flows, the rate cannot normally be manipulated over the medium term without consequent adjustments to, or consequences for, other dimensions of monetary conditions. Where exchange controls are in place (usually administered by the central bank) the authorities may have somewhat greater influence, though the long-term effectiveness of controls in economies with substantial external trade is moot.

It is not possible to fix both the exchange rate and domestic monetary conditions at the same time. Through much of their history, central banks have chosen, or been required, to maintain a fixed exchange rate, relative to either gold, another currency, or a basket of currencies. This choice of regime is typically the responsibility of government rather than the central bank. The choice has a profound effect on the operation of the economy, through the impact on prices, and for long periods of time has been seen, in effect, as the monetary policy tool of choice, whether because of the powerful nature of the consequences for economic behavior or because of its relative simplicity. It has been seen as particularly helpful where innovation erodes the meaning and usefulness of monetary and credit aggregates as indicators of monetary policy.

In any event, the central bank will usually be responsible for implementing the financial transactions needed to fix or manage the rate, either using foreign exchange reserves on its own balance sheet or on a government account. Such reserves may be either owned outright or borrowed. These transactions involve a wide range of counterparties, often spread around the globe, and participation in and knowledge of numerous different markets. This places a premium on close international relationships. The need to foster those relationships was one of the driving forces behind the very early globalization of central banking.

This world has become more complex from both policy and operational perspectives because of the very widespread move over past decades toward floating exchange rates managed in a variety of ways. This move took place because fixing the rate proved impossible, either because the reserves to maintain a fixed parity were no longer adequate or because the consequences for the economy were no longer acceptable. But the alternative of leaving the exchange rate to be broadly market determined is not straightforward either.

As Goodhart notes,[8] there is no generally accepted model of the determination of exchange rates in the short to medium term. Relative inflation rates may be relevant, and purchasing power parity may eventually be restored in the long run, but so slowly as to be beyond current policy horizons. Although academic attempts to explain exchange rate fluctuations continue,[30] Goodhart suggests that modeling the exchange rate as a random walk remains the standard to beat. He goes on to say that there is no great confidence in our knowledge of the transmission mechanism whereby monetary policy affects the exchange rate either. He notes that one of the few stylized facts in this field, that exchange rates would appreciate in response to an increase in interest rates, has been called into question in recent years. Insofar as international capital flows have become increasingly equity, rather than debt, related, a rise in interest rates could, he suggests, reduce rather than encourage inward capital flows.

In general, though, at least for small and medium-sized economies, it was thought for a time that one of the main transmission channels for monetary policy into the domestic economy was via the effect of interest rates on the exchange rate and hence on inflation.

Nevertheless, a kind of "Washington Consensus" grew up that, wherever possible, countries should focus their monetary policy on domestic price stability more directly and allow their exchange rates to float freely, without imposing controls on capital movements. As exceptions to this, small, open economies with little capacity or credibility to maintain domestic price stability through an independent monetary policy could still adopt a fixed rate, in some cases administered by a currency board.

The Asian crisis of 1997–98 gravely weakened this view, as countries that had robust exchange controls in place managed to weather events better than those, such as Thailand, whose currency had long been informally pegged to the U.S. dollar, so that Thais had assumed there was little or no exchange rate risk and were unable to cope with a depreciation when it occurred. The result was a combination of a resumption of pegged exchange rates, a reluctance to lift exchange controls on capital flows, export-led expansion, a massive increase in foreign exchange reserves, and a corresponding relaxation of domestic monetary conditions. The market consensus was that only countries with massive foreign exchange reserves could withstand a concerted assault by speculators.

Meanwhile, the fluctuations in bilateral exchange rates between the core industrialized countries have been large and often not easy to relate to fundamental explanations. The position is now that, in a world where all the main participants operate primarily to establish domestic price stability and leave their exchange rates floating freely, the resulting fluctuations in exchange rates may be large and, quite frequently, dramatically so. In the last three months of 2008, for example, the rates between the dollar, euro, sterling, and yen oscillated remarkably. Such volatility is not new but came as a shock after a period of relative calm in foreign exchange markets. The disruptions to profit margins and trade flows created by short-term volatility on a large scale are considerable. The shifts in prices they engender may well influence inflation rates by amounts outside the range of recent experience.

This leaves the question as to whether it is possible at all in a country aiming at price stability, and without capital controls, to have a secondary mechanism for influencing the exchange rate. The main mechanism that may work is "sterilized intervention." This has been found to be challenging. There may be unhelpful results for domestic interest rates, the sums available for intervention may be small relative to the size of the market flows, there is uncertainty as to whether the intervention may be effective, and there is a risk that losses will be incurred.

Whether or not, and if so when, to intervene can be the subject of intense debate between the finance ministry, who will generally be responsible for overall strategy, and the central bank, who will typically have to engage in the relevant market operations. The finance ministry will normally be able to overrule the central bank in principle, but in practice will be hesitant to do so because the central bank will usually argue from a position of greater technical expertise.

The current question, as Goodhart explains, is whether, with the emergence of twin currency poles following the rise of the euro after an extended period of dollar dominance, changes in sentiment toward, or against, one or other might spark off fluctuations in capital flows and exchange rates that could prove damaging to the world economy.

At present, central banks and finance ministries are unhappy about the excessive volatility of both real and nominal exchange rates but they do not really understand what causes this volatility and they are evidently unwilling to use intervention to mitigate it, in large part because they doubt the latter's efficiency. (In March 2009, however, Switzerland became the first major Western economy to seek to influence its exchange rate through intervention for some years.) While this is a commonly shared view, such volatility, when it occurs, can be uncomfortable and threaten to unsettle efforts otherwise targeted elsewhere, such as on prices. It leaves, as in the United Kingdom in the second half of 2008, difficult decisions as to whether interest rate policy should directly aim to stabilize the exchange rate in the nearer term, rather than rely on inflation forecasts that may be rendered invalid by unwelcome exchange rate movements in the future. When exchange rates become volatile, the already-challenging effort to trade off the range of purely domestic variables becomes even more demanding.

Concern grew, for instance, through 2008 that the appreciation of the euro may be causing damage to the export sector and to activity in general. De Grauwe[31] argues that the ECB's minimalist interpretation of its mandate is damaging. The ECB interprets its responsibility for price stability in such a way that only if exchange rate movements threaten price stability does it need to act. Implicitly, it argues that exchange markets are efficient and that therefore the exchange rate always reflects economic fundamentals. De Grauwe believes that the ECB should intervene in the foreign exchange market and oppose exchange rate developments that are out of touch with economic reality in order to send a signal. Such calls for direct exchange market intervention are not yet widely supported. However, if more extreme market movements persist, so will calls for monetary policy judgments to place greater weight on exchange rate developments. This will mean reverting to the more complex decision-making models of only a decade and a half earlier.

But before considering the ways in which monetary policy frameworks may need to be revised in light of the experiences of the credit crisis, we should examine the second pillar of central banking: financial stability. It is in that area that the greatest weaknesses in the late-twentieth-century model have been revealed. How could an institution like the Federal Reserve, revered in the early years of the decade as a body with almost mythical powers over financial markets, and thought to have tentacles reaching into every systemically significant financial institution, have presided over the biggest and most costly crash for eighty years?

Financial Stability

The financial disasters of 2007-9 brought the role of central banks in financial markets back into sharp focus, after a period in which a narrow price stability objective had held pride of place. The authorities were unclear how to react when the crisis began in the summer of 2007, and were again wrong-footed by the meltdown in the fall of 2008, following the failure of Lehman Brothers. It was widely argued that there was a need for a fundamental rethink of how central banks monitor trends in financial markets, how they provide liquidity and other forms of support to those markets in times of stress, and how they should relate to other financial regulatory authorities.

Before considering the changes in approach to which the crisis points, we should review what central banks had been doing in the name of "financial stability," and why it fell short. In the years leading up to the crisis, central banks talked extensively about financial stability, published financial stability reviews, renamed sections of their organizations to emphasize the importance of financial stability—and yet the financial system came close to collapse in 2008. What went wrong?

In fact, while the recent crisis has been unusual in its severity and breadth, it is striking just how many financial crises there have been over the last thirty years, and quite how costly they have been in fiscal terms. Caprio and Klingebiel[1] of the World Bank identified 117 systemic banking crises that have occurred (in 93 countries) since the late 1970s. In 27 of the cases the eventual fiscal cost was over 10% of GDP (figure 3.1). The crisis that began in 2007 will certainly far exceed that threshold in a number of countries.

As we have explained, there is no bright line between monetary and financial stability: the two are closely, indeed inextricably, linked. Monetary policy takes effect only through financial markets; financial firms and markets are in turn critically dependent on what is happening in the real economy. Within central banks, however, monetary stability and

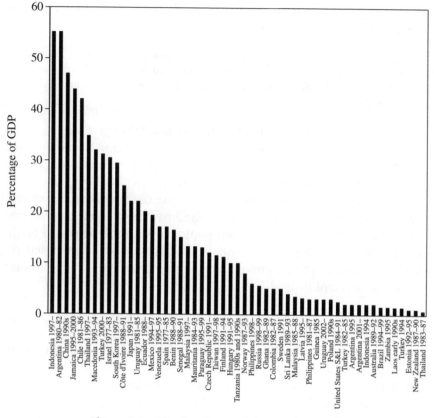

Figure 3.1. The fiscal cost of financial crises.[1]

financial stability have been considered separately for some time. In 1994 the Bank of England split the organization into two wings, named in that way. The division was accentuated in 1997 when two separate deputy governors were appointed—a separation that proved to be a mistake. But before explaining why that is so, and how a closer linkage between the two stabilities can be established, we should examine how the concept of financial stability emerged.[2] We also go on to explore the link with supervision, where we have some sympathy with the description by Padoa-Schioppa[3] of financial stability as "a land in between" monetary policy and prudential supervision.

Given the extensive debates surrounding financial stability in recent years it is surprising to note that the term itself came into general use quite recently, though of course the concept of systemic risk has been

debated for decades. In a paper on "defining and achieving financial stability," Allen and Wood observe that[4]

> The Bank of England used the term in 1994 to denote those of its objec-
> tives which were not to do with price stability or with the efficient func-
> tioning of the financial system. We are not aware of any earlier usage
> of the phrase.

In fact, the convention establishing the OECD in 1960 gave the organization the objective of achieving the highest possible growth and employment "while maintaining financial stability," but the term was not widely
used thereafter. When Alan Greenspan discussed banking crises in a
1996 paper on risk management he did not use the term at all.[5] Yet today
it would be hard to find a speech on the financial system, by a central
banker or regulator, which was not peppered with references to financial stability. New international organizations have been created that are
exclusively devoted to its pursuit. For a time, finance ministers around
the world talked of little else.

Definitions and Measurement

Unfortunately, while the term is extensively, even incontinently, used,
it has no clear definition. Indeed it may be one of those expressions
which, to paraphrase Paul Krugman writing on the competitiveness of
nations, has passed from jargon to cliché without moving through the
usual intermediate stage of meaning.

After reviewing the literature in 2004, and examining the Bank of England's role, Charles Goodhart concluded that "There is currently no good
way to define, nor certainly to give a quantitative measurement of, financial stability."[6] Similarly, de Haan and Oosterloo reviewed the activities
of a wide range of central banks and reported that there was "no unam-
biguous definition of financial stability or systemic risk, and that generally the responsibility is not explicitly formulated in laws."[7] Furthermore, they noted, "there is considerable heterogeneity in the way central
banks pursue their financial stability objective" and they pointed to a
lack of clarity in the accountability and oversight of the function, which
often contrasted sharply with the focused arrangements in place for the
monetary responsibilities of the institution. Some central bankers have
themselves revealed unease. Lars Heikensten of the Swedish Riksbank,
for example, acknowledged that the concept is "slightly vague and difficult to define."[8] In 2005 the European Central Bank noted that "Financial

stability assessment as currently practiced by central banks and international organizations probably compares with the way monetary policy assessment was practiced by central banks three or four decades ago—before there was a widely accepted, rigorous framework."[9] That is a realistic assessment: it is a pity that no significant consequences flowed from it at the time.

By comparison with the apparent certainties of price stability, financial stability is hard to capture. Aspachs et al.[10] offer a neat taxonomy of the problem. It is far more difficult to define and measure financial stability. Only limited progress has been made on forecasting bouts of financial turbulence, and very little indeed has been made on assessing their likely severity. Quite apart from these technical problems, there are doubts about what tools might be used to maintain or promote financial stability, and about the means of holding the central banks or other agencies accountable for its delivery. There is an almost infinite number of possible financial instruments, as against the very narrow range of monetary policy tools. Furthermore, the use of different instruments affects different firms or economic agents in diverse ways, making such use of more than technical interest.

Efforts have nonetheless been made to produce a working definition. In 2005 the ECB talked of "a condition where the financial system is capable of performing well all of its normal tasks and where it is expected to do so for the foreseeable future."[9] But the first half of the definition adds little, and in the second the question of who "expects" in this context, and on what basis they do so, is left unclear. In 2008, the ECB had a second try:[11]

> Financial stability can be defined as a condition in which the financial system...is capable of withstanding shocks and the unravelling of financial imbalances, thereby mitigating the likelihood of disruptions in the financial intermediation process which are severe enough to significantly impair the allocation of savings to profitable investment opportunities.

While the new definition is somewhat more precisely specified, it has a contingent, post-crisis flavor.

The Swiss National Bank has also proposed a definition, ending up in a similar place: "A stable financial system can be defined as a system where the various components fulfil their functions and are able to withstand the shocks to which they are exposed."[12] Pressed in Parliament in July 2008 to offer his own definition, Mervyn King said[13]

> I would think of financial stability as a period during which the payment system worked normally and the ability of households to mediate their savings into real investment in the economy at home or abroad operated normally.

It was an impressive off-the-cuff response—one does not get advance notice of questions in the British Parliament—only slightly undermined when he went on, "But the question is—what is normally?" and did not offer an answer.

Surprisingly, the Icelandic central bank offers one of the most substantial diagnoses, making use of a definition initially proposed by Andrew Crockett[14] when he was general manager of the BIS. The Icelandic Bank argues as follows:[15]

> Financial stability requires (i) that the key institutions in the financial system are stable, in that there is a high degree of confidence that they continue to meet their contractual obligations without interruption or outside assistance; (ii) that the key markets are stable, in that participants can confidently transact in them at prices that reflect the fundamental forces and do not vary substantially over short periods when there have been no changes in the fundamentals.

Once again, there are awkward judgments subsumed in the definition, but it gives a helpful sense of what the bank is trying to assess. Unfortunately, the Icelandic financial crisis of September 2008 showed that the bank and the Icelandic regulator had failed comprehensively to convert their analysis into action. Icelandic banks had been allowed to expand overseas well beyond the capacity of the Icelandic authorities to support them.[16] That failure had important consequences for financial markets and their regulation throughout Europe, as we shall discuss later.

Others outside the world of central banks have tried to give more specificity to the definition. Rick Mishkin,[17] an academic who has also served on the Federal Reserve Board, proposes "the prevalence of a financial system, which is able to ensure in a lasting way, and without major disruptions, an efficient allocation of savings to investment opportunities."

There is an attractive clarity and simplicity to this definition, but Allen and Wood[4] identify two difficulties. First, "no-one would say that savings were allocated efficiently to investment opportunities in the Soviet Union, but the Soviet Union did not suffer from financial instability, except right at the end of its existence." Second, the definition is not easy to apply in practice. It is not possible to know until after the event, if indeed then, whether or not savings have been efficiently allocated to investments.

Another, rather more detailed, definition was proposed in 2003 by Michael Foot,[18] then a Managing Director of the United Kingdom's Financial Services Authority. He suggested that a financial system might be considered stable if four conditions were met:

- Stability in the value of money.
- Employment close to its natural rate.
- Confidence in the operation of key financial institutions and markets.
- No relative movements in asset prices that would in time undermine the first three conditions.

Foot's definition has the merit of being largely observable, though an element of judgment is unavoidably present in the assessment of asset price movements and of how large moves need to be to threaten stability. It has the additional virtue of bridging the worlds of monetary and financial stability. The main weakness is that the creation of conditions that promote full employment, in particular, owes much to a range of other policies, notably in relation to the labor market, which take us a long way from the normal concerns of central bankers and regulators. If we define financial stability very broadly, to include aspects of the functioning of the real economy, then we might find it difficult to disentangle the contribution made to it by the financial authorities.

In the circumstances, it is tempting, and some central banks have been thus tempted, to eschew attempts to define stability and to focus instead on what we mean by instability. We may not be able to produce a clear definition of our desired state of the world, but we may nonetheless be able to identify malfunctions. In the nineteenth century, Bagehot defined a crisis as a situation in which "the Bank of England is the only institution in which people have confidence."[19] In the summer of 2008 we approached such a state of affairs in London and New York. But we might hope for a definition that gives us a little advance warning before that unhappy point is reached.

Some central banks have chosen, privately, to determine a list of regulated firms that they regard as systemically significant, as a way of deciding how to focus their efforts. The U.S. Treasury has now proposed the establishment of a special regulatory regime for such firms. The difficulty with this approach is that in different circumstances the failure of different institutions can either generate systemic failure or not. The concept of "too connected to fail" has entered the vocabulary of regulation since the collapse of Lehman Brothers. And the prospect of the failure of a significant number of small firms, as in the Savings and Loan crisis in the United States or the post-BCCI "small" bank crisis in the United Kingdom, can be just as threatening. So "systemic," when applied to a firm, is a contingent not an absolute qualifier.

Allen and Wood take a different tack. They are concerned to avoid incorporating into a definition of instability losses that may be incurred by individuals as a result of their own risk-seeking behavior. As Mervyn King was, at the beginning of the crisis, they are conscious of the need to avoid moral hazard. So they develop what we might call the "innocent bystander" test. They define episodes of financial instability as "episodes in which a large number of parties, whether they are households, companies or governments, experience financial crises which are not warranted by their previous behaviour." In other words, "a distinguishing feature of episodes of financial instability is that innocent bystanders get hurt."

This is, in principle, an appealing approach, and it is certainly helpful, when regulators and central banks consider the case for intervention, to ask whether this definition is met. The rescues of Northern Rock in 2007 and Bear Stearns in 2008, neither of which would necessarily have been regarded before the crisis as systemically significant institutions, can only be justified by reference to such a test. The authorities in London and New York must have concluded that the risks to savers and investors elsewhere, if these banks failed, were severe. While they may not have looked "too big to fail," they may well have been "too connected to fail." But the test is not straightforward to apply. In the subprime case, for example, were the investors in securitizations seeking higher yields really innocent bystanders? Were they aware of the risks they were running, or *should* they have been aware? It is also less helpful in determining whether the system, or a number of individual firms, is coming under such strain as to justify preemptive action.

In that context the work done in the Swiss National Bank, and elsewhere, to develop a kind of "stress index" may be more promising than continued efforts to craft a pithy definition of what is bound to be a complex concept—far harder to define than price stability. The ECB also undertakes a vulnerabilities exercise that attempts to capture the potential impact of both exogenous and endogenous risks.[20]

In the academic world, Goodhart and others have attempted a similar exercise, but one that aims to have more predictive content.[21] Their

"Metric for Financial Stability" is based on data on the probability of default on bank loans, with an adjustment using bank equity prices as a leading indicator of bank profitability. Their view is that an index along these lines, and they recognize that their work is very preliminary in nature, could be the basis for forward-looking provisioning that might dampen financial crises in the future. (We explore this concept further in chapter 5 when we discuss what is now called macroprudential supervision.) Fell and Schinasi[22] have proposed a rather broader approach, which they describe as identifying a "corridor of financial stability," like an exchange rate target range. They propose a set of indicators that would help to determine whether the system as a whole is inside or outside the corridor.

STATUTORY RESPONSIBILITIES

In the light of these definitional and measurement problems it is perhaps not surprising that few central banks have a clear statutory duty to pursue financial stability, even though many now describe it as one of their core purposes or "critical responsibilities."[23] When they carried out their survey in 2005, de Haan and Oosterloo noted that only in Portugal was financial stability incorporated in statute,[7] though a number of countries have recently been given new mandates in the area, whether statutory or nonstatutory.[24] The Maastricht Treaty makes it clear that the responsibility for financial stability in the EU does not lie with the ESCB, without specifying where it does lie, but it places an obligation on the ESCB to cooperate with those other authorities that are responsible.

Following the Northern Rock crisis the British government decided that the Bank of England's stability objective should be put into legislation. Its previous mandate, for "the overall stability of the system as a whole," was enshrined in a letter from the chancellor of the exchequer (Gordon Brown) to the governor, dated May 20, 1997,[25] and in the Tripartite Memorandum of Understanding with the Treasury and the Financial Services Authority. But after several months of endeavor, the new chancellor, Alistair Darling, decided that the legislation would not in fact expand materially on the earlier mandate. In a letter to the chairman of the Treasury Committee of the House of Commons, John McFall, on June 19, 2008, he said, "in the forthcoming banking legislation we will set out a high-level statutory objective for the Bank of England to ensure financial stability." Ensure is a remarkable word in this context, and a dangerous hostage to fortune. But, he went on:[26]

> Whereas a monetary policy objective can be set out in clear operational terms through a quantitative inflation target, financial stability is a concept that is harder to define and measure. Any attempt to do so in primary legislation would result in an objective which could subsequently prove inflexible in dealing with the fast-changing nature of global financial markets. So we will set out a high-level objective for financial stability in the legislation, and then define it operationally.

The aim was to force the Bank to give greater weight to financial stability when taking decisions about liquidity provision, and even on interest rates, though without overtly changing the monetary policy mandate. The Treasury were frustrated by the Bank's reluctance during the second half of 2007 to introduce a "general liquidity facility," and indeed by its overall reluctance to intervene in the banking market.

The government went on to explain that a subcommittee of the Bank's Court would be responsible for the new duty, and the Bank's executive would be accountable to that body for its delivery. But the subcommittee will be chaired by the governor so, as the Treasury Committee pointed out, the line of accountability runs from the governor back to himself. In the light of this we might doubt whether the change will turn out to be of great significance in the affairs of the Bank. There are well-grounded suspicions that, while other aspects of the legislation are substantive, the idea of a statutory objective was introduced as a political initiative that was preferable to the acknowledgment that the Treasury made mistakes of judgment in the Northern Rock affair in failing to require the governor to lend to the bank earlier (or, indeed, in not lending to the bank themselves) and in delaying the announcement of government backing for deposits in Northern Rock—a delay that was a material factor in causing a run on the bank by retail depositors. Senior Bank of England staff pointed out at the time that without a new tool to deliver it, a statutory financial stability objective was unlikely to make much difference to the way the Bank operates in practice. The governor subsequently put the point more colorfully:[27]

> To achieve financial stability the powers of the Bank are limited to those of voice and the new resolution powers. The Bank finds itself in the position rather like that of a church whose congregation attends weddings and burials, but ignores the sermons in between . . . it is not entirely clear how the Bank will be able to discharge its new statutory responsibility if we can do no more than issue sermons or organise burials.

In this formulation he implicitly dismissed the idea that changes in interest rates might sometimes have a financial stability justification.

From this brief survey we might identify a broad consensus that financial stability is a core function of the central bank but that it cannot be defined in terms other than broad and general ones that give little guidance on policy or action, and indeed that it could even be dangerous so to do.

But below that broad consensus there are several contentious areas where opinions and practices differ. They center on the tools central banks need to pursue such an objective with some chance of success, and how they should structure themselves to carry out the responsibilities implied. How can emerging imbalances and tensions be identified? How transparent should central banks be about their concerns over stresses and strains in the system? Is there a risk that by drawing attention to those concerns they will create the very problems they seek to avert? There is a clear risk that the central bank will forecast ten of the next three crises, and will gain a reputation as a little boy who cries wolf. What precise tools do they need? How should they deploy them? What information does the central bank need and how should it secure that information? Is it essential, from a financial stability perspective, for the central bank to have some direct responsibility for banking supervision, or is it enough for it to have a general oversight role, collecting data from the direct supervision authority or authorities? Finally, and most controversially, how far should financial stability concerns influence monetary policy decisions, where the prevailing ideology has dictated an exclusive focus on retail prices?

To seek to answer these questions, we should first look in a little more detail at what central banks have been doing so far in the cause of financial stability—or at least at what they have been saying they are doing. Much of this information is contained in financial stability reviews, which are now published regularly by many of them. The declared aim of these reviews has been to identify emerging tensions in the financial system. They hinted, for instance, at the vulnerability of several institutions to a hiatus in wholesale funding, but they did not anticipate the dramatic liquidity consequences of the subprime crisis and, while there were some warnings of credit risks, there were none that came close to forecasting the scale of the crisis that ensued. Why not?

FINANCIAL STABILITY REVIEWS

The first central bank financial stability review (FSR) was published by the Bank of England in the summer of 1996. It was conceived, at least in part, as an attempt to assert the Bank's continued involvement in financial regulation, as it was suspected that a new government, to be elected in 1997, might wish to restructure the regulatory system, after a series of mishaps in both banking and securities markets. The Bank of England's own reputation had suffered from the failures of BCCI and Barings. (Davies was responsible for the launch of the FSR: Green was also involved.) A second objective was to raise the standard of public debate on financial stability issues.

In the first respect the innovation was wholly unsuccessful and the Bank was stripped of its responsibilities for banking supervision the following year, but it was surprisingly influential in other ways. The example was widely copied by others. According to a review by Martin Cihak[28] of the IMF, by the end of 2005 almost fifty banks were publishing FSRs, and many others were actively considering publication.

Some central banks remained hesitant. Cihak reports discussions with nonpublishers of FSRs who argue that financial-sector issues are too sensitive to be discussed openly and that "the publication of a central bank analysis at a time of increasing risk to financial stability might precipitate the very shocks or crisis that the central bank was trying to avoid." They also argue that, since the central bank does not hold all the levers for delivering financial stability in its own hands, it may be misleading to produce a review that implies that the institution has responsibilities that it does not have. Finally, there are concerns about whether adequate resources are available to produce high-quality analysis.

These increasingly seem to be minority concerns. A more reasonable worry today is that the number of FSRs is escalating to such an extent that the impact of any individual review may be very modest indeed, or possibly even counterproductive. The number of FSRs, and the onset of chronic financial instability, seem to be positively correlated! Almost all OECD countries, and a number of others, publish them, usually twice a year. There are now twenty-five regularly produced FSRs in Europe, thirteen of them by central banks in the euro area, where the ECB itself adds another. There is a risk of redundancy at best and confusion at worst. It is hard to avoid the conclusion that in the euro area wide-ranging FSRs have become part of the justification for the continued existence of substantial National Central Banks in individual member countries who have lost their monetary policy responsibilities to the European Central Bank.

What reasons do the banks themselves give for publishing FSRs? In 2007, Oosterloo et al. reported, on the basis of a survey of central banks themselves, that three main reasons are advanced:[29]

- To contribute to the overall stability of the system.
- To increase the accountability of the financial stability function.
- To strengthen cooperation on financial stability issues between the various relevant authorities.

These are conventional and politically correct responses, and we may take them with a pinch of salt, especially the accountability point. It is more interesting to analyze the content of the reports, as both Oosterloo et al. and, separately, Cihak have done. Oosterloo et al. focus on the extent to which the FSRs incorporate the Financial Soundness Indicators (FSIs) that have been developed by the IMF in an attempt to provide a comparable basis for assessing the relative health of different countries' financial systems. The core set includes statistics on deposit takers, while a broader group includes figures on nonbank financial institutions, real estate markets, and so on. The IMF recognizes that these data can only be guidelines, but it has encouraged member countries to calculate them on a harmonized basis and to release them quarterly.

Strikingly, the central banks that publish FSRs are sparing in their publication of the FSIs. On average, a central bank FSR includes only a third of the FSIs, and only 53% even of the core indicators on deposit takers. Almost 80% of them do publish core indicators on capital adequacy, which lie at the heart of the Basel Capital Accords, but only 16% publish all three indicators relating to the asset quality of the banking sector. Half of all central banks publish no indicator at all on liquidity, and almost 90% do not publish data on the net open position in foreign exchange. The diversity of practice is hard to explain. It is not related to the relative sophistication of the markets or banks involved. For example, Poland publishes 50% of the full set of indicators, while De Nederlandsche Bank reveals only 10%. As Oosterloo et al. neutrally observe, "this analysis suggests that central banks have some scope to improve on the public availability of FSIs." It is likely that, following the crisis, more will do so.

Cihak takes a more subjective approach. He has designed an assessment framework for FSRs that incorporates twenty-six principles (see table 3.1), ranging across clarity about the aims of the document, the coverage (for example, does it cover the risks that may emerge in the financial sector as a whole or is it focused on one subsector only), the consistency of the assessment approach over time, etc. Reviewing forty-seven countries' FSRs against these principles, he grades them on a four-point scale, from fully compliant with the principles (graded 4) to not

Table 3.1. The proposed "CCC" framework for assessing FSRs.

	Clarity	Consistency	Coverage/contents
A. Aims	A1. The definition of financial stability should be clearly indicated. A2. The aims of the report should be clearly indicated.	A3. The definition of financial stability should be a standard part of the report, presented consistently across reports. A4. The statement of aims should be a standard part of the report, presented consistently across reports.	A5. The definition of financial stability should cover both the absence of crisis and resilience to crises. A6. Financial stability should be defined both in general terms and in operational terms. A7. The aims of the report should be comprehensive.
B. Overall assessment	B1. The overall assessment should be presented clearly and in candid terms.	B2. The overall assessment should be linked to the remainder of the FSR. B3. There should be a clear link between the overall assessments over time, making it clear where the main changes took place.	B4. The overall assessment should cover the key topics.
C. Issues	C1. The report should clearly identify the main macro-relevant stability issues.	C2. The coverage of issues should be consistent across the reports.	C3. The coverage of the financial system should be sufficiently comprehensive.
D. Data, assumptions, and tools	D1. It should be clear what data are used to arrive at the results presented in the report. D2. It should be clear what assumptions are being used to arrive at the results presented in the report. D3. It should be clear what methodological tools are being used to arrive at the results presented in the report.	D4. The results should be presented in a consistent manner across the reports.	D5. The report should use available data, including those on individual institutions. D6. The report should use the available tools.

Table 3.1. *Continued.*

	Clarity	Consistency	Coverage/contents
E. Structure and other features	E1. The structure of the report should be easy to follow. E2. Other features of the report—such as its length, frequency, timing, public availability, and links to other central reports—should be designed to support its clarity.	E3. The structure of the report should be consistent across time to make it easier to follow for repeat users. E4. The other features of the report should be designed to support its consistency.	E5. The structure of the report should allow covering the key topics. E6. The other features of the report should be designed to support its coverage.

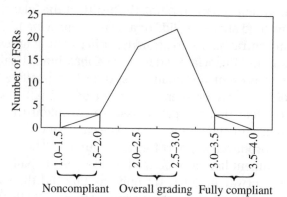

Figure 3.2. How do existing FSRs compare with the proposed criteria.[28]

compliant at all (graded 1), and concludes that many of them are incomplete and inadequate (figure 3.2). Very few include all the principles he sets out.

What explains the differences in coverage and depth between the FSRs published by different central banks? Cihak finds, unsurprisingly, that the gradings are positively correlated with both economic development and the size of the financial sector, and that the reviews tend to improve over time. A number of central banks are clearly learning by doing in this area. Most interestingly, he finds that "gradings are on average higher for central banks not directly involved in day-to-day supervision, partly reflecting that the overall assessments are more candid." This conclusion offers some support to those who argue that a central bank without direct responsibility for institutional supervision may take a more objective and critical view of financial-sector trends, rather than being primarily concerned with defending the record of its supervisors and maintaining confidence in the banks it oversees, even when that confidence might be misplaced.

It is clear from both these analyses that the concrete benefits delivered by FSRs are so far very modest. They may have informed public debate, but there is little evidence that they have been effective as early warning systems, or that they have changed behavior in the financial authorities or in firms themselves. Reviewing the editions published in 2006, when the imbalances that led to the credit crisis in 2007 were becoming starkly evident—with risk premia at record lows, credit growth escalating, and asset prices in unknown territory—Cihak finds that "virtually all (96 percent) started off with a positive overall assessment of the soundness of the domestic system (characterizing the health of the financial system as being, e.g., 'in good shape,' 'solid,' or at least 'improving')." This strongly suggests that central banks are, frankly, either poor at assessing emerging tensions in the financial system or, as Cihak himself suggests, they "may prefer to present the financial system in a positive light, partly because problems may be seen as a result of bad policies, and partly because of the fear that a negative assessment might trigger a decline in the confidence of the system." An external review of the Norwegian FSR in 2003[30] produced support for this argument. The reviewers noted that the government had been obliged to intervene to bail out insurance companies in Norway in 2001, yet only in 2002 did the FSR recognize that the sector had gone through a turbulent period. While the problems were being addressed, the central bank's financial stability function was silent.

Those who were involved in drafting FSRs during the period acknowledge some of these criticisms. They do not think their quality or prescience can be measured by statistics on coverage of IMF indicators. They maintain that a careful reading suggests they were, overall, far from Panglossian in tone. They draw attention to the legitimate concern to avoid publishing a laundry list of worries that might, but probably would not, crystallize. How high should the threshold of confidence be before a central bank highlights a potential problem whose identification might itself cause a collapse of confidence? While acknowledging these anxieties, we nonetheless conclude that central banks should in future err more on the side of pointed analysis and be less afraid to be precise about emerging risks and imbalances.

So we conclude from this assessment that in the first area of potential activity in pursuit of financial stability—the public identification of emerging issues—many central banks have been performing poorly. Their FSRs are too bland and fail to highlight emerging stresses that might alert private-sector participants to the risks they are running, and might cause them to modify their behavior, in a timely way. Indeed it is often unclear at whom the reviews are addressed, and there is little evidence that they are even read by those in private-sector firms, especially by the members of their boards, who might need to act on them.

There seems little point in this booming industry of financial stability analysis if it is to be sanitized, with any potentially risky observations removed. What is worse, participants in international meetings convened to discuss financial market stress, whether at the BIS or in the Banking Supervision Committee at the European Central Bank, report that this lack of candor is replicated in those forums, with national central banks reluctant to admit, even to their counterparts overseas, that there are any potential problems in their banking system.

Another related problem is that many existing FSRs seem to pay little attention to the global reports produced by the IMF, the BIS, and the FSF. Since 1999, following the Asian financial crisis, the IMF has produced its own *Global FSR*. Unfortunately, perhaps partly as a result of the sensitivities of its board members with respect to their own countries, the IMF has been very cautious in drawing attention to emerging tensions in the system. In a speech on the reform of the IMF in 2006 Mervyn King asked rhetorically if it had followed Keynes's injunction to engage in "ruthless truth-telling."[31] King's own answer was clear. The phrase, he says, does not "conjure up memories of any of the international meetings I have attended." His point is reinforced by an examination of the IMF's views on some of the financial market developments that led to the crisis. The April 2006 edition of the *Global FSR* commented on credit default swaps:[32]

> There is growing recognition that the dispersion of credit risk by banks to a broader and more diverse group of investors, rather than warehousing such risks on their balance sheets, has helped make the banking and overall financial system more resilient. The improved resilience may be seen in fewer bank failures and more consistent credit provision. Consequently the commercial banks may be less vulnerable today to credit or economic shocks.

The BIS has at times been more outspoken, and it was certainly more forceful than the IMF in advancing its view of the asset and credit bubbles that burst in 2007. We discuss the role of the BIS, both generally and in this specific case, in chapter 10. The FSF produced a regular private assessment of vulnerabilities in the financial system for its members from 1999 onward, using staff resources from member central banks and regulators. Yet there is little sign that these assessments have informed the FSRs of most individual countries in a useful way.

While it would be unrealistic to expect central banks, or indeed anyone else, to be able to forecast the nature and especially the timing of future crises with any accuracy, and while acknowledging the risk of warning too frequently, there is a clear need for stronger linkages between the IFIs and individual central banks, and for greater candor on the part of both. Without that, the continued explosion in the number of FSRs will deliver diminishing, and even perhaps negative, returns. There have been regular calls from G7 leaders, notably Gordon Brown, for an effective early warning system to identify emerging crises. The FSRs published so far have not fulfilled that objective, partly because the content has been opaque and partly because the warnings (often oblique) have not resulted in any precautionary actions. The G20 summit of April 2009 instructed the FSF's successor, the Financial Stability Board, to "collaborate with the IMF to conduct Early Warning Exercises to report on the build-up of macroeconomic and financial risks and the actions needed to address them." It remains to be seen whether this process will be any more effective than its predecessors. The FSB will need to be far bolder than its predecessor in the future.

In the United Kingdom the tripartite arrangements provide a forum for the Bank of England to highlight emerging risks. Yet issues like the financial stability implications of growing wholesale funding of the U.K. banking system, and particularly the vulnerable position of Northern Rock, were apparently not raised in that setting, even if there were veiled references to them in the FSR.

So it is clear that simply writing elegant prose, dotted with multicolored graphs, has little impact. If no consequences flow from the analysis, and if the analysis itself is sanitized, there is no useful purpose served by all this activity. Some would go on to argue that the answer is straightforward. They maintain that the problems have been accentuated by a gradual tendency to narrow the responsibilities of central banks, and specifically to remove their direct supervisory powers. Surely, the argument runs, for the financial stability responsibility of a central bank to carry any weight, the bank must itself be the supervisor of the banking sector, which allows it both to acquire superior insights into the system's vulnerabilities and to act directly on concerns it might have about, for example, the amount of capital in the system. How valid is that argument?

CENTRAL BANKS AND BANKING SUPERVISION

All central banks contribute to financial stability through their influence on banking regulation relating to liquidity and capital. G10 central banks have always been members of the Basel Committee on Banking Supervision, whether or not they have direct responsibility for institutional supervision in their own country. (Since 2009 a number of emerging-market and other central banks have also been included.) So they have an input to the crucial task of setting the framework for capital reserving. But the question of whether or not a central bank should also be responsible for the direct supervision of individual institutions remains highly contentious, and international practice varies widely. It is generally acknowledged that central banks need information on the banking system, both because the banking system is the principal transmission mechanism for monetary policy and because of the risk of financial instability. But whether that information needs to be collected by the central bank itself, through direct relationships with banks, and whether or not they need to be engaged in the grubby day-to-day business of supervising individual institutions is less clear.

Central banks have always had an interest in the soundness of individual banks in that they have been concerned about the viability of their counterparties. In some cases, as with the Bank of England, that evolved into direct oversight of their balance sheets, carried out through the Discount Office in which other banks discounted their bills. As Capie et al. point out, "such supervision over the banking system as was carried out by the Bank of England was undertaken by one senior official on a part-time basis."[33] Not until the late 1970s did this function take on a separate life and begin to employ a significant number of staff. Elsewhere, dedicated agencies were set up. In the United States the Office of the Comptroller of the Currency was established in 1864, half a century before the Federal Reserve itself was founded. Other countries like Germany, Canada, and Sweden also established government agencies outside the central bank. So there has never been a standard model of bank oversight in operation around the world.

In our guide to global financial regulation[34] we set out the state of play internationally on this fraught question, as it was then, and briefly explored some of the arguments that had led different countries to the solutions they had reached. No consensus view can be found. We pointed out that in 2006, out of a sample of 143 countries, in 50 of them the central bank has no supervisory responsibilities and in a further 29 it shares banking supervision responsibilities with another agency, while in 64 countries it does have the prime responsibility. A more recent, larger sample, quoted in chapter 2 above, shows that around 60 central banks have no supervisory responsibilities and 120 have some or all of the supervisory task allocated to them.

We noted that the trend, especially since the creation of the United Kingdom's Financial Services Authority, had been toward regulatory consolidation, and that where regulatory responsibilities had been consolidated in a single entity, that entity was typically outside the central bank, except in some smaller jurisdictions. By 2006, forty-nine countries had set up integrated regulatory authorities, thirty-nine of them outside the central bank. We were aware at that time of a number of other countries that were reconsidering their regulatory arrangements and several were moving toward an integrated scheme outside the central bank. But in a number of cases the credit crisis, and especially the very visible problems in the U.K. banking system, has caused these reexaminations to be put on hold. After a long period of relative calm in global banking markets, in which the possibility of disorderly bank failures seemed to have receded to a more remote horizon, issues related to bank rescues and the provision of lender of last resort support once again assumed prominence, and the links between supervisors and central banks again appeared crucial.

In the United Kingdom the Conservatives announced in July 2009 that, if elected, they proposed to reverse the regulatory consolidation of a decade earlier and to return to the Bank of England not just banking but also insurance supervision. (Their proposals would abolish the FSA in its current form and replace it with a consumer protection agency and a market regulator, though the structure of the latter was left unclear. These arrangements would be unusual internationally and the British system would interface awkwardly with international groupings.) In the United States the Obama Administration proposed that the power of the Federal Reserve should be extended to the supervision of all firms that could pose a threat to financial stability, even those that did not own banks. That idea has proved controversial in Congress and among the other regulators. At the time of writing, the outcome is unclear.

It is therefore timely to reexamine the arguments for and against brigading banking supervision alongside the other uncontested responsibilities of the central bank for monetary policy, payment system oversight, and the provision of emergency liquidity assistance and lender of last resort facilities.

Practices in the United States and the United Kingdom differ markedly on this important issue, and indeed on many others, such as the nature of deposit protection arrangements and the appropriate role for the central bank in the payment system (see below). So the arguments can be well described by reference to the contrasting positions taken in Washington and London.

The Federal Reserve has long argued that it is essential for a central bank to maintain a role in banking supervision, even though its own role has in fact covered only a part of the banking system. The Federal Reserve shares the responsibility for regulating and supervising the U.S. financial system with a number of federal and state government agencies. It supervises state-chartered banks that are members of the Federal Reserve System, the U.S. operations of foreign banks, and, in some cases, the foreign operations of U.S. banks. It also serves as the umbrella supervisor of all bank and financial holding companies, though the bank subsidiaries of those holding companies are often supervised by other agencies. For example, the commercial banking activities of holding company subsidiaries with national bank charters are supervised by the Office of the Comptroller of the Currency. But although their coverage is partial, and the result of several accidents of history, the Fed has long argued that it is essential for a monetary authority to have some direct links with the banking system, not only for financial stability reasons but also to assist with the conduct of monetary policy. A paper published by the Federal Reserve Bank of Boston in 1997 argued that[35]

> Confidential supervisory information on bank ratings significantly improves forecast accuracy of variables critical to the conduct of monetary policy, which supports the argument that central banks should have bank supervision responsibility.

The validity of this analysis is contested by others.

Shortly after his appointment as chairman of the Federal Reserve, Ben Bernanke articulated a trenchant defense of the Fed's role, with explicit reference to the British government's decision to separate supervision from the Bank of England.[36] He argued that "The Fed's ability to deal with

diverse and hard to predict threats to financial stability depends critically on the information, expertise, and powers that it holds by virtue
of being a bank supervisor and a central bank." While acknowledging
the partial coverage that the Fed's shared powers give it, he noted that
"The Fed's supervisory activities provide it with a window onto financial institutions that it does not regulate and onto developments in the
broader financial markets." So, through the directly supervised entities,
the Fed can acquire knowledge about entities supervised by others, and
indeed about unregulated firms like hedge funds. He noted, further, that
given that the Fed lacked explicit legal authority to oversee systemically
important payment systems, its powers in that area "derive to a considerable extent from its bank supervisory activity." So banking supervision
in practice plugged a legal gap in relation to payment systems.

He further maintained that at times of financial stress, while

> some of the expertise that proved most valuable was derived from the
> Fed's non supervisory activities...nevertheless, examination authority
> and the knowledgeable and experienced examinations staff have often
> proved essential.

In its provision of liquidity in previous financial crises, especially after
the September 11 terrorist attacks, the Federal Reserve

> benefited from its knowledge of liquidity management practices of key
> institutions, their funding positions, and their financial conditions, as
> well as from its ability to evaluate the collateral provided by institu-
> tions requesting funds. This information and expertise, gained in part
> through its supervisory role, allowed the Fed to supply the needed liq-
> uidity efficiently and without undue risk.

Overall, his conclusion is that

> the supervisory authority of the Fed has significant collateral benefits
> in helping it carry out its responsibilities for financial stability...and,
> when financial stresses emerge and public action is warranted, the
> Fed is able to respond more quickly, more effectively, and in a more
> informed way than would otherwise be possible.

(It is not clear that these structural advantages helped the Fed to identify
the problems with structured debt, or off-balance-sheet vehicles, that
were at the heart of the financial crisis that originated in its jurisdiction.)

While Bernanke pegged his speech on a reference to the U.K. reforms
a decade earlier, and while the Northern Rock episode clearly posed a

challenge to the reformed U.K. structure, his speech could also easily be read as an attack on the structure of the European Central Bank, which has no banking supervision responsibilities of any kind. Yet we might note that the ECB responded quickly and effectively to the liquidity crisis in the summer of 2007. Indeed, in the early stages its responses were faster and more decisive than those of the other central banks crucially involved. The absence of information gleaned from its own direct supervision activities did not seem to be a drawback in that case. The ECB argues that the existence of some central banks within the euro area who do have supervision responsibilities gave it the essential "DNA" to sense the appropriate actions to take.

On the other side of the debate, two sorts of arguments have been presented. First, there is the case in favor of regulatory integration, bringing together the supervisors of different types of financial firm in one agency. Second, there are specific arguments advanced against giving the monetary authority direct responsibilities for banking supervision.

In principle, these arguments may be separated, though they tend to come together, since few central banks have shown enthusiasm for taking on direct responsibilities for the supervision of nonbank financial institutions. So far, if we set aside institutions like the Monetary Authority of Singapore and the Irish central bank, in rather small jurisdictions, only one sizable central bank, De Nederlandsche Bank in Amsterdam, has been prepared to extend its reach into the prudential supervision of insurance companies and securities firms. And it did so only after losing its monetary policy responsibilities to the European Central Bank. It is possible that other national central banks in the euro area may now be prepared to go in that direction, notably those in Spain, Italy, and perhaps France. There are powerful arguments for combining the prudential supervision of banks and insurance companies. More cynically, it may be sensible to use the central bank for this purpose if no other function for the institution can be found and its staff cannot be transferred. Proposals in the United States and the United Kingdom could also move in the same direction.

The first set of arguments, for regulatory integration, are well set out in two papers by Clive Briault, formerly of the Financial Services Authority.[37,38] The points he makes are as follows.

- The growth of financial conglomerates has blurred the boundaries between subsectors of the financial industry and the traditional functional approach no longer matches the structure of either firms or markets.

73

- There is therefore a clear need for regulatory oversight of a financial conglomerate as a whole.

- While it may be possible to manage this oversight through a lead regulator approach, a single regulator is able to generate a number of efficiency gains and there are important economies of scale and scope, as well as a simplification of the overall relationship between the firm and the regulator.

- A single regulator should be more efficient in the allocation of scarce regulatory resources, using a system of risk-based supervision.

- A single regulator ought to be in a position to resolve inevitable conflicts between the objectives of prudential soundness and consumer protection.

- A single regulator strengthens accountability as the responsibility for the oversight of any individual firm is clear.

Empirical evidence to prove or disprove these arguments is hard to find. Arguably, the global financial crisis has demonstrated that all structures are equally ineffective. But shortly before the crisis erupted, Cihak and Podpiera of the IMF attempted to assess the performance of the different models then in operation.[39] They attempt an assessment of whether integrated supervision is associated with higher quality of regulation and lower cost.

Their primary proxy for regulatory quality is compliance with international regulatory standards, as assessed by the IMF in their now-extensive program of Financial Sector Assessment Programs. In addition, they look at (pre-crisis) nonperforming loans as a proxy for banking system quality. They find that integrated regulators comply more effectively with international standards (figure 3.3). Furthermore, they assert that "countries with integrated supervisory agencies enjoy greater consistency in quality of supervision" and that "this greater consistency is not associated with diluting the overall quality of supervision, as on the contrary... integrated supervision is associated with a high overall quality of supervision." On the other hand, "integrating supervision does not seem to be associated with significant reduction of supervisory staff."

Their conclusion is that "integrated supervision may be associated with substantial benefits, particularly in terms of increased supervisory consistency and quality." The study is of some interest, but the proxy for regulatory quality is doubtful. Formal compliance with global standards

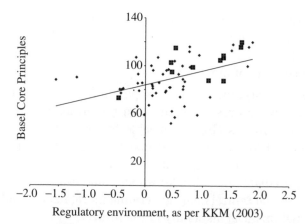

Figure 3.3. Basel Core Principles compliance
and degree of regulatory integration.[39]

is a good starting point, but in itself it says little about the quality of enforcement.

The second set of arguments, related to the problems of combining prudential supervision of banks and monetary policy, do to some extent overlap with the arguments for a single regulator: if banking supervision is left in the hands of the central bank, and if the central bank is reluctant to take on other forms of oversight because of a fear of dilution of effort, or of implicitly extending the safety net to nonbanking institutions, then the claimed benefits of a single regulator cannot be achieved. But there are four further arguments against incorporating banking supervision into the central bank.

- There could on occasion be a conflict of interest that might tempt a central bank to loosen its monetary policy stance because of concerns about the financial health of the banks it regulates, which might put price stability at risk, to the disadvantage of the economy as a whole. Buiter argues that this issue did arise in the United States in 2007–8, and that the Fed overreacted to financial-sector concerns: "cognitive regulatory capture of the Fed by Wall Street resulted in excess sensitivity of the Fed not just to asset prices but also to the concerns and fears of Wall Street more generally."[40]

- A loss of credibility could arise from perceived regulatory failings and this may damage the central bank's reputation and therefore its authority to conduct monetary policy.

- Supervisory responsibilities imply a different type of accountability, and a different and closer relationship with the political authorities, which may cut across the independence a central bank needs in the conduct of monetary policy.[7]

- There is an argument for the separation of lender of last resort and supervision responsibilities on the grounds that a lender of last resort that is also responsible for ongoing supervision may be tempted to intervene in support of an institution—in part to cover up the inadequacy of its own supervision. This might therefore mean that nonviable institutions could be inappropriately supported by the central bank, generating moral hazard and therefore potential financial instability in the future.

For a decade, from 1997 to 2007, these arguments appeared to be gaining ground in international debates, as evidenced by the growing number of integrated regulators. An awareness that the U.S. regime was over elaborate, costly, and confusing, and the apparent growth of London's market share in mobile international financial business, contributed to a growing view that the British government had stumbled on a successful formula. (The 1997 reform was not proceeded by a White Paper, or any consultation process, and its timing was dictated by the monetary policy reform that was the government's top priority at the time.) The FSA, with its streamlined staffing, risk-based regulation, and principles-based framework, was widely admired. A series of reports in the United States on their own regulatory scene, some commissioned by politicians anxious about job losses in New York, drew attention to the many advantages of the U.K. model.[41] Integrated regulation became the "flavor of the month."

The failure of Northern Rock in the summer of 2007 was an unpleasant shock to the international reputation of the new London model of regulation. Northern Rock was a purely domestic mortgage bank that had grown rapidly over the previous three years, at times accounting for almost a quarter of all new mortgages issued. By the summer of 2007 its balance sheet was over £100 billion in size. Its growth had been fueled by aggressive use of an innovative, if by no means unique, funding model, based on securitizations through off-balance-sheet vehicles. It relied on securitization for some 80% of its funding—a far higher percentage than any of its competitors. When the liquidity crisis hit, the bank was no longer able to securitize its growing mortgage book and did not have adequate access to wholesale markets to carry the exposure on its own books. It was obliged to seek assistance from the Bank of England.

After a period of reluctance, during which the governor argued that to rescue a bank from the folly of its own excesses would create moral hazard and promote instability in the future, the Bank advanced around £30 billion of short-term funding in conjunction—perhaps rather late in the day—with a government guarantee of the deposits. The authorities then sought to sell the bank to a private-sector bidder or consortium, but by the end of the year it proved impossible to do so and it was taken into public ownership, as many had argued was inevitable.

The nationalization outcome was embarrassing enough for a Labour government that had come to office on the basis that nationalization was no longer part of its policy platform, but the circumstances of the failure were, perhaps, even more difficult to present. There was a strong perception that the authorities had acted indecisively, and with inadequate coordination. Answers given by the three authorities to the Treasury Committee and to Parliament did not convince the Committee, or public opinion, that the system had worked well. There were strong rumors that the Bank of England had been reluctant to provide support, and that the Bank, the FSA, and the Treasury had taken very different views. It was not clear who was in charge when the crisis hit. The tripartite arrangements, enshrined in the memorandum of understanding published in 1997 and revised in 2006, looked to many to be unclear and ineffective.

There was also much criticism of the characteristics of the U.K. deposit protection scheme, which gave 100% protection to retail depositors only on the first £2,000, with 90% protection up to £35,000. The scheme was also a post-funded mechanism, which depended on a post-event levy from surviving banks. And the absence of a special resolution scheme, which could allow the early payout of retail creditors, generated uncertainty about the speed at which depositors would be paid out, even if a deposit was guaranteed. These fears contributed to the retail run on Northern Rock.

Subsequently, an internal audit report published by the FSA itself[42] highlighted many inadequacies and weaknesses in the supervision of Northern Rock. It had been categorized as a retail institution in a reorganization of the authority in 2003-4 and supervised alongside insurance companies, while the principal risk to its business model lay in its reliance on wholesale funding in the securitization market. Concerns expressed within the authority about the funding model and the rapid growth of the institution had not been followed up. The report led to a major overhaul of that part of the FSA. A National Audit Office review, focusing primarily on the Treasury's role, confirmed that the Treasury had not been well equipped to handle the failure of a large bank, and indeed had been aware of the flaws in the bankruptcy procedures for some years.[43] No parallel review of the Bank of England's role has been undertaken but it was widely assumed that there were lively disagreements within the Bank on the position of Northern Rock and the case for liquidity support for a potential purchaser. A leak of the imminent provision of large-scale assistance to the BBC created conditions of such uncertainty that retail depositors queued to withdraw their money—the first run on a bank in the United Kingdom for over 150 years. When the Federal Reserve facilitated the rescue of Bear Stearns by J.P. Morgan with a line of credit exclusive to J.P. Morgan, criticisms of the Bank's reluctance to do the same in London were revived. On the other hand, when the Californian bank Indymac suffered a bank run in July 2008—in spite of the existence of the Federal Deposit Insurance Corporation with its huge fund, a special resolution mechanism, and a 100% deposit protection scheme up to $100,000—that suggested that the earlier praise in London for the U.S. system may have been overdone.

For the purposes of this argument, the key consequence of the Northern Rock affair was that the question of central bank responsibility for supervision was reopened. Members of Parliament on the Treasury Committee, leading opposition politicians, and others argued that the government's reform could now be seen to have been a mistake, and that banking supervision should be returned to the Bank of England. In its majority report, the Treasury Committee made a slightly different suggestion, which would have created a kind of parallel regime within the Bank of England.[44] At the other end of the argument, there were suggestions that, while the division of responsibilities in the tripartite agreement was unsatisfactory, the direction of change should be to give more responsibilities to the FSA, making it the effective lender of last resort.[45] Another point that emerged in the postmortem, which should not have been a surprise, was that the tripartite MOU was asymmetrical. Influenced by the Johnson Matthey affair, it provided that the Treasury could veto the provision of support by the Bank but could not mandate it. The Treasury perception in the past was that the Bank was too ready to support its banking clients. Yet other aspects of the 1997 reforms could be seen as distancing the Bank from banks, though under Eddie George there was little sign of that distance. By 2007, however, the institution's bias went in the opposite direction, and the Bank did not leap to the support of the commercial banks in difficulty. The Bank itself also noted that the provision of lender of last resort facilities made it vulnerable to the contagion effect from bank failure, even though it had lost supervision to the FSA. The damaging effect of the crisis on the Bank's reputation was measured by the regular tracking surveys of credibility for monetary policy purposes. That confirmation reinforced the arguments of those who believed that the Bank neglected the banking system at its peril.

In its own response the government concluded that there should be no shift in the formal responsibility for supervision.[46] Instead, the government focused attention on reforms to the deposit protection scheme, which was perceived to be too restrictive and too slow in operation, and on the creation of a special resolution regime for failing banks, which clarified the position of depositors in the event of a windup and would facilitate an earlier payout to depositors. The rational concern of retail depositors was that their funds could be tied up in a lengthy bankruptcy procedure, even if they were eventually paid out. The government also imposed some changes on the Bank of England itself, to strengthen its focus on financial stability through the creation of a new committee of the Bank's Court. That committee was described as a mechanism for holding the governor to account on financial stability matters. The subtext seemed to be a hope by the Treasury that it would override a reluctant governor in a future Northern Rock case. Yet, as we have seen, the committee is to be chaired by the governor himself. Other changes, of a more cosmetic kind, were made to the Bank's governance structure. In May 2009 the size of the Court was reduced, and more members with financial-sector experience were to be appointed. These reforms partially reversed changes made by Gordon Brown in 1997.

While the government did not explain the reasons for these changes with any clarity, it was perceived that the Bank had, in the previous few years, moved too far away from financial markets. Meetings between senior officials and leading bankers had been cut back. In the past, governors met an advisory group of bank chairmen regularly. Those regular meetings were abandoned after 2003, in favor of an annual dinner that precluded serious discussion. Mervyn King was determined to move away from the past notion of the Bank as "mother hen" of the City, sometimes indeed acting as a kind of spokesman for the banks to government. He also abandoned the Bank's third "core purpose" as it was known: a rather loose objective that gave it a license to intervene in city matters wherever it chose—often in ways that were much welcomed by the private sector.

At the same time, the Bank's senior staffing had changed. Many of the staff with greatest experience of the financial sector had transferred to the FSA a decade before. At the time of the crisis the two deputy governors were both former Treasury officials, neither of whom had live financial market experience. The most senior official with recent expertise on financial market issues had recently retired, and staffing levels in the financial stability wing of the Bank had been cut back. The government showed little concern about these changes when they happened, but its conclusion after Northern Rock was that they had affected the Bank's sensitivity to market developments and that that, rather than any fundamental structural flaw, was behind the debacle, and indeed behind the broader failure of the U.K. authorities to respond to the strains and imbalances in the financial system that developed in the years 2004–7 in particular.

In his review of the U.K. regulatory system, and its performance in the run-up to the crisis, Adair Turner diagnosed the reason for the failure to respond to the buildup of risks as follows:[47]

> The Bank of England tended to focus on monetary policy analysis as required by the inflation target, and...that analysis did not result in policy responses (using either monetary or regulatory levers) designed to offset the risks identified.... The FSA focused too much on the supervision of individual institutions, and insufficiently on wider sectoral and system-wide risks.... The vital activity of macro-prudential analysis, and the definition and use of macro-prudential tools, fell between two stools...the problem was not overlap but underlap.

He recommended a number of ways in which the future relationship between the Bank and the FSA could be defined, but not a fundamental review of their respective responsibilities. Prime Minister Gordon Brown also rejected structural change. The Conservative opposition commissioned their own review by James Sassoon, a former senior Treasury official, who had at one time been responsible for the tripartite structure.[48] This report recommended improvements to joint working, which went in the direction of the Turner proposals. It also questioned whether the new legislation brought in to strengthen the Bank of England's role in financial stability had in fact put in place the basis for a sensible relationship between its financial stability and monetary policy responsibilities. Sassoon also opened up broader questions of regulatory structure without recommending a particular alternative. However, the Conservatives finally decided on radical structural change, including moving banks and insurance companies back under the direct supervision of the Bank of England and creating a Financial Policy Committee alongside the Monetary Policy Committee that would be responsible for the overall stability of the financial system and for operating macroprudential regulation (to which we return below). They argue by reference to the Obama Administration's proposals for the Federal Reserve—even though those proposals were conceived to compensate for the absence of an integrated supervisor in the United States.

Was the Labour government correct to take the view that no fundamental reform of the structure of responsibilities was required or did the Northern Rock affair demonstrate more fundamental flaws in the U.K. arrangements that it was difficult for the government of the day, having been responsible for introducing them, to acknowledge?

Before answering these questions we should travel back west across the Atlantic, where the whole question of the U.S. financial regulatory structure has been opened up. There were many concerns about the Byzantine U.S. system before the crisis erupted, but the events of 2007-8, and especially the SEC's unsure response, gave new impulse to the case for change, which had previously faced seemingly insuperable political obstacles. The then Treasury secretary Hank Paulson launched a "blueprint for regulatory reform" in March 2008.[49] In introducing it he noted that the

> current regulatory structure was not built to address the modern financial system with its diversity of market participants, innovation, complexity of financial instruments, convergence of financial intermediaries and trading platforms, global integration and interconnectedness among financial institutions, investors and markets.

He noted that the functional division at the heart of the U.S. system

> is at odds with the increasing convergence of financial service providers and products. It creates jurisdictional disputes among regulators, and it is a likely result that some financial services and products were exported to more adaptive foreign markets.

The conclusion the U.S. Treasury reached, having assessed different international models, was to recommend an approach based on objectives, which would link the regulatory structure to the reasons for regulation. So they proposed three separate regulators: one focused on market stability across the entire financial sector (the Federal Reserve); a regulator focused on the safety and soundness of those institutions supported by a federal guarantee; and a regulator focused on protecting consumers and investors.

The details of how the consumer protection regulator would be constructed are not relevant here. From the perspective of financial stability, Paulson argued that the Federal Reserve was the natural choice for that task, but that in future the Fed's role "would continue through traditional channels of implementing monetary policy and providing liquidity to the financial system." This role "would replace the Fed's more limited role of bank holding company supervision." So while the Fed would have the authority to roam across the financial system for information, it would no longer be involved in direct institutional supervision, as it had been in the past. So, far from concluding as a result of the previous nine months of market turmoil that the Bernanke argument for a direct role in institutional oversight had been strengthened, the U.S. Treasury argued the reverse. It argued that the market stability, or financial stability, regulator needed a broad vision and access to the whole of the financial sector, but that it did not need to be engaged in day-to-day activities in relation to what was, after all, only a subset of deposit-taking institutions that, in turn, were a subset of those firms that could create threats to the stability of the system.

Shortly after its publication, market events added force to the Paulson analysis. The Fed concluded that it could not allow the failure of a relatively small broker–dealer, to use the anachronistic phrase still in use in Washington, and engineered a rescue of Bear Stearns. At the same time, access to the discount window for investment banks was extended, which implied a regulatory relationship between the Fed and the investment banks that had not existed in the past. The SEC was nervous but accepted the inevitable, with a remarkable acknowledgment of the shortcomings of the functional approach to which it had clung for so long. Announcing a new Memorandum of Understanding on information-sharing with the Fed, Chris Cox (chairman of the SEC at that time) said:[50]

> Years ago, when the dividing lines between commercial and investment banking were bright, the high level of coordination we are establishing today was not a priority for the U.S. government. But today, the interconnectedness of mortgage and lending markets, credit derivatives, securitizations, and counterparty relationships requires the U.S. government to adopt a more coherent and coordinated approach.

In September 2008 the regulatory frontiers shifted in an even more fundamental way. The U.S. authorities decided not to rescue Lehman Brothers. The reasons for this fateful decision are still not wholly clear. The New York Fed was well aware of the risk of serious instability if a large broker–dealer went down. They went to great lengths to engineer a rescue by Bank of America and then, when they refused to be involved, by Barclays. Some argue that the refusal of British regulators to allow Barclays to guarantee Lehman's trades when the market opened, without consulting shareholders, was the crucial point that scuppered the deal.[51] Others maintain that Barclays themselves, in the course of their due diligence, decided that it was unwise for them to proceed. Without a potential purchaser, Tim Geithner, then the president of the New York Fed, maintained that "the Fed just did not have the legal authority to act."

The Lehman Brothers failure precipitated a major crisis of confidence in almost all U.S. financial institutions. The remaining investment banks, Goldman Sachs and Morgan Stanley, came under particular pressure and were soon at risk of bankruptcy themselves. Merrill Lynch found timely refuge in the bosom of the Bank of America, a maternal embrace that the latter came soon to regret. The Fed's response was to facilitate an emergency conversion of both the remaining large "broker–dealers" into "bank holding companies," subject to Federal Reserve oversight and with broader and deeper access to the Fed's support facilities. Thus a whole category of institution disappeared in a matter of weeks. The Fed's consolidated oversight led quickly to a reduction of leverage on the part of the investment banks. By the end of 2008 their leverage ratio was around half what it had been a year earlier and it fell further in 2009. The change in status means that they are now able to take retail deposits. It also led to the removal of the SEC from its position as consolidated supervisor, a role which it had never carried out with great enthusiasm.

These changes, unplanned as they were, added force to the arguments for regulatory reform. It became commonplace to argue that the U.S. system was damaged beyond repair and needed comprehensive overhaul. The near-collapse of AIG, supervised by the New York State Insurance Commissioner and the office of the Thrift Supervision—an odd couple— added pressure for the creation of a federal insurance charter. The failure of AIG was perhaps the most dramatic illustration of the dysfunctionality of the U.S. system.

Some academic critics of the U.S. system went further. Howell Jackson of the Harvard Law School argued for the creation of a U.S. Financial Services Authority that would be consistent with, and complement, the expansion of the Federal Reserve Board's role in overseeing market stability.[52] He set out a four-phase approach to reform beginning with enhancement of the coordinating role of the President's Working Group on Financial Markets. The Committee on Capital Markets Regulation, chaired by Hal Scott of Harvard, produced a comprehensive report on the global financial crisis in May 2009 that again recommended the creation of a U.S. Financial Services Authority, though it would differ markedly from the U.K. version in that the Fed would continue to set capital requirements.[53]

It was always highly unlikely that the Scott or Jackson approaches would find favor in Congress, or indeed that the Paulson blueprint would be implemented in full. There are many vested interests, both institutional and political, in the American system that would make an integrated model of the kind the Treasury had advocated difficult to achieve. Battle lines had already been drawn and by the time the Obama Administration outlined its own proposals in June 2009 many of the rationalizing elements of the Paulson proposals had lost traction. There was strong resistance to a merger of the SEC and the Commodity Futures Trading Commission. The state insurance regulators were hostile to the idea of a federal charter for nationally significant insurance companies. The regional Federal Reserve Banks saw their role diminishing if federally chartered banks were removed from their purview, even if the governors in Washington themselves could see advantages in the broader role envisaged for the Fed.

In March 2009, ahead of the G20 summit, the Obama Administration produced an outline of its own proposals for institutional reform.[54] The first element was to create a "single independent regulator" with responsibility for systemically important firms and critical payment and settlement systems, regardless of whether those firms owned a depositary institution. The main characteristics of systemic importance were identified as the financial system's interdependence with the firm, its size, its leverage (including its off-balance-sheet exposures), its degree of reliance on short-term funding, and, crucially, its importance as a source of liquidity and credit for the real economy. The regulator's focus would in future be on what the firm did, and the potential for it to create systemic risk, and not on its legal form (a reflection of the approach taken in the United Kingdom's Financial Services and Markets Act).

Intriguingly, the statement did not immediately identify the Federal Reserve as the existing institution best placed to take on this role, though some of the criteria are close to the core concerns of central banks.

However, at the same time, a separate statement was issued, confirming the Fed's critical responsibilities in the fields of financial and monetary stability.

In the event, after some months of deliberation, the new Administration came out in favor of a new role for the Federal Reserve.[55] In issuing the paper describing the approach they boldly appropriated the URL www.financialstability.gov. Although some consolidation of banking supervisors was proposed, through the creation of a national bank supervisor to supervise all federally chartered banks, the Fed was given responsibility for the consolidated supervision of all companies that owned a bank, and of all large, interconnected firms whose failure could threaten the stability of the system. Thus, although the creation of a federal insurance supervisor was resisted, a large complex group like AIG could no longer escape consolidated supervision.

The Obama proposal did not quite amount to giving the Fed an overarching responsibility for financial stability. Instead, a new Financial Services Oversight Council, chaired and staffed by the Treasury and including the main federal financial regulators, would be set up to identify emerging risks in firms and markets, fill gaps in supervision, and facilitate policy coordination and dispute resolution. This arrangement is a cousin of the United Kingdom's's Tripartite Committee, as it brings together the monetary, fiscal, and supervisory authorities. This makes sense, as the crisis has highlighted the interdependence of the three functions in the prosecution of both monetary and financial stability.

In the euro area developments took a different course, though the preservation of a strong role for the central bank in supervisory policy was a common element. A European Systemic Risk Board under the aegis of the ECB was created, as proposed by Jacques de Larosière (this is discussed in greater detail in chapter 7). The Board can issue risk warnings of a general or specific kind, addressed to the Council of Ministers, or to one of the EU-wide committees of supervisors (which are to be characterized in the future as "authorities").

In both cases, therefore, after some flirtation with a structure that would leave authority for financial stability in the exclusive hands of the central banks, a tripartite framework has been proposed, recognizing that monetary, fiscal, and regulatory powers may need to be used, in different combinations at different times, and that a coordinating framework was therefore essential.

So how has the financial crisis left the argument on the appropriate role for central banks? We think that it has not fundamentally altered the balance of the arguments set out in our earlier guide, though in London it did point to weaknesses in practice and in coordination. In fact, the key failing was political—the Treasury's reluctance or inability to take timely decisions on bank support or depositor guarantees. The crisis certainly also produced a strong argument in the United Kingdom and the United States for resolution of the long-outstanding question of bankruptcy procedures for banks and investment banks, and of the status of depositors in those procedures. It also revealed that the political appetite for a deposit insurance scheme based on an element of coinsurance was very modest indeed. The case for reform of deposit insurance was, as a result, strongly made out. There is no point in a regime of coinsurance if the government is to underwrite deposits 100% in the event of a bank failure, as it did in the case of Northern Rock, and as many other governments have since done.

But as far as the role of a central bank in supervision is concerned, our conclusions are as follows.

- No single model of supervision is clearly superior to all others. There are examples of single regulators that work well, and examples of hiccups in those regimes. Equally, some central bank supervisors seem to have performed well. In other cases, the additional insights they were supposed to possess have made little difference.
- We now have it on the authority of the U.S. Treasury that a system based on the legal form a firm takes has many drawbacks, and the earlier defenses of the U.S. system by successive Fed chairmen have been abandoned. The U.S. system has been found wanting in crisis conditions.
- The process of integration of different subsectors continues apace, and argues for, at the very least, formal structures of cooperation between different regulators, as the Fed and the SEC have belatedly acknowledged. The new Financial Services Oversight Council should fill that gap.
- The lessons from the crisis are focused on the nature of lender of last resort provision, the importance of robust oversight of liquidity, the need for early preemptive action and rapid resolution mechanisms for failing banks, and the importance of depositor protection schemes in which retail depositors have confidence, rather than on regulatory structures.

- The crisis also points to the importance for a central bank of good links with regulators, on the one hand, and with market participants, on the other. A central bank that begins to behave like a monetary policy institute, as the Bank of England had arguably begun to do, risks finding itself dangerously behind the game when a crisis strikes.

- Central banks clearly need individuals in senior management positions to have experience of, and an instinctive understanding of, the dynamics of financial intermediation, including both banking and securities markets, and the use made of securities markets by other intermediaries, especially insurance companies.

- Carrying out the day-to-day tasks of prudential regulation of individual institutions is neither necessary nor sufficient to create the understanding of financial stability, and the threats thereto, that a central bank needs. Indeed it may serve to reduce the institution's objectivity and candor. But the central bank does need first-hand knowledge of systemically important institutions, focusing on their liquidity, funding, and capital adequacy. It should equip itself to obtain that knowledge, even if some duplication of regulatory oversight is thereby created.

- A form of tripartite structure is inevitable, bringing together regulators (whether within or without the central bank), the monetary authority, and the fiscal authority. The Canadian and Australian systems, which incorporate such arrangements, performed well in the crisis, suggesting that the U.K. structure was not to blame, rather the way decisions within it were made.

We continue to see advantages in an integrated model of regulation, whose ultimate justification has not been undermined by the crisis, and in separation of frontline regulation from the monetary authority, though in the particular circumstances of the euro area we can see attraction, in the case of countries with a functional breakdown still in place, in the Dutch model, where integrated prudential regulation is collocated with the operational, if not the policymaking, arm of the monetary authority. It is particularly attractive in circumstances in which politicians do not have the courage to engineer a move of staff from the central bank to an outside agency, which was essential in constructing the FSA. (The fact that the main Dutch banks entered the crisis in as vulnerable a state as any gives pause as to the effectiveness of De Nederlandsche

Bank as a supervisor, but does not necessarily invalidate the structural case.)

As the *Financial Times* argued in a leading article in June 2008:[56]

> Over the past 40 years, the guardians of financial stability within central banks have lost power to markets and to international commercial banks. Most of all they have lost power to the monetary policymakers within their own institutions. Monetary policy is high profile and of constant interest; financial stability hits the headlines in a crisis once or twice each generation. The risk that it becomes a backwater is constant. Nonetheless, monetary policy and financial stability cannot be separated . . . the challenge is to build a central bank where the two functions can coexist.

We agree.

But we do not think they can coexist usefully as two separate "wings," to use the old Bank of England terminology. The analysis of financial market developments, captured in FSRs, has not often influenced debates in the MPC. A similar disjuncture is also visible in other countries. By the same token, bank supervisors, even when they are in the central bank, often have little awareness of the monetary policy dimension. This is clear from their contributions in international committees. The need is to integrate the core functions of the central bank, so that the two forms of stability can be seen as interconnected. We discussed some of the practical implications in our discussion of monetary policy and asset prices.

But defining the composition and remit of a new-style financial stability operation in a nonsupervisory central bank is not straightforward. In our view it should, at least, perform the following functions:

- It should develop a robust set of indicators of financial stress that will act as the underpinning of a frank and pointed FSR. We note that nonsupervisory central banks have a better record of producing frank FSRs.
- It should coordinate its work closely with the IMF, FSB, BIS, and the other central banks in systemically important centers.
- It should patrol the regulatory frontier, seeking market intelligence from both regulated and unregulated firms, and identifying the need to adjust the frontier from time to time.
- It should regularly assess the opportunities for regulatory arbitrage (a function that is much harder for supervisors, with their inevitable focus on regulated firms, to perform).

- It should contribute to the assessment of the need for counter-cyclical capital requirements (see the section on macroprudential oversight in chapter 5).
- It should develop its own list of systemically important firms, whether regulated or not, and regularly debate that list with the line supervisors.
- It should ensure that wholesale markets are resilient to the failure of a major counterparty, including, for example, settlement arrangements for OTC derivatives, collateral arrangements in repo markets, or margining practices.
- It should feed its views on financial-sector stresses into the monetary policy process. If there is no link between monetary and financial stability, the argument for a formal financial stability role for the central bank is much reduced. So stresses in the financial system, "excess" growth of credit, and the inflation of asset price bubbles need to be seen as political justification for changes in interest rates.
- It should make a substantial contribution to policy on capital, liquidity, and operational risk in the key global committees.

Financial Infrastructure

Whether or not they have the statutory responsibility for banking supervision, central banks play the key role in the day-to-day functioning of the
financial system. They are, almost everywhere, the authorities empow-
ered to provide liquidity to the banking system. They are also often the
overseers of payment systems, and the linked settlement systems for
securities and foreign exchange. Sometimes they manage government
debt, though the practice has become less widespread in recent years.
In each case, the crisis has challenged previous assumptions about the
responsibilities that central banks should have in these areas, and how
they should carry them out.

These functions are sometimes carried further and expressed as a
general responsibility for the smooth functioning of financial markets
in a central bank's jurisdiction. That may also translate into a quasi-
promotional role, as the central bank seeks to ensure that its own offer-
ings, and those of financial firms in its financial center, are internationally competitive.

LIQUIDITY MANAGEMENT

As Philip Turner explains in "Central banks, liquidity and the banking
crisis,"[1] one of the functions of financial intermediation is to liquify illiquid investments. He quotes Keynes as observing that "capital markets
provide liquidity to make investments which are 'fixed' for the community more 'liquid' for the individual." This is true for banks as well as for
capital markets more generally. It is a natural role of banks to be illiquid
themselves, and for that reason it has long been a core function of central banks to deal with the circumstance in which a bank has to repay a
short-term deposit or other liability unexpectedly and cannot liquidate
its loans or investments to do so.

Liquidity problems were at the heart of the financial crisis that began in the summer of 2007. The change occurred very rapidly. In late 2006 conditions were very easy; there was talk of "excess" liquidity seeking a good home. But liquidity can be at its most vulnerable when it appears strongest. Defenses designed by firms to cope with their idiosyncratic risks may be of limited use when market-wide liquidity is under stress. Liquifying assets, increasing retail deposits, and slowing asset growth are often impossible when all banks are trying to do the same thing. The strains were first visible in the mortgage and structured credit markets, as investors shunned new securitizations, resulting in a wave of involuntary reintermediation. That in turn put pressure on the liquidity position of banks and broker–dealers. The first signs of the emerging crisis were seen in the asset-backed commercial paper market in the early summer of 2007, when issuers began to find it difficult to roll over existing issues, and impossible to issue new paper. Investor nervousness was especially evident in relation to off-balance-sheet vehicles related to banks, notably structured investment vehicles. Some were liquidated and others migrated back to the balance sheets of their sponsors, aggravating their funding problems. Liquidity demand surged, while investors were nervous about their banking counterparties, creating a sudden and protracted disruption in the interbank markets.

The disruption, and the continuing liquidity strains, were evident from the unprecedented widening of spreads between overnight and three-month rates. In normal times, three-month Libor rates are usually a few basis points above overnight rates, but from late July 2007 there was a rapid and sharp widening, reflecting both investor preference for liquidity and rising risk premia, in part driven by uncertainty about where the subprime and other losses lay. The credit and liquidity dimensions of the crisis were therefore very closely linked, and the relative contribution of each is hard to assess. The BIS conclusion was that[2]

> The behaviour of Libor banks' credit default swap spreads vis-à-vis Libor overnight index swap rate spreads suggests that, while credit concerns have indeed played a role in driving interbank rates through the turmoil, liquidity factors have accounted for much of the dynamics.

The Bank of England publishes and monitors, in its FSR, an index of market liquidity based on three factors:[3]

- tightness, as measured by bid–offer spreads for gilts, foreign exchange contracts, and FTSE 100 equities;

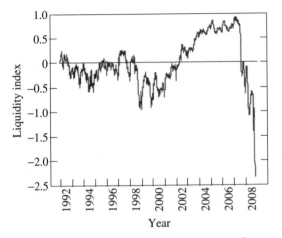

Figure 4.1. Financial market liquidity.[3]

- depth, based on an assessment of the size of trades possible without impacting market prices; and
- premium, a measure of the prospective premium in the corporate bond market as a compensation for liquidity risk.

The index trended upward from 2000 to the middle of 2007 (figure 4.1) and was at historic highs in the early part of the year, before declining very sharply from August onward. The fall was remarkable, but the historical record shows that the buildup of liquidity tends to be a gradual process while downward adjustments are often sharp—albeit not always as precipitous as the movement in late 2007.

Central banks reacted to these developments in what the BIS themselves called a number of "extraordinary and unprecedented ways." In all cases they engaged in interventions on an unusual scale and at longer maturities. Most also, sooner or later, broadened the range of collateral they were prepared to accept. (In the ECB case the range was already much broader than in the United Kingdom or the United States.)

The ECB was, in fact, the first to react, on August 9, with a huge injection of liquidity, front-loaded at the start of its maintenance period (it was unwound later). The Federal Reserve held late supplementary auctions the following day. The Bank of England did not change its liquidity operations in August, maintaining its limited range of assets accepted as collateral. As late as mid September the Bank rejected the case for general injections of liquidity against a wider range of collateral on the grounds that to do so "would encourage in future the very risk-taking that has led us to where we are." Underlining the point—with an oblique but acid reference to Chuck Prince of Citibank who said, just before he was forced to resign, that while the music continued to play his bank was "still dancing"—the governor maintained[4] that "the provision of large liquidity facilities penalises those financial institutions that sat out the dance, encourages herd behaviour and increases the intensity of future crises."

Mervyn King attracted some criticism for this unforthcoming stance. Larry Summers accused him of being a moral hazard fundamentalist who misunderstood the insurance analogy.[5] Others argued that the Bank's tough line, and failure to appreciate the scale of the crisis, aggravated the difficulties faced by Northern Rock and helped to precipitate its collapse. At the least, it made management of the crisis considerably more difficult. It could also be said to be at variance with the Bank's traditional policy, as set out by Eddie George in 1993, that when the Bank intervenes shareholders lose everything, senior management lose their jobs, but the institution survives.[6]

Even the exceptional market interventions by the Fed and the ECB were not successful in reducing the three-month spread, which continued to be an expressive indicator of market dysfunctionality. The central banks then shifted their focus to the direct provision of term funding. The Bank of England offered larger three-month tenders, the ECB added a six-month tender facility, and the Fed introduced a new term auction facility. These measures significantly increased the proportion of term funding in the total facilities made available to the market.

There was a coordinated effort to relieve liquidity pressures in December 2007, organized by the Fed, the ECB, the Bank of England, and the Swiss National Bank. But once again these arrangements proved inadequate. The problems were exacerbated by liquidity hoarding by the banks themselves, which further reduced the pass-through to nonbanks. The authorities' actions were criticized at the time as being "too little too late." Nouriel Roubini argued that the provision of liquidity to only depository institutions would not be enough. As he pointed out,[7]

> The severe liquidity and credit problems affect today a financial market dominated by non-banks that do not have direct access to the liquidity support of the Fed.... They are now at risk of a liquidity run as their liabilities are short-term while many of their assets are longer-term and illiquid...so monetary policy is totally impotent in dealing with the liquidity problems and the risks of runs on liquid liabilities of a large fraction of the financial system.

This critique, rejected at the time, was broadly accepted by the Fed in March 2008, when the near-bankruptcy of Bear Stearns compelled them to intervene directly in the funding of investment banks for the first time. The Fed made available a large overnight nonrecourse loan to J.P. Morgan through the discount window to allow it to take on the obligations of Bear Stearns. At the same time, recognizing the risk of further instability, and using its power to provide exceptional financing in "unusual and exigent" circumstances, the Fed established a new Primary Dealer Credit Facility through which it would in future be able to lend to an investment bank (and indeed other corporations) if the latter could not find needed credit from its commercial banking counterparties. The securities lending program was also changed, with the creation of a new term-lending securities facility.

The justifications offered by the Fed for this unusual move were revealing. Tim Geithner, then the president of the New York Fed, acknowledged that the earlier moves had not solved the problem.[8] He attributed that failure to the changing structure of financial markets over the previous thirty years and the move away from a bank-dominated system to one in which "credit is increasingly extended, securitized and actively traded in a combination of centralized and decentralized markets." There had been a dramatic increase in the amount of financial intermediation occurring outside the core banking system. As a result, investment banks "now perform many of the economic functions traditionally associated with commercial banks, and they are also vulnerable to a sudden loss of liquidity." The rescue of Bear Stearns could therefore be justified on conventional grounds: had the firm been allowed to collapse there would have been collateral damage for a range of innocent bystanders. Geithner rejected the charge that additional moral hazard had been created on the grounds that the shareholders of Bear Stearns had suffered a massive loss (though the subsequent settlement provided an amount per share almost five times larger than the Fed had initially envisaged). For reasons not fully explained at the time, or since, the U.S. authorities took a different approach in September 2008 when Lehman Brothers failed.

The Bear Stearns rescue was heavily criticized, by Buiter among others,[9] though Summers took the view that he would also not have wished to carry out the experiment of seeing what the consequences of an investment bank collapse would be.[10] We saw the dramatic consequences of such a collapse in September. But the remarkable aspect of the justification offered by Geithner was its long-term nature. If he is right in his analysis of these long-term trends, why had there been no earlier change in the way the Fed provided liquidity to U.S. markets? The collapse of Drexel Burnham years earlier had shown just how exposed an investment bank could be to a liquidity run. And if even the smallest of the major investment banks could not be allowed to fail, why had it not been subject to proper oversight before? The Bear Stearns rescue was, therefore, a watershed, and a recognition that the U.S. authorities had been operating according to an outdated model of intermediation and regulation—one, furthermore, that they themselves knew to be obsolete. The implications for the U.S. regulatory system are far-reaching.

Elsewhere, the ECB did not change its facilities again, though it did continue to provide huge volumes of support at the beginning of each maintenance period. It was able to make a virtue of the fact that it already accepted a broader range of collateral than its counterparts, partly because its liquidity arrangements were a compilation of those it inherited from the central banks that had come together to form the European System of Central Banks. The characterization of its support facilities as the "litterbin of last resort" did not deflect it.[11] The Bank of England did, under pressure from the banks, revise its own scheme significantly in April 2008, introducing a special liquidity scheme that greatly broadened the range of assets accepted as collateral, and lengthened the terms of support provided.[12]

As the crisis developed through the fall and winter of 2008, and especially after the failure of Lehman Brothers, the authorities were obliged to intervene in the markets on a larger and larger scale, and to take even more extensive collateral, as the debt markets stubbornly refused to reopen. The central banks became, in a sense, market-makers of last resort. In the United Kingdom the Treasury, through the Bank of England, guaranteed certain kinds of bank debt. But liquidity provision quite soon proved insufficient, and solvency support from governments was needed. In almost all developed countries direct injections of capital into systematically important banks resulted in either de jure or de facto nationalization of large parts of the system of financial intermediation. It became clear that in the exceptional circumstances of the credit crisis the traditional central banking toolkit had proved inadequate. As more banks tried to liquidate their positions, prices fell further, and liquidity problems turned into severe concerns about solvency. As Paul Tucker put it, central banks had moved on from the familiar, historic role of lender of last resort and needed to look at other instruments, in effect becoming the market-maker of last resort, or even the capital provider of last resort.[13] Some commentators even described this role as "market-maker of first resort." (See Turner[1] for a detailed analysis of the various techniques adopted and their implications.)

So the consequences of the crisis for central banks in their role as providers of liquidity to markets (and indeed for regulators) have been highly significant, and have caused them to rethink the principles and practice of liquidity management, by reminding them yet again that banks are structurally illiquid institutions. Three interlinked sets of issues arise:

- How can commercial and investment banks' own liquidity management be improved to introduce more robust shock absorbers into a system that has been shown, as it often has in the history of banking, to be dangerously unstable?

- How can the regulatory oversight of liquidity be strengthened? How should liquidity regulation be adapted to take account of central banks' own operational practices? What are the cross-border implications of changes in individual countries' practices?

- How do central banks' arrangements for liquidity support need to be changed to accommodate the changes in credit creation and intermediation that Geithner described?

Liquidity Management in Banks

Banks, and other financial institutions, got a nasty surprise in 2007. Assumptions they had made about the continuous availability of interbank funding for solvent firms were proved to have been overoptimistic. Banks found themselves without stocks of high-quality assets that they could quickly turn into cash. Northern Rock and, later, Halifax Bank of Scotland were the most visible and dramatic cases among U.K. commercial banks. The problem spread through the banking systems of North America and Europe. A review by regulators in the main financial centers identified many weaknesses in liquidity management, even in the biggest global firms.[14] Some had no internal incentives in place to manage liquidity, and business lines were often not charged for building contingent liquidity exposures. Treasury functions were frequently not closely aligned with risk management processes. Contingency funding plans were based on incomplete information, and the potential liquidity needs of off-balance-sheet vehicles were ignored. This sorry catalog of failings came as a shock to boards and even to senior management.

In the short run the conclusion reached by many was that they should protect their own sources of liquidity at all costs. This individually rational strategy contributed to the continuation of the crisis, as interbank markets became heavily constricted. Banks declined to lend to long-standing counterparties, which made the problem worse.

In the longer term firms concluded that they needed to work on greater diversification of funding sources, which in turn may involve greater diversity of asset portfolios. A report by the Institute of International Finance summarized the lessons learnt.[15] Furthermore, internal assessments by firms themselves demonstrated that liquidity concerns had not been properly reflected in internal pricing mechanisms. Trading desks whose strategies depended heavily on access to short-term interbank financing had not been charged a realistic price. Some of the changes needed to correct these deficiencies were obvious. Firms need to create incentives for business lines to recognize the liquidity risks inherent in their business models. That is particularly true in the case of asset securitizations. Banks should also stress test liquidity risk management. In particular, they should understand the conditions in which their balance sheets might expand during times of market stress and they should prepare contingency plans.

But however prudent and cautious firms may be in the short term there will always be a temptation for them to economize on liquidity, or liquidity insurance more generally, especially in view of the pressure on banks to increase profits and return on equity. Holding short-term liquid assets is costly, and experience shows that the half-life of lessons from near-death market episodes is surprisingly short. In more normal times the powerful incentives to economize on holdings of cash and low-yielding liquid assets will reassert themselves. So the challenge for supervisors and central banks is to underpin the prudent behavior to which intermediaries now say they are firmly committed. Indeed banks may for a time have been recklessly prudent in the immediate aftermath of the crisis, but if they are not to begin dancing again when the band strikes up once more, this new prudence will need to be underpinned by revised supervision arrangements that will operate effectively in peacetime as well as in war.

SUPERVISION OF LIQUIDITY

Banks have a strong financial incentive to minimize their holdings of liquid assets. The amount they actually hold at any time is largely determined by the opportunity cost and their perception of risk. The state of the cycle is therefore influential, and there is evidence that banks systematically hold less liquidity in an upturn and more in a downturn. They are also, however, influenced by their perceptions of the likelihood of lender of last resort support being made available. It is not easy to measure that effect, though there are case studies that cast light on it. Banks in Argentina reduced their liquidity measurably when the central bank implemented a repo agreement at the end of 1996 that strengthened its ability to assist the market.[16] Using the Fitch ratings of U.K. banks as a proxy for the likelihood of LOLR support, Aspachs et al.[17] conclude that "the greater the potential support from the central bank in case of liquidity crises, the lower the liquidity buffer the banks hold." They are also influenced by their expectations of the future course of interest rates. Diamond and Rajan have shown that the incentives for banks to become illiquid increases with the expectation that future interest rates will be low. They comment:[18]

> With global savings pouring in, and with the Federal Reserve emphasizing its willingness to pump in liquidity and cut interest rates dramatically in case of a sharp downturn (the so-called Greenspan put), it is not surprising that banks are willing to take liquidity risk.

So there is some empirical support for Mervyn King's moral hazard argument. There is therefore a clear case for intervention by supervisors to require banks to hold more liquidity than they would otherwise, as part of the implicit "social contract" between the banks and the authorities.[19] Governments allow banks to engage in more maturity transformation by offering the prospect of liquidity support, but the risk of the need for that support crystallizing is mitigated by obligations placed on them to hold buffers of capital and liquidity. Those buffers will need to be stronger in future, to offer greater protection to taxpayers, who have been obliged to undertake expensive rescues.

Charles Goodhart, the historian of the Basel Committee, has pointed out that the declared intention of the Committee on its formation in the 1970s was to underpin the capital and liquidity adequacy performance of the main international commercial banks.[20] But notwithstanding the trenchant academic criticisms of Basel II, the Committee's record in relation to capital is far stronger than it is in relation to liquidity. The first capital accord did reverse the downward trend in capital adequacy, but there was no parallel accord to underpin bank liquidity. Supervisors found it difficult to reach international agreement on the subject. While they continued to reflect unproductively, banks continued to run down their liquidity stocks. Fifty years ago, around 30% of British clearing bank assets were held in the form of highly liquid instruments: largely cash, Treasury bills, and short-dated government debt. By 2007 they held about 0.5% in cash and perhaps another 1% in other traditional liquid assets.[21] There was "guidance" issued by the Committee in 2000, but this fell well short of a mandatory regime, and the guidance appears to have had little or no impact.

Since the crisis, the Committee has attempted to fill the gap. Indeed it was firmly told to do so in April 2008 by the FSF[22] on behalf of the G7 finance ministers. The outcome was a set of "principles for sound liquidity risk management and supervision," first issued in June 2008[23]—a very rapid turnaround for the Basel Committee. After a short consultation period, a slightly revised version was issued in September 2008. The language of the principles is suitably tough. Words like "vigorous" "strong," and "robust" pepper the text, and supervisors are encouraged to "intervene in a timely manner" to address deficiencies.

This tough talk, however, proved to be a substitute for tough action, as is often the case. The detail of the principles is less impressive. There is a remarkable lack of analysis and calibration. Indeed the only numbers in the report are ordinal: there are seventeen numbered principles. Of course it is hard to dissent from the fine sentiments expressed. Who can disagree with the idea that a bank should ensure that "it maintains sufficient liquidity, including a cushion of unencumbered, high quality liquid assets, to withstand a range of stress events"? Or that it should have "a robust framework for comprehensively projecting cash flows arising from assets, liabilities and off-balance-sheet items over an appropriate set of time horizons"? But if these principles are not turned into hard-edged operational guidelines, they are unlikely to change behavior.

The report said many eminently sensible things about liquidity policies and the role of the banks' boards, and about the need to consider liquidity in different currencies (dollar liquidity was a particular problem for European banks in 2007), which in fact closely parallel the recommendations by the Institute of International Finance. But the Committee hedged its bets heavily on off-balance-sheet vehicles. Structured investment vehicles were at the heart of the problem for many banks, and when their liquidity requirements fell back on the sponsors they were surprised to find that their balance sheets and funding needs were growing, contrary to the assumptions that lay behind their funding models. The paper said only that the question of whether or not they should be consolidated for liquidity purposes should be decided on a case-by-case basis. More importantly, the Committee was silent on the fundamental question of whether banks should now reverse the trend toward holding a smaller and smaller proportion of liquid assets. In the case of capital, the first accord was entirely clear about its headline objective: banks should, overall, strengthen their capital base. Even the second accord, criticized in other respects, began from the presumption that supervisors should not be seeking to reduce the system's capitalization overall. Rather it should be seeking to ensure that capital was better distributed in relation to a more sophisticated and fine-grained understanding of risk. As for the quantum of liquidity, the Committee appeared to be agnostic on whether or not more is required. It limited itself to the observation that "liquidity problems are typically low frequency but potentially high impact events."

Undoubtedly, setting liquidity standards is more difficult than determining capital adequacy. Confidence is an elusive element in the equation, subject to irrational factors. Liquidity is contingent on how a bank is positioned structurally in the interbank market, among other things. All this makes liquidity harder to model than capital. But the latter has benefited from a much higher investment of *intellectual* capital, particularly by central banks. Goodhart warns against the danger of mandatory minimum liquidity standards by reference to the metaphor of

> the weary traveler who arrives at the railway station late at night and, to his delight, sees a taxi there who could take him to his distant destination. He hails the taxi, but the taxi driver replies that he cannot take him, since local bylaws require that there must always be one taxi standing ready at the station. Required liquidity is not true, usable liquidity.

But he nonetheless argues that there is a need for some kind of methodology to measure the degree of maturity transformation and to assess stock liquidity. This exercise has not yet been undertaken by the Basel Committee.

In a consultation paper issued in December 2007, the FSA attempted to get closer to an assessment of how much liquidity a bank should hold.[24] It argued that it is in principle possible to calculate a distribution of the risk of failure of a bank through illiquidity at any point in time, and then to determine a risk appetite on the part of the supervisor (and perhaps the bank itself). In other words, the supervisor can require the bank to hold liquidity at all times so as to reduce the risk of failure on the grounds of illiquidity to, they suggest, 1 in 200 per year. Michael Foot argues that this ratio is far too high. Banks fail for reasons other than insufficient liquidity, so a 1 in 200 event just because of a liquidity shortfall might be consistent with an unacceptably high rate of failure overall.[25] But the principle of setting a risk appetite, and deriving a liquidity requirement from that, is reasonable. Foot sees the key criterion as being to "ensure that the minimum liquidity required provides enough time for any bank above a minimum size to be rescued or closed in an orderly fashion." It is unfortunate that, internationally, no progress seems to be being made toward an agreed regime. Supervisors have not so far been able to translate this objective into a practical requirement. With only fine words available from supervisors, considerable weight will continue to fall on central banks as the last-resort providers of liquidity.

As the scale of the crisis became clearer, regulators became tougher. In October 2008 the Bank of England published proposals for a further reform of its market operations.[26] In future, there will be four main avenues of assistance:

- A reserves averaging scheme for eligible banks, with reserves remunerated by the Bank if they remain within a target range.
- Operational standing facilities, available on demand at a modest premium rate.
- A "discount window facility" through which banks may borrow gilts for up to thirty days, for a fee, against a wide range of collateral.
- Open market operations through short- and long-term repos offered through both variable-rate tenders and outright purchases.

In parallel, the FSA published its own proposals for enhanced liquidity requirements[27] which would require banks to hold significantly larger proportions of their balance sheets in the form of highly liquid assets in the future. One of the explicit aims of the new policy is that it should "act as a check on unsustainable expansion of bank lending, during favourable economic times." It would also produce "less reliance on short-term wholesale funding, including on wholesale funding from foreign counterparties." This was an implicit recognition that the previous regime had allowed imprudent reliance on wholesale funding. Changes of this kind, if and when implemented, will have an impact on the structure of market rates. Central banks will have a close interest in them because of the potential consequences for the monetary transmission mechanism.

In his review of the regulatory response to the banking crisis, Adair Turner, the new chair of the FSA, went further.[28] He argued that it was "essential to restore liquidity regulation and supervision to a position of central importance," and he proposed a "core funding ratio" expressed as retail deposits plus long-term wholesale funding as a percentage of total liabilities. The ratio (as operated for some time in Hong Kong and Singapore) could be a backstop rule or an indicator to identify overall macroprudential risks. As Turner recognizes, tightening liquidity requirements in this way would imply less maturity transformation than would otherwise occur, with some economic cost. This might, however, be a price worth paying to strengthen the resilience of the system.

CENTRAL BANKS AND LIQUIDITY

The central lesson of the crisis from the liquidity perspective was well described by Geithner in his apologia for the Bear Stearns rescue:

> We need to redesign the set of liquidity facilities that we maintain in normal times, and *in extremis*, in the United States and across other major central banks. And these changes will have to come with a stronger set of incentives and requirements for the management of liquidity risk by financial institutions with access to central bank liquidity.

He also called for "a stronger set of shock absorbers, in terms of capital and liquidity" in institutions that are critical to the functioning of the market.

Progress toward the second objective has been slow, but the liquidity facilities of the major central banks have already been revised in a number of respects, as detailed by the BIS. The problem is that in their collective response to the crisis the central banks were pushed into measures that go further than they would have wished in normal times. While they may have clung too long to the moral hazard argument while the house was on fire, as if in the insurance world, as the Bank of England certainly did, they have now become market-makers of last resort for a wide range of risky assets, and even the close haircuts imposed on some of them may not fully compensate for the additional risks they have taken on. As Mervyn King argued in June 2008,[29] central banks needed to learn from the experiences of the previous year and put in place a liquidity facility that worked in all seasons—both normal and stressed. That facility needs a pricing structure that encourages banks to manage liquidity risk prudently. The haircut arrangements in place are not fine-grained enough to produce such incentives: they are in place primarily to protect the central bank's own balance sheet at times of stress.

Tucker[13] summarizes the goal as being

> To reduce the cost of disruptions to the liquidity and payments services supplied by commercial banks. The Bank does this by balancing the provision of credit insurance against the costs of creating incentives for banks to take greater risks, and subject to the need to avoid taking risk onto its balance sheet.

At the same time, the facility needs to overcome the stigma problem that plagued the use of central bank facilities through the crisis. Banks reasonably feared that the knowledge that they were using a "special" facility—one put in place, in the words of the Federal Reserve Act, to deal with only "unusual and exigent" circumstances—would create a crisis of confidence among their other counterparties. Some institutions have made a practice of using the available facilities at times when they may not have been obliged to use them, and have sometimes been encouraged to do so, to create an assumption that they are available to be used; others have shunned them, making the effect on the interest rate curve less powerful.

One potential response to the stigma effect is to make such assistance secret. But while it seems that it might well have been possible for the Bank of England to make an emergency loan to Northern Rock without immediate disclosure (and it subsequently did make massive undisclosed loans to Royal Bank of Scotland and Halifax Bank of Scotland), it seems unlikely that, on a continuing basis, liquidity operations can be undisclosed for very long. There are grounds to believe that, in the EU at least, the provisions of the Market Abuse Directive would preclude undisclosed assistance over an excessively extended period, because shareholders would be misled about the condition of their investment. The trend over many years has been toward greater transparency in central bank operations, and greater use of market prices, so to resort to the former practice of clouding the central bank's actions in "decent obscurity" would be to swim against the tide. It was always assumed in the past that, if the central bank's objective in providing support is to help the system as a whole, there would be few grounds for complaint about discreet support for a troubled bank. The arrival on the scene of large-scale short-sellers has challenged that assumption. Secret support for a failing institution may threaten the profitability of the trades, and potentially give grounds for legal action.

Goodhart argues that we should take a different tack.[30] The problem begins, as he sees it, with "a continuing and misplaced reverence for the

Bagehot dictum that central banks should only lend to individual banks at a penalty rate." This is bound to generate a stigma. His solution is to require all banks to borrow an initial tranche of funds from the central bank at all times. The cost of this initial tranche would be deliberately low, indeed it might even be zero. The pricing of additional borrowing would be varied by scale and duration, and the quantum available for an individual institution would be set as some percentage of eligible liabilities. The sizes of the tranches available, and the pricing attached to them, could be varied. So at a time of liquidity stress the bank could increase the size of a given tranche to effect an easing in liquidity. The instrument could be exercised by the new Financial Stability Committee of the central bank, or whatever the decision-making body on financial stability is called, giving it a usable tool, which it does not currently have. The amounts of funding available to each bank would be published in advance, though utilization of the facility would only be disclosed after the event.

Goodhart's scheme is a bold attempt to solve the stigma problem, if somewhat complex in operation. We can, however, see problems with it in practice. What if the initial amount is not enough? What if a bank considers that it needs a tranche that is appreciably larger than the going rate? There would still be a risk that the market would discover the tranche in which an individual bank was borrowing.

The involvement of central banks in a wider range of instruments has also muddied the waters when making a distinction between intervention to provide liquidity to individual banks or alternatively to the market as a whole. There have also been purchases of instruments, such as commercial paper or corporate bonds, that have the additional and quite different motive of stimulating activity in those markets. These activities raise questions of accountability. Does central bank independence stretch that far? We think not, and note that in the United States, while the Fed has used its umbrella power to act in "unusual and exigent circumstances," it will in future need the prior approval of the U.S. Treasury secretary.

There is also an important cross-border dimension. International banking business often involves three central banks: the central bank in the country where the bank is conducting its business; the central bank where the bank is headquartered; and the central bank of the jurisdiction that the currency used comes from.

As Turner explains, the question of which central bank should take responsibility for emergency liquidity has always been difficult. The issue was extensively discussed among central banks in the early 1970s when the investment of the large oil surpluses in the foreign branches of banks increased the risk of a general liquidity problem if there was a significant withdrawal of short-term funds. Which central bank should be responsible for the liquidity problem: the home or the host? After much debate the G10 central bank governors concluded in 1974 that "it would not be practical to lay down in advance detailed rules and procedures for the provision of liquidity." This remains the formal position, though it became the general presumption that the host-country central bank would have the initial responsibility for providing liquidity support to a foreign bank, but that the home-country central bank might become responsible very soon after such support became necessary.

This cross-border aspect has relevance in relation to the question of whether liquidity can be regulated on a national or international basis. The answer will depend on how likely it is that agreements can be reached on the resolution of cross-border banks that face failure. If agreement is unlikely, the regulators will want to ensure that each bank in its jurisdiction has enough liquidity onshore. If liquidity requirements are tightened on a national basis, then it will have an inhibiting effect on the scale of cross-border business. So there is a clear risk that steps taken to tighten national liquidity regimes may hinder trade and investment flows, if no overall global approach is agreed. Addressing this is a task for the Financial Stability Board.

The currency angle is also important. In the recent crisis many banks found themselves in difficult funding positions where currencies were mismatched. To help mitigate these problems, cross-border swap operations were put in place enabling central banks with limited foreign exchange reserves to lend foreign currency to their own banks, as well as reducing other disturbances in domestic money markets. Such swaps were conducted on a very large scale so that by late 2008 outstanding usage of foreign exchange lines by the ECB, the Bank of England, and the Swiss National Bank exceeded $300 billion.

It remains to be seen whether the new arrangements now in place, which have been constructed to give banks an incentive to manage their own liquidity more effectively in future, will prove adequate. In a crisis, there is little need to encourage banks to hoard liquidity: from 2007 to 2009 they did so overenthusiastically, if anything. The test comes when credit conditions return to normal. When the band strikes up again, will the dancers again cavort with gay abandon as they did from 2004 to

2007? Or will the new, tougher regulatory requirements act as an effective constraint?

PAYMENT SYSTEMS

The second area in which central banks may contribute to financial stability is in the oversight of systemically important payment systems. Certainty that when payments are made they will also be received is, as we suggest in chapter 1, one of the assumptions that society makes when engaging in economic activity. Yet that assumption is also fragile. The systems that central banks oversee include "clean" payment systems (like CHAPS in the United Kingdom) and those, like Euroclear, that involve linked flows of cash and securities. Their traditional aims have been to promote safety and certainty, economic efficiency, and adaptation to the changing needs of innovative financial markets. They are also banks themselves, and they could not undertake the transactions on the balance sheet through which they implement monetary policy if there was uncertainty about the completion of those transactions. Final settlement of transactions is ultimately undertaken through payments involving the central bank's own liabilities.

Members of payment systems are exposed to liquidity as well as credit risk when they incur credit exposures to other members of the system. The system may act as a transmission mechanism for financial problems in one or more members, creating a domino effect that may cause contagion to other participants. Indeed the system itself may be a source of systemic risk through operational failure or malfunction.[31] The different types of risks that may arise have been helpfully codified by the Bank of England.

Many enhancements to these systems, long desired by central banks, have been introduced in recent years, largely made possible by technology improvements. In particular, the introduction of real-time gross settlement, even if it took decades to achieve, has helped to eliminate the buildup of settlement exposure and of so-called Herstatt risk (the risk that in foreign exchange trading one party will deliver foreign exchange while the other counterparty fails to do so) between financial institutions as a result of the exchange of high-value payments and securities settlements.

As a comprehensive response to these potential risks the G10 governors oversaw the drafting of a set of "core principles," by the Committee on Payments and Settlement Systems (CPSS) in Basel, for systemically important payment systems in 2000.[32] Central banks are formally committed to these principles, which were also endorsed by IOSCO on behalf of securities regulators, but while the framework has been widely accepted, the practical role played by different central banks in their domestic payment systems varies widely.

In an extensive review published in 2003, Tanai Khiaonarong of the Bank of Finland identified three main models of involvement (though there is a degree of overlap between them in individual countries):[33]

(1) The minimalist approach, in which the private sector takes precedence in promoting payment systems efficiency, with the central bank's role limited to providing settlement account services, collateral, and liquidity facilities. The systems in use in Australia, Canada, Finland, and the United Kingdom are examples of this approach.

(2) The competitive approach, exemplified by the United States, in which the public and private sectors compete, but in which the central bank owns and operates interbank funds-transfer systems, recovering its full costs from the participants.

(3) A public service philosophy, in which the central bank owns and operates a majority of, if not all, interbank funds-transfer systems. The system used in Thailand exemplifies this third strategy.

From an efficiency perspective, Khiaonarong strongly prefers the first approach. He finds that it is "more efficiency enhancing than the competitive and public service approaches, due to higher cost-reducing effects, stronger private-sector involvement, and the avoidance of the central bank's conflicting role as a regulator."

A similar conclusion was reached by Green and Todd of the Federal Reserve Banks of Chicago and Minneapolis respectively. They argue that[34]

> A recommended strategy involves specialization in providing services where the central bank has a comparative advantage—notably services directly related to providing a comprehensive, secure system of accounts for interbank settlement...the strategy would have the Fed rely on means other than direct service provision to help ensure that services are provided efficiently and equitably.

Again, one argument advanced, and reinforced elsewhere[35] by Green, is that if the Fed is a major participant in the system, and hence a beneficiary of it, this argues against the Fed as its regulator.

While these arguments rest primarily on the efficiency case for low-key central bank involvement, they overlap with the financial stability argument.

Traditionally, payment system oversight was regarded as part and parcel of the relationship between the central bank and its counterparties, and not necessarily as a separate function, but as banking supervision was split away from central banks, some, like the Reserve Bank of Australia, began to formalize their role. In Australia the 1998 Payment Systems (Regulation) Act gives the RBA formal powers to regulate the systems and determine risk control and efficiency standards, though in the Australian case the regulation has in the event focused heavily on access and competition rather than on financial stability issues.[36] Indeed, the RBA is specifically charged with using its powers in a way that "will best contribute to... promoting competition in the market for payment services." Green is strongly of the view that this is not an appropriate role for the central bank, and is far better left to the competition authorities. Most other countries seem to implicitly take this view as well.

While it is generally true that the oversight of payment and settlement systems has become more distinct and formal over the last fifteen years, there remains a remarkable diversity of practice in terms of what powers banks have and how they exercise them. Of the major developed-country authorities, in five cases—the ECB, Germany, the United Kingdom, Japan, and Sweden—the responsibilities are set out in a statute or, in the case of the ECB, a treaty. In another four countries—Canada, Hong Kong, the Netherlands, and Singapore—there is specific legislation related to oversight that gives the central banks distinct responsibilities. Seven others have partial powers, but these stop short of full oversight responsibility. In the United States the Fed has derived its powers from a series of enactments related to other functions, such as banking supervision, but has hitherto lacked a focused set of powers. Its "Policy on payment system risk" is expressed in nonstatutory form.

With the deference and respect that central bankers like to show to each other in public, a CPSS report in 2005[37] presented this diversity without comment, though it noted that "the effectiveness of oversight is likely to depend on there being an appropriate match between those responsibilities and the tools the central bank has to carry out oversight." It is hard to avoid the conclusion that there is great scope for tidying up the legislation in many places. Of course legislating in this area is rarely likely to be a top political priority (though a crisis can make it so, as it has in the United Kingdom and in the United States).

Among the options on offer, the Canadian model is attractive. The Bank of Canada does not own or operate payment or other clearing or settlement systems, though it does maintain settlement accounts and provides final settlement. Its oversight role is clearly set out in the Payment Clearing and Settlement Act of 1996. As the Bank of Finland paper notes, "the Canadian payment system has been regarded as one of the most efficient in the world."

In the United Kingdom, the Bank of England has long relied on informal oversight, as described under the 1997 MOU, though that merely codified what had long been understood to be the position. In 2000, a report for the government by Don Cruikshank recommended that a new authority should be set up explicitly to regulate payment systems, but his concerns were primarily with competition and access rather than with systemic risk.[38] He believed that the clearing banks had resisted new entrants and maintained a cosy cartel, which a new competition authority could deal with by mandating open access for all economically significant systems. The Bank successfully resisted the proposal to establish a separate authority. But the informal position in which the Bank found itself came to seem as increasingly anomalous. In June 2007, Governor Mervyn King described this as "unfinished business" from the MOU. Informal powers could only go so far, he said.[39] "To have responsibility without power is the misfortune of the bureaucrat," he went on. The Banking Act of 2009, stimulated by the need to respond to the Northern Rock crisis, regularized the position, after a decade of masterful inactivity on the government's behalf.

In our view codification of the powers available, and the way in which those powers might be exercised, is welcome and would be valuable in other jurisdictions. It would meet the laudable commitment to transparency enunciated by the CPSS (and to which the ECB has since responded with a comprehensive report on its oversight activities) and would mark a further move away from the "governor's eyebrows" approach to central banking, which is increasingly anachronistic in today's financial markets.

After long defending the Fed's informal role[40] there were signs in 2009 that the U.S. authorities recognized the problem. In congressional testimony in March[41], Tim Geithner, the Treasury secretary, noted that federal authority was incomplete and fragmented, and concluded: "We need to give a single entity broad and clear authority over systemically important payment and settlement systems and activities." But the complexity of doing so was demonstrated in the following sentence: "Where such systems or their participants are already federally regulated, the authority of those federal regulators should be preserved and the single entity should consult and coordinate with those regulators." So while the problem was acknowledged, the simple solution of giving new authority to the Federal Reserve to oversee payment, clearing, and settlement systems was only finally proposed in June 2009 as part of the Obama Administration's reform package.

The interest of central banks in the safety of payment and settlement infrastructure was further reinforced by the structural risks confirmed by the crisis in the arrangements for over-the-counter (OTC) derivatives markets, and they have put increased pressure on market participants to replace bilateral arrangements with central counterparties (CCPs), forcing all transactions onto the same platform or set of platforms. This will reduce risk, though a CCP can still itself fail and needs to be brought under some form of oversight.[42] Some market participants have resisted these proposals on the grounds that they may inhibit competition. In our view, given the malfunctions demonstrated in the crisis of 2007–8, when many complex, bespoke bilateral deals proved difficult or impossible to unwind, they are well-justified on risk-reduction grounds.

FINANCIAL SYSTEM EFFICIENCY

Central banks' responsibility for market infrastructure has often extended far beyond narrow payment and settlement issues, and they have been interested in and involved themselves in many other aspects of the functioning of a modern financial center.

For the most part, this involvement has developed in an unplanned way. Often the central bank has identified a problem and simply stepped in to fix it. On other occasions, market participants themselves have invited the bank's participation. As an active market participant, and one usually unbound by tight budget constraints, it is often able to act expeditiously and independently. The range of ad hoc tasks that central banks have taken on in the past is remarkable: oversight of self-regulatory organizations or exchanges; honest broker in trade disputes; manager of insolvency or debt workouts; interface between the markets and the government; promotion of the local financial center; leader of trade missions; even, in the United Kingdom, direct developer of settlement systems—the Bank of England took over the leadership of the London Stock Exchange's ailing plan to dematerialize securities, which led to Crest. (This last example has now been emulated by the ECB in its own Target 2 Securities project.)

When the Bank of England tried in the early 1990s to define its own role in this area, faced with confusion and some overlap within the institution, it adopted the formulation of a "third core purpose," to promote the efficient functioning of the financial system, alongside its monetary and supervisory roles. While they have not categorized them in quite the same way, other central banks have typically carried out many of these functions alongside their other, more formally specified tasks.

Over time, with the greater emphasis on the use of law to resolve disputes, and the ever-widening scope of statutory regulation to replace self-regulatory organizations, some elements of this role have fallen away. Also, active involvement as a market promoter can be inconsistent both with the degree of independence needed for the monetary role and with the degree of distance and objectivity needed in the supervisory area. Cheerleaders for a financial center will usually wish to attract as many institutions as possible to that center. The regulatory gatekeepers will often wish to turn some doubtful applicants away. These responsibilities therefore have to be kept separate. There are still quite often cases where central banks sponsor and support promotion agencies. In our view this is undesirable. But there are nonetheless many opportunities for a central bank to promote sensible enhancements to the market's infrastructure in ways that do not cut across monetary or financial stability responsibilities. The Federal Reserve-led initiatives to promote more rapid settlement of derivatives and to increase on-exchange standardization of contracts are good examples. They are now being turned into a formal regulatory framework. So some flexibility to intervene to promote market efficiency, in the interest of the bank's principal functions in relation to the reliability of financial transactions, is valuable. It is wrong, however, to see it as a distinct core purpose sitting alongside the other two. If an intervention cannot be justified by reference to either monetary or financial stability, it is unlikely to be appropriate for the central bank to be in the lead.

Debt Management

In their comprehensive review of the institutional arrangements for public debt management, Currie et al. of the World Bank note that "until the late 1980s, public debt management tended to be considered an extension of monetary policy."[43] As debt levels rose in many OECD countries, following the expansionary fiscal policies of the 1960s and 1970s, the implications for inflation of high government debt became of central concern. So it became widely accepted that the central bank should not facilitate higher borrowing through "printing money." As Currie et al. show,

> This thinking led to clear and narrow price stability objectives for central banks, to their greater independence from the government and to the prohibition for central banks to finance the fiscal deficit. Debt issuance to parties other than the central bank became the sole way to finance the deficit. This was also the logic under which the Maastricht Treaty forbade overdraft facilities and other types of credit facilities for governments, or the direct purchase of government securities in the primary market by the future ECB or EU central banks.

This approach in turn led many of those countries in which the central bank remained the agency that issued and managed public debt to rethink. Where governments borrow exclusively on open markets, at market rates, it is easy to separate government funding from central bank liquidity management. A BIS survey of forty-one central banks in 2008 showed fewer than a quarter with government debt or asset management responsibilities.[44] Some countries set up freestanding agencies under the ministry of finance, or managed debt in a department of the ministry. In some cases the separation of the bank from debt policy was gradual. In other cases, as in the United Kingdom, the separation was sudden, and announced with some fanfare as part of the reorganization of financial oversight and monetary policy in 1997. The government, at the time and subsequently, advanced three reasons for the establishment of a new Debt Management Office:[45]

- That both debt policy and its implementation should be, and be seen to be, unaffected by short-term monetary policy considerations. A central bank with monetary policy independence might be thought to have insider information on the future course of interest rates, which might make potential purchasers of debt suspicious.
- To guard against potential conflicts of interest between debt management and monetary policy that could undermine the objective of minimizing the cost of financing the deficit.
- The general desire to create a clearer allocation of responsibilities among the public bodies responsible for financial policies.

This change was barely controversial at the time. It was submerged under what were seen as more significant moves to create a single regulator and a new Monetary Policy Committee. Although there were those within the Bank of England who regretted the move, the governor accepted it as a condition of independence on interest rates, seen as the greater prize, for which sacrifices of other functions could be justified.

The U.K. statement of policy gradually became the orthodoxy, supported by other research.[46] Advice given to emerging-market countries by the IFIs suggests that "professionalism and accountability can best be achieved when debt management is assigned to an agency that is separate and autonomous from the political process."[47] But practices still vary, even within the EU. Among euro area members, around half, including France, manage debt through offices within the Treasury, without formal delegated authority, while the rest, led by Germany, have established special debt-management offices to which operational responsibilities are delegated.[48]

In the euro area no central bank has the task. It is seen as incompatible with the degree of independence from government required by the Maastricht Treaty. Outside it the Danish central bank, for example, retains the responsibility for central government debt management on behalf of the Ministry of Finance. They defend their role as "an efficient way to solve some of the unavoidable needs for the coordination of issues related to monetary and fiscal policies."[49] They argue that coordination is essential, whether or not there are separate authorities, and that the potential conflicts can be avoided if the policy rules are clear. Critics point out, however, that the Danish case is unusual, in that their monetary policy amounts to a fixed link with the euro, so it is arguable that the central bank does not enjoy policy freedom in the usually understood way.[50]

But this broad consensus was challenged in the crisis of 2009, when the Federal Reserve and others began to buy in public debt, to ease monetary conditions further once the zero interest rate band was reached. Some argued that the advent of "quantitative easing made the separation of duties look distinctly odd." In evidence to the Treasury Committee, Charles Goodhart said that he would "sack the Debt Management Office" and simply not issue gilts for a period, thus achieving the same end.[51] Tim Congdon of Lombard Street Research characterized the process whereby the DMO issues debt, while the Bank buys it in, as "quite idiotic." If the Bank ran the DMO it would simply issue fewer gilts in the first place and achieve monetary easing by buying bank debt.[52] It is recognized within the Bank that without the acquiescence of the DMO the Bank cannot control the pace of quantitative easing.

There is no doubt that in the extreme circumstances of 2009 the separation of duties in operation in most developed countries was effectively overridden. It is clear in retrospect that the claims made, especially in the United Kingdom, for the eternal superiority of a system in which policies on interest rates, and on debt management, were rigorously separated for all time have been revealed to be operational only in "normal" times. We doubt it would make sense in the longer term to return debt management to the central bank. What is required, however, is more effective coordination of functions, and a recognition that monetary and financial policies cannot be put in distinct boxes. When the system is under severe stress, all levers must be at the disposal of the authorities, irrespective of the organizational location of powers.

In all these areas, therefore, the crisis revealed the need for reform in the way central banks go about their business. But the biggest flaw in the approach taken by the monetary authorities in the run-up to the explosion was the failure to react to bubbles in the housing market and in other asset markets. We turn now to that controversial issue.

Asset Prices

Perhaps the fiercest controversy in the world of central banking in the last few years has centered on the extent to which monetary policy should respond to changes in asset prices—whether equities, property, or, most particularly, housing. The arguments for and against doing so rumbled on through the early years of the century, in Basel, the IMF, and the scholarly journals, and burst into the open in late 2007, as the severity of the credit crisis began to be understood. The issue lies at the heart of the critique of central banking in the Greenspan years, which has now become more fully articulated.

The strong-form version of that critique maintains that the crisis was "made in the Fed." Steve Roach, the former chief economist of Morgan Stanley and a longstanding critic of Alan Greenspan, does not mince his words:[1]

> Central banks were asleep at the switch. The lack of monetary discipline has become the hallmark of an unfettered globalization. Central banks have failed to provide a stable underpinning to world financial markets and to an increasingly asset-dependent global economy…it is high time for monetary authorities to adopt new procedures—namely taking asset markets into explicit consideration when framing policy options…. As the increasing prevalence of bubbles indicates, a failure to recognize the interplay between the state of asset markets and the real economy is an egregious policy error.

Roach's call for a shift away from "one-dimensional fixation on CPI-based inflation" has been reinforced by arguments that the CPI has been giving false readings as a result of the entry into the traded economy of huge new super-competitive nations—especially China. Competition from China held down prices of traded goods, and indeed the wages of manufacturing workers, while leading participants in financial markets grew incontinently rich, recycling excess liquidity created by central banks misled into a belief that inflation had been conquered and that a productivity revolution was under way. The critics consider that this reading of inflation was fundamentally wrong. The CPI itself was really "Chinese Price Inflation"[2] held artificially low by the Chinese export boom. In fact, during the so-called Great Moderation a massive expansion of credit was under way, which in turn led to mispricing of risk and asset price bubbles, all under the noses of central bankers myopically monitoring their narrowly defined inflation objectives.

Indeed the period demonstrates an interesting asymmetry. Central banks used imported low, or even negative, inflation to declare victory in hitting their inflation targets while running a relatively loose monetary policy—as measured by the low level of real interest rates, for example, or by the Taylor rule—for much of the 2000s. (The Taylor rule specifies by how much a central bank should change interest rates in response to the divergence of actual from potential GDP and actual from target inflation. Specifically, it says that the interest rate should be one and a half times the inflation rate, plus half the GDP gap, plus one.) But when commodity prices rose they argued that it was necessary to exceed the target for a period.

Taylor himself has produced a strong critique of Fed policy from 2001 onward. He points out that interest rates in the United States were, from the end of 2001, held significantly below the level that his rule would have indicated (figure 5.1). Indeed by 2004 rates were fully three percentage points lower—what he describes as "an unusually big deviation," going on to say that "there was no greater or more persistent deviation of actual Fed policy since the turbulent days of the 1970s." He argues that this deliberately loose monetary policy, implemented in response to a fear of Japan-style deflation, was the direct cause of the house price boom and subsequent bust. He further shows that European countries in which the deviation from the rule was greatest experienced similar house price bubbles.[3] (Defenders of the Fed suggest that here was another motive at play, namely fear of collapse of the bond market and consequential damage to the banks with long bond positions—a kind of financial stability concern.)

Less aggressive critics than Roach and Taylor acknowledge that the judgments that central bankers made from 2001 to 2007 were defensible, and that it is unreasonable to expect them to manage asset prices as they control consumer price inflation, but nonetheless argue that they could have done more than they did to moderate the massive escalation in asset prices and credit expansion that preceded the crash of 2007. While accepting that many central banks have a narrow statutory

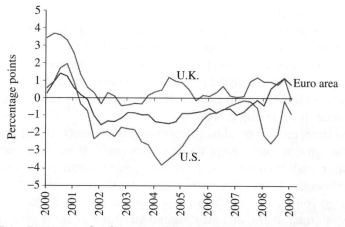

Figure 5.1. Deviation of policy rates from the Taylor rule. Source: OECD data taken from Charlie Bean's Schumpeter Lecture at the Annual Congress of the European Economic Association, Barcelona, August 25, 2009.

obligation to meet an inflation target, the welfare losses that have resulted are so great that some risks could and should have been taken in an attempt to head them off. Sushil Wadhwani, who was an external member of the Bank of England's MPC for three years, believes his colleagues were captives of an outdated, almost religious belief in efficient markets:[4] "They would rather carry out inflation forecast-targeting policy on the assumption that financial markets are efficient and there are no bubbles." The idea that financial markets might exhibit serious and sustained dysfunctionality was alien to them. The assumption had to be that prices were reflecting fundamental factors of supply and demand. Who were they to question their sustainability?

Willem Buiter, also a former external member of the MPC, says the same about the membership of the Committee, which in his view had[5]

> quite a strong representation of academic economists and other professional economists with serious technical training and backgrounds. This turned out to be a severe handicap when the central bank had to switch gears and change from being an inflation-targeting central bank under conditions of orderly financial markets to a financial stability-oriented central bank under conditions of widespread market illiquidity and funding illiquidity.

Robert Shiller has advanced a related critique, pointing to the dramatic moves in asset prices in the early years of the century, which were quite unprecedented and impossible to justify by reference to supply and demand, in the case of housing, or earnings, in the case of equity prices. He points to a version of what he calls "group think" that blinded central banks to the unsustainable nature of the trends observed.[6] We can identify another asymmetry here, which is sometimes known as the "Greenspan put." When asset prices rise, the central bank ignores "exuberance" and lets the good times roll. Yet when prices fall, that can be a justification for relaxing policy.

At the time, most central bank governors did not accept the argument that asset prices were giving dangerous signals. It would be wrong to suggest, though, that there was one single view within the central banking community. Inside the central bank tent, so to speak, there were dissenting voices, some of them articulate and strident. Bill White, the chief economist at the BIS, also argued strenuously for a greater focus on credit expansion and asset prices, and did so well before the crisis hit. Surely, he argued, there was a point at which it was possible to identify mispricing and bubbles?[7] Why could interest rate policy not take some account of the risks posed by escalating asset prices, just as it did with other risks to inflation and growth? BIS economists became closely identified with the proposal that the monetary authorities, even those with a tight inflation objective focused on retail prices, should have been prepared to "lean against the wind" of asset price escalation. The phrase became associated with a particular critique of the Federal Reserve orthodoxy, generally supported at the time by the Bank of England. (Though it is fair to say that the Bank did maintain interest rates at a rather higher level than the Fed in the run-up to the correction.)

White went on to argue that there were stronger grounds, even stronger than in earlier periods, for looking at financial-sector developments, and their potential to threaten rapid and sustainable output growth, as new indicators that ought to help guide the conduct of monetary policy.

White concluded that the many benefits of stable prices did not extend to excluding financial-sector shocks and that, just as there was a willingness to tolerate the first-round effects of negative supply shocks on inflation, there should perhaps be a willingness to tolerate deflation arising from positive supply shocks. Having accepted that the status quo had brought many benefits in terms of the Great Moderation, White argued that, with a monetary policy focused on price stability, the endemic procyclical characteristics of the financial system, demonstrated over the centuries, would only meet with resistance to the extent that they triggered inflationary pressures. He thought that responding to the subsequent downturn following the bursting of a credit bubble through asymmetrically easier monetary policies could set the stage for a new set of imbalances, unless these policies were reversed promptly, which might not be easy. If positive supply-side shocks were also accentuated by easier credit conditions, then policy could actually positively enhance the usual procyclical tendencies in the financial system. The pursuit of similar policies in successive financial cycles might, for an extended time, maintain output growth and price stability, but could also compound the underlying financial exposures. Unless the regime was changed there was a risk of disruptive deflation, along with equally disruptive adjustments in financial markets.

White proposed that the policy framework needed to be changed. He suggested that the policy horizon should be pushed out far beyond the then-conventional two years to see the full effects on prices of financial imbalances accumulated over many years. Recognizing the costs of cumulating financial imbalances, constraints would have to be put on policies designed solely to deal with today's problems, given that they risked creating significantly larger problems in the future.

He recognized that such a shift posed major political challenges. In particular, it would not be easy to convince those affected by higher rates that tightening was required: not to resist inflation over the traditional horizon but to avoid an undesirable disinflation over a still longer period. It was not easy to identify serious imbalances sufficiently robustly or to gain recognition for the fact that overextended personal or corporate balance sheets could result in a reduction in economic growth to rates well below potential.

At the same time, monetary policymakers would need to explain why they should undershoot near-term inflation targets in order to respond to emerging financial imbalances and should be expected to explain, not why they had missed a short-term inflation target, but why they had chosen not to respond to what might be seen as a dangerous buildup of such imbalances. Such steps would demonstrate greater symmetry over the credit cycle. Greater resistance in upswings would obviate the need for asymmetric easing in the subsequent downturn and all the associated problems arising from holding policy rates at very low levels for sustained periods.

White could see that it could be difficult to make these changes. "One hopes that it will not require a disorderly unwinding of current excesses to prove convincingly that we have indeed been on a dangerous path," was his prescient conclusion in early 2006.

Andrew Crockett, the general manager of the BIS, and in effect the G10 governors' most senior hired hand at that time, articulated a version of this argument himself, in 2003:[8]

> In a monetary regime in which the central bank's operational objective is expressed exclusively in terms of short-term inflation, there may be insufficient protection against the buildup of financial imbalances that lies at the root of much of the financial instability we observe. This could be so if the focus on short-term inflation control meant that the authorities did not tighten monetary policy sufficiently preemptively to lean against excessive credit expansion and asset price increases. In jargon, if the monetary policy reaction function does not incorporate financial imbalances, the monetary anchor may fail to deliver financial stability.

In a paper that rejected the argument out of hand, Charlie Bean, now deputy governor of the Bank of England, stigmatized Crockett's argument as "the heterodox view."[9] In Bean's view a forward-looking inflation-targeting central bank should bear in mind the longer-run consequences of asset price bubbles when setting current rates, with no need for an additional monetary response to asset price movements.

The central bank response to this heterodoxy, both before and during the crisis, was robust—though not quite universally so, as we shall see. As might be expected, Alan Greenspan himself led the counterattack. He challenged every link in the chain of argument. In his view it was not possible to identify when a bubble was inflating, and even if it were possible so to do, a monetary policy response would be ineffective. Referring explicitly to "leaning against the wind" he asserted that "I know of no instance where such a policy has been successful."[10] He further maintained that it would almost certainly be undesirable to attempt to respond in a way that might constrain markets and hinder the processes of innovation. Instead, central banks should forget about preventive measures and focus on policies to mitigate the fallout when a crisis occurs and ease the transition to the next expansion. On this view, while liberalized capital markets may well be prone to booms and busts (and there is evidence that the incidence of busts is growing), the net result remains positive in terms of economic welfare. Attempting to interfere directly in the process of the creative destruction that accompanies these intermittent crises would be unwise and counterproductive.

These contrasting points of view seem to admit little possibility of accommodation. Yet there are more recent signs that central banks, faced with the massive value destruction of the years 2007–9, are becoming more pensive about their record. There are signs that some are taking a less strident line—though in this particular area Greenspan himself has continued to offer an unrepentant apologia pro vita sua. (His celebrated apology related rather to what he now sees as a misplaced belief in the ability of private-sector firms to act effectively in the defense of their shareholder's interests.) It is therefore worth picking through the details of the dispute to see if the outline of a new and potentially more effective approach might emerge—one that does not compromise the success achieved in anti-inflation policy but gives somewhat greater weight to financial stability.

To do so it is useful to parse the argument into a series of issues on which different points of view are advanced. On the first two, the germs of a revised consensus can be identified. Divergences open up on the later questions. Finally, we offer our own view on the way forward.

Question 1. Should central banks target asset prices?

Here there is a large measure of agreement. The locus classicus of the case for taking more account of asset prices in the setting of monetary policy, by Cecchetti et al.,[11] says that "it is important to emphasize that...we are recommending that while [central banks] might react to asset price misalignments, they must not target them." So the argument is not about adjusting the definition of inflation on an ad hoc basis as asset prices fluctuate—it is about how far decision makers should take account of asset price misalignments in setting interest rates and in determining the appropriate inflation forecast horizon. Advocates of leaning against the wind believe that central banks seeking to smooth output and inflation can do so more successfully if they set rates with an eye toward asset prices in general, and misalignments in particular.

Question 2. Should the measure of inflation targeted include an element of asset price, and particularly house price, inflation?

As Goodhart points out[12] this is a crucial question as, if asset price changes are not incorporated in the measure of inflation that the authorities are enjoined to stabilize, they may express well-founded anxieties about asset price inflation from time to time but lack a framework within which to respond to them in an effective way. His argument is that the case for incorporating a measure of house price inflation into the targeted rate is far stronger than it is in the case of equity prices. The link between equity price rises and subsequent changes in retail price inflation is weak, whereas the relationship between house price movements and subsequent output and inflation is much stronger. Alchian and Klein[13] and others argue that a correct measure of inflation should include asset prices because they reflect the current money prices of claims on future, as well as current, consumption.

Yet the current definition of inflation used in the United Kingdom and in the euro area excludes any element of housing costs. In the United Kingdom the target rate was changed from the RPI, which did include an element of imputed house rental, to the CPI, on the model of the Harmonised Index of Consumer Prices used in the euro area, in 2003. The potential risks inherent in the change were little remarked upon at the time, except by Goodhart and other academics. Some central bankers welcomed the change. John Vickers, when he was chief economist of the Bank of England, argued that while policymakers might wish to draw on asset price information, asset prices should not be in the targeted measure of inflation—largely on the grounds that volatility would be transmitted to the price measure, complicating measurement and accountability.[14]

Since then, the Bank of England has changed tack and has accepted that it would be preferable to change to a measure that did incorporate an element of housing costs. The question is in the hands of, or perhaps in the long grass at, Eurostat, as it has been for some years. It is hard to understand why progress has been so slow, even acknowledging the conceptual problems and the difficulty of establishing a set of metrics that take account of the different types of housing tenure and finance across Europe. Mervyn King himself has expressed public frustration with the lack of urgency displayed.[15]

So there also appears to be an emerging consensus on this point after a period in which central banks favored a more restricted definition of consumer prices. But just how sizable an element of housing costs should be incorporated in the target rate is likely to prove far more controversial. In the United States, the index includes an estimate of the price of owner-occupation based on a survey of rental costs. Cecchetti has calculated the impact on U.S. inflation were that element to be replaced by an index of home sale prices.[16] The effect is dramatic. Over five years from 2000 recomputed inflation would have been three quarters of a percent a year higher than under the CPI index used (figure 5.2). In the United Kingdom, the effect would have been even greater: the recomputed RPI including house price inflation would have been between 2% and 4% a year higher over the last decade (figure 5.3).

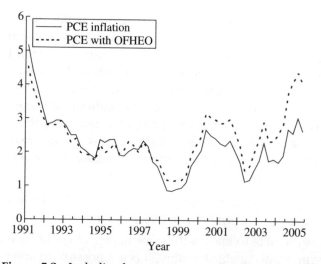

Figure 5.2. Including house prices in inflation measure.[16]

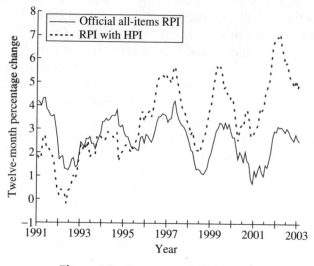

Figure 5.3. Recomputed U.K. RPI.[16]

It is unlikely that a recomputation on that scale is what King has in mind. And one might question how useful it would be to respecify the index in this way. Would the Bank of England have kept interest rates significantly higher for some time on these grounds? Only if they were persuaded that there was indeed a serious misalignment, and on that question opinion is divided. So while some readjustment of the index might be helpful as a signaling mechanism, it is highly unlikely that the adjustment would be anything like as dramatic as Cecchetti's calculations imply. Of course a preemptive rise in rates earlier in the bubble *would* have been likely to reduce its scale: indeed that would have been its purpose. And the effect would be greater if economic actors expected policymakers to react in this way. But the addition of some element of housing consumption within the index does not solve the problem of how monetary policy, or indeed other policies, should react to sharp changes in house prices: if there is no immediate pass-through to core inflation, for example.

Question 3. Is it possible to identify serious price misalignments, and are they of legitimate concern to monetary policymakers?

Unless it is possible to know with some degree of confidence that asset prices are in unsustainable territory, it is not possible to know how, if at all, to respond to them.

Some say that it is quite impossible to know, *ex ante*, whether or not a bubble has inflated. Ben Bernanke, before he joined the Federal Reserve, was a skeptic, noting in a paper written with Mark Gertler that[17] "advocates of bubbles would probably be forced to admit that it is difficult or impossible to identify any particular episode conclusively as a bubble, even after the fact." He went on, nonetheless, to acknowledge that "episodes of irrational exuberance in financial markets are certainly a logical possibility, and one about which at least some central bankers are evidently concerned." Greenspan's position on this point is curious. When he made his celebrated comment about irrational exuberance in December 1996 he appeared to have reason to believe that prices (at that time the principal concern was with the level of the Dow Jones Index) were misaligned. Perhaps the subsequent experience—the index continued to rise for some years after his gypsy's warning—caused him to rethink. He now argues that it is impossible know when misalignments occur and that central banks should limit themselves to a focus on policies that mitigate the fallout when it occurs.

Others strongly dispute the argument that misalignments cannot be identified. Cecchetti argues that there are long-run measures that can help to identify mispricing. In the equity markets extravagant price/earnings ratios that could not be explained by changes in dividend policies or a fall in the equity risk premium were a powerful leading indicator of trouble in the dot-com boom. More recently, a dramatic fall in the risk premium on high-yield bonds, which ran for a couple of years at something close to half its long-run average, was a strong sign of mispricing there. In the case of housing there are price/earnings ratios, and perhaps more importantly price/rental income ratios, that point to the likelihood of downward shifts. The growth of credit aggregates may also be helpful in identifying unsustainable asset price increases. These indicators cannot be used as automatic triggers, and misalignments may persist for some time (as they did in the U.S. and U.K. housing markets). But, as Wadhwani contends, the uncertainties are no greater than in many other areas in which the monetary authority has to take a view on the basis of highly uncertain assumptions: "it is not obvious to me that it is any easier to estimate the output gap than to identify bubbles."[4]

These arguments, combined with the dramatic effect on opinion of the credit crisis, are clearly influencing views within monetary authorities. Bernanke's attitude is now somewhat more nuanced. He has accepted that there can be circumstances in which asset price fluctuations are of legitimate concern to policymakers and that there can be sources of non-fundamental price fluctuations that can be identified. One of the sources is what he calls "poor regulatory practice," whereby through explicit liberalization, or perhaps through the exploitation of opportunities for regulatory arbitrage, credit availability is radically enhanced, with consequential effects on asset prices. This condition, which he described in 2000, seems to have been amply fulfilled in 2005–7. Credit creation outside the banking system escalated dramatically through the use of securitization and resecuritization and through the exploitation of off-balance-sheet vehicles that attracted a lower capital charge. Credit standards were relaxed, especially in relation to borrowing for house purchase in the Anglo-Saxon economies and in relation to leveraged private equity deals. That relaxation should have been an additional warning sign.

The second possibility is indeed irrational behavior by investors, which he concedes may be observed from time to time. And he accepts, furthermore, that booms and busts in asset prices have important effects on the real economy. His concern is not so much the so-called wealth effect, whereby household spending is depressed by falling net worth, but the balance sheet channel. Firms and households use assets as collateral for borrowing. As asset prices fall the value of that collateral falls, generates an unplanned increase in leverage, and impedes access to further credit. Financial firms "which must maintain an adequate ratio of capital to assets can be deterred from lending...by declines in the value of the assets they hold." This perfectly describes the painful adjustment process of 2007–8, which was highly resistant to post-event changes in interest rates. It is therefore surprising that Bernanke was not more concerned by what he saw in 2006, and more ready to act. Of course he inherited a policy stance from his predecessor that was inimical to this kind of analysis. But it also seems that he, along with his colleagues in the other major central banks, was not persuaded that interest rate changes were an appropriate response to a house price bubble, even one that showed every sign of reaching alarming proportions. This leads us leads to the next question—one on which opinions differ starkly.

Question 4. Even if we can identify misalignments, and believe that some price adjustment is bound to occur, is it right to use interest rates to try to moderate the expansion and bring forward the adjustment?

It is striking how often in this debate, which may seem arcane to many observers, the opposing sides caricature each other's positions in the worst tradition of political point scoring. So advocates of the use of the interest rate weapon prefer to use the nonthreatening metaphor of "leaning against the wind," suggesting nothing more hazardous than a brisk walk in a warm overcoat on a breezy morning. Those who resist it typically raise the stakes by talking of the risks of trying to "prick bubbles," which sounds an inherently more hazardous activity, likely to be accompanied by loud noises and collateral damage. So Wadhwani,[4] for example, talks of a gentle "tilt" in policy to reduce the risks of further inflation of an emerging price bubble, while Bernanke[17] argues that there is no such thing as "safe popping," and that "bubbles can normally be arrested only by an increase in interest rates sharp enough to materially slow the whole economy." His argument is based on his reading of the inappropriateness of the Fed's policy in the period leading up to the Wall Street crash of 1928 (of which he is a distinguished historian), when the main effect of a tight monetary policy was to slow the economy rather than to prick the equity price bubble. The Fed, he says, "passed into the control of a coterie of aggressive bubble-poppers." He has no intention of repeating the same mistake. As Keynes put it:[18]

> A rate of interest, high enough to overcome the speculative excitement, would have checked at the same time every kind of reasonable new investment. Thus an increase in the rate of interest as a remedy for the state of affairs arising out of a prolonged period of abnormally heavy new investment, belongs to the species of remedy which cures the disease by killing the patient.

Elsewhere, though, he does say that he agrees that to raise the rate of interest during a boom may conceivably be the lesser evil.

In Bernanke's view, and the point is repeated regularly by his colleagues in the United States and elsewhere, the scale of interest rate changes needed to make a significant impact on a price bubble, whether in the equity or property markets, would be so large as to threaten the health of the economy overall and would inflict greater damage on economic welfare than a policy of benign neglect followed by aggressive easing to mitigate the adverse consequences of the crash, if and when it comes.

Inflation-targeting banks also argue that it would have been impossible to justify holding rates higher than they were, in response to concerns about asset prices, at a time when inflation on the chosen indicator was comfortably within the target range. Certainly it would have been hard to justify the kind of large rise that, they say, would have been necessary to make a significant difference. A quarter of a point here or there would not have done the trick. The Bank of England points out that inflation did run below the range for a period in 2004–5, in part as a response to concerns about house price inflation. (But it is hard to find much evidence in the MPC minutes to prove that this was in effect a "leaning against the wind" policy.)

Elsewhere, however, we can find such evidence. The Reserve Bank of Australia explicitly justified its interest rate policy by reference to inflated house prices, and it appears to have had some impact on moderating their further growth. The Riksbank in Sweden was even clearer about its decision making. Lars Heikensten, the former governor of the Riksbank, wrote:[19]

> With house prices increasing drastically, risks for the real economy have been perceived to be bigger. On a few occasions in 2004–05 the Riksbank did for that reason not follow a strict inflation-targeting rule. We "leaned against the wind," in the sense that we did not take rates down as quickly as we could have done considering the outlook for inflation alone.... We explicitly referred to asset prices in our published minutes, press releases and speeches—and received some criticism for that.

The Riksbank believes that their actions did have a helpful effect on the expansion of asset prices in Sweden, though the country did not avoid a fall in 2008. The ECB, too, maintains that it takes asset prices into account in the monetary pillar of its analysis—though faced with a highly divergent pattern of asset price movements across the euro area the practical consequences may be limited.

So there is a clear fault line here within the central banking fraternity—though in public both sides are generally keen to play it down. The experience of 2007–8 strengthened the hands of those who favor lean-ing against the wind, and the language used by governors has begun to change, but the Greenspan tendency is not down and out. Indeed with the greater freedom available to a former central banker, Greenspan has been active in defending his position, both in the press and between hard covers.[20] Even in the summer of 2009 Mervyn King was unrepen-tant. He argued that while maintaining price stability "did not prevent a recession induced by a financial crisis," nevertheless "diverting mon-etary policy from its goal of price stability risks making the economy less stable and the financial system no more so."[21] This suggests that the Bank of England will not in practice allow its monetary policy to be influenced by its new financial stability mandate, legislated in 2009.

Both sides are agreed, though, that interest rates are not the only weapon that can be used. Even central banks that paid little attention to bank regulation before the crisis have begun to take more interest in capital requirements. This leads us to the fifth question.

Question 5. How does consideration of the exchange rate alter the analysis?

If countries raise interest rates primarily to limit domestic asset price increases, unwanted exchange rate appreciation could result, with poten-tially damaging consequences for trade, output, and investment. This has been a dilemma for some open-economy countries and can have global implications if U.S. interest rates are raised for this motive. It has heightened the pressure to seek out other policy measures that might affect asset prices in the desired way without having the additional effect of generating major shifts in exchange rates.

Question 6. Should we try to find and use other mechanisms to moderate extravagant credit expansion and associated asset price bubbles?

Almost all central bankers would now answer yes, in principle, to this question, whether or not they believe that interest rate changes should also in some circumstances be used to that end. Indeed some seem to argue that while it is not possible for central banks as monetary authori-ties to spot a bubble, bank regulators should certainly be able to do so. A more sophisticated version of the argument, advanced by a senior gov-ernor, is that the burden of proof on bank regulators is not as high as it is on monetary policymakers. Regulators contest the point, highlight-ing that regulatory decisions are in some countries subject to judicial appeals, unlike interest rate moves. The certainty needed to raise inter-est rates, given the likely impact on economic activity as well as on asset prices directly, is higher than is needed to justify a precautionary rise in capital ratios for banks active in the markets whose behavior is of concern. So regulators can afford to take a chance, now and again, with fewer downside risks. Macroprudential adjustments to ratios are therefore a preferable response to bubbles. In a BBC interview in December 2008 John Gieve, then of the Bank of England, made the argument that

> one of the main lessons (of the crisis) is that we need to develop some new instruments which sit somewhere between interest rates which affect the whole economy and activity, and individual supervision and regulation of individual banks.... We need to develop something which bridges that gap and prevents the financial cycle and the credit cycle getting out of hand.

Our view is somewhat different. Raising capital ratios as a precautionary move will also affect the economy as a whole unless regulators use some kind of sectoral approach: raising capital requirements only in relation to mortgage finance, for example, which is likely to be a politically unpopular move. There is an argument, based on the Modigliani–Miller theorem, that reducing bank leverage should not increase the overall cost of capital for banks, as their riskiness is thereby reduced. But taxation affects this calculation significantly, and it assumes a smooth transition to a lower average return on equity for banks. So increased capital requirements are likely to increase the effective cost of credit, and thereby to reduce investment and growth. Any form of credit rationing will feed through into prices through interest rate changes, which will themselves affect the monetary stance. So a macroprudential mechanism is not an easy option and it should not be seen as wholly distinct from monetary policy adjustments. It may nonetheless be justified as a useful additional tool.

Conclusions

But before considering the regulatory dimension, and how to fill the gap Gieve identifies, how should we conclude on the "leaning against the wind" arguments?

In our view it is clear that central banks must pay more attention to asset price bubbles than they have in the recent past. The output costs of bubbles are large. The IMF estimate that equity market busts are typically associated with a 4% GDP loss, while sharp house price adjustments generate output losses twice as large.[22] So house price bubbles are more worthy of attention, especially, as is usually the case, where they are linked to rapid credit expansion, whose unwinding may directly damage the functioning of the financial system and hence the transmission of monetary policy. We agree with those who argue that[23]

> accommodating monetary policy over the period 2002–5, in combination with rapid market innovation, would seem in retrospect to have been among the factors behind the run-up in asset prices and consequent financial imbalances—the (partial) unwinding of which helped trigger the 2007 market turmoil.

As Bean of the Bank of England now concedes, "the events of the past couple of years have clearly tipped the balance in favour of taking preemptive action."[24]

We are not persuaded by the argument that bubbles cannot be identified *ex ante*. Of course assessing price misalignments is not an exact science, but nor are many other aspects of monetary policy. All interest rate judgments are based on an assessment of risk, and on the consideration of a range of possible outcomes. There are indicators that can be used to identify potential misalignments, as Cecchetti points out.

Furthermore, we believe that asset prices should be identified as an explicit factor in the consideration of policy. It was, for example, a mistake in the United Kingdom to exclude housing costs from the CPI, and an element of those costs should be reincorporated into the index as soon as possible. This would help to explain policy responses that are rooted at least in part in observed price movements.

It is not enough to say that an inflation-target regime can, without amendment, take full account of asset price moves. Inflation forecasts are usually based on assessments of likely inflation at a horizon of two years. It is possible, in principle, to imagine a regime that looks at longer horizons, to allow the possible long-term impact of asset price misalignments to feature explicitly in decision making. Indeed the *BIS Annual Report 2008/09*[25] supports such an approach. Lengthening the time horizon substantially may complicate the exposition of policy more than would a statement that explains that on occasion policy will be influenced by asset prices and credit expansion, and why. A policy reformulation along these lines does not seem to us to pose any significant threat to the clarity of inflation targeting, which is a legitimate central bank concern.

Both the Swedish authorities and those in Australia have justified rate changes along these lines in the past, with what seem to have been beneficial effects. Nor do we think that this amounts to an attempt to "prick bubbles." We do not accept that very large increases would necessarily be needed to have an impact on asset price movements. The impact on expectations of a more explicit attitude to asset prices may in itself have an impact on price movements, and we see monetary policy as just one of a range of possible responses. We do not think, however, that an interest rate response can be excluded on the grounds that it is too difficult, or too dangerous. Nor do we accept the argument that interest rates affect the economy as a whole, whereas raising capital ratios does not. A change in capital ratios is also a blunt instrument. Much credit is created outside the banking system, and any repricing of credit, however engineered, will have broad macroeconomic effects. The dangers of allowing bubbles to inflate for too long have been vividly demonstrated in the last two years. A policy that attempts to respond in some way to extreme asset price moves (in either direction) and to related developments in credit could enhance overall macroeconomic stability.[26] It is one important way in which monetary and financial stability aims can and need to be brought together. As the IMF Research Department under Olivier Blanchard has argued, "the mandate of monetary policy should include macrofinancial stability, not just price stability."[27] After all, as the BIS points out, macroeconomic stability is built on the foundations of a stable financial system.

We do not know precisely what former Fed Chairman William McChesney Martin thought about popping bubbles, but his famous suggestion that the Fed should take away the punch bowl just as the party gets going could be interpreted as support for the general idea.

The Role of Regulation

None of this should be read as implying that we reject the case for regulatory policies that try to work more directly on asset prices themselves. The argument for more explicitly countercyclical adjustments of capital ratios is well-made, though we find it interesting that central banks have rediscovered the link between monetary policy analysis and banking regulation only in the aftermath of the crisis. There was little sign of such interest in the years of expansion. The case developed by White, Borio, and others at the BIS was given little support by the Fed or other major monetary authorities. It is hard to avoid the conclusion that the new focus on regulatory policy is something of a smokescreen to conceal other policy errors, especially in monetary policy. Furthermore, although the second capital accord, Basel II, with its generally procyclical bias, is often presented as a purely regulatory intervention, it was in fact developed in the early years of the century with the central banks firmly in charge of the process through their chairmanship, and oversight, of the Basel Committee.

In his defense of the Fed's policy leading up to the crisis, Mishkin argues in favor of maintaining the monetary policy mixture as it was before, in which central banks should look at asset prices and adjust policy as required to achieve maximum sustainable employment and price stability, but with no explicit role for asset price moves themselves.[28] This seems dangerously complacent, especially as the changes he would like to see in regulatory policy are so vague as to be meaningless. He calls for a new regulatory framework that "should be structured to address failures in information or market incentives that contribute to credit-driven bubbles." How? Well, more research is required. Indeed it is. And as former regulators (and central bankers) we are acutely conscious of the need not to ask the regulatory system to bear a greater load than it can sustain. Surely part of the burden of responding to financial instability must be borne by the central banks in their monetary stability role? The demand for credit must be influenced by the level of interest rates, even if that is not the only factor.

Before considering the regulatory arguments further, there is one additional dimension of the problem that should be mentioned.

Our assessment, and indeed most of the academic literature on the point, proceeds from the assumption that in each monetary policy jurisdiction there is a set of asset classes whose prices are likely to move together. Of course we know that house prices behave in different ways in different parts of the United Kingdom and the United States, but it is possible within an integrated economy to disentangle the reasons for regional price differentials based on relative economic prosperity. So it is generally meaningful to refer to the Case–Shiller index in the United States and the Halifax or Nationwide indices in the United Kingdom.

Within the euro area this approach works much less well. Real house prices have behaved in remarkably different ways in different euro area countries over the last decade. On average, prices in the original twelve members have risen by just under 50% in real terms since the exchange rates were fixed in 1997. But in Germany prices have risen scarcely at all, while in Spain real prices had risen almost 120% by 2007 and in Ireland the rise was some 170% (figure 5.4). (In both cases prices have fallen sharply since.)

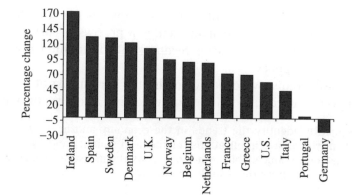

Figure 5.4. Real increase in house prices over the last decade. Source: David Miles (derived from the ECB, National Statistical Offices, the IMF, the European Mortgage Federation, the Italian Ministry of Infrastructure, and Morgan Stanley Research).

So while house price rises in Europe as a whole have not been such as to cause concern to the ECB, and could not have been used as a justification for preemptive tightening, there are individual countries in which the bursting of the housing bubble is bringing painful economic adjustments in its wake. In these circumstances the burden of policy response necessarily falls on areas other than monetary policy. Indeed it may be necessary in those countries to consider more aggressive use of targeted capital regulation at the national level; changes in tax policies relating to transfer taxes (stamp duty) or to mortgage interest relief where that applies may also be necessary. This may be just one dimension of the problem of a "one-size-fits-all" monetary policy for a diverse area that exhibits few of the characteristics of an optimal currency zone. But it is a particularly acute problem at present, and one that may require an idiosyncratic response.

Macroprudential Oversight

We have argued that monetary policy decision makers in central banks should pay more attention in the future to the creation of credit, both within and without the banks, in reaching decisions on interest rates. But the interest rate weapon is powerful and blunt. There will be circumstances in which it will be more appropriate to act directly on the expansionary appetites of banks themselves, through adjusting capital requirements. We have to recognize, though, that the application of additional capital requirements for macroeconomic reasons, not directly related to the risk positions of individual banks, is not straightforward and would require new participants and new processes. Furthermore, as explained above, there would be feedback effects to interest rates and hence monetary policy.

The recently rediscovered jargon in this territory speaks of "macroprudential oversight," defined in the Turner Review as oversight that is[29]

> designed to identify the trends in the economy and in the financial system which have implications for financial stability and as a result for macroeconomic stability and to identify the measures which could be taken to address the resulting risks.

The term "macroprudential" is not at all new, with the G10 central banks devoting much attention to "macroprudential policy" as long ago as the mid 1980s.[30] It was probably devised in the Bank of England in the context of the deliberations of the G10 governors group chaired by Alexandre Lamfalussy in 1979. That group was charged with the examination of different possible approaches to limiting the growth of banks' international lending. The Bank of England representatives in the group argued strongly for the microprudential aspect of banking supervision to be placed in a wider context and put forward a number of proposals including changes in capital ratios, control of banks' country risk exposure, and maturity transformation. The Lamfalussy group then consulted the predecessor to the Basel Committee of Banking Supervisors, who rejected the proposals not only for technical reasons but also because of the lack of prudential justification for increases in capital requirements. They were also concerned about a potential conflict between macroeconomic and prudential aims. Intriguingly, in the light of current debate, the chairman of the group of supervisors advancing this view was Peter Cooke, also of the Bank of England. So even within a supervisory central bank views could differ markedly. The debate, unresolved then, has resurfaced.

If it is accepted that, in future, central bankers and supervisors should try to incorporate an understanding of the state of asset and credit markets into their decisions on capital requirements, with the aim of "leaning against the wind" of unsustainable booms, then we need to consider by whom, and on what grounds, decisions to require more capital would be made. The answers to these questions depend on precisely what the ambition is. One can imagine prudential supervisory interventions designed to "protect banks from the cycle," or ones that are designed to reduce the contribution to instability by the financial sector: "protecting the cycle from the banks." At the extreme would be attempts to seek to moderate the business cycle itself, by inducing banks to lean against it. In our view the ambition should be the more limited one of dampening the impact of booms and busts in the banking system on the wider economy, which points to a lead role for regulators, supported by central banks where they are separate.

In order to deal with competition issues it would be essential for a framework for these decisions, if not the decisions themselves, to be made on an international basis—it would be unreasonable, and contrary to the spirit of the Basel process, for a bank in one country to be put at a disadvantage by its domestic supervisor imposing a macroprudential adjustment when others were not doing so, unless it were clear that the economic circumstances were very different in its country. On the other hand, there are indeed differences from country to country, and these would need to be taken into account. As figure 5.4 shows, in the decade up to the start of the credit crisis, real house prices rose by over 60% in the United States and by over 100% in the United Kingdom, yet they fell slightly in Germany. So a common framework is required, but one that can be adapted to the circumstances of individual banks. In the case of global banks operating in many different markets through branches or subsidiaries, there will be a need for host-supervisor adjustments to be agreed by the home supervisor, which will not be easy, though the decision by the G20 summit to create supervisory colleges for the largest global institutions could create a decision-making framework within which those judgments could be reached.

The existing international capital regime, Basel II, provides a way of thinking about how such a framework might work. Pillar I sets a basic capital requirement for the bank based on an assessment of loss probabilities related to its own portfolio of loan assets. Pillar II provides for decisions on individual capital requirements to be set, bank by bank, by reference to the idiosyncratic risks of their credit portfolios and the quality of their management. But there is no place in the accord at present for a supervisor to take a view that, however high the quality of a bank's book might appear to be, risk spreads have narrowed too far and asset prices have escalated in a way that will be unsustainable for borrowers. Since the calculations of probabilities of default, and losses given default, are essentially historical, even where supervisors seek to apply them on a "through the cycle" basis, they are not forward-looking and they carry the risk of procyclicality. So a supervisor looking at the balance sheets of mortgage banks in the United States and the United Kingdom early in 2007 might well have considered that a reduction in capital requirements could be justified, on the grounds that housing loan losses had been very small during the previous decade—a period of rapidly rising house prices. Yet in retrospect we can see that the level of house prices reached in 2007 was unsustainable.

Three questions arise. How do we know when asset prices are out of line? Who would make such an assessment, if one were to be made? And how would we adjust capital requirements, on an equitable basis, were we to decide that it was appropriate to do so?

The honest answer to the first question is that it will not be possible to be certain of price misalignments in advance. But many elements of prudential regulation are similarly uncertain. Supervision is also a business in which calculated risks must be taken. Supervisors are regularly required to make judgments on the basis of imperfect information, and uncertain forecasts, as indeed are monetary policymakers. As we have argued in the monetary policy context, to say that it is simply impossible to identify asset price bubbles, and that all that can be done is to mop up afterward, is a counsel of despair. Furthermore, academic analysts, and indeed some central banks, have begun to develop metrics that show promise in identifying mispricing and incipient financial stress. There is an emerging technology on which to build. Much further work is needed, of course, but there is time to produce a workable scheme: asset price booms are not likely to be a pressing problem for supervisors and banks in the next couple of years.

The second question is also difficult. One obvious answer would be to say that this should be a job for the Basel Committee, on the grounds that the Committee devised the new accord and should therefore be responsible for adapting and implementing it. Unfortunately, the Committee has not demonstrated the fleetness of foot that would be required to make the judgments necessary. It took almost a decade to produce Basel II. And while the Committee's meetings typically start with a *tour de table* during which countries describe developments in their jurisdictions, the focus is more on regulatory developments than on macroeconomic ones. Even supervisory central banks do not send macroeconomists to the Committee. They send people well-versed in the often mind-numbing detail of the risk buckets.

So, while it would clearly be for the Committee itself to agree a formal codicil to the accord to admit of macroprudential adjustments if this were necessary, we do not consider it to be the right body to make decisions in real time on the case for overall adjustments to bank capital.

Indeed, surprisingly to outsiders, the Basel Committee spent very little time in the revision of the accord considering how much capital, in aggregate, should be required in the banking system. It made an assumption at the start of the process that the quantum of capital, overall, was broadly appropriate and concentrated almost all its attention on how that capital should be distributed. No serious macroeconomic analysis lay behind that decision, which began as a kind of planning assumption but gradually assumed the status of unchallengeable doctrine. It was also forgotten that, if capital requirements are set that there is no discretion to run down in bad times, banks will need to hold substantially more in good times if they are to have flexibility when times are hard. Otherwise they could be faced with the need to raise capital urgently just when this might be most difficult.

By late 2008 the shortcomings had become apparent and the G20 leaders commissioned work to put in place more effective prudential arrangements, involving finance ministries, central banks, and accounting standard-setters, as well as banking supervisors.

The academic community has also entered the debate. The transposition of any assessment of the evolution of credit, asset prices, risk spreads, and so on into an agreement to raise capital requirements would require the exercise of careful judgment. Goodhart and Persaud[31] have argued that, instead, an automatic mechanism should be introduced, whereby each bank would have a basic allowance of asset growth, linked to the country's inflation target and long-run GDP growth rate. Asset growth above this rate would be given a higher weight in the calculation of capital requirements, providing an automatic dampener on the growth of a bank's balance sheet. They propose, as a sighting shot, that capital adequacy requirements would be raised by 0.33% for each 1% "excess" growth in bank asset values. So, if a bank grew its assets at a rate of 21% above its allowance, its minimum capital requirement would rise from, say, 8% to 15%.

We are not attracted by the idea of an automatic escalator of this kind. Indeed we are suspicious of any approaches to supervision that seek to remove judgment from the process. There can be unsafe banks whose assets are declining relative to the market, perhaps because counterparties are suspicious of them. While unusual market share growth can be a good indicator of poor pricing or credit decisions, or of a risky funding strategy as in the case of Northern Rock, it may also be an indicator of superior management and better business focus. An automatic stabilizer of this kind could ossify market shares and indeed offer protection to sleepy banks, whose competitors would be constrained from taking share from them. There would be a risk of returning to the days of lending ceilings and "window guidance," which were discredited decades ago. It might have the paradoxical effect, in the longer run, of weakening the banking system.

In the wide-ranging *Geneva Report on the World Economy 11*[32] Goodhart, Persaud, and others presented further possible techniques for adjusting capital requirements by adjusting the normal microprudential capital ratios by a coefficient relating to the macroprudential assessed risk. They argue that the best measures of an institution's contribution to macroprudential risk are, in addition to its rate of expansion, its leverage and its maturity mismatch (taking into account market liquidity at times of stress) and that these factors be combined to generate an additional capital requirement for each bank. The precise calibration of such adjustments would be complex and judgmental. Other ideas, such as adjusting capital requirements over time for the deviation of the rate of growth of GDP from its long-term average, were advanced in a CEPR report in 2009.[33]

The G20 made a start on trying to devise new arrangements in April 2009.[34] They resolved that, until global recovery was assured, the international standard for the minimum level of capital should remain unchanged, and existing buffers above the minimum should be allowed to decline in deteriorating economic conditions. But they decided in principle that, once recovery was under way, prudential regulatory standards should be tightened. The FSB, the Basel Committee, and the BIS Committee on the Global Financial System, working with the accounting standard-setters, should work on a new approach that would mitigate procyclicality, including a requirement on banks to build buffers of capital in good times, which could be drawn down when conditions deteriorate. These recommendations included a mandate to the Basel Committee to address observed shortcomings in the risk models used by firms as part of the Basel II process, in stress testing, and in the use of credit ratings. They also tasked the accounting standard-setters with reviewing the provisioning and valuation requirements that some had seen as exacerbating the crisis.

Adjusting capital requirements to the state of the economic cycle will be very difficult. Decisions to impose higher capital requirements would require courage on the part of economists and supervisors. But if the assessments were agreed by central banks from a broad range of countries, they would have authority and would give line supervisors the cover they need to impose unpopular "taxes" on their banks. We need to recognize that, at bottom, a macroprudential tool is a tax—and one whose cost would largely be passed through to borrowers and savers. Now would be the right time to introduce a system of this kind, when the memories of the crisis are fresh and the wounds still raw.

We can see, therefore, that a macroprudential override is more than a theoretical possibility. But the technical and political difficulty of agreeing a new mechanism should not be underestimated. Some of the advocates do not seem to appreciate the delicacy of what is proposed. A higher capital requirement is a tax on the banking system, or a rise in effective interest rates, or a bit of both. It will not be popular when imposed, especially as, by definition, it would be introduced at a time of economic optimism, when the need for tightening might be hard to explain. It is the famous punch bowl problem in a different form. A continuing strong political commitment by the G20 finance ministers would certainly be required to make such an exercise successful.

LEVERAGE RATIOS AND QUANTITATIVE CONTROLS

The G20 also decided in April 2009 that risk-based requirements should be supplemented with a single, transparent, non-risk-based measure that is internationally comparable, that properly takes account of off-balance-sheet exposures, and that could help to contain the buildup of leverage in the banking system. Some authorities have used leverage ratios in the past, and others were already moving in that direction. The Canadian Office of the Superintendent of Financial Institutions applies a maximum gross leverage ratio of 20:1. The Swiss banking regulator added a new leverage ratio to its existing capital requirements in December 2008.[35] The Swiss are particularly concerned about the absolute size of their two major banks in relation to Swiss GDP, so a constraint on overall leverage, even if it is not risk based, is attractive to them.

Leverage ratios have divided the international regulatory community for some time. Their advocates, who have included some of the U.S. bank supervisory agencies, have argued that they are a useful adjunct to the model-based determinants of capital requirements, as a relatively simple constraint on the growth of banks' balance sheets relative to their capital. Critics, which in the past included U.K. supervisors (in both the Bank of England and the FSA), argued that a leverage ratio can have a perverse effect in creating an incentive for banks to invest in more risky assets in order to generate higher returns for a given quantum of leverage.

There are also awkward definitional questions: notably the treatment of off-balance-sheet exposures. (A useful discussion of leverage ratios, dynamic provisioning, and other potential countercyclical measures can be found in the Bank of England's FSR for October 2008.[36])

Turner concludes that the arguments for imposing a gross leverage ratio are compelling and that the FSA will argue in favor of an international agreement on definition and level. It may be that a consensus emerges on this point. But it is not clear that a leverage ratio would in itself deliver the needed additional capital in exuberant times. Certainly it did not do so in the United States in the past. We believe that a new mechanism will be needed to have a more effective countercyclical impact. It is therefore encouraging that the introduction of leverage ratios is seen by the G20 and the FSB as an integrated part of a broader package of measures to rectify shortcomings in the previous arrangements.

Turner also examines the case for some other quantitative restrictions (on loan-to-value rates in the mortgage market, for example) without reaching a firm conclusion. The past U.K. experience of quantitative credit controls through the control of terms of borrowing was not encouraging, though in some other countries it is believed that house price escalation has been contained by this means. In our view they need to be justified on consumer protection, rather than prudential, grounds and are unlikely to be a major bulwark against the kind of financial crisis recently experienced, which spread to countries both with and without these restrictions in place.

The broad conclusion here must be, however, that these potential interventions cannot be seen in isolation. They will all affect credit conditions. In each country there will be a need for coordination between the functions of regulation and monetary policy, wherever the operational responsibilities are located in institutional terms. This interdependence carries some implications for central bank independence—a subject to which we now turn.

Structure, Status, and Accountability

INDEPENDENCE

The movement toward central bank independence has seemed unstoppable in recent years. In Germany it was a postwar reaction to prewar hyperinflation. Elsewhere it was largely a reaction to bouts of inflation in the 1960s and 1970s. As Cukierman has pointed out, "There is mounting evidence that the legal independence of most central banks in the world has increased during the nineties to an extent that appears to be a veritable revolution in central bank legislation."[1] In a survey by Fry et al., carried out for the Bank of England in 2000, 71% of banks say they enjoy independence without significant qualifications (though in developing countries the figure is only 57%).[2] Indeed, as Lastra says, "central bank independence has become a kind of 'graduation issue for countries wishing to exhibit or consolidate their credentials in monetary stability and fiscal restraint.'"[3]

It now seems to be received wisdom that price stability and economic performance are both enhanced by independence, or at least that price stability is maintained while economic growth is not adversely affected— a rare economic "free lunch," one might say. As Buiter argues, "A commitment to price stability through the pursuit of an inflation target by an operationally independent central bank has become the canonical model of monetary policy in an open economy with a floating exchange rate."[4]

Independence was not, however, historically linked to an inflation target. Since 1951 the Fed has enjoyed a high degree of insulation from political interference, while in Europe the movement toward monetary union required member states to legislate to free their central banks as a precursor to membership of the Eurosystem. While no U.K. government has yet seriously intended to join EMU, the departure of sterling from the ERM created a dynamic that led to Bank of England independence in 1997 (de facto) and 1998 (de jure).

So have we reached the end of history on this issue? Is there anything to say other than that if a country seriously wants to pursue price stability, central bank independence—whether with or without a specific target—is the necessary and sufficient precondition?

Not quite. Just as Francis Fukuyama's prediction proved premature, there are grounds for believing that the debate on the status and responsibilities of central banks is not over. We say that for three reasons.

First, if we look more closely at the landscape we find that there are many different interpretations of independence. The differences between the statutes of the ECB, the Bank of England, and the Fed are marked, and there are intriguing variations elsewhere too: notably in New Zealand, Australia, and Canada, to say nothing of the diversity of practice in emerging markets, which we consider later. There are lively arguments about which model is superior, and indeed about whether all of them are sustainable in the long run.

Second, there are signs of political discontent. Especially in the EU, politicians of all persuasions have begun to show frustration with their inability to influence interest rate decisions, and with the degree of discretion given to the ECB—even though their governments were of course responsible for the detail of the Maastricht Treaty that enshrines that independence. It may be that the degree of independence granted to the ECB, which follows the Bundesbank model, is greater than is comfortable in the political economies of several other European countries. We should also note that the ECB has some quasi-political responsibilities, too, such as the public advisory role it has in relation to new applicants for membership of the euro area and its power to comment on new legislation in the economic and financial spheres. Buiter's view is that "the institution has neither the political legitimacy nor the analytical competence to play such an important part in a quintessentially political and analytical decision."

Third, while the Anglo–American consensus may be near complete, there are academic critics elsewhere who remain to be convinced that independence as presently defined is the right model, and their criticisms have become more strident as the consequences of the financial and economic crisis that began in 2007 have become clearer. In an aggressive polemic called *The Incendiaries* (this is our translation: the book is only available in French), Patrick Artus of the Sorbonne and the École Polytechnique argues that the responsibilities of central banks should be more effectively coordinated with other social and political objectives and that independence was conceived as a reaction to the inflation of the 1970s and is no longer appropriate in the changed conditions of the twenty-first century. His contention is that within the euro area, governments have reacted to monetary union, and to the absence of exchange rate adjustments, in one of two ways: by cutting unit costs (Germany) or by compensating for losses of competitiveness through running excessive deficits (Italy, Portugal, Greece). Both are, in his view, deflationary strategies in the long run, as in the latter case private agents see the prospect of higher taxes in the future and therefore reduce their spending today. So central banks with an exclusive focus on inflation are fighting the last war: "The argument that independent central banks are a bulwark against the inflationary bias of governments seems to have become very difficult to defend."[5] If the ECB persists in its policies, according to Artus, the consequence could be the breakup of the euro area, or a lengthy period of Japanese-style stagnation.

Other less polemical critics have argued that the credit crisis has demonstrated the need for more effective coordination of monetary and fiscal policies, and shown that central bank independence must always be qualified. They have maintained that a government's inability to instruct the central bank to respond to a sharp downturn makes crisis management more difficult. These criticisms were especially sharp in the United Kingdom in the summer of 2008 when the Bank of England was slow to respond to the accelerating recession. It is also clear that in circumstances in which the conventional weapon of monetary policy can no longer be used—the zero interest rate bound—further action must be coordinated by the central bank and the finance ministry working together. At that point the notion of independence becomes heavily qualified, especially in relation to earlier efforts to outlaw the monetization of government debt. The scale of quantitative easing must be agreed with the finance ministry. In the United Kingdom in 2009 the total sums available to the Bank of England were clearly determined by the Treasury, while the tactics were left to the MPC. The fact that the Debt Management Office is a separate agency outside both the Treasury and the Bank makes close coordination inevitable.

It is therefore worth examining whether the case for independence remains strong, and also whether the emerging criticisms point to lessons for the future, especially in terms of accountability and transparency, and in terms of the necessary interactions between the central bank and the fiscal and regulatory authorities.

THE EVOLUTION OF INDEPENDENCE

Although, as we saw, the numbers of independent banks escalated sharply in the 1990s, the idea of an independent monetary authority was hardly new. Montagu Norman campaigned for it throughout his quarter century as governor of the Bank of England. Emile Moreau, then governor of the Banque de France, noted in his diary in 1926 the trenchant views on the subject that Norman had put to him on a visit to London:[6]

> In his view politicians and political institutions are in no fit state to direct with the necessary competence and continuity this task of organization which he would like to see undertaken by central banks, independent at once of governments and of private finance. Hence his campaign in favour of completely autonomous central banks, dominating their own financial markets and deriving their power from common agreement among themselves.

It is interesting to note that Norman emphasized independence from private finance, as well as from government. That point is less prominent in debates on independence today, though Blinder attaches importance to it. "Central banks should assert their independence from financial markets just as vigorously as they assert their independence from politics" he argues.[7] In the case of the New York Fed, Wall Street bankers are involved in the selection of a president, which looked odd in 2009, given the banking sector's heavy dependence on the institution for financial support.

This also raises the question of whether monetary authorities should have responsibility for the oversight of financial firms or be at a greater distance from the financial sector. The Bundesbank long argued that it was inappropriate for the central bank to oversee the banking sector, on the grounds that it could then be tempted to prioritize its interests over those of other sectors of the economy in setting interest rates. We reviewed the validity of those arguments in chapter 4.

Norman made little headway with his campaign for independence during his lifetime, and indeed shortly after he stepped down as governor the government took the Bank into public ownership, which at the time seemed a decisive move away from independence. It was fifty years before another Labour government passed a new Bank of England Act which gave the Bank the authority to set short-term interest rates. Indeed, although the Bundesbank was endowed with strong de jure independence, ironically under the influence of British officials in postwar Germany, until twenty years ago most central banks still functioned as semidetached departments of their ministries of finance. Their staff were better paid, a point that always rankles with finance ministry officials. But the use of their policy instruments was typically coordinated with other government policies to achieve a range of government objectives such as growth and a high rate of employment, with exchange rate, balance of payments, and public debt financing aims subordinated to them.

Many countries nonetheless achieved satisfactory price stability, either because their governments and central banks worked well together to contain inflationary pressures or because they pegged their currencies, under the Bretton Woods system, to the U.S. dollar or the pound sterling. In the United States the de facto independence of the Federal Reserve was substantial and the inflation record generally good, which created a stable anchor for many other countries.

But this good inflation performance broke down in the 1970s: spectacularly in the case of Latin America and significantly in the United States and parts of Europe. The Bretton Woods institutions designed to safeguard nominal stability were no longer performing that function effectively. That failure, combined with the gradual globalization of capital markets and the dismantling of controls on capital flows, prompted a search for new types of discipline on inflation.

Over the last two decades a new consensus has emerged, both in the academic literature and among policymakers and practitioners. Cukierman summarizes that consensus as follows:[1]

> The primary responsibility of the central bank is to assure price stability and financial stability. Without prejudice to these objectives the Bank should support the economic policies of government. To achieve its main objective the Bank is given instrument independence. Delegation of authority to a non-elected institution should be accompanied by accountability and transparency.

Why did this consensus emerge? The simplest answer is based on time horizons. Because the effect of interest rate decisions on output and inflation emerges only after a considerable (and uncertain) time lag, those who make those decisions do not see the impact of the choices they make for some time—possibly on the other side of an impending election. The temptation for a politician to delay an unpopular decision, or bring forward a popular one, may be irresistible. There are many examples of interest rate reductions ahead of an election that generated inflation after it. An even more important factor is that disinflation has the cost–benefit profile of long-term investments. The costs are born up front; the benefits accrue over time. The pressures on political decision makers make it hard for them to make rational decisions faced with that unappealing trade-off.

If politicians find it difficult to make these decisions, and if it is rational for them to use interest rates to further their political ambitions, why might they choose to deny themselves that possibility and hand over power over those decisions to an unelected agency? Why is a government willing to make that binding commitment but not the commitment to price stability itself? Buiter and Sibert offer an answer:[8]

> There are occasional, infrequent interludes of "extraordinary politics" or windows of constitutional opportunity, during which otherwise opportunistic actors can commit themselves to enact certain broad, quasi-constitutional principles or rules, embodied in institutions. They make this commitment, despite knowing that, once the constitution and associated institutions have been established, the authors of the constitution will, in the course of "ordinary politics," regret their earlier commitment.

They may be right. Certainly many elected officials have been prepared to delegate powers in this way. But there remains a mystery, as Blinder remarks. Why have governments not been prepared to make the same trade-off in relation to tax policy, where there are similar technical issues and political pressures from interest groups that politicians find it hard to resist? The answer may be that tax policies inevitably have very visible distributional as well as macroeconomic consequences, and elected politicians are not prepared to hand these over to officials.

Whatever the political motivation, can it be demonstrated that better decisions do in fact emerge from an independent institution not subject to the pressures of the electoral timetable, and that the self-sacrifice is worthwhile? The evidence, both theoretical and empirical, while not unequivocal, suggests that de facto and de jure independence are associated with lower inflation, though the direction of causality is not easy to establish.[1,9,10,11] There was a clear shift to a lower-inflation environment around the world as the independence movement grew—well before the disinflationary pressures from China and India began to make themselves felt.

But the nature of independence is crucial. Where independence is purely legal, and where governor turnover around elections suggests that political influence on the central bank remains powerful, the evidence is, as one might expect, far weaker. Institutions that are supposedly independent but do not have the financial resources to act decisively also perform poorly. (We discuss the conditions for financial independence in chapter 9.) Overall, however, independent banks seem to be less ready to accommodate inflationary nominal wage increases, as the theory would predict.[12]

Furthermore, there is no evidence that this improved inflation performance is bought at the cost of output, other than in the short run. A number of studies have shown that for developed economies, certainly, real growth and central bank independence are unrelated. It may also be true that, in the even longer run, there will be a positive impact on growth potential, as price stability improves the quality of decision making by firms and individuals through reducing uncertainty, but it is enough for the purposes of this argument to establish that independence and price stability do not seem to come at a long-run cost in terms of output or employment. This is not to say that independent central banks are not capable of policy error. There is a risk that they may fall into the hands of "inflation nutters," as Mervyn King memorably described those hard-liners who might wish to stick to an inflation target come what may. That risk appeared in stark form in 2008, in the United Kingdom and in the euro area. Some would say, indeed, that it crystallized over the summer of that year, when both the Bank of England and the ECB remained preoccupied by the risks to their inflation objectives even in the face of mounting evidence of a severe recession. This is an important reason for looking carefully at the nature of the central bank's remit and its decision-making structure.

As Alan Blinder has said, independence is a vague concept, capable of a number of different interpretations.[7] Appointment procedures differ, as do the financial arrangements within which central banks operate. The most important variable, though, is the nature of the goals that the central bank is mandated to pursue, and how tightly they are defined by the government. Stanley Fischer characterizes the key distinction as being between banks with goal (or target) independence and those with only instrument independence.[13] He recognized that even this typology was not watertight, and that there is in practice a spectrum of options. However, as he says,

> A central bank with a mandate for price stability but no numerical targets has more goal independence. A central bank has instrument independence when it has full discretion and power to deploy monetary policy to attain its goals.

The indices of independence that have been developed by several different researchers suggest that there are significant differences between the monetary institutions of the G7.[14] On all of these measures the ECB is the most independent central bank and the Bank of Japan the least. On the goal/instrument axis, the ECB has a price stability mandate enshrined in the Maastricht Treaty and is able to determine its own definition of price stability. The Federal Reserve is mandated with the goals of maximum employment, stable prices (as it defines them), and, more unusually, moderate long-term interest rates. The instruments are defined in the mandate as "long-run growth in monetary and credit aggregates." In practice, of course, both the ECB and the Fed operate, at least in normal times, through determining interest rates, though there is a potential congressional override of the Fed's decision (which is very difficult to invoke in practice). The Bank of England has instrument independence but the government defines the inflation target. Again there is the possibility of a governmental override in extreme circumstances. So far that override has not been invoked, though there were suggestions in the early fall of 2008 that the Treasury gave serious consideration to doing so. Correspondence between the Treasury and the Bank in 2009, in the context of quantitative easing, reaffirmed the government's continued support for the Bank's discretion, but in terms that reminded the governor of the primacy of the Treasury's role.

There have been, and continue to be, lively debates among academics and practitioners about the merits and demerits of these different arrangements. But how differently, in practice, do these central banks behave? It is arguable that when inflation is low there is little difference in practice. The Bank of England's current government-set target is to keep inflation at 2% with a tolerance band of plus or minus 1%. Both the Fed and the ECB operate without the precision of a numerical inflation target. The ECB aims to keep inflation below but close to 2%, an asymmetrical target, while the Fed is assumed to be targeting 2%. The ECB also continues to refer to its "second pillar" in the form of a monitoring range for monetary growth. One should not exaggerate the practical consequences of these differences. For a number of years the inflation performance in the three monetary areas was broadly comparable. But the distinctions do have consequences. It is observable that the ECB is more often criticized by politicians for its interest rate decisions than is the Bank of England. This may in part be due to the difficulty of setting a single interest rate for sixteen countries with very different economic structures. But it also seems to be related to the very high degree of independence the ECB enjoys. Politicians feel they have no purchase on monetary policy whatsoever. Artus links his critique of the ECB specifically to this absence of political influence. This concern lies behind repeated French attempts, so far resisted by the Germans, to strengthen the political institutions of the euro area and to establish a finance ministers grouping that can more effectively influence the ECB.

If politicians in the United Kingdom criticize the Bank, they must say whether they are disagreeing with the Bank's technical judgment on interest rates, which is a high hurdle, or with the target itself, in which case they must make representations to the chancellor of the exchequer, who is able to change it if he or she wishes and has the political support to do so. (In fact, the target has been changed once since 1997, when the range was recentered on 2% rather than 2.5%. This happened when the inflation index was changed from the RPIX—including a measure of housing costs—to the CPI, which so far does not.) In the euro area this important distinction does not apply, leaving the ECB more exposed to criticism.

In the case of the Federal Reserve, criticism is more complex because of the dual mandate, which does not incorporate any notion of hierarchy between the objectives for employment and prices. Since the Fed itself is responsible for reaching a judgment on the trade-off, it has greater policy flexibility than the Bank of England or the ECB. While the Bank of England can decide to alter the policy horizon in response to an exogenous shock—in other words, it can decide to tolerate divergence from the target inflation path for longer on the grounds that bringing inflation back to the target quickly would impose unacceptable output costs in the short run (as it did in 2008-9)—it is obliged under the current arrangements to explain the deviation in a public letter to the chancellor. In response to such letters the chancellor ritually reminds the Bank that, subject to maintaining price stability, it also has a responsibility in relation to growth and employment. In fact, however, during the lengthy divergence from the target range during 2008-9, which was clearly attributable at least in part to an exogenous shock from oil and commodity prices, the government did not adjust the target range, which raises a question about the way in which the regime will operate in practice in the longer term. If the target was not changed in these circumstances, apparently because of the potential impact on inflation expectations, then one might ask under what circumstances it would be altered.

APPOINTMENTS

When we describe central banks as independent we are using an imprecise term. It might be preferable, indeed, to talk of autonomy. Their independence is often constrained by objectives set by government, and by a variety of accountability mechanisms. And, of course, appointments to top management positions are made by government. It is hard to imagine that they could be made by anyone else. The practice of appointment varies. In a majority of central banks the head of state appoints the governor, based on a proposal from elsewhere in the government; elsewhere, the head of state both nominates and appoints.

In some places it is customary for a government to inherit its leading central bankers from its predecessors, and for them to serve out their term. In other cases, notably in many emerging-market countries, it is common for governors to be replaced when the government changes. Our focus here is primarily on how appointments are made to the major developed-country central banks, whether there is evidence that politicians seek to influence the conduct of monetary policy through those appointments, and which processes are in practice most effective at insulating central banks from short-term political interference.

The Federal Reserve System is constructed in a highly complex way, appropriate for a federal state, which means that political power over appointments is highly distributed. The Federal Open Market Committee is the key interest rate setting body. It has twelve voting members. Five of them are presidents of the District Reserve Banks. The New York president is a permanent voting member; the other four seats are filled by rotation from the other eleven banks on a constituency basis, weighted by historical economic factors, which has the effect of allowing the presidents of Chicago and Cleveland to serve more frequently than the others. Those presidents are in turn appointed by the boards of the Reserve Banks, made up of bankers and borrowers from the district. The Federal Reserve Act calls for the majority of each board to be from the "borrowing public," but the appointments must be approved by the board of governors in Washington. That approval is not automatic. Some recent propositions by the District Boards have been sent back by Washington for reconsideration.

The Federal Reserve Board itself, with seven governor members, is appointed by the president of the United States, with the advice and consent of the Senate. Its members nominally serve fourteen-year terms but rarely do so in practice. The Federal Reserve Act, which legislated these arrangements, provided for two appointments per presidential term, but each of the last five presidents has appointed at least three governors. This complex structure, introduced in 1913 and reformed in 1935, when the Treasury secretary and the Comptroller of the Currency were removed from the Board,[15] reflects the political need to set a balance of power between the federal government and the states, between the Administration and Congress, and between politicians and bankers. The system has remained essentially unchanged for over seventy years, although the complexity of the process for securing agreement on names means that there are often unfilled vacancies on the board of governors, especially near the end of a presidential term, and this can alter the balance between Washington and the districts.

The European Central Bank's governance similarly reflects a balance between the center and the member states, and the structure clearly owes something to the example of the Fed. There is an Executive Board, which is made up of a president, a vice-president, and four other members. They come together with the governors of the countries that participate in the monetary union in the Governing Council, which sets interest rates. (There is also a General Council that includes the governors of non-EMU members of the EU. The General Council is more a dignified than a useful part of the constitution, however, and the governor of the Bank of England rarely attends.) Executive board members are appointed to staggered, eight-year, nonrenewable terms by the heads of state of EU countries, on the recommendation of the Council of Ministers (ministers of finance in this case), who are required to consult the European Parliament and the Governing Council of the ECB.

The comparison with the Fed is not straightforward, and in practice the heads of state or government are dominant in the process. Neither the Governing Council nor the European Parliament has been able to exercise any material influence on the appointments that have been made. Heads of state also, of course, appoint their national central bank governors, who make up the balance of the membership of the Governing Council. So far there has been no case of any effective dissent by the European Parliament, or by the ECB itself, whereas in the United States the Senate's preferences have frequently been a significant influence on the outcome, even though the Senate cannot propose candidates of its own. When in 1996 President Clinton sought to appoint Felix Rohatyn, a well-known advocate of a less restrictive monetary policy, a fierce response from Senate Republicans caused Rohatyn himself to withdraw.

The dominance of the heads of state has not prevented controversy. The appointment of Wim Duisenberg as the first ECB president was accepted by the French only on the understanding that Jean-Claude Trichet would succeed him, and when Duisenberg decided to remain in office rather longer than Chirac wanted, there was an acrimonious row in which Duisenberg complained of being treated by Chirac as a "little functionary." That dispute was eventually resolved when Duisenberg stepped down at a time of his own choosing, but before the end of his term. Then, in 2003, the Italian government, in the EU presidency seat, tried to secure agreement to a change that would have allowed the Council of Ministers to change the composition of the Executive Board by majority vote, rather than by unanimity. That assault on the ECB's independence was firmly rejected by Trichet and not supported by other members of the Council of Ministers.

In the case of the United Kingdom all members of the Monetary Policy Committee are appointed by the government (though nominally the governor and his two deputies are Crown appointments). The governor can exercise some influence over the appointment of his two deputies and the other two executive members of the Bank of England staff who sit on the MPC (as was evident in the summer of 2008 when Mervyn King insisted on his own choices for deputy governor and chief economist, over the wishes of the Treasury and members of the Bank's own Court of Directors). For the first ten years of the new arrangements both the external and internal members were appointed by Gordon Brown without external advertisement or competition, contrary to normal practice for other senior public appointments in the United Kingdom.

The reputational problems experienced by the Bank over the winter of 2007–8, when it was argued that the fact that both deputy governors were former Treasury officials, imposed on the institution over better-qualified internal candidates with more knowledge of financial markets, made the government less willing to impose its choices. So in 2008 Brown's successor as chancellor of the exchequer, Alistair Darling, announced that in future the positions would be advertised and that there would be a formal process of selection involving a selection committee with independent members, though the final decision would be made by the chancellor. The role of Parliament in these processes is curious. Formally speaking, members of parliament have no role. The government have always rejected the idea that the Treasury Committee should be entitled to hold formal confirmation hearings. The Committee itself has nonetheless adopted the practice of summoning newly appointed members and writing a short report on their suitability. Indeed in one case—that of Christopher Allsopp, an Oxford economist—the Committee concluded that he was not a suitable appointee. The Government went ahead and appointed him anyway.

These differences can be partly explained by the different constitutional contexts, but not entirely. The question that concerns us here, however, is whether the different models of appointment give politicians the opportunity to influence monetary policy, with potentially damaging consequences for price stability.

The answer is not straightforward. We must first presume that a president, or a government collectively, has a firm point of view about the tightness or otherwise of policy and, second, that it is possible to know in advance how a given appointee will in fact behave when given the responsibility to set interest rates. In advance, the only evidence available to the government may simply be the candidate's reported comments on the passing economic scene, if even those are available. Kelly Chang has attempted to answer this difficult question in relation to both the Fed and the ECB.[16] She models the preferences of FOMC members, essentially by using the preferences they turn out to express while in office. She then uses these to assess whether, in appointing them, a president has shifted the balance of view on the Committee in the direction he is assumed to favor. The revealed presidential preferences for loose or tight monetary policy do not follow party lines. Of the presidents she studies, Clinton emerges as the advocate of the tightest policy and George Bush (the elder) as the advocate of the easiest. It is hard to escape the conclusion that there is a risk of circularity in the argument. A president is deemed a tight money advocate because he appoints people who are positioned on the tighter side of the FOMC, and is therefore seen to have influenced policy in his preferred direction through the appointments he made.

But, with these caveats in mind, Chang's conclusions are inherently plausible. She finds that presidents do seek to influence policy through the character of the appointments they make. "Politicians," she says "may delegate monetary policy authority to the Fed, but they have never taken a completely hands-off attitude towards it." However, she finds that the complex balance that surrounds Fed appointments, and the careful phasing of vacancies, limits the ability of any Administration to influence policy decisively. No branch of government fully dominates the process, and as with the Supreme Court, presidential terms are not long enough to allow an individual to appoint a full FOMC in his image. A president can nudge the balance of opinion in one direction or another but not radically change it in short order.

In the case of the ECB the problem of determining the prior preferences of the appointing body, the EU heads of state, is complex in a different way because of the number of countries involved and the larger (and, over time, varying) number of voting members on the Governing Council. To assess the prior preferences of the heads of state involved in the selection of Executive Board members, Chang takes the average five-year inflation rate before the country entered the monetary union as their desired state of the world (a doubtful assumption in a few cases). She then asks whether the appointment of the first members of the Executive Board by the heads of state had the effect of shifting the center of gravity toward easier-money countries, since there were more heads of state to the easier side of the central point than to the tighter side. In fact their choices did not shift the central point, suggesting that the veto power of tighter-money countries was strong. In our view it may also have reflected the view that the declared purpose of EMU was to share the price stability achieved in the deutsche mark zone with the rest of the EU. It was therefore not a surprise that the addition of two more "loose-money" countries—Portugal and Greece—also failed to affect the balance. The governments of those countries were not content with their pre-EMU inflation performance and wanted to improve it. Her conclusions are that in the ECB context it is very hard to use the appointment process to loosen monetary policy and that the unanimity rule means that the status quo at the outset, dictated by the Germans in particular, is extremely difficult to dislodge. The behavior of the ECB in practice over the last decade would seem to support that conclusion. So while the appointment process does not include quite the elaborate checks and balances in place in Washington, it is difficult for any individual or group to manipulate it effectively.

The U.K. situation is quite different, as we have described. There are no checks and balances in place. Up to now, the appointment power has lain almost exclusively in the hands of the government—and indeed in the hands of one man. Hix et al. at the London School of Economics have tried to assess the extent to which appointments (of external members of the MPC) have in fact been used to influence the direction of policy.[17] Again they use the recorded votes of MPC members to assess their position on what they call a "dove-hawk" or "ease-tightness" spectrum. They then examine the appointments made by the government between 1997 and 2007 to see whether any pattern emerges. They believe it does:

> Even allowing for the uncertainty surrounding our estimates, we found evidence to suggest that there may have been an influence upon appointment policy, but that this influence was conditional upon fiscal policy. Specifically, it appears that when public spending was restrained

in the run-up to elections, the chancellor may have used MPC appointments to induce a more stimulative monetary policy (ensuring a more favourable economic climate) replacing existing MPC members with more dovish individuals.

On this analysis the U.K. system is potentially more vulnerable to political manipulation than are either the U.S. or EMU arrangements. So far, that vulnerability has not been translated into a measurably weaker inflation performance, but the risk is there. It remains to be seen whether the new procedures for selecting external members, announced in June 2008, will have any impact on the profile of new appointments. They should make it more difficult for the chancellor to pack the Committee with his friends. But the process still falls well short of the best practices adopted elsewhere in the British public sector, where independent assessors take part in the appointments process to ensure that decisions are made in relation to objective criteria. Confidence in the United Kingdom's anti-inflation policy would certainly be enhanced by measures to remove the risks that Hix et al. have identified. We would do well, however, to recall the observation in the U.S. National Monetary Commission's report in 1908 (available via the Federal Reserve Bank of St. Louis). Congress set up the commission to report on "what changes are necessary or desirable in the monetary system of the United States." It went on to recommend the Federal Reserve System. In their commentary on the Bank of England, which they examined as part of their fieldwork, the authors noted that "the important place which the Bank of England holds in the financial world is due to the wisdom of the men who have controlled its operations and not to any legislative enactments."

TERMS AND TERM LIMITS

Around the world, relatively few central bankers are subject to term limits. The Riksbank survey to which we referred earlier identified that in 70% of the countries sampled there were no term restrictions: governors can in principle be reappointed without limit. In only 4% of cases are no reappointments possible; these cases include the ECB and the Bank of Spain. For around one quarter there are two- or three-term restrictions.

The question of limits interacts, of course, with the decision made on the appropriate length of a governor's term. Here, also, international practice varies. The modal term is five or six years. Over the last decade, in practice the average term for central bank heads in developed countries was 5.2 years, compared with 4.8 years in emerging markets. There is a positive relationship between governor turnover and inflation. In other words, the shorter the governor's achieved term of office, the higher the inflation rate. But the direction of causation is unclear: long-serving governors may be more independent and effective, or high inflation may be the motive for a governor's replacement.

The arguments in these areas are finely balanced. Most would agree that short-term limits are undesirable, whether or not reappointment is possible. If it is not, then the bank is likely to find it difficult to build up experience and expertise. If reappointment is possible, then short-term appointees may feel under pressure to act in a way that "pleases" the government of the day. (The U.K. Monetary Policy Committee, with three-year terms, may be a case in point.) There is a case, therefore, for relatively long terms for governors and other senior decision makers—at least long enough to cover more than one electoral cycle. If the governor is not subject to reappointment in an election year, that is likely to promote policy stability. There may also be an argument for a backup limit on the length of time a governor may serve. The examples of very-long-serving leaders such as Montagu Norman or Alan Greenspan are not encouraging. In the later years of their terms they became more autocratic and less receptive to dissenting arguments.

ACCOUNTABILITY

There is a tight link between independence and accountability. As Lastra[3] observes,

> democratic legitimacy is a prerequisite for an independent central bank.... They regulate price levels, which is one of the most fundamental powers of government, and one of the most practical concerns of the public at large.

While governments may rationally decide to hand over control of interest rates to technicians, they should also wish to set up mechanisms to assess the skill with which they have exercised that discretion. In Blinder's words,

> Independence and accountability are symbiotic, not in conflict. The latter legitimizes the former within a democratic political structure.

Here the arrangements in place for the major central banks also differ markedly, partly as a result of their design and partly because of the political context in which they work. De Haan and Eijffinger have compared the legal accountability of the G7 institutions. Their conclusions are summarized in table 6.1.

Before examining these frameworks we should note, though, that we are talking about a weak version of accountability. In the central bank context accountability typically implies a duty to explain the reasons for decisions, after the event, and to answer questions on them. But rarely do any consequences, whether financial or otherwise, flow from these accounts. In most countries central bankers can be dismissed only for incapacity or gross misconduct, and not for incompetence. (That is fortunate for some.) So in the absence of any penalties or rewards the incentive effects of accountability arrangements are bound to be modest.

The U.K. framework of accountability is in a sense the most straightforward. It is also the most rigid. If inflation moves outside the target range set by the government, the governor must write a letter to the chancellor explaining why this has happened and what his plans are for ensuring that the rate moves back into the acceptable territory. For the first nine years of the new regime no letters were written and Mervyn King quipped that the art of letter writing was dead, but in 2006 a letter was required, and another one was needed in 2008–9, as inflation stayed above the target range for some time. Note that the obligation is symmetrical, and an explanation is also required if inflation falls below the range. The government is required to reply, either accepting the Bank's explanation and rectification plan or rejecting it and requesting a different approach. So far the replies have not challenged the Bank's actions. No serious differences of view between the government and the Bank have opened up, at least not in public. The Bank is also required to attend regular hearings in front of the Treasury Committee of the House of Commons—a committee that has grown in importance over the last decade. Indeed the independence of the Bank has been the most powerful factor in giving it greater importance than before. In the past, the Bank was largely accountable, in private, to the Treasury. Now the governor appears far more frequently in Parliament.

In the case of the Federal Reserve, Congress has long been the principal locus of its accountability. In his biannual Humphrey-Hawkins testimonies the chairman has reported in detail to the Senate Banking Committee and the House Committee on Financial Services. The status of Congress makes these occasions of the highest significance. In the past one heard few claims in the United States that there was an accountability, or a democratic, deficit in relation to the Fed, though the question

157

Table 6.1. Comparing the (legal) accountability of various central banks.[11]

Various aspects of accountability	Bank of Canada	Bank of Japan	Bank of England	Federal Reserve System	ECB
1. Does the central bank law stipulate the objectives of monetary policy?	Yes	Yes	Yes	Yes	Yes
2. Is there a clear prioritization of objectives?	No	No	Yes	No	Yes
3. Are the objectives clearly defined?	No	No	Yes	No	No (Yes)
4. Are the objectives quantified (in law or based on documents grounded in law)?	No	No	Yes	No	No (Yes)
Subtotal on *ultimate objectives of monetary policy*	1	1	4	1	2 (4)
5. Must the central bank publish an inflation or monetary policy report of some kind, in addition to standard central bank bulletins/report?	Yes	No	Yes	Yes	No (Yes)
6. Are minutes of meetings of the governing board of the central bank made public within a reasonable time?	No	No	Yes	Yes	No
7. Must the central bank explain publicly the extent to which it has been able to reach its objectives?	Yes	Yes	Yes	Yes	Yes
Subtotal on *transparency*	2	1	3	3	1 (2)

began to surface in 2009 in relation to its role as lender to the private sector.

In the euro area such criticisms are commonplace. The ECB faces an unusual problem. The European Parliament remains a weak and poorly

Table 6.1. *Continued.*

Various aspects of accountability	Bank of Canada	Bank of Japan	Bank of England	Federal Reserve System	ECB
8. Is the central bank subject to monitoring by Parliament (is there a requirement—apart from an annual report—to report to Parliament and/or explain policy actions in Parliament)?	Yes	Yes	Yes	Yes	Yes
9. Has the government the right to give instructions?	Yes	Yes	Yes	No	No
10. Is there some kind of review in the procedure to apply an override mechanism?	Yes	Yes	Yes	Yes	No
11. Is the central bank able to appeal against an instruction?	No	No	No	No	No
12. Can the central bank law be changed by a simple majority in Parliament?	Yes	Yes	Yes	Yes	No
13. Is past performance a reason for dismissal of the central bank governor?	No	No	No	No	No
Subtotal on *final responsibility*	4	4	4	2	1
Total on accountability	7	6	11	6	4 (7)

organized body. Its own legitimacy is challenged. In many states of the union only a third, or fewer, of voters bother to turn out in European elections. Members of the European Parliament are often of poor quality—they are frequently politicians who have failed to secure a seat in their domestic parliaments. While both Wim Duisenberg and Jean-Claude Trichet have appeared more regularly in front of the Parliament than they are required to, they can do little about the lack of what the French term an "interlocuteur valable." Perhaps the Parliament will one day acquire the stature to take on that role but that may take some time.

Duisenberg did not help to strengthen the mechanism when he explained that when it came to comments made by European parliamentarians on monetary policy decisions, he heard but he did not listen. Trichet has been more careful in his public pronouncements. Accountability to governments in the EU is also complex. The president is appointed by the European Council, though in a way that does not inspire confidence in the process. The first president, Duisenberg, was the head of the predecessor body, the European Monetary Institute, where he had been selected by his central bank colleagues rather than by elected officials. Politicians did not regard that as giving him an automatic right to the ECB job, while the central bank governors certainly did.

The ECB president, once appointed, cannot appear in national parliaments, and must clearly not be seen to be dancing to the tune of the government of an individual member state. So the ECB is condemned by its environment to be accused of a lack of accountability. And the fact that the Bank is able to produce its own definition of price stability makes it, in a sense, judge and jury in its own court. (See chapter 7 for further discussion of the ECB regime.)

Even if it were possible to reach international agreement on the superiority of one of these models, or on a blend of the three, there is little prospect of legislative change. In the United States, while there may be change in the Fed's regulatory responsibilities, there is no chance of removing the dual mandate. The credit crunch removed such support as there may once have been for a more rigorous, inflation-focused definition of the Fed's remit. Before he took office Bernanke was a noted enthusiast for formal inflation targets, but it is inconceivable now that he could secure congressional approval to implement one in the United States. It would be seen as demotion of the employment objective, which would be politically impossible to defend, especially at a time of economic difficulty. The argument that price stability is the dominant aim of the Fed, and that an inflation-target regime can still allow sufficient flexibility to cope with output shocks, would be hard to advance.

In the United Kingdom the government reviewed the legislation affecting the Bank of England after the Northern Rock affair and found no reason to change the inflation-target regime. At times in 2008–9 they may have regretted reaching that conclusion, as the Bank delayed interest rate cuts until it could produce an inflation-target-oriented justification for them. The government would have preferred earlier cuts in an attempt to offset rises in unemployment. A dual mandate on Fed lines would have made that easier to achieve. While the Conservative opposition have made proposals to change the appointment procedures for members of the Monetary Policy Committee, they have not so far suggested a dual mandate, or proposed to delegate target independence to the Bank or indeed to return control of interest rates to the Treasury.

In the EMU, any change to the statutes of the ECB would require treaty amendment. The difficulties surrounding ratification of the Lisbon Treaty show that the chances of treaty amendment are currently close to nil. That is unfortunate. In our view the ECB would be better placed in the long run were it to work within a framework more like that of the United Kingdom, with an inflation target set by the Council of Ministers. But even if legislative change is off the agenda, there is nonetheless scope for central banks to help themselves by making their decision making, and the way in which they communicate with politicians and the public, more transparent.

TRANSPARENCY

Transparency was historically not coded into the DNA of central banks. As Karl Brunner[18] put it in 1981, they were

> traditionally surrounded by a peculiar and protective political mystique [that] thrives on a pervasive impression that central banking is an eso- teric art. Access to this art and its proper execution is confined to the initiated elite. The esoteric nature of the art is moreover revealed by an inherent impossibility to articulate its insights in explicit and intelligi- ble words and sentences.

Buiter[19] refers to the priestly tradition of monetary policy: "monetary policy is a cult whose high priests perform the sacred rites far from the prying eyes of the non-initiates." Robin Leigh-Pemberton, when gover- nor of the Bank of England, reinforced the stereotype with his reference to decisions of the Bank being taken "in decent obscurity," while Alan Greenspan played to the same gallery, with tongue firmly in cheek, when he observed that if his congressional inquisitors thought they had under- stood him they were almost certainly wrong. He was, perhaps uncon- sciously, echoing a former deputy governor of the Bank of England who explained to the Macmillan Committee in 1930 that "it is a dangerous thing to start to give reasons." Another favored conceit was "construc- tive ambiguity"—keeping the market guessing. (We discuss the culture of central banks later, in chapter 10.)

On the face of it the mood has now changed, at least in the lead- ing institutions on which we are focusing attention here. These witty defenses of opacity are no longer as amusing as they once were, in light of the perception that the Fed made important and very costly policy errors in the run-up to the crisis. Transparency is the new orthodoxy: almost as positive a word as stability in the governors' lexicon. Governors rarely now praise obscurity, even when they are being economical with the truth. Seventy-four percent of them now consider transparency to be a "vital" or "very important" component of their monetary policy framework,[2] though the enthusiasm is less evident in emerging markets. While as little as fifteen years ago the Fed did not even disclose its interest rate decisions at the time they were made, that would now seem extraordinary behavior. Most would, at least on the record, sign up to Alan Blinder's conclusion that "the bank should reveal enough about its analysis, actions and internal deliberations so that interested observers can understand each monetary policy decision as part of a logical chain of decisions leading to some objective(s)."[7]

Dincer and Eichengreen[20] show that the central banks of all large, systemically significant countries have increased the transparency of their policymaking and operations over the last twenty years. They review fifteen subindicators of transparency—including macroeconomic and inflation forecasting and the publication of minutes and voting records—to construct an overall index. Their conclusion is that there has been significant movement in the direction of greater transparency, and that transparency is typically greater in countries with strong and stable political institutions, and in democracies. They also show that more transparency in monetary operations "is associated with less inflation variability though not with less inflation persistence."

Why this new commitment to openness? There are two sets of reasons: the first is political in nature, the second relates more directly to the price stability objective itself.

The political reasons relate to the problem of independence and accountability that we have discussed. Accountability, as we have seen, is the other side of the coin of independence, and accountability cannot be effective unless the objectives the central bank is trying to achieve are clear. Furthermore, the public cannot assess the quality of the bank's analysis and economic reasoning unless they know what it is. So transparency is part of the way in which the central bank maintains and protects its independence. The formal arrangements differ from country to country. They are most rigorous in the United Kingdom, where the Bank is obliged by law to publish an *Inflation Report*, and to publish the minutes of its Monetary Policy Committee. Broadly similar obligations bite on the Federal Reserve, but the Maastricht Treaty imposed no such requirements on the ECB, although it does in practice publish information like that produced by the Fed and the Bank of England. The president makes an "Introductory Statement" at the press conference held after each Governing Council meeting.

The economic case for transparency rests on expectations theory. Financial markets, in particular, will be influenced not only by the interest rate decision today but also by what they expect interest rate decisions to be in the future. Those expectations about the future level of short-term rates will influence the long bond rate today, which is an important element of the transmission mechanism. So the argumentation surrounding a rate decision, and the balance of opinion on the decision-making body, may be as important as the immediate decision itself. There is evidence that as central banks have become more transparent the markets have proved better at anticipating future moves, and as a result monetary policy has become more reliable and fast acting.[21]

The same expectation impact may be seen in wage and product markets. Wage bargainers and price-setters will alter their behavior more quickly if they, or the commentators they read, can better anticipate future actions by the monetary authorities. If market participants think like the central bank, the latter will find it easier to manage expectations more effectively. There are further arguments, too, relating to the quality of decision making. If decision makers know they are obliged to articulate a public defense of the choice they have made, they will need to ensure that their decisions are intellectually coherent. To quote Blinder again, "sound policy is explicable; muddled policy is not."

Blinder is also helpful in proposing a taxonomy of transparency—a taxonomy that helps to identify the differences in theory and practice that still obtain. He distinguishes between transparency about goals, about methods, and about decisions and decision making.

We have described the differences in goals that derive from the different legal mandates under which the major central banks work. Looked at from the perspective of transparency, the Bank of England has the clearest mandate, and Blinder therefore prefers it. He praises the ECB, too, for having provided explicit clarification of its definition of price stability. The Fed's objectives, by contrast, he finds too obscure. The Federal Reserve Act directs it to pursue "maximum employment, stable prices, and moderate long-term interest rates." The Fed has chosen not to amplify these aims with any great precision, preserving flexibility but sacrificing transparency. Former Fed governor Larry Meyer has argued that the Fed could, without sacrificing too much room for maneuver, be "more transparent about their estimate of the unemployment rate that is consistent with maximum sustainable employment."[22] On the other hand, at times of crisis, the Fed's balanced objective allows it greater flexibility. The employment objective is not subordinate to price stability and may be used as a justification for cutting rates.

Transparency about methods is Blinder's second category. This relates primarily to the central bank's forecasts. Should they be published? The key argument for doing so centers, once again, on expectations. Central bank forecasts are likely to be given more than usual weight by private economic actors, and therefore may influence behavior. The counterargument is that decision makers may not wish to bind themselves for the future, as circumstances change. There is also the practical problem of gaining agreement on the part of a large and diverse group (especially in the case of the FOMC) to a single set of assumptions and forecasts. That is particularly true when it comes to the projected path for interest rates. Should the forecast include an estimate of what the monetary authority itself will do in the future, be based only on unchanged rates, or assume some path for rates derived from market expectations using the swap curve? Mishkin believes that it would in practice be impossible for a committee to agree a forecast on a regular basis.[23] Goodhart agrees.[24] Indeed Mishkin argues that publishing a projection for official rates "will complicate the communication process and weaken support for a central bank focus on long-run objectives."

But, although there are complications, research shows that there is value in publishing official forecasts of some kind. One study contends that the publication of detailed forecasts reduced inflation in a sample of eighty-three countries, even after controlling for other economic characteristics like GDP per head.[25] So there is some empirical support for the proposition that official forecasts influence behavior in a helpful way.

Different institutions have tried to resolve this conundrum in different ways. The Fed publishes a staff forecast. So does the Bank of Japan. The Bank of England publishes a forecast in its *Inflation Report*, but it is one that in effect includes a range of possible outcomes. The *Inflation Report* reflects the views of MPC members but captures the range of uncertainty by producing fan charts of the likely outcome for inflation, up to two years ahead, on two different bases: a conventional assumption of unchanged rates and an alternative based on market expectations of future rates, derived from the swap curve. These fan charts have subsequently been copied elsewhere, and do appear to have made public commentary more balanced, with better understanding of the nature of the uncertainty policymakers face. The Reserve Bank of New Zealand, which led the way on inflation targeting, produces a forecast that is based on an assumption of interest rate changes the Bank expects to make in the future—rather easier to do when there is only one decision maker: the governor. So, while differences in practice remain, the direction of travel is clear: toward greater transparency.

The third dimension—transparency about the decision making itself—is the most difficult and reflects divergent practice at the heart of the monetary policy process. Again, though, it is an area in which practices have changed rapidly over the last few years.

In the case of the Federal Reserve, FOMC minutes are published a few weeks after the meeting and the votes of individual voting members are revealed (not all those who attend the meetings are entitled to vote—the regional Fed presidents rotate the rights to vote among their number). The full minutes are now made public after a five-year lag. The reasons given for dissenting votes are very brief, however, and reveal little about the arguments advanced in support of them. It is also the case that dissents from the majority view are relatively rare. Only when a member strongly disagrees with the majority line is a vote of dissent recorded, and the terminology of "dissent," with its implication of heterodoxy, is in itself revealing.

At the Bank of England a vote is taken at each meeting of the MPC and the results are disclosed when the minutes are published, two weeks later. Those minutes give some detail on the points made by the majority and by those who would have preferred a different result. The votes of each member are also revealed. So the evolution of voting behavior can be a further guide to the market on the way the Committee's thinking is changing, though critics argue that individual voting can have the opposite effect, introducing "noise" into the system and both excessively personalizing the process and creating confusion. The Bank of Japan now also publishes board votes and minutes, and an official forecast. But a broader survey of international practice[2] shows that in only three other countries are voting records published: Korea, Poland, and Sweden. Some argue that publishing blow-by-blow accounts of contentious discussions among committee members can have the effect of heightening asset price volatility.[25]

The ECB does not disclose the minutes of its Governing Council meetings, at which interest rate decisions are taken. In this, and in many other things, it takes its cue from the Bundesbank, which published its minutes only after thirty years. The Bank argues that decisions are reached by consensus and that the guide to policy appears in the statement issued at the time of the decision, when the president also gives a press conference to explain the background. Critics argue that the ECB is therefore not as informative as the other central banks. Can it be that there are never dissenting voices on the Governing Council? Does the statement really reflect the views expressed or was it drafted beforehand by the ECB staff? While the practice of indicating the Council's future bias has begun to be adopted, especially under Trichet, this amounts to materially less transparency than in London or Washington.

Defenders maintain that the results have been as good as in the United States or the United Kingdom, and that there is little or no evidence that the markets have been confused. Quieter voices argue that the methodology, while not perfect, is more appropriate for the circumstances of a new monetary union than a more transparent, vote-based system would have been. In the early years of the union might there not have been a serious risk, if their votes had been disclosed, that the governors of national central banks would have been obliged to vote in line with the needs of their local economy rather than taking account of inflationary pressures in the euro area as a whole? The NCB governors are in a curious position. They are appointed to the Governing Council on the basis that they will exercise their votes on a personal basis, in the interests of price stability in the entire euro area. Yet they are appointed to their "day jobs" by national governments and serve on the ECB ex officio. As Geraats[26] argues, "voting opacity could be desirable for a monetary union in which the central bank reappointments are made by national governments, as is the case for the ECB." It would appear that in spite of its curious structure the ECB has created a collegiate atmosphere, to a greater extent than might have been foreseen at the outset at least. We discuss below whether the initial settlement may need to change as more new members join.

COMMUNICATIONS

It is clear that what central banks disclose is important, but does it matter how they do it? In other words, do the channels of communication they use make a difference?

Although the theory would strongly suggest that it must, as policy is thought to work in part through influencing expectations, the evidence is mixed and is not easy to interpret. There is extensive academic literature on the point, whose conclusions are ambiguous. Recently, economists have chosen to focus attention on the impact of different types of statement and news release on interest rate expectations, through interest rate futures. They assume that if the bank is providing new information to the market, that should show up in an increase in the variance of interest rate futures prices on the day of the communication.[27] They recognize that it is impossible to know whether or not the change is the one the central bank hoped to see, and that the measurement only reflects the presence of new information, not its accuracy. However, if genuinely new information is being imparted, there ought to be some price movement.

Connolly and Kohler summarize the results of a range of studies carried out in different countries and apply the methodology to a panel of economies: Australia, Canada, the euro area, New Zealand, the United Kingdom, and the United States.[28] Their conclusions are that in comparison with other macroeconomic news (output figures, industrial trend surveys, etc.), "central bank communication is not a large contributor to overall movements in interest rate futures," and that communications from the bank typically add only a few basis points to the standard deviation of rates on the days they occur. There is, however, a marked difference in the impact of different types of communication. Commentaries following interest rate decisions, whether in the form of a press conference or otherwise, monetary policy reports (inflation reports and forecasts), and testimony at congressional or parliamentary hearings all have some influence on market expectations. The Humphrey–Hawkins testimonies are especially significant in the United States. In the United Kingdom the MPC minutes are significant, and do move markets, while the *Inflation Report* has little effect on expectations, perhaps because the minutes are released quite quickly. MPC minutes in effect include evidence on the Committee's future "bias" through disclosure of the voting balance.

Speeches by governors and senior officials in the central bank, by contrast, have much less impact. Only in Australia and, mildly, the United States is it possible to identify any impact on the market. Even when speeches on subjects other than monetary policy are excluded, the impact on the markets is invisible. This will come as a disappointment to the gubernatorial fraternity, and especially to their speechwriters. If the Bank of England is in any way representative, a huge amount of effort goes into preparing speeches for the governors and other members of the MPC. There may be an educational purpose to this effort, but as far

167

as influencing expectations is concerned they need not bother. There is at the same time a risk of confusion if a large number of individuals speak for a central bank: "A central bank that speaks with a cacophony of voices may, in effect, have no voice at all."[29]

GOVERNANCE

The way institutions behave in practice is also influenced by their governance structures, whatever formal legal autonomy they enjoy. Those structures differ markedly from country to country. Some of those differences are explained by the different tasks assigned to the institution, others by the legal and governance context within which they operate.

The IMF have surveyed almost one hundred institutions to map their board structures against their degrees of policy freedom.[30] More heroically, they have attempted to categorize the functions of different boards, identifying five different types of role a board might play: advisory, supervisory, policy, management, and implementation (see table 6.2). The picture that emerges is confusing. In practice, many boards have more than one function. In our view a simpler distinction is between determining policy (in other words, setting interest rates (normally) or managing the exchange rate (where the central bank itself does so)), continuing oversight of the institution's affairs, and day-to-day management and operations.

The oversight role may or may not involve some formal involvement in management issues, perhaps including determining the overall budget and staff complement. It certainly involves the core functions of audit and risk management, usually together with a role in determining the remuneration of senior staff. In jurisdictions with a tradition of unitary boards, the role is likely to be somewhat broader; in countries where corporations typically have two-tier board structures, the borderline between oversight and management may be drawn in a different place. These differences are of lesser importance than the core distinction between oversight and policy. To illuminate the different approaches taken to both, and to try to identify good practice, it is useful to focus on the details of a few institutions: firstly the Federal Reserve and the Bank of England.

OVERSIGHT

It is conventional to talk of the "Anglo-Saxon model" of capital markets. The French like to do so. In practice there are many differences

Table 6.2. Numbers of members in different boards (end of 2003).[30]

	Percentage of laws in each group						Governor is chairman		Number of laws surveyed
	≤3	4-6	7-9	10-12	≥13	Total	Yes	No	Total
Policy board	4	28	50	10	8	100	92	8	50
with multiple functions	2	18	28	8	4	60	56	4	30
Implementation board	4	28	47	11	10	100	87	13	95
with multiple functions	1	18	26	5	6	56	47	9	54
Advisory board	—	10	10	40	40	100	70	30	10
with multiple functions	—	—	—	—	20	20	10	10	2
Supervisory board	1	23	46	14	16	100	74	26	98
with multiple functions	1	14	27	5	8	55	45	10	54
Management board	14	52	24	5	5	100	86	14	21
with multiple functions	—	15	14	—	—	29	24	5	6

Note: Certain functions may be performed by several governing bodies, but only the body with the primary responsibility is included in this survey. Figures may not add up; for instance, if the supervisory function is performed by the governor. Percentage figures are rounded.

between the systems in place in the United Kingdom and the United States, not limited to the fact that, to the British eye, American profit-and-loss accounts are presented back to front and upside down.

Different approaches to corporate governance, and especially to the structure of leadership, are another fault line in so-called Anglo-Saxon capitalism. In the United States, most corporations are still run by a combined chairman and chief executive. In the United Kingdom, the unitary model of corporate control is frowned upon. While corporate governance codes do not absolutely mandate a separation of the roles, they are about as negative on the practice as they can reasonably be, and in almost all cases the roles are now separated in large companies, with a chairman in charge of the board and a chief executive officer managing the affairs of the company on a day-to-day basis. Few U.S. corporations split the role, in spite of much recent evidence of the dangers that can result from the excessive concentration of power in the hands of one individual. A similar contrast is visible in the governance arrangements for the Federal Reserve and the Bank of England. At the Fed, the chairman is evidently in executive charge of the institution as a whole, not just of the FOMC, which sets interest rates, while at the Bank of England, following the Bank of England Act 2009, a nonexecutive director chairs meetings of the Bank's Court, which oversees the management of the Bank. The governor, of course, continues to chair the MPC.

While the formal change at the Bank occurred very recently, the practical arrangements were in fact altered in 2003, with the appointment of Mervyn King as governor. The Bank of England Act 1998 mandated the creation of a nonexecutive committee of the Bank's Court, chaired by a lead nonexecutive director, but it left the chairmanship of the Court in the hands of the governor. That remained the case under Governor Eddie George. The nonexecutive committee oversaw the setting of salaries, and the other "housekeeping" functions—audit, risk, etc. In 2003 Mervyn King changed things. He asked the lead nonexecutive to chair the meetings, though since the legislation still required the governor to chair Court, there was a formal, five-minute session at the end of each meeting to meet the legislative obligation. The Treasury accepted this device as a practical method of bringing the Bank's governance closer to best practice in the private sector without the need for a change in the law. Then, when legislation affecting the Bank was proposed for other reasons, following the failure of Northern Rock, the Court of Governors was reformed, reducing the number of members and formalizing the nonexecutive chairmanship, so that the governor is now no longer even nominally in the chair. The chairman has an office in the Bank and is expected to devote a substantial amount of time to its affairs.

The Bank of England is not alone in separating the roles in this way, though the significance of the chairman role is much greater than is typical elsewhere. Several other countries have supervisory boards in place, to oversee management. Such an arrangement is in place in Austria, Belgium, Denmark, and Hungary, for example. In Singapore, too, there is a board chaired by a former prime minister, while the Monetary Authority of Singapore is run by the managing director. In some recent cases where governance has been reformed, such as in Iceland, New Zealand, Norway, and Switzerland, the opportunity has been taken to split the post of governor from that of chairman of the supervisory board. But in other major institutions, notably the Bank of Japan and the ECB, the governor/president is in sole charge, with oversight mechanisms structured in different ways. ECB salaries, for example, are set by a special committee of six wise persons, half of whom are appointed by the Governing Council and half by the European Council of Ministers.

Those who support a division of roles argue that the public policy roles of a central bank require governance arrangements that balance autonomy and accountability, which points to the need for a supervisory board to represent the public interest within the institutional structure. If that is the role of the board, then it is appropriate for it to be chaired by someone other than the governor. A nonexecutive chairman is likely to promote freer discussion, and more searching questioning of the executives. Those with experience of both models maintain that such a difference was observable when the change was made. The fact that the governor does not chair the board enhances its credibility as an oversight mechanism. The chairman can also act as a buffer between the bank and the government. With an independent chairman in place it is more difficult for the ministry of finance to lean on the bank on budgetary or pay issues, which are an important element of independence.

Opponents, and there are many among the ranks of governors, argue that it is not appropriate to apply a corporate governance model designed for private corporations to a central bank. In the case of a private company there is the potential for a conflict of interest between the shareholders and the executive management, especially in the case of a projected takeover. No such conflict should apply in the case of a central bank, where the task is to pursue statutory responsibilities, and there is no reason for a supervisory board and the executive to reach a different view on the interpretation of the statute. Indeed, if they do, that is a recipe for confusion. Whereas it is accepted that some independent oversight is needed, especially in relation to the budget and salaries, that can be provided by external auditors, perhaps appointed by government, or by a subcommittee of the board on which the governor does not sit.

We do not find these latter arguments persuasive. In view of the importance of the functions delegated to independent central banks, they should be held to the highest standards of corporate governance. The risks to credibility where questions are raised about the conduct of a governor can be serious, as the unhappy cases of Ernst Welteke at the Bundesbank and Antonio Fazio at the Banca d'Italia demonstrated. Both were forced to resign after publicity about entertainment and gifts. The fact that Fazio himself chaired the board of the Banca d'Italia made it difficult for the bank to reach the conclusion that for long seemed inevitable, following the disclosure of his too-close relationships with Italian commercial banks and interference in a cross-border takeover. The lengthy delay before he was removed from office was damaging for the reputation of the bank.

We therefore share the conclusions of Lybeck and Morris that the majority of a board primarily responsible for supervising the central bank should constitute nonexecutive members, or outside individuals, and that the governor should not be chairman of a supervisory board. We do not favor the presence of government officials or ministers on such boards, on which Lybeck and Morris are neutral. There is a risk that responsibilities and authority are blurred. It is important that the board owes its principal loyalty just to the Bank, as long as it is pursuing its legal objectives. Government representatives are bound to have other considerations in their minds. We do, however, share Lybeck and Morris's view that it is helpful if the underpinning legislation is clear about the respective responsibilities of different types of governing body. Their survey reveals considerable confusion in practice about where specific duties lie. The appropriate division of responsibilities may differ somewhat from place to place, but we can see a bright line between policy on the one hand and oversight of management on the other. Giving responsibility for the hygiene factors of governance, including budgetary control, to a board with strong nonexecutive representation can be helpful in practical terms, and can also defend the bank against accusations of profligacy and ethical failings.

POLICY-MAKING STRUCTURES

Very different considerations apply to the boards or committees that make monetary policy decisions. Lybeck and Morris's survey shows that in almost half the central banks they surveyed, government officials are voting members of policy boards. That is undesirable, though a nonvoting member may be a useful channel of communication.

But in the case of policy boards a number of other considerations also apply. How many members should they have? Is there, indeed, any advantage in having a board rather than an individual? If a board is set up, what type of people should be appointed to it? How should they reach their decisions? On all these points there is wide diversity of practice, even in the large developed economies.

Until the last couple of decades, central banks did not operate explicit schemes of collective decision making. Many still simply played an advisory role in relation to governments on interest rates. But even those who had decisive powers normally vested the decision-making authority in individual governors, who may or may not have consulted their colleagues. Part of the revolution in practice over the last two decades has been a movement toward making monetary policy by committee. A few banks still operate a single-decision-maker system, notably those in Israel and New Zealand, arguing that individual responsibility creates the strongest form of accountability. But a survey of eighty-eight banks in 2004 showed that seventy-nine made monetary policy by committee.[31] Many switched from the single-decision-maker model to a collective model at the time of independence. There is no example of a bank moving in the opposite direction. Even in countries where the governor remains legally responsible, as in Canada, India, Malaysia, and South Africa, decisions are now made in the context of committee meetings that involve a vote or the formation of a consensus.

One obvious reason for favoring a committee over an individual is to protect against the risk that policy becomes subject to the idiosyncratic preferences of a dictatorial individual. As the BIS governance review points out, "society is reluctant to delegate state power to an individual."[32] A second reason is that the pooling of knowledge ought to lead to better decisions. There are powerful general arguments generated elsewhere in the social sciences, often in the management departments of business schools, that point to the superiority of group over individual decision making, and most governments have implicitly accepted these arguments. Blinder has attempted to produce specific evidence of the superiority of group decision making in the context of monetary policy.[33] He conducted an experiment using a group of economics students who were required to simulate monetary policy in a laboratory setting. Each of the students made decisions on interest rates in a simulated economy, both as an individual and as part of a five-man committee. The students would be rewarded for keeping inflation as close as possible to 2% and the unemployment rate at 5%. (The detailed specification of the experiment was clearly influenced by the Federal Reserve's objectives.) The economy was subject to random shocks in each simulation.

The results were striking. Groups outperformed individuals by a clear margin. The differences were highly significant statistically, and large enough to be economically important. Furthermore, there was no evidence that the groups made policy more slowly or reacted more slowly to changed circumstances. The average lag in monetary policy reactions was about the same in each case. So groups make superior decisions, and do so no more slowly than individuals. Gerlach-Kristen offers an elegant theoretical explanation of both phenomena.[34]

Blinder's groups were made up of five students. In the real world the most common size for a policy board or Monetary Policy Committee (MPC) is between five and ten members.[31] The FOMC has twelve voting members, though it has nineteen speaking participants. The Bank of England MPC has nine members, as does the Bank of Japan Policy Board. The Canadians make do with six, while the ECB now has twenty-one voting members of the Governing Council. (Their aim is to limit the number to twenty-one, as we shall see.)

What are the determinants of these size differences? Not surprisingly, population is a factor: the larger the size of a country, the bigger the rate-setting committee of its central bank tends to be.[35] Countries with open and democratic political institutions tend to have large decision-making bodies, while countries with autocratic structures have relatively small MPCs. Curiously, landlocked countries have smaller boards (and smaller navies too, no doubt). We cannot generate a hypothesis that explains this phenomenon. More independent central banks have relatively larger boards, but with members who serve relatively shorter terms.

There is no hard-edged analysis that points to the optimum size for an MPC. On the one hand, there are arguments related to efficient information processing in favor of a larger number of participants—though, as Blinder points out, virtually all the data that matter to decision makers are common knowledge, making this a weak argument. A more significant case can be built on the notion that a larger number of board members should involve a broader range of experiences and perspectives and hence be better at dealing with uncertainty. On the other hand, decision making is likely to become more difficult as board size increases. Discussions at the board take longer, and there is a risk that suboptimal decisions are reached under pressure of time. Beyond a certain point there is a risk that individuals "free-ride" on the analysis of others, and that the value of additional viewpoints is small, or conceivably nonexistent.[36]

Two central banks have acted on the assumption that it would be a mistake to increase the size of their MPC further. Before monetary union, the Bundesbank, faced with a large increase in its MPC following German reunification, concluded that the increase in size that would have resulted had all the new Länder been given a seat "would have greatly complicated that body's decision-making processes" (see www.bundesbank.de). More recently, the ECB noted that an increase in the number of members of the Eurosystem could influence the Governing Council's capacity for timely and effective monetary policymaking.[37] The European Council therefore resolved in 2003 to limit the future number of voting members to twenty-one, on the declared grounds that "there is a need to maintain the Governing Council's capacity for efficient and timely decision making in an enlarged monetary union." As soon as the number of members of the Governing Council exceeds twenty-one (i.e., reaches six Executive Board members plus sixteen or more national governors), a rotation system was to be put in place. This new system involves a complex weighting of member countries by GDP, which results in less frequent membership of the Council on the part of smaller member states. That trigger point was reached when Slovakia joined the monetary union on January 1, 2009.

Is it possible to conclude that there is a maximum size beyond which an MPC is bound to become inefficient, or indeed a minimum size to provide adequate protection against "groupthink"? Probably not. The appropriate size is likely to depend on the size and heterogeneity of the monetary area, and also on the way in which the MPC makes its decisions—the issue to which we now turn our attention.

DECISION MAKING

The issue that has generated the most heat among practitioners and academics in recent years is the optimal decision-making process—if it is accepted that some form of committee is to be preferred. In part, the heat has been generated by somewhat strident advocacy by the British government, and the Bank of England, of the MPC model, with its individual voting and published voting records. (The British model is also unusual in another respect. In most countries, the policy board is also responsible for other functions, including the management of the bank. The U.K. MPC is responsible exclusively for monetary policy decisions.) Unsurprisingly, that advocacy has caused others to defend their own models. The advocates of the British system maintain that the MPC maximizes accountability as the votes of individuals are registered and gives the market leading indicators of the Committee's tendency through the regular publication of the balance of votes, thus helpfully influencing expectations. Critics say that the process is over-engineered, that it over-personalizes what should be an objective process, and that it may mystify the market rather than enlightening it, by creating confusion about who speaks for the Bank, especially when, as has happened now on a number of occasions, the governor finds himself in the minority. This point may have some significance as was shown in August 2009, for example, when the governor was outvoted on the quantity of asset purchases the Bank should undertake.

Blinder offers a useful way of thinking about this controversy.[38] He argues that in fact a spectrum of practice can be observed, from individualistic to collegial committees, with the Bank of England at one end of the spectrum, along with the Swedish Riksbank, and the ECB at the other extreme. The Bank of Japan is closer to the individualistic model and the Fed is closer to the collegial model. Individualistic committees are more straightforwardly democratic. The processes may be, in Blinder's words, "quite messy, because the group process thrives on, indeed requires, differences of opinion." The group may find it difficult to agree what to do. A series of split votes may give the impression that the committee does not know what it is doing. A committee may reach a majority decision but have difficulty in producing an agreed explanation of it, given the divided opinions. The Bank of England typically does not produce an agreed post-meeting statement for that reason. This may mean that the process of getting the markets to think like the central bank, one of the key aims of transparency, is more difficult in the individualistic model.

Blinder may exaggerate the messy-process point. In fact, the proceedings of the MPC are carefully structured. The main meeting is preceded by lengthy presentations of the latest evidence by Bank staff, and the Committee dine together on the night before. The Committee uses the dinner for a general discussion about the evolution of the economy since the last meeting, in the light of what they have heard and read.

At the meeting itself the Deputy Governor for Monetary Policy normally speaks first and makes a proposal. (This orchestration was agreed when King was in that role.) Other members then speak, in no set order. They may, at that point, give their view on the interest rate decision, or they may wait until the end of the round to do so. The governor usually speaks last and ends his intervention with the proposal that is put to the vote (which may not necessarily be the one put forward by his deputy at the start but very often is). A simultaneous vote is then taken. In principle, this procedure could allow the governor always to be on the winning side if he so chooses. In practice, on three occasions so far he has chosen to vote with the minority. That did not happen under Governor George, perhaps because on those occasions when he felt very strongly he gave his view to the Committee at the start of the meeting. Critics argue that if the governor is in the minority it is difficult for him to then represent the Bank's view in public forums, and that since it is the governor, not the Committee as a whole, who must write to the chancellor to explain any divergence from the target, he may find himself having to explain that the target would have been met had the Committee taken his line. That has not so far happened, and may be a far-fetched scenario.

The counterargument is that, in practice, the public response to the governor's minority position was muted. The alternative to the governor being prepared to vote with the minority on occasion is, logically, that if he is expected to always vote with the majority, his vote would not count at all, or that he should act autocratically, seeking to bully a majority of the Committee to support his point of view. These are reasonable points, but the question of how the system would operate if the governor were to find himself in a minority position for a long period is still open. It is not clear that he could continue to lead the Bank effectively in public were that to be the case.

Do these arguments point to the superiority of the collegial approach? Not necessarily. First, Blinder subdivides committees into what he describes as "genuinely collegial" and "autocratically collegial" committees. He asserts (and he spent two years as vice chairman under Alan Greenspan) that under Greenspan's chairmanship the FOMC was an autocratically collegial committee. Writing in 2004 Blinder said:

> Nowadays Alan Greenspan's mythic status is so intimidating that his opinion always prevails. Persuasion is almost automatic; all Greenspan needs to do is open his mouth.

Dissent was an act of moral, as well as intellectual, courage, as some of those who dissented attest.

The formal procedures of the FOMC differ from those of the MPC in significant ways. There are eight meetings a year, not twelve—perhaps a trivial point, though most past and present MPC members in the United Kingdom believe that they meet too often and that the legislation, which mandates monthly meetings, should have allowed more flexibility. There is a staff forecast available for each meeting, and voluminous data. At the formal meeting all participants (including those district presidents who do not have a vote at that time) express a view on the economic situation in an initial round of comments. They may, at that time, also offer a view on the direction of policy but are not obliged to do so. The chairman then presents a proposal and participants comment on it in turn. Finally, a vote is taken, with the chairman voting first, followed by the vice chairman and the other voting Committee members in alphabetical order.

It is clear that this structure gives the chairman much greater authority than is the case at the MPC. Some studies suggest that the chairman has a disproportionate influence on the process, by virtue of the procedures used, and that he effectively exercises as much as 40–50% of the voting weight in Committee decisions.[39] While there may be votes against the chairman's recommendation, those votes are, significantly, termed "dissents," and carry quite different baggage from that of an MPC minority vote. In practice, approximately one dissenting vote is registered in every third meeting: a low rate. The president of the New York Fed never votes against the proposition put by the chairman, suggesting prior discussion. And former members of the Committee say that there is an informal agreement that there should never be more than a couple of dissenters at any one time, to avoid diminishing the authority of the chairman.

There is evidence, indeed, that the incidence of dissent declined from the time when a decision was made to publish the transcripts of FOMC meetings, in 1993.[40] Empirical analysis shows that policymakers then became less likely to express verbal disagreement with Greenspan's proposals. This suggests that there are circumstances, especially where the policy committee is controlled by a dominant chairman, in which greater transparency of decision making may prevent the full and frank discussion needed to make the best decisions. Indeed the publication of transcripts seems to have had the effect of allowing even greater dominance by Alan Greenspan.

Blinder, who left the Fed after disagreements with the chairman, argues that under Greenspan the Committee became more autocratic than ever. Greenspan, he says, is "about as dominant a chairman as you are ever likely to see," though he acknowledges that there were a few occasions on which he modified his position slightly, perhaps by allowing a free vote on the so-called "bias." The Committee still acts as some kind of check on the chairman, as members may speak out in public, and sometimes do, but the cards are stacked in his favor. Where the chairman is wrong there is a clear risk to policy. We consider elsewhere whether, in practice, Greenspan's dominance was excessive in the early years of this century and whether that led to a seriously flawed policy.

The third model is the "genuinely collegial" model. Blinder considers the ECB Governing Council to be a working example of this model, in which the chairman seeks out and perhaps builds a consensus and then persuades recalcitrant members to go along, resulting in something that is presented as a unanimous decision.

It is hard to know whether this assessment is correct. The ECB's procedures are in this respect much less transparent than those of the Fed and the Bank of England. They have given no public explanation of the way in which the policy proposition put to the Governing Council is developed. Anecdotal evidence from participants suggests that there is in practice an inner group, whose composition has changed over time, that precooks the proposal. In the early years the key players were Wim Duisenberg, the Executive Board member responsible for the economic divisions of the bank, Otmar Issing, Tommaso Padoa-Schioppa, and the heads of the Bundesbank (Tietmeyer) and of the Banque de France (then Trichet). It was unkindly said that Duisenberg was the least important of the group, as a man whose previous monetary policy decision making at De Nederlandsche Bank had amounted to taking telephone calls from the Bundesbank. When Welteke took over at the Bundesbank the German influence declined for a while, but Axel Weber has reasserted it. Within the ECB, Lucas Papademos, a considerable economist, is also very important, along with some other governors, including Draghi of Italy and Orphanides of Cyprus, a former Fed economist.

In his political history of the euro,[41] David Marsh concludes that there has already been a significant change of regime at the ECB, with the transition from Duisenberg to Trichet:

> Trichet brought far greater decisiveness to the Council than Duisenberg, who confined himself largely to summing up and presenting the conclusions afterwards. Trichet steers meetings with a rigour lacking

under his predecessor. During Duisenberg's stewardship of the Council, Trichet coined the phrase, "We are a team, the chairman is the coach"—a slogan that, under his firm leadership, fell into disuse.

So the practical difference between the Fed and the ECB may not be as great as Blinder suggests, especially now that Bernanke is the chairman. It may therefore be that Greenspan's era marked the high watermark of autocratic decision making.[29]

What conclusions might we reach from this discussion?

An easy conclusion might be, to adopt a cliché beloved of central bankers defending their idiosyncrasies, that one size does not fit all. But there do seem to be persuasive arguments to suggest that a committee structure is likely to produce better decisions than an individual, as long as the committee is not effectively dominated by one person. The answer to the latter problem may lie partly in term limits. It is odd that in the United States the Constitution forbids a president from holding office for more than two terms, while a Fed chairman may go on and on. A maximum of two terms of seven years would seem to be a sensible precaution against the overdominant individual. There would also be merit, in all three cases studied here, in measures to open up the appointment process to external scrutiny.

The question of voting is more complex. We can see arguments for both a consensual model and for a formal, publicized, voting model as in the MPC. The former may well be more suitable at present for a monetary union, where the political environment is such that voting members could find themselves almost mandated by national governments to vote in a particular sense at times of economic stress. This conclusion reflects the anomalous position of national central bank governors that we have described. Over time it may be possible for the ECB to evolve toward a more transparent structure, but the first step should be to publish minutes that expose the arguments presented on all sides without identification of individual advocates. That would build confidence in the process by showing that counterarguments had been considered and would assist further in influencing expectations.

The ECB statutes do in fact provide for decision making by voting if need be. So far decisions have been made by unanimity or broad consensus defined by the president. Nout Wellink of De Nederlandsche Bank is one who thinks this may change in the future. As he told Marsh,

> The reason why there have been no votes up to now has been partly to create a feeling of consensus and collegiality during the early years. There is now less reason to be sensitive on that issue.

The current Fed procedures have less to be said in their favor. The terminology and disclosure of dissents is not helpful, especially when we know that the number does not fully reflect the balance of opinion. In those circumstances, transparency, which is normally to be preferred for the reasons we have set out, can have perverse effects. The Fed would be wise to move toward a model less heavily focused on the chairman.

Finally, the procedures in place in all three institutions are not obviously well-suited to handling the complex interactions involved in quantitative easing, or indeed the kind of interdependencies that are emerging between interest rate decisions and decisions on macroprudential supervision. In the United Kingdom, a new Financial Stability Committee has been put in place to deal with the latter, but this risks reinforcing the distance between monetary and regulatory policies that contributed to the crisis. In each case, a better mechanism for linking the two types of policy decision is required. We return to this question in chapter 12.

Europe: A Special Case

The creation of a monetary union between eleven of the member states of the EU in 1998 was perhaps the most ambitious central banking project ever contemplated. Although countries have shared a common currency before, for instance through the medium of a currency board (as in the East Caribbean and West Africa), the interlinking of central banks on this scale is without precedent, particularly given the complexity of the activities brought together and the different characters of the national central banks, many of them steeped in idiosyncratic historical tradition. By 2009, sixteen countries had joined the euro area (the most recent, Slovakia, entered on January 1, 2009) and six more are at various states of readiness for membership (though there is a severe risk that the crisis will make it very difficult for them to meet the Maastricht criteria). Of the EU member states only the United Kingdom, Denmark, and Sweden had not made a political commitment to join. The market turmoil began to shift opinion in Sweden and Denmark in 2008, however, as the risks of remaining outside the zone became apparent. Iceland, not a member of the EU, began to talk actively of membership. The United Kingdom, by contrast, remained aloof. Sterling's steep decline against the euro over the winter of 2008-9 was widely seen in London as a helpful offset to recession rather than as a sign of vulnerability.

BUILDING THE MONETARY UNION

The construction of the European Central Bank and the Eurosystem is a fascinating case study that exposes many of the issues about the nature of central banking today in a stark form.

The decisions taken at the outset about the nature of the currency union, and the institutional arrangements that would underpin it, about which responsibilities should be merged and which should not, about what should be identical across jurisdictions and what should not, and about how much power should be concentrated at the center and what should remain in the national central banks all posed fundamental questions about the nature of central banking. National arrangements differed, each based on historical experience and evolution, the diverse nature of local banking systems and financial markets, the precise relationship between finance and government and indeed the wider political environment, and differing relative priorities based on the preservation of sound money or on ensuring that the provision of finance met wider social objectives.

The political background is important because the creation of the euro had strong political as well as economic motives. The economic motive was straightforward. Elimination of foreign exchange risk for intra-area transactions, it was argued, should boost trade, competitiveness, and growth. But for some of those driving the project—certainly for President Mitterrand and Chancellor Kohl—it was as important that a single currency would force greater political collaboration between states and be the motive power of a stronger federation. Mitterrand also saw the single currency as a means of reducing each state's vulnerability to movements in the capital markets. Why, he asked, should the state[1]

> be at the mercy of volatile capital which does not represent any real wealth, or creation of real goods? It is an intolerable immorality.

The fact that currency union was a marriage that did not provide for the option of divorce was seen as a concrete way of minimizing, and perhaps eliminating, the risk of armed, or commercial, conflict between European nations. States would need to collaborate because the breakup of the currency would be almost impossible to contemplate. A state could clearly defect from the euro area if the overwhelming political will to do so was present, but the economic and financial costs would be immense, particularly for a country leaving as a result of perceived weakness.

The political motive was so powerful that it may have blinded some of the founding fathers to what the commitment to a single currency involved in practice. Some of the principal architects certainly did not understand, for instance, that interest rates would be more or less uniform. They imagined that, though exchange risk would be eliminated, national interest rate structures would carry on much as before, with different financial conditions according to the state of the national economy. As Karl-Otto Pöhl, the former Bundesbank president, has said, at the time of the Delors report, which defined the architecture of monetary union, the French "were more keen on a system where currencies would remain separate but where the parities would be underpinned by large-scale central bank intervention."[1]

The implicit model for the new ECB was the Bundesbank, which had the anti-inflation credibility needed for the new institution. The decision to site it in Frankfurt was made in order to emphasize the strength of that connection. But the differences in national central bank functions meant that no single model of central banking could easily be adopted. The need to write a description of the ECB into the treaty creating these wholly original arrangements required an unusual degree of clarity about what the functions of the central institution would be. Most central banks have evolved over time: the ECB had to be brought into being fully fledged with a constitution set out clearly in treaty language. At the core was the issue of currency, including the production of notes and coins on the one hand and their backing by the monetary authority on the other. Then there was the conduct of monetary policy: the mandate given to the ECB related solely to inflation, though the Bank is enjoined, without prejudice to the objective of price stability, "to support the general economic policies of the Community"—policies that include a high level of employment.[2] The Bank was established with a very high degree of insulation from political interference. It has both target and instrument independence.

Lastly, an exclusive role was given to the ECB in relation to the oversight of payment systems—a customary central bank role even if it is not always legally specified. That role has been gradually extended over time to the direct provision of payment systems, first through Target 1 and then using the much more centralized Target 2 arrangements, which are now in turn being extended to include a settlement system known as T2S (Target 2 Securities). All of these services are provided in some jurisdictions by the private sector, sometimes in competition.

These responsibilities were broadly agreed. In particular, the strong-form independence of the ECB was seen as essential if the new currency was to achieve market confidence. Countries in the deutsche mark zone wanted to maintain the credibility of the Bundesbank, which had given them price stability for many years. Countries that had not benefited from that stability were keen to create it.

The ECB's responsibilities as defined in the treaty do not, however, include any kind of banking supervision role or even any explicit responsibility for financial stability. In the negotiations leading up to the creation of the ECB this was hard-fought territory between very different schools of thought. There were those who thought that banking supervision was an integral part of central banking and so should move to the new body; those who thought that it was indeed a customary role of many central banks but that, because the supervision of banks, and ultimately their support, was a matter of such national interest, it could not be assigned away to a supranational body; and those few who felt that formal responsibility for supervision should be independent of monetary policy as a matter of principle. At that time the Bundesbank, which had the greatest influence on the new architecture, was in the last camp (though it was always engaged in the practicalities of supervision): its views have since changed markedly.

The outcome was that supervision was not included within the ECB's objectives, but Article 105 (5) of the Maastricht Treaty assigns to the Eurosystem as a whole the task of "contributing to the smooth conduct of policies pursued by the competent authorities relating to the prudential supervision of credit institutions and the stability of the financial system." The treaty also gives the ECB a formal role, both consultative and advisory, in the rule-making process. It must be consulted on any new Community legislation relating to financial regulation. Lastly, provision was made for a simplified procedure through which "specific tasks concerning policies relating to the prudential supervision of credit institutions and other financial institutions with the exception of insurance undertakings" could be entrusted to the ECB, without amending the treaty, if the member states unanimously agreed that this should happen.

It was never wholly clear what this somewhat opaque language was intended to mean in practice, nor how this would fit in with the law- and policymaking functions of the European Commission, the Council of Ministers, and the European Parliament. It was the outcome of prolonged negotiations between people with quite different intentions. The lack of clarity about just who has responsibility for financial stability has contributed to a good deal of sterile debate in the last decade. Tommaso Padoa-Schioppa, a founding Executive Board member of the ECB and subsequently Italian finance minister in the Prodi government, interprets it as "a last resort clause which might become necessary if the interaction between the Eurosystem and national supervisory authorities turned out not to work effectively."[3] He is probably right. Unanimous agreement to hand new powers to the ECB is only likely to emerge in crisis conditions, if the system is perceived to have failed. So far that has not (quite) happened, though there are influential voices in the largest euro area banks that maintain that the system has shown that it is not equipped to cope with the failure of a large institution, and that furthermore it imposes high regulatory costs on pan-European firms obliged to respond to a plethora of different regulatory agencies. These arguments were heard more loudly in 2008, when a number of European banks failed or had to be rescued by their governments and the ECB began to consider mounting a case for the activation of its contingent power. The consequence was indeed a new framework for financial stability oversight, which we discuss below.

THE INSTITUTIONAL ARCHITECTURE

The overall structure of the arrangements for managing the euro has two parts: a unitary European institution, the ECB itself, and the national central banks (NCBs), who collectively comprise the European System of Central Banks (ESCB), which includes all EU member states, and the Eurosystem, which consists of the EU countries that have adopted the euro.

The ECB itself has an Executive Board consisting of a president, a vice president, and four other members appointed for nonrenewable terms of eight years. (The initial appointments were of different lengths to allow staggered appointments in future.) The Executive Board run the ECB on a day-to-day basis, manage its central staff in Frankfurt, and—despite coming from different economic schools and having varying political persuasions and different personal skills and temperaments—have the capacity to form a cohesive center. They are bound together by their close physical proximity at the summit of the Eurotower (a new headquarters is under construction), by frequent face-to-face meetings, and by a sense of European mission in the face of the diversity of approach and opinion to be found among the national governors.

They each have executive roles but, rather like European commissioners, they are not necessarily appointed primarily to fulfill a specified function and fitting people to jobs is therefore a challenge for the president.

By contrast, the governors of the national central banks are appointed according to national arrangements. They are usually appointed by government but are also subject to independence criteria that mean that, once appointed, they remain accountable to their national parliaments or governments as the case may be, but in theory must not be subject to inappropriate national pressure, at least in relation to their ECB roles.

They invariably have some concurrent national responsibilities: sometimes very important and burdensome ones, such as for banking supervision. This means that they have split responsibilities. Some of their roles carry weighty accountability and indeed legal responsibility toward their national parliament and legal system, while for monetary policy their responsibilities are exercised purely at the European level. Each of the potential models of regulatory organization can be found in the EU and this has been a complicating factor when attempts have been made to achieve more effective pan-European coordination.

It could be argued that the NCBs are now not in fact central banks at all, as the core central banking functions in monetary policy are vested at the European level in the ECB or in the person of the individual NCB governor when acting as a member of the Governing Council. The ECB sets interest rates and provides euro liquidity. Where the NCB is not the banking supervisor, and is in a jurisdiction with small money and capital markets, it is, arguably, little more than an economic observatory. The prime role of the staff is to brief their governor on conditions in the euro area in preparation for meetings of the Governing Council or the new European Systemic Risk Board. It would certainly be possible for NCBs to move more explicitly in that direction were they so to choose. None has done so to date, and they present themselves in public as "full-service" central banks, rather than operating arms of the ECB.

Monetary Policy

The challenge the ECB faces in the monetary policy field is unparalleled. Indeed, many thought before its creation that it would prove impossible to set an interest rate appropriate for such a diverse currency union, and that any attempt to do so would create such strains that the union would quickly implode. As Henrik Enderlein puts it, the central problem is that the ECB provides a monetary policy for a country that does not exist.[4] That is why there were so many decades between the earliest discussion of a European single currency and its implementation. The first serious consideration of the construction of a European monetary union came from the Werner Committee, which reported in 1970. The Committee proposed a central bank structure on the lines of the U.S. Federal Reserve but also placed great emphasis, under German influence, on the need for a high degree of budgetary convergence before a single currency was attempted.[5] Werner saw serious risks in a single currency area if adequate fiscal stabilizers were not available to respond to asymmetric shocks. While the European Council broadly accepted the report, the outcome was in fact a series of attempts to promote currency alignments, rather than a single currency. Enthusiasts saw these attempts as

187

steady and deliberate steps toward EMU; others saw them as possible endpoints.

Outside Europe the project baffled many observers, especially in North America (and the balance of opinion in London remained skeptical throughout). In 2006 Alan Greenspan, recalling the buildup to EMU, said: "I didn't think it was going to happen. I am surprised that it worked, and didn't think it would last."[6] (In view of the post-crisis reassessment of Greenspan's reputation, perhaps the architects of monetary union should have been encouraged to know he was a skeptic.) Martin Feldstein of Harvard saw such a serious risk that monetary policy would be set in a manner inappropriate for important economies that he warned that EMU could lead to war in Europe. In a private discussion a Canadian finance minister once observed to the then governor of the Bank of England that he found the plan incomprehensible. Canada found itself with a single currency, but the economy was so diverse across its regions that the stance of monetary policy was wrong for most of the country for most of the time. As often as not, if there was a boom in Ontario there would be depressed conditions in British Columbia or the Maritime Provinces, or vice versa. As a result the Bank of Canada usually had no choice but to strike a balance that left the monetary stance too easy for some regions and too tight for others. But at least there was some compensation through the federal budget and reasonable labor mobility. In the EU even these mitigating factors were far more muted. Much of this analysis was shared by many central bankers in Europe, notably in the Bundesbank. The MacDougall report,[7] which examined what might be needed in terms of fiscal stabilizers, argued in 1977 that a much larger central EU budget would be needed in a single-currency zone. Indeed MacDougall argued for a budget of up to 25% of EU GDP to be controlled centrally, compared with just over 1.2% at present.

There was no political enthusiasm for anything approaching that degree of budgetary centralization. The size of the Commission's budget has barely been increased in relation to EU GDP in the intervening thirty years. Nonetheless, in the late 1980s a second and more determined attempt to design a monetary union was attempted. The Delors Commission can be seen in retrospect as the high point of European federalism. Delors himself chaired a committee—which included Jacques de Larosière, Karl-Otto Pöhl, and the then governor of the Bank of England, Robin Leigh-Pemberton—to explore what practical steps were needed to implement the vision set out by Werner. The Delors report[8] of 1989 described a three-stage approach that would lead to a single currency at the end of the century. In spite of turmoil in the foreign exchange markets in the early 1990s the plan was completed more or less to time. That owed much to the leadership and diplomacy of Alexandre Lamfalussy, the first head of the European Monetary Institute, the precursor of the ECB, who had also been a member of the Committee. The emphasis was, however, on the monetary rather than the economic dimension of EMU (a distinction drawn originally by Werner). In other words, the institutional arrangements needed to manage a single currency were put in place without the fiscal convergence and coordination that the Germans had earlier argued were essential prior conditions. And the decisions on first-round membership, when Italy and Greece were admitted on short-term evidence of convergence, were clearly political in nature. It was considered impossible to construct a monetary union without Belgium, whose debt to GDP ratio was as high as Italy's, which effectively meant that the Italians had to be included, even though the Germans and others harbored serious doubts about their readiness—doubts that have been reinforced by more recent developments.

For that reason, and because of the inherent difficulty of the project, there were many voices, especially in London, prophesying doom. John Major, as prime minister, famously described Delors's calls for early implementation of EMU as having "all the quaintness of a rain-dance and about the same potency."[9] The Bank of England too remained institutionally skeptical. The two governors who followed Leigh-Pemberton, Eddie George and Mervyn King, were both hostile to British membership of the monetary union. Nonetheless, its officials, following in a long tradition of close Bank of England involvement in EU affairs, remained closely engaged in the technical construction of the project and subsequently produced a series of detailed reports[10] on practical issues related to the introduction of the euro that proved of considerable value to the central banks that did join the Eurosystem.

But despite skepticism in the United Kingdom, and on the other side of the Atlantic, and despite the lack of sustained economic convergence among the first wave of members, the arrangements articulated in the Maastricht Treaty have served for ten years without the kind of internal crisis that many had predicted. Technically, the euro has been an astounding success, with none of the teething problems forecast. Inflation averaged 2.1% a year in the first decade: above the ECB ceiling, but only trivially so. While there were concerns about euro weakness in the first two years of its existence, it subsequently strengthened considerably against other major currencies. The euro has gained broad international acceptance and begun to assume a greater significance in the investment portfolios of other central banks and sovereign wealth funds. Estimates suggest that the euro accounted for 18% of official foreign currency reserves in 1999 but over 26% in 2007.[11] Part of this rise can be explained by valuation effects, but Jean-Claude Trichet, in particular, has established the global credibility and status of the ECB presidency. The ECB's prompt reactions to the liquidity crisis in the summer of 2007 won admirers in European financial markets, notably in London—though not a sufficient level of admiration to overcome the London market's continued antipathy to the adoption of the single currency in the United Kingdom.

In retrospect it can be seen that the euro's first decade was a propitious one for the launch of an untried experiment. Economic conditions were mainly benign and inflationary pressures relatively subdued. It remains to be seen whether the euro area will remain as comfortable, and the ECB's policies as well accepted, with the ending of the period of unprecedented economic calm and ready liquidity that has coincided with the euro's first ten years. There are ominous signs that with the onset of recession politicians are more ready to criticize the ECB, and even the structure of the Eurosystem itself. President Sarkozy of France has proposed enhanced arrangements for economic governance in the euro area designed to force the ECB to listen directly to representatives from governments. Chancellor Merkel of Germany was outspoken in her criticism of the ECB, and other central banks, in the summer of 2009, breaking with a longstanding political tradition in Germany.

It is still arguable that, while the euro has worked well in practice, it does not work in theory. The euro area does not score well in relation to the standard economic criteria for optimum currency areas and there are increasing signs that some of the tensions that concerned earlier critics have merely been dormant rather than having been resolved. Little progress has been made on the coordination of fiscal policy. Expansion of the zone will make these problems worse. It will put the existing policies and practices under stress. We consider below how the ECB, and the other bodies, may need to adapt.

The monetary policy task has been delicate and complex. In the first place, the euro area is extremely diverse economically, with regional centers and markets that develop independently, whether in terms of activity, of inflation in terms of goods and services, or of inflation in property values, all of which vary over time. The ECB needs to make a judgment about where matters stand on average and how they are likely to evolve on average. Of course, this is normal for a central bank in a large diverse economy, though it is aggravated by obstacles, practical and otherwise, to the free movement of capital and labor, which do not exist in other geographically large monetary zones. It is inevitable that at any one time interest rates will be too high for some member states and too low for others. The ECB is therefore bound to face criticism. The high degree of independence it has is both an advantage and a disadvantage in these circumstances. It is advantageous in that politicians may not impose their will on the ECB, or easily dislodge its management. It is disadvantageous in that, since the ECB sets its own objective, politicians feel disempowered and react accordingly.

In France, especially, politicians of the left and right have been free with their criticisms. Sarkozy criticized the July 2008 decision to raise rates from 4% to 4.25% as "at best pointless, at worst totally counterproductive." (In retrospect, he had a point.) More seriously, his advisers were said to believe that granting independence to the ECB had been a "historic error," and that a new economic government in Europe was absolutely necessary as a counterweight.[1] Laurent Fabius, a former Socialist prime minister, called for a "more pragmatic and less dogmatic 'monetary policy'." He went on to say:

> I have seen these remarkable people at the European Central Bank. That left a negative impression, because I saw in their views, perhaps to strengthen their power, that they were concerned only with inflation. Growth and employment didn't really concern them.

Jacques Delors reinforced the point: "The ECB president puts too much emphasis on inflation rather than on the total parameters affecting the economy."

It is tempting to think that some of these critics did not quite understand the nature of the animal they created in the Maastricht Treaty, which precisely requires the bank to focus narrowly on price stability. German politicians, with their Bundesbank history, understand the situation more clearly, and have shown great impatience with the French. Finance Minister Peer Steinbruck pointed out:

> There is no possibility that France can succeed in reducing the ECB's independence...these criticisms by Nicolas Sarkozy have no effect. I do not know why he rattles the cage like this—it is completely idiotic.

So politicians are powerless to move, and it is not open to the ECB to hand back its target independence to the Council of Ministers, which could not be done without revision of the treaty. But it could revise the specification. An asymmetric target, with only an upper bound for inflation, is open to misinterpretation and does not give the Bank enough flexibility to adapt to external shocks without appearing to have failed in its objective. As de Grauwe argues, while the ECB has demonstrated some flexibility, there is, as a result, "too large a discrepancy between the announced policy strategy and the policy actions of the ECB and this discrepancy damages its credibility."[12] He and other academic economists argue that it should explicitly adopt a symmetrical target. He also argues that the ECB would be wise to downgrade the monetary pillar of its price stability objective. Since 1999 the growth rate of euro area M3 has been above the indicated range most of the time. This overshoot may yet prove to have been at least part of the reason for the regional asset price bubbles in Spain and elsewhere.

It would also be possible, without treaty change, for the president of the ECB to mimic the accountability arrangements of the Bank of England, to offset the accusation that it is judge and jury in its own cause. Thomas Mayer of Deutsche Bank[13] has suggested that Trichet could write to the head of the Eurogroup (the finance ministers of the euro area countries) when inflation moves outside the target range, explaining how soon and at what cost inflation can be brought down again.

Adaptations of this kind would be helpful to the ECB. In spite of its success, there is no guarantee that the next decade of its existence will be easier than the first—indeed the reverse is likely to be true. It is striking that in the first decade of the euro the economic performance of different countries has diverged.

Average inflation rates have varied a lot. That may not in itself be wholly surprising as some countries, notably Ireland, Spain, and other newer entrants to the EU, have been engaged in a catch-up process. But the most remarkable development has been the changes in real exchange rates and competitiveness across the Union (figure 7.1). Germany, which arguably joined at an overvalued exchange rate, has improved its relative unit labor costs year on year. Italy and Portugal have done the reverse, failing to control domestic costs or to enhance productivity. These trends, if they continue unchecked, are likely to impose strains on the euro. There have already been political calls in Italy for withdrawal, though the practical consequences of doing so would be dramatic and the immediate costs certainly very high. One consequence is that current account imbalances within the euro area have grown. Some argue that this is a positive sign and that capital is therefore flowing to the cheaper

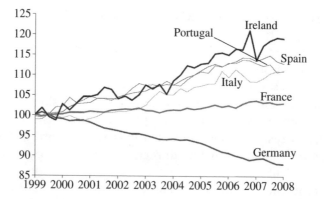

Figure 7.1. Real exchange rate relative to the euro area.
Source: Oxford Economics/Haver Analytics.

countries. But there is so far little sign that this inflow of capital is generating new and competitive investment, certainly in the larger countries, such as Italy and Spain.

Budget deficits, too, have varied greatly. Spending disciplines on individual member states are weaker than they were before EMU, as the spreads on their debt are still narrower than they were, though they widened during the crisis and credit default swap prices rose very sharply. That is partly because the ECB accepts similarly rated public-sector debt from all member states on the same basis.

The economic consequences of the financial crisis put increasing stress on a number of the constituent economies. The severe loss of competitiveness by Italy, Portugal, and Greece cannot be mitigated by exchange rate depreciation, while the collapse of credit bubbles in Spain and Ireland cannot be mitigated by rapid cuts in interest rates.

This led to mounting tension over monetary policy, even though the ECB loosened monetary conditions by increasing its balance sheet by over 50% in a year. Rising spreads on government paper in smaller and less competitive EU countries were only attributable to concerns about credit risk. The debate on possible withdrawal resurfaced.

Although currencies have been split in the past, this has been under very constrained circumstances with few cross-border assets or liabilities and where it was relatively politically uncontroversial to identify which assets and liabilities were to be assigned to the new currency. This is most unlikely to be the case in relation to the euro. The task of identifying which euro assets or liabilities should in future be, say, in new lire or new drachmae would be both technically and politically fraught, particularly in circumstances where the purpose of the exercise was to allow the separating currency to depreciate. Even if achieved, it would almost certainly lead to defaults that would compound the difficulties. It is only conceivable that separation could take place when there was already serious social and political breakdown.

This leaves, then, the burden of adapting to major slowdown to other tools. These are essentially major supply-side reforms in countries that have hitherto resisted them and/or a massive increase in the central EU budget to facilitate transfers to regions in depression, which will be politically difficult.

These problems cannot all be laid at the door of the ECB, but they greatly complicate the monetary policy task. The ECB is faced with the additional challenge that it is limited in the way in which it can interact with other policymakers. In particular, it has no national fiscal counterpart that can play a role in handling regional differences that monetary policy cannot hope to address. This challenge was recognized from the outset.

FISCAL POLICY IN THE MONETARY UNION

The laudable intention was to try to articulate an integrated fiscal policy that would be the standard counterpart of monetary policy. From the central bank's perspective, profligate fiscal policies make it more difficult to conduct a stability-oriented monetary policy.[14] At a national level, high deficits and public debt reduce the scope for governments to use fiscal policy to stabilize domestic demand: markets may be concerned about the sustainability of public finances and excess government borrowing can also contribute to inflationary pressures. In EMU the elimination of exchange rate movements has weakened the mechanisms through which financial markets exert discipline on national fiscal policies. Furthermore, the spillover effects of borrowing in one country on other countries in the euro area are likely to be greater. The costs of "excess" borrowing may be at least partly spread across the entire currency area.

In the preparation phase of EMU these arguments were sufficiently convincing for a fiscal rule to be enshrined in the Maastricht Treaty. Article 101 prohibits monetary financing of deficits by the ESCB, while Article 103 states that neither the European institutions nor member states shall be liable for another member state's financial obligations. Article 104 obliges member states to avoid "excessive deficits" assessed against the reference values of 3% of GDP for the deficit and 60% of GDP for debt. Breaches of the reference values trigger an Excessive Deficit Procedure, which can ultimately lead to financial sanctions.

To bring some structure, and indeed reality, to these requirements, not least in the face of cyclical developments, it became necessary to devise a fiscal agreement, known as the Stability and Growth Pact, that incorporated a process both to analyze fiscal positions and to deter and correct excessive deficits. The SGP made economic sense but, unfortunately, brute politics intervened. The SGP was conceived by the Germans largely as an attempt to constrain the feared profligacy of the Italians. When the SGP also began to constrain Germany itself, and France, its provisions were watered down. In its own review of the first decade of the euro, which produced a positive, even at times gushing, verdict on the new currency, the European Commission nonetheless accepted that the Eurogroup had not yet proved capable of taking real leadership on budgetary issues. In particular, "commitments to consolidate budgetary positions during the good times have not always been reflected in budgetary decisions."[11] The report argues for a strengthening of the Eurogroup as a political and fiscal counterweight to the ECB. Enlargement of the euro area makes this more important than ever.

However logical, these calls run up squarely against the reluctance across Europe, after a series of failed referendums on changes to the Treaty, to envisage any new transfers of power to central institutions. It is arguable that EMU itself was agreed at a time of unusual enthusiasm for the "European ideal," and that many of the consequential changes to policy and practice needed to underpin it are now not politically practical.

The article in the treaty banning the ECB from the monetary financing of fiscal deficits is not a standard provision for a central bank, and it has featured in the debate about the merits of quantitative easing through the purchase of government debt. It was seen as being of particular importance to a federal central bank, not just because it would assist the new ECB in establishing its credentials but also against the background of fiscal diversity. However, these arrangements mean that there is a natural tension between the ECB and euro area finance ministries, singly and collectively, of a character that does not arise elsewhere but that impinges both on the substance of its policymaking and on its accountability, to which we return below. So far it is difficult to maintain that the Byzantine, and largely ineffective, process for debating fiscal plans at EU level has put disproportionate pressure on monetary policy, but strains emerged as the recession of 2008 unfolded. Some countries found their debt downgraded by credit rating agencies, in spite of their membership of the monetary union, which created pressure for spending discipline—Ireland being an obvious example.

In formulating monetary policy the ECB must take an approach based on inflationary conditions in the euro area as a whole, despite its heterogeneity. It is therefore crucial that the members of the Governing Council take decisions not as representatives of their own country but as members of a collective team responsible for the whole area. Duisenberg asserted that "the members of the Governing Council consider the interests of the euro area as a whole; they do not represent their individual countries."[15]

In this there is some similarity with the FOMC arrangements in the United States, where a regional Reserve Bank president will bring to the table both regional expertise and nationwide perspective. However, the position of a national central bank governor in the euro area is rather different because of their position within their own country: they are usually appointed by a national government and have accountability to a national parliament. (The Federal Reserve Districts are deliberately not coterminous with any political authority.) The natural pressures on them to vote for the monetary stance that best suits their own country can be intense when it is an outlier from the euro area average. In order to address this, the independence of each governor is critical, with consequences for the transparency of decision making. The ECB has so far taken the view that if the votes of individual governors were disclosed, they would come under pressure to vote in accordance with the economic conditions in their home country. We discuss the merits of that argument below.

The individual members of the Governing Council have certainly equipped themselves to take their euro area responsibilities seriously. They have increased resources at the national level to brief themselves on conditions elsewhere in the euro area, sometimes in addition to local analysis, sometimes partially to replace it. This has had the result that analytical resources overall have increased significantly even though there are fewer decisions to make. This in turn raises an interesting question about how much analysis is enough to make an adequate decision in relation to a relatively simple choice: whether to change interest rates or not and, if so, by how much. We might also ask what sense it makes for all the central banks to be expending resources analyzing each others' economies. Weak budget constraints have allowed National

Central Banks to increase expenditures in this area without transparent justification.

But the more fundamental questions are whether the ECB structure sets an appropriate balance between the center and the regions and whether it provides a framework for efficient and effective decision making. The two points are linked but may be analyzed separately.

While the ECB structure, as we have explained, owed a lot to the Bundesbank and the Federal Reserve, in fact it differs from both in terms of the balance of power within a federal system. The ratio of regional votes to central votes is much larger. With fifteen national members, the ratio of regional votes to central votes is 2.5:1, compared with 0.71:1 at the Fed (seven governors and five regional Fed presidents) and 1.1:1 in the pre-1999 Bundesbank.[16]

It is also notable that in the case of the ECB the principle of one man (usually) one vote was enshrined in the Maastricht Treaty. So among the founding members Luxembourg had the same weight in decision making as Germany. The post-Nice arrangements for rotation make a small impact on this misalignment, as smaller countries will rotate off the voting roster more often, but the impact is modest. Helge Berger[17] has calculated a "misrepresentation index" based on the sum of the squared difference between regional vote shares in the Governing Council and relative economic size. He has compared the ECB on that index with the Fed and the pre-1999 Bundesbank. In 2001 the index reached a value seven times higher than for the FOMC or the Bundesbank Council. Even after the 2003 reform the index will stay very much higher indefinitely (the precise number will depend on the order of new countries entering: entry of all the Baltic states before Poland joins would push it up even higher).

Does this matter if, as Duisenberg claimed, all the national governors take a euro area perspective? Yes, because there is evidence that they may not be as nationality blind as he asserted. Meade and Sheets[18] have analyzed the voting records of governors and Reserve Bank presidents in the Federal Reserve System. They find that regional conditions do influence voting behavior. For example, FOMC voters dissenting from the majority view, in favor of lower rates, were from districts with unemployment rates higher (or lower for votes in favor of higher rates) than the national average. Similar results were found in the Bundesbank.[19] Given the lack of individual voting records in the ECB they cannot duplicate that analysis for Europe as a whole, but they do find that interest rate decisions have almost invariably reflected the majority votes that would

197

have been cast based on a similar assessment of national versus Europe-wide unemployment rates. So there is a risk, if the system remains as it is, that a policy that does not reflect the needs of the greater part of the euro area could be imposed based on the votes of governors representing a small share of euro area GDP.

Both the Bundesbank and the Fed worked over time to reduce the mis-representation index. The Fed's introduction of an asymmetrical rotation scheme in the 1930s had that effect, as did the redrawing of Bundesbank districts in the 1950s and again after German reunification. Indeed the 2003 change in Europe, modest though it was, can be seen as a contradiction to the view that all governors act in the interests of the totality. If Duisenberg were right, there would have been no need for reform. The reform still leaves the ECB's decision making badly unbalanced. (Note, however, that when the Governing Council votes on financial issues relating to the ECB itself, only the NCB governors vote, with their voting power weighted according to the share each holds in the capital of the Bank.)

The Governing Council is also very large by international standards. With a euro area membership of twenty-four, there would be twenty-one voting members and thirty people entitled to speak, compared with twelve and nineteen, respectively, in the Federal Reserve and only nine in the Bank of England MPC. It is hard to argue that there is a precise number above which clear decision making becomes very difficult, but this looks to be at the top end of what is feasible.

All these factors mean that decision making for the ECB differs from that in other central banks and is presented differently. As we have explained, the analysis at each policymaking meeting is put forward by a member of the Bank's Executive Board and is then debated. The board member is without national affiliation and represents a view for the euro area as a whole. It is clear that the proposition put forward is one that has the support of the Executive Board as a whole and will also have been discussed with key NCB governors. Though there is no public information on the point, insiders say that there have been no instances so far of the original recommendation being overturned as a result of discussion in the Governing Council. This point is hard to verify as the debate leaves behind no public record in the form of minutes. The convention that the position of individual Governing Council members goes unreported remains strictly respected, even privately, and no voting is recorded or disclosed. The dynamics within the council have been the subject of both political and academic discussion.[20] Although national positions remain secret, to reduce pressure on individual governors, even the cloak of anonymity may not prevent them from advancing a national case.

While this process lacks the integrity and equity of the MPC process in London, it may be a realistic way of offsetting, in practice, the misrepresentation effects we have described. Though the center is weak in terms of voting power, the Executive Board has retained the right of proposition, which is crucial. And it seeks to ensure, through informal means, that its proposals stand a strong chance of acceptance.

THE ECB AS A BANK

The ECB is not just a monetary authority: it is also, of course, a bank and banker to the banks. It conducts the market operations through which monetary policy decisions are implemented and supplies liquidity to the banking system with a wide range of counterparties through the medium of the national central banks. Banks operating in the euro area, whatever their national origin, may be counterparties of the Eurosystem. The process of constructing these arrangements, effectively overnight, when the euro was launched produced a smoothly functioning money market virtually instantly, but it was achieved mostly by virtue of compromises that meant that the standards for acceptance of collateral were set so as to accommodate virtually all the kinds of instrument accepted as eligible by any one of the preexisting central banks. As Buiter has pointed out, "the set of eligible collateral for open market operations and at the discount window and the set of eligible counterparties were defined as the union rather than the intersection of the previous national sets."[21] Agreement could not be reached on a more limited set because each NCB, which remains responsible for implementing these operations, was anxious to maintain support arrangements suited to their "own" banks. So the variety of instruments accepted as collateral was much more diverse, and probably of greater risk, than is the case with the Federal Reserve or the Bank of England, at least before the crisis. This has led from time to time to suggestions of insufficient discipline on the part of the ECB both from within the system and from outside it. It had the happy consequence, however, that, when the liquidity crisis of the second half of 2007 struck, the ECB found itself better endowed with vehicles to provide liquidity readily across the system. It did not need to make structural changes to cope with the greater market volatility as the Fed and the Bank of England did.[22] There were suggestions that, faced with continuing liquidity pressures, some banks exploited this flexibility inappropriately, perhaps even with the encouragement of their local central bank or supervisor, by deliberately issuing securities targeted at securing ECB funding. Partly as a result, the ECB has since cut back on the range of instruments it will accept.

By contrast, the ECB is different from other central banks in that it has a generally clearer approach than others in seeking to make a distinction between solvency and liquidity support. Liquidity support may in due course lead to losses, but the ECB seeks to distinguish between liquidity, which is controlled at the center, and solvency, or suspected solvency, support, which must be provided at the level of the NCB, backed by its own finance ministry. There is, understandably, no provision for loss sharing between countries when support is given to an individual bank— so any support that may lead to loss has to be given at the risk of the local central bank. The local central banks may in turn need to lay off the risk with the local fiscal authorities. In this respect the arrangement at the ECB level is different from that at other central banks who, while still wanting to avoid risk, will at least understand that they may have to bear any loss in full.

Do these special arrangements required to distribute responsibilities in the euro area mean that there is unusual uncertainty about the LOLR arrangements? Not necessarily. It is rather that the division of functions between monetary policy operations and the provision of liquidity, and individual bank solvency support, is laid bare. Generally, this transparency is helpful. There is much confusion in public debate about the resources of the central bank. While the credibility, and credit, of a central bank is usually accepted without question, at least in major economies, its finances depend ultimately on the finance ministry and its taxing powers. This became painfully apparent in the Icelandic crisis of 2008. That episode pointed to the concern, which does not arise logically from the single currency but is frequently voiced in this context, that there are large pan-European banks headquartered in small jurisdictions whose central bank and finance ministry might be unable or unwilling to underwrite them, especially if the losses that threaten their viability have arisen elsewhere? This is in principle a problem of the growth of cross-border banking, especially within the single financial market, not of the single currency, but it is posed particularly starkly in circumstances where the ECB is providing liquidity support yet does not have a direct view of the bank's likely solvency. Some argue that because the closure of an international bank would be likely to generate cross-border spillovers, and because some small European countries might be unable to finance the bailout of their very large banks, central-ization of crisis management is needed.[23] In 2008, recalling a meeting of the European Council of Economics and Finance Ministers at which the decision to establish the ECB was being discussed, former Italian finance minister Giuliano Amato described the governors as behaving like ostriches.[24] The governors had warned that in the event of a sys-temic crisis Europe lacked a competent authority but had then required reference to this to be removed from the communiqué because it could create anxiety among markets and investors.

The fact that the ECB does not have supervisory responsibilities under the Maastricht Treaty, while many national central banks do, also requires responsibilities to be clear. Thinking on this within the Eurosys-tem itself has evolved, with views differing according to national back-ground. For those who thought that supervision was an integral part of central banking it seemed natural that the ECB should have some kind of role in supervision, even if it did not itself take over the role of pan-European banking supervisor (though a few supported that idea as well). However, no governments were prepared to surrender supervision of "their" banks to a supranational central bank—still less one that was constructed with a very high degree of independence and with limited accountability. The result is that national arrangements for supervision remain in place and are quite diverse. As we have seen, in some cases the NCB is solely responsible for banking supervision, as in Italy, Spain, and the Netherlands; in others the NCB continues to perform supervisory activities but final authority lies elsewhere in an integrated regulator, as in Austria and Germany; in yet others responsibility lies formally out-side the central bank, but with central bank involvement through dual executive roles or provision of resources, as in France and Belgium, or with no formal role at all, as in Luxembourg or Finland.

These diverse arrangements have been the subject of a continuing debate about the relationship between the supervisory, financial stabil-ity, traditional central banking, and monetary policy functions of central banks. Some of the positions taken are grounded in logical arguments. In other cases it is hard to avoid the conclusion that the primary objective is to retain a function for the NCBs that will secure their futures and contin-ued employment opportunities for their staff. In 2001 the ECB itself took a formal position on the subject,[25] though it is not entirely clear on what basis it claimed the right to intervene in issues of national responsibil-ity. The ECB conclusion at that time was that the arguments against com-bining monetary and supervisory responsibilities—which had concerned the Bundesbank, and some governments, in the past—were not forceful within the euro area, given that the ECB and not the NCBs now holds the monetary policy responsibility. The conclusion they reached was that "when viewed from a Eurosystem perspective, the attribution of extensive supervisory responsibilities (i.e., both macro and micro-prudential) to NCBs is likely to prove beneficial."

In fact, where an NCB has a supervisory role, its governor wears two hats: one as an independent monetary policymaker in the Governing Council with euro area-wide obligations and club loyalty; and another as supervisor fully accountable under national legislation and trustee for the aspirations of the national central bank, its staff, and local stakeholders.

It can readily be seen that the interests of the ECB and its staff, who are primarily charged with monetary policy, and those of the NCBs and their staff, who are primarily charged with supervision, may diverge. Contested territory has included the extent to which those responsible at the European level for monetary policy and market operations need to know about the position of individual banks or national banking systems. Senior ECB staff do not believe they are always fully informed about the position of individual banks, even where they are important counterparties of the Eurosystem. There is a natural tendency for national supervisors to present a rosy (or indeed simply unrealistic) view of the institutions in their care. The ECB's reasonable concern is that it may have extended large facilities to a bank through the discount window on which it could lose money if the bank failed. In those circumstances the losses would be shared by all members of the Eurosystem, based on the GDP key. Profits and losses at the ECB go back to member states in proportion to the percentages of euro area GDP that they generate. Other member states could be expected to react with hostility to losses incurred in that way.

To cope with this problem Goodhart and Schoenmaker[26] recommend the establishment of a new mechanism to intermediate between home and host supervisors and to develop a new approach to fiscal burden-sharing. In principle, bank recapitalization could be organized by the ECB and financed through its own seigniorage revenues. They recognize that there is little enthusiasm for the use of this mechanism. Their recommendation is therefore for an *ex ante* agreement on burden-sharing based on the proportion of a problem bank's business that resides in each country in which it operates. They are right that there is no easy solution to this problem at present, and that resolution of a failed bank after the event would be extremely difficult. Mayes et al.[27] propose an alternative scheme based on a "Prompt Corrective Action" methodology agreed in advance by supervisors across the EU, which in turn would require much greater harmonization of supervision practices and decision making than is the case today. The agreement at the Economic and Financial Affairs Council (ECOFIN) to work toward the introduction of pan-European supervisory colleges for systemically important firms is unlikely to resolve the problem. Each national supervisor is well aware that it will be expected to do everything possible to protect national stakeholders.

A more detailed plan has been developed by the Centre for European Policy Studies.[28] They argue that the crisis has demonstrated that the model adopted so far in the single financial market is fundamentally flawed. If banks are to be allowed to operate on a pan-European basis in future, with a single authorization, there needs to be a pan-European regulatory authority, backed by a federal lender of last resort. Otherwise the single market may break up, as national authorities seek to protect their own depositors. (There were examples of measures of this kind in 2008, notably in Ireland.) They recommend the establishment of a European Financial Institute, on the model of the European Monetary Institute that prepared the ground for the EMU. In due course that would lead to a European System of Financial Supervisors backed by a European Resolution Trust, which might recapitalize insolvent banks.

So far, there is inadequate political support for a federal solution. Ministers instead favor the establishment of Colleges of Supervisors for systemically significant firms, and a multilateral MOU to formalize the exchange of information across borders. But the powers of the Colleges are unclear, and 113 separate authorities have signed the MOU, vividly illustrating the balkanized character of EU financial regulation. This can only be an interim, second-best solution. If a member of a College of Supervisors finds early evidence that a bank in his/her jurisdiction is in trouble, s/he has every incentive to hide such evidence to help ensure that the position of creditors in that jurisdiction is secured. The several collapses, and near-death experiences, at European banks that the ECB has witnessed over the last eighteen months have shown that a new mechanism is required.

The European Commission recognized the problem at the end of 2008 and asked Jacques de Larosière to review the structures of regulation in Europe, with the assistance of a small committee made up almost entirely of central bankers. His report[29] begins with the blunt assertion that "the

European Union's framework today remains seriously fragmented." In wording reminiscent of the Paulson critique of the U.S. arrangements, he pointed to competitive distortions, regulatory arbitrage, the incompatibility between the regulatory system and the way firms themselves manage their risks, and the difficulties involved in handling institutional failures. It amounted to a damning indictment. Remarkably, therefore, both the United States and the EU had found that their regulatory systems were found seriously wanting in a crisis.

The diagnosis, however, was less contentious than the recommended solutions. The report was unusually revealing in that the attempts by EU institutions to lobby in their own interests were laid bare. It explained that the ECB had, as it had also done a few years before, made a bid to play a major role in both macroprudential and microprudential supervision. The ECB argued that it should become responsible for the direct supervision of cross-border banks in the EU, or only in the euro area. Alternatively, the ECB could oversee colleges of national supervisors.

In spite of the predominance of central bankers in the de Larosière group, it rejected this extravagant bid for power on the part of the ECB, arguing that "adding micro-supervisory duties could impinge on its fundamental mandate" and that in the case of a crisis the Bank would then be heavily involved with governments, which "could result in political pressure and interference, thereby jeopardising the ECB's independence." This is a powerful argument. Also, of course, a number of NCBs have no domestic responsibilities for supervision, which would greatly complicate the task. Finally, the specific exclusion of insurance companies from the ECB's remit (in the Maastricht Treaty) would make an integrated approach to prudential supervision impossible.

It is surprising that the ECB—even though opinion in the Governing Council was divided on the point—made such a strong pitch for a role in the supervision of individual institutions. It suggests a lack of appreciation of the political sensitivities of bank regulation and, indeed, a lack of understanding of the implications for the ECB's own accountability of taking the job on. The remarkable degree of independence on monetary policy enshrined in the Treaty is inconceivable in the regulatory world, as de Larosière well understood. Fortunately, the Committee protected the ECB from the potentially disastrous consequences of its own unrealistic ambition.

By contrast, and in our view correctly, de Larosière did see a new and more important role for the ECB in the macroprudential area and recommended the establishment of a new European Systemic Risk Council, to be chaired by the president of the ECB and to include all the central banks of the EU and the chairs of the sectoral regulatory committees. This committee would fulfill in Europe some of the functions of the global Financial Stability Board, as reconstructed after the G20 summits. It would effectively supersede the Banking Supervision Committee, which has always been an uncomfortable, and little used, part of the regulatory architecture. Unfortunately, the composition of the ESRC as proposed by de Larosière was very "central bank heavy." Did it really make sense to think of a pan-European observatory of systemic risk that excluded non-central bank supervisors from the formal decision making? At the time of writing the precise membership and functions of the new committee were still under discussion. These will need careful attention if the committee is to fulfill its mandate effectively and command the respect of the regulatory community.[30]

In parallel, he proposed that the committees of regulators set up following the earlier Lamfalussy report[31] should become "authorities," though without a change in the treaty their authority is in fact rather limited. The aim would be to deliver greater consistency and efficiency of regulation across the continent. The economic benefits of so doing could be considerable. Pan-European firms complain bitterly about the compliance costs of doing business in Europe.

These proposals together posed a challenge to governments, like the United Kingdom's, that had long resisted further transfers of powers and responsibilities to what is, in shorthand, known as "Brussels," wherever the new authority might physically be located (and the banking authority would in all likelihood remain in London, where the existing Committee of European Banking Supervisors is located). The ESRC would also require the Bank of England to become more engaged with the ECB than it has been for the last decade.

In May 2009 the Commission proposed implementing the de Larosière proposals, albeit with some amendments. European supervisors could attend the ESRC alongside central bankers, but as observers only. In London this was seen by some as the thin end of a sinister federalist wedge. In June the European Council broadly endorsed the de Larosière plan, though not without difficulty. Arguing for the United Kingdom, Gordon Brown said that he could not accept a situation in which supervisors in other member states could impose requirements on the United Kingdom that might involve a fiscal cost. So a qualification on that score was agreed, and many other details were left to be resolved later. The plan agreed may strengthen the oversight of financial stability at

European level, and promote greater regulatory harmonization, but without a change in the treaty the fundamental problem at the heart of the single financial market cannot be resolved. There is no genuine pan-European regulation to match the shape of European banks, and no EU-wide mechanism to support ailing institutions financially.

THE ROLE OF THE NCBS

As the report pointed out, in this and in other areas the relationship between the ECB itself and the NCBs is structurally uneasy. It has already evolved considerably in the direction of greater centralization as the logic of the single currency has driven forward greater integration. This has been most tangible in the construction of ever more centralized payment, and now settlement, systems. Nevertheless, the existence of the ECB is a natural threat to the NCBs because it has removed from them their core monetary policy function and it is easy to see a logic that could transform the NCBs into operational branches of the ECB. Much of what was hitherto done at national level is either not needed at all, because it either is or could be done at the center, or is needed on a far smaller scale. Intra-euro area foreign exchange reserve and exchange rate management disappeared at a stroke; the contribution made by the analysis conducted by a provincial branch of an NCB of local economic conditions no longer carries the same weight within the euro area as a whole; operational decisions that were taken locally are now subsumed within decisions taken centrally by others; and so on. As a result, jobs and status are under constant threat and every fresh development involves a negotiation between the Executive Board and the governors about who precisely will perform a function and where.

The NCBs have adopted a number of different defense strategies. Many have cut back their branch and regional operations significantly, particularly where international comparisons indicated major discrepancies in resourcing. It became difficult to explain why central banks without monetary policy functions in countries like France or Germany needed six or seven times the number of staff needed by, say, the Bank of England, even allowing for differences in noncore responsibilities. Often, though, this was as much in response to domestic pressure arising out of the sense that, even if it was perhaps justified in the past, a central bank no longer needed a string of historic palaces across the country (as is the case in Italy) to perform its basic role.

At the same time, a variety of strategies was evolved by NCBs to preserve the integrity, and size, of their organizations. In some cases, these strategies involved acquiring fresh roles at the national level. In others, the strategy has been to capitalize on existing specialist strengths to provide a service to the Eurosystem as a whole. In many cases, these strategies were evolved in the face of efforts to use the opportunities to substantially diminish the power and size of the national central bank on the grounds that many of its functions had been subsumed by the ECB. (See chapter 10 for more detail on the disproportionate size of central banks in Europe.)

Although some central banks had argued, as had the Bundesbank, that there was a conflict between holding the responsibility both for monetary policy and for supervision, because of the potential temptation to ease policy to support banks if they were under pressure, as the ECB has itself pointed out, any such conflict disappeared with the transfer of monetary policy decisions from the NCBs to the ECB. Conveniently, this came at around the same time as the trend for integrated regulators to be established outside the central bank increased. The way was therefore open to argue that the existing NCB infrastructure could be built upon, not just to support an existing role in banking supervision, as in Austria or Germany, but also to expand the role by absorbing other responsibilities.

This was achieved most rapidly in the Netherlands, where De Nederlandsche Bank took on insurance supervision so as to eventually become an integrated prudential regulator. This was not without a fight as some argued that combining these functions in the central bank would create an overmighty and inadequately accountable body, given the independence granted to the governor as part of the process of creating the Eurosystem. These arguments eventually failed in the face of clarification of the fact that independence only pertained to the governor's role in the Eurosystem and could be separated from his accountability in relation to his purely national supervisory responsibilities.

A further argument, of greater force in the Dutch case than in others, was that the Dutch financial system was so concentrated in both the banking and insurance fields that the central bank's responsibility for the stability of the financial system meant that, if supervisory responsibility were to be placed elsewhere, the central bank would still need to engage in much duplicative activity. (The question of the division of responsibility for financial stability between the NCBs and the ECB is one we return to below.)

In other countries yet other strategies were devised by central banks to protect their interests. In Belgium, for instance, although the decision was taken to create a separate integrated financial supervisor, after much debate a number of its key executive roles were assigned to central bank executives, exercising two roles concurrently in the separate organizations.

Progress in adapting the role of the central bank has been much less rapid elsewhere. In France, where the existing banking supervisor was effectively, if not legally, part of the Banque de France, the central bank initially resisted proposals for the banking supervisor to merge with the insurance supervisor because there were political suggestions that this should only be done if banking supervision were taken out of the central bank.

Over time the Dutch example has increasingly been seen to be acceptable (in spite of the poor record cf the Dutch regulatory authorities revealed by the financial crisis, in which ABN Amro and Fortis proved to be among the most vulnerable institutions in the world, while ING also needed government assistance). So the threat to a continuing substantive role for the NCB has receded. At the time of writing there are firm proposals to merge insurance regulation with the existing banking supervisory function of the central bank in both Spain and Italy so as to form integrated prudential regulators, and a similar proposal is gaining momentum in France. At the same time, in the former two countries some existing market conduct functions would be moved into a strengthened securities regulator, though in France the recognition that prudential and conduct of business issues are closely intertwined means that the split is unlikely to be as clear-cut as it is in the Netherlands. Given the difficulty of moving staff out of the central bank, this may be a rational strategy even for those who are persuaded of the benefits of regulatory consolidation.

Another way in which the NCBs have sought to preserve their identity is by developing specialisms within the system and by providing services to the system as a whole rather than leaving these as the province of the ECB. In this respect there has been some correlation with the distinct specialization of the different Federal Reserve Districts. In the operational field of payment, and then settlement, systems, a small number of central banks have taken the lead in developing new systems and then providing the technology on which these systems are based. Thus the Bundesbank, Banque de France, and Banca d'Italia have led the work on Target 2 and have been joined by the Banco d'España in the ongoing effort to develop T2S.

There have also been attempts to justify building an influential role through expertise in research for the euro area as a whole. Four research departments are said to be in a different league from the others: those in Italy, the Netherlands, Portugal, and Spain. Insiders think this partly came from the standing of the prior agencies. This would certainly account for Portugal, Spain, and Italy, where in each country the respective central bank was a major organization held in great respect and employing well-paid staff with considerable social standing. Surprisingly, the French and German central banks are considered way behind, but they have both made recent efforts to catch up. One reason these otherwise-major institutions are behind could be that the respective organizations were traditionally seen as more representative of bureaucratic officialdom as distinct from having the social and intellectual standing of the other banks mentioned. We discuss a more systematic evaluation of central bank research in chapter 10.

The relationship between the ECB and the NCBs does not yet appear to have been settled. On the one hand, the pressure for further integration of infrastructure so as to continue to reap the maximum economic benefit from the creation of the euro and the evident scope for further cost savings in the face of duplication point toward pressure for further centralization. At the same time, NCBs will continue to fight for a substantive separate existence. Indeed, to a certain extent the whole system depends for its legitimacy on the national accountability of the individual governors, who correspondingly need to have sufficient substance, and to be seen to have it, in order to play their roles at both the national and ECB level. The role of NCB governor is already clearly less powerful than it was ten years ago and it may be the case that, once the present generation of governors has moved on, the position will attract candidates of lesser substance except where there is a role as a financial supervisor, which still has a position of prestige at the national level. The Dutch central bank, which seems to have internalized the long-term consequences of EMU earlier, and more comprehensively, than most other central banks, has recognized that need. Its president, Nout Wellinck, who spent much of his career on the economic and monetary policy side of the bank, has converted himself into an international expert in banking supervision and has become chairman of the Basel Committee. It is not so easy to discern a long-term institutional strategy elsewhere.

CONCLUSIONS

It is widely understood that EMU has not reached a stable equilibrium and must evolve. The European commissioner with responsibility for monetary policy, Joaquin Almunia, introducing the Commission's ten-year review of the euro, said: "EMU is not finished. It is unfinished business. It needs to be further developed."[32] But in which direction? Is there a need for stronger fiscal stabilizers at European level? An economic government for the single-currency zone? The logic is powerful, though not everyone would agree. Erik Jones argues that "the need to organise some sort of European fiscal stabilization as a response to asymmetric shocks is a myth."[33] Economic policymaking should be treated as a matter of common interest, which argues for more coordinating mechanisms but "does not entail every member state doing everything the same way."

We think it inevitable that the Eurosystem will evolve toward a more centralized model, which will incidentally make it even less likely that the United Kingdom will wish to join, though Jones is realistic in thinking that a common fiscal policy is so far away that we need to think about other models of coordination. There will be strong efficiency arguments in favor, even though the NCBs are in a position at present to resist major changes. There are also equity arguments for a reduction in the economic misrepresentation we have described. For now, the NCBs are also repositories of expertise, which the ECB cannot quickly duplicate. But in the longer term that will change. Ambitious young European central bankers today are bound to be attracted to Frankfurt and the ECB, which is where the power lies and the action is. It will become harder and harder for the NCBs to attract and retain top talent while their role is purely advisory. The monetary policy departments are already clearly subservient to the ECB's. The financial stability departments, even though given a new advisory role through the European Systemic Risk Board, similarly do not feed directly into those who make decisions on the provision of liquidity support.

In twenty years' time there should be half the number of central bankers in Europe. The remaining NCBs will, in addition to being operating branches of the ECB, primarily be prudential supervisors, where they have that responsibility, and monetary policy think tanks, where they do not. Perhaps it is reasonable that the process should take some time. The ECB needed some breathing space to build up its own credibility. But it is time the larger NCBs, in particular, accepted even more explicitly that they need a new institutional strategy, and one which involves carefully managed contraction. In the meantime, there are many talented staff who are increasingly, and uncomfortably, aware that they are under-employed. Barry Eichengreen, reviewing the early history of the Federal Reserve to identify lessons for the euro area, said the history[34]

> should be read as a cautionary tale.... It points to the advisability of reducing the existing European central banks to mere branch offices of the ECB or of eliminating them entirely.

If they are to avoid that fate, NCBs have work to do.

At the same time, the financial crisis has revealed the risks inherent in the patchwork arrangements for banking supervision, in particular. It has shown that very large pan-European banks cannot in future be head-quartered in small member states, where governments may not be large enough to stand behind them. Some individual banks had balance sheets that were several times larger than the GDP of their home country. Effective ad hoc collaboration, after initial stumbles, produced a workable solution in the case of Fortis, which involved dismembering the institution. There could easily have been other more difficult cases. And for a time member-state governments adopted beggar-thy-neighbor policies involving discriminatory guarantees of domestic bank deposits (most egregiously in the Irish case).

The crisis therefore revealed the need for stronger central institutions and a coordinated approach to the oversight of systemically important banks. The current proposals for colleges of supervisors seem unlikely to be adequate for the task, and in due course a supranational regulator of some kind will be needed. The de Larosière proposals are an important next step, particularly in relation to rule making, but they are unlikely to be the end of the story. A move to some form of single regulator will be another challenge to the U.K. approach, especially if a government even more suspicious of European engagement is elected in 2010.

Central Banking in Emerging Market Countries

Central bank governors typically occupy grand premises. The theory is that such premises inspire confidence in the public—though commercial banks have now generally abandoned their own marble halls. The contrast between the grandeur of the central bank and the squalor of the Ministry of Finance is often striking, not least in Japan, where the Ministry is a rabbit warren with officials working a dozen to a room, often sharing desks and even chairs. Before the Treasury's refurbishment it was similarly true in London, and even now there is no comparison between the Governor's Parlours and the modest lodging of the permanent secretary to the Treasury. Washington is something of an exception, reflecting the traditional parsimony of the American public sector. The chairman of the Federal Reserve is well down the list of governors in remuneration terms, and his office is similarly modest. The Federal Reserve may be powerful but in the past the view was that it should be kept aware of its status as subordinate to the wealth-creating titans of Wall Street.

Practices vary in emerging markets, though they tilt more toward the chandelier-and-gilt school than toward the Fed's functional approach. In Argentina, where financial crises are a way of life, the Reserve Bank occupies heavy and imposing premises in the oldest part of downtown Buenos Aires, with an enormous banking hall on the ground floor. (There is also a revolving door for governors, who last little more than a year on average.) The Bank of Mexico owns several of the oldest palaces in the capital. The governor of the Central Bank of Libya may have the most striking accommodation of all. His bank's premises were built by the Italians in the Mussolini era and his office remains as it was seventy-five years ago, with heavy baronial style furniture, fasces decorating the brass-studded doors, and a view of the Mediterranean facing toward Sicily. But a similar approach to decor does not mean that emerging-market central banks may easily be compared to their OECD counterparts. As Guillermo Calvo of the Inter-American Development Bank says in his survey:[1]

> "A nice art collection and quiet surroundings do not a First World central bank make," should be the motto of every central banker in emerging market economies.

We should be aware of the dangers of treating emerging market countries as a single class. Some, like Uruguay, have central banks whose foundation predates that of the Fed by many years. In others, notably the transition economies of the Former Soviet Union, brand new institutions were set up in the 1990s. Nonetheless, we can identify some common themes and linked challenges.

One prior question is whether a developing country should have a central bank at all or whether it should simply have a currency board. A paper written for the London Institute of Economic Affairs in 1996 argued that central banking had so far proved to be a failure in many cases and that most central banks in developing countries have been unable to provide high-quality currencies. On this argument the real choice for developing countries is between a low-quality currency under central banking and a high-quality currency under a rival monetary system.[2]

Others take a different view. In 1999 the Bank of England commissioned a survey of ninety-four central banks (the economies of which make up around 95% of world GDP) that produced a rich database of their institutional structures, legal bases, and policy objectives.[3] There have been changes in some cases in the intervening decade, which have been described, for example, in a series of IMF papers, but the conclusions of that survey remain broadly valid.

In many respects, EMC central banks have, not surprisingly, followed trends in developed countries. "Price stability," the authors note, "is now the dominant ethos of monetary policy." They point to a growing trend toward transparency and the publication of targets, whether for inflation, money growth, or the exchange rate, though such targets are used more frequently as a policy benchmark than as a rigid rule. Only a small minority of banks specify objectives for growth or employment, and those objectives are increasingly seen as a consequence of, rather than an alternative to, low and stable inflation. Financial-stability concerns also appear as important aspects of central banking in EMCs, to a greater extent than before. Overall, they conclude,

> From the perspective of an observer of central banking even ten years ago, this represents a remarkable convergence in the approach to policy, and one that has contributed to delivering lower and more stable inflation throughout the world.

They focus attention on the more recent period, while the Institute of Economic Affairs paper's pessimistic verdict is based on a longer run of years.

This comforting conclusion may be true at a very high level, but the survey also reveals a wide diversity in practice, and a deal of confusion about how different targets and objectives relate to each other. A number of respondents say they have exchange rate, money, and inflation targets, working in parallel within an overarching framework. It is not easy to see how such an approach can be consistent with anchoring expectations, as the trade-offs made between these targets from time to time are complex and unpredictable. Fry et al.[3] say that their results "show that [credibility] is achieved through a discretionary strategy employing a combination of transparency and explanation." Of course central banks are unlikely to say, in response to a survey whose results will be published, that their policy frameworks lack credibility, but we need to interpret the results using a few more pinches of salt than are employed by Fry.

The questions we should ask are the following.

- What trends can we identify in both the legal status of EMC central banks and in their operating independence (which may diverge from each other more than in developed countries)?
- Similarly, how have the monetary policy frameworks in use been changing?
- What can we learn about the relative success and failure of different strategies in both areas, and the circumstances in which those successes, in particular, have been achieved?
- And, most importantly, what does this analysis tell us about how EMCs should now be thinking about how their central banks should be further reformed and improved?

INDEPENDENCE: DE JURE AND DE FACTO

In legal terms, more and more EMC central banks have been granted independence in respect of monetary policy decisions in recent years. But it is necessary to examine quite what that legal independence means in practice. A cottage industry of indices of central bank independence has been developed over the last decade, with four different scales now in use. The first, and perhaps the best known, was articulated by Cukierman, but Grilli, Masciandro, and Tabellini (GMT)[4] have since produced a slightly different analysis. De Haan and Kooi, and Fry et al. for the Bank of England, have also produced slightly different indices, but these do not add materially to the earlier measures.

The GMT index helpfully makes a distinction between political and economic autonomy. Political autonomy refers to the ability of the central bank to select the final objectives of monetary policy; economic autonomy is an indicator of the extent of the central bank's discretion in the use of instruments, notably the interest rate, to achieve the objective, by whomever it may be set. The Cukierman index is more complex to describe but has the advantage of being somewhat older, and therefore of providing a better basis for assessing trends over time.

Using a combination of these indices, and a sample of EMCs, the IMF concludes that from 1991 to 2003 both political and economic autonomy increased sharply.[5] (They draw a distinction in this work between emerging markets like Russia, South Africa, and Brazil on the one hand, and developing countries like Armenia and Guatemala on the other, but the results are broadly similar for each group of countries.) The trend toward increased autonomy has been as marked in both sets of countries as it has been in the OECD. Indeed, on the face of it, the level of autonomy on both counts is now close to what was typically the case in OECD countries at the beginning of the 1990s, though more progress toward autonomy has been made in the design of the instruments of policy than in the political framework. On the political front, while governors are typically still appointed by governments, the practice of them holding political office simultaneously has now all but disappeared, and formal government vetoes over monetary policy are now rare. On the economic front, central bank lending to the government is now far more tightly constrained, where it is allowed at all, and even where it is possible it is usually now provided at market rates.

The IMF's researchers also identify a trend in the evolution of legislation that depends on a country's stage of economic development:

> At an early stage of economic development the law aims to protect the central bank from political interference. In a subsequent stage, the one in which emerging markets are now situated, greater focus is given to instrument autonomy, suggesting that the objective is to safeguard de facto autonomy for an institution that enjoys a high level of de jure

autonomy. The process concludes with a final push on political autonomy, characterized by greater autonomy in the appointment of governors and longer terms of office; even less political interference in the formulation of monetary policy; and stronger provisions to protect the central bank in case of conflict with the government.

Why has this happened? The IMF is not a neutral analyst. Fund staff have recommended central bank independence consistently in their advice to developing economies for many years. But they see the principal reason as being the growing consensus that economic performance can be improved if price stability is assigned to the central bank as its prime objective and if the scope for monetization of government deficits is strictly limited. So, they conclude, "today we can see an approximately equal distribution of autonomy among countries, irrespective of the level of economic development."

TRANSITION ECONOMIES

Further support for this proposition can be found in an analysis of central bank formation and reform in transition economies in the former Soviet Union and Eastern Europe.[6] In an assessment of twenty-six former socialist economies Cukierman et al. find that reforming governments were ambitious in their approach to their central banks, influenced in some cases by Western economists and central banks themselves, who provided technical advice and support. The Bank of England's Centre for Central Banking Studies advised many transition-economy countries. By 2001 these countries had created central banks with levels of legal independence that were substantially higher, on average, than those of developed countries during the 1980s. Some of the results look a little curious. On the legal independence scale they use (yet another index), Belarus has a score more than three times higher than New Zealand (0.73 versus 0.24). Armenia's central bank is more than three times as independent as the Bank of England on this measure. These rankings assume that we may take the statute as a close proxy for operational practice. As we know from experience elsewhere, independence is not a binary issue. Even institutions like the Fed and the Bundesbank have had to continue to earn their independence, as Alan Greenspan has always argued, and it can take time for the political and public understanding of the bank's role to develop.

But while we may be skeptical of the reality in some cases, and of the apparent precision of the rankings, once again the legal trend is clear, and the more recent the reform the more independent the bank is under law. That is necessarily the case for countries on a track toward EMU, who must meet the tough criteria in the Maastricht Treaty, but it is also true for former Soviet Union countries, who are as unlikely as the United Kingdom to join the euro area in the foreseeable future. Indeed Armenia and Belarus are, in legal terms, stronger candidates for membership than the United Kingdom on the basis of this analysis.

In the transition economies these reforms coincided with a gradual reduction in inflation, and an acceleration of growth rates, though the record is somewhat confused by the impact of the removal of price controls, so inflation frequently rose in the first stage of reform before falling back later. It is difficult to disentangle the impact of central bank reform from other factors at work as the former socialist economies shifted toward a market economy, but the introduction of largely independent monetary authorities was certainly an important element in the reform agenda.

Latin America

A more fine-grained assessment of reform in Latin America, again by IMF researchers, produces more compelling evidence of the global trend, and also of the impact of central bank institutional reform on inflation.[7]

In 1990, average inflation across Latin America reached a rate of 500%. The damaging economic consequences of hyperinflation provided a strong stimulus to the search for new mechanisms to ensure a greater measure of price stability. Since then, a series of reforms have been introduced, country by country, to enhance the independence of their central banks. On the Cukierman index the average score increased from 0.427 to 0.774. The degree of independence on this measure still varies, with Peru at the top with 0.862 and Brazil, where an independent bank was legislated earlier, on 0.641. But the direction of change is clear, and there is some persuasive evidence that central bank independence is a significant factor in explaining the radically improved inflation performance across the region.[8] More recently, populist regimes in Venezuela, Bolivia, Argentina, and Ecuador have thrown this progress into question. Inflation has begun to rise again, and political interference in central bank decision making has reappeared. So the prospect for monetary and financial stability in Latin America is once again clouded.

Africa and the Middle East

It is less easy to generalize about the position in Africa. The Bank of England survey suggested that there had been some progress in legislating for greater independence, though not on as uniform a basis as in Latin America. The relationship between the central bank and government is covered in more detail in the BIS publication "Central banks and the challenge of development."[9] Tito Mboweni, the governor of the Reserve Bank of South Africa until November 2009, offered an optimistic reading at the end of 2004[10] claiming that "since the beginning of the 1980s, African countries have generally moved to more market-based financial systems with greater autonomy and accountability applying to central banks," though he acknowledged that, at that time, South Africa was the only African country with an explicit inflation target.

A number of African countries belong to currency unions. The Central Bank of West African States and the Bank of Central African States have existed since 1959 and are responsible for the two monetary unions known as the Colonies Francaises D'Afrique Franc Zone. Monetary unions are also being considered elsewhere in (anglophone) West Africa, and in the Southern African Development Community—though Zimbabwe, with recent inflation in eight figures, is not the only country that would find joining a monetary union quite a challenge.

In the Middle East and North Africa (MENA), where most countries have in the past pegged their currencies to the dollar in spite of the growing significance of their trade with the European Union, a trend toward at least de jure independence for the central bank can be observed. As Ghassan Dibeh[11] observes, "most MENA countries have either adopted or are in the process of adopting economic and financial reforms that include the conduct of monetary policy and the role of central banks in the process of monetary policy making." The degree of independence adopted varies considerably from country to country, with Lebanon at the top of the league and Syria at the bottom.

Once again, however, the distinction between de facto and de jure independence should be made. Gisolo[12] points out that the de facto independence in Israel is much greater than the position de jure, which is the opposite of the case in the Palestine Monetary Authority, mainly due to the delicate sociopolitical situation and to the fact that Palestine does not issue its own currency. Broadly, there is an emerging negative relationship, albeit a weak one, between independence and inflation, though the legal changes are so recent that one must be cautious. There is also a loose positive relationship between independence and economic growth, though, again, the period of time involved is not long enough to give confidence in the results. It is also not easy to disentangle the influence of political autonomy on the one hand and economic autonomy on the other—two factors that are by no means closely correlated.

Asia

In Asia it is similarly difficult to determine a clear trend in the political and legal autonomy of central banks. In some cases, as in Thailand, there have been explicit reforms. In Hong Kong and Singapore the monetary authorities operate currency board regimes in close consultation with the government. In other countries the relationship between the central bank and the government remains complex and ambiguous. This is true, in quite different ways, in both India and China, the two most important emerging economies, where governments clearly influence monetary policy choices directly—especially in China.

The People's Bank of China (PBOC), which incorporated almost the whole of China's financial sector until the 1980s, has been substantially reformed in recent years. Three new commissions—for banking (the China Banking Regulatory Commission), securities (the China Securities Regulatory Commission (CSRC)), and insurance (the China Insurance Regulatory Commission)—have been created to take on the regulatory functions, and both commercial and development banks have been carved out and turned into distinct entities. The banking system, beset by massive nonperforming loans (NPLs) at the beginning of the century, has been greatly strengthened and recapitalized with large equity injections from the government, first, and subsequently from international equity investors. The transformation has been remarkable, though there is still work to do, especially in the case of the huge Agricultural Bank of China. The economic slowdown that began in late 2008 also threatened to bring about the reemergence of new NPLs, especially in the overheated property market, but Chinese banks looked more robust than most as the recession bit—a tribute to the efforts made to strengthen their capital base in the preceding five years.

The PBOC now has a narrower set of functions, of which by far the most important is monetary policy, though the legislation also provides that it "shall...prevent and mitigate financial risks and maintain financial stability." Both Governor Zhou Xioachuan and Governor Dai Xianlong before him have been positioned as prominent governors on the world stage. Zhou's impressive command of English, his extensive experience of financial markets (before taking over at the PBOC he was the chairman of the CSRC), and his willingness to debate policy openly with his counterparts in Basel and elsewhere has earned him a high reputation. Overseas, he is clearly seen as the spokesman for China's financial policies, standing alongside Bernanke or Trichet. His grasp of monetary and financial issues is also impressive. In 2009 he began to publish a series of papers on international financial reform, including a provocative note on the scope for the SDR to replace the U.S. dollar as a global currency.[13]

The domestic reality is somewhat different. People's Bank governors are not as highly placed in the hierarchy as their overseas reputations imply. The law governing the PBOC states that "under the guidance of the State Council, the People's Bank of China formulates and implements monetary policy, prevents and resolves financial risks, and safeguards financial stability." And there is no doubt about the controlling role played in practice by the State Council. While the PBOC is the body in charge of the implementation of monetary policy, decision-making power lies firmly with the State Council. A common characterization of the relationship, offered by researchers at the Hong Kong Monetary Authority, is that[14]

> the PBOC proposes but the State Council disposes, and may sometimes respond to a recommendation by implementing measures other than those put forward by the Bank. Action may be taken by another agency, or in another form.

Monetary policy has essentially been driven by the fixed or, more recently, slowly crawling exchange rate peg, with the PBOC focusing on credit and money conditions through open market operations, changes in the discount rate, and reserve requirements. The monetary base is formally the operating target, with the growth of money and bank lending as explicit intermediate targets.

The move to a somewhat more flexible exchange rate regime, which began in 2007, has put this framework under strain. Inflation rose markedly in 2008, in response to rising oil and commodity prices, before falling back. China is now too large an economy, with idiosyncratic dynamics and huge domestic financial markets, for an exchange rate target to operate as a comfortable anchor. IMF researchers have recommended a move toward operational independence for the People's Bank, as a precursor to the eventual adoption of a domestic inflation target:[15]

> The crucial requirement is that the People's Bank be granted instrument (operational) independence. Operational independence is necessary because the PBOC must have the authority to move its policy instruments aggressively on short notice without permission from other government agencies.

Such a move would entail a greater reliance on policy interest rates and the adoption of a short-term interest rate as the operational target.

It may be argued that the Chinese authorities are already edging in that direction. Certainly there is little transparency at present about the People's Bank's policy objectives. They announce money supply growth targets but change them from time to time, and there is nothing approaching a predictable cycle of decisions on interest rates or reserve requirements. But there is evidence that, in practice, the Bank is operating with an eye to a price stability aim. In an attempt to deduce a monetary policy rule from observed changes in reserve polices and interest rates, the Hong Kong Monetary Authority find that the PBOC's policy actions are more closely related to deviations of CPI inflation and broad money growth from declared targets than to output gaps. These findings, they say, "are consistent with a characterization of the monetary policy framework in China as one of 'implicit inflation targeting'."[14]

Whether China will move toward a formal IT regime in the near future is uncertain. They have considered the implications internally but have concluded, for now, that it would be difficult to determine a credible range and stick to it, given the amount of monetization of economic transactions that were previously not market based that is still under way. In those circumstances they believe that a rigid commitment to price stabilization could impede reform. The question remains under review but the Chinese government's priority has been to maintain a competitive exchange rate, in the interests of its exporting sector. A shift to a domestic inflation objective would cut across that overriding policy aim.

The Reserve Bank of India (RBI) was established under the Reserve Bank of India Act of 1934, on a model that owed something to the constitution of the Bank of England at that time. The basic objective of the Bank was described then as "to regulate the issue of bank notes and keeping of reserves with a view to securing monetary stability in India and generally to operate the currency and credit system of the country to its advantage." While the RBI was nationalized in 1949, the underpinning legislation has not been changed since 1934. There is therefore no explicit price stability target.

The Act provides that the government may give directions to the Bank. That provision has rarely been used, but the government has retained its primacy in monetary policymaking through controlling all appointments to the bank's decision-making board and in other less formal ways. Invited to characterize the relationship between the RBI and the Ministry of Finance the last governor, Dr. Reddy, acknowledged the Bank's subservient status:[16]

> In the given legal and cultural context, while making every effort to give its views, either informally or formally, but as unambiguously as possible, the RBI generally respects the wishes and final inclination of the government.

Over the last two decades, as India has gradually liberalized its economy, the RBI has gained more autonomy, particularly in its oversight of financial markets, and has gradually withdrawn from providing concessional finance to priority sectors of the economy, but there has been no legal reform that prohibits either that or the automatic monetization of deficits, which was practiced before 1997.

Several reviews, commissioned by the RBI itself or by the government, have drawn attention to this unsatisfactory position. The Advisory Group on Transparency in Monetary and Financial Policies sharply criticized the institutional arrangements for monetary policy under the 1934 Act, which it described as anachronistic, and urged early reform.[17] The government was not persuaded of the case and continued with its gradualist approach, choosing to retain political discretion in Delhi rather than implementing any formal devolution of power to the RBI in Mumbai. As a result policy has remained imprecise, and observers of the Indian scene note that "the RBI remains very elusive as to what is being targeted and how the target is being attained."[18]

More recently, the Committee on Financial Sector Reforms—set up by the Ministry of Finance under Raghuram Rajan of the University of Chicago, and including several leading Indian bankers—has also argued for legislative change. Their recommendations covered a wide range of areas, including the regulatory structure and the direct controls still in place on financial markets. In relation to the RBI specifically they concluded that it "should formally have a single objective, to stay close to a low inflation number, or within a range, in the medium term and move steadily to a single instrument, the short-term interest rate (repo and reverse repo) to achieve it."[19]

So far, the government has made no commitment to implement the Rajan recommendations but it is clear that, over time, pressure for legal reform is building up and opinion within both government and the Reserve Bank is edging toward the introduction of an IT framework. Although the inflation record has not been bad in recent years, hovering around 6% in the years before the current financial crisis, India is paying a price for the lack of clarity about the RBI's objectives.

POLICY FRAMEWORKS

In spite of the ambiguities and uncertainties, therefore, and bearing in mind some skepticism about what independence means in some places, we can identify a clear global trend toward central bank independence. It would, perhaps, be surprising if we could not, given the enthusiasm with which the IMF has embraced the idea and the working models on offer in the OECD.

There is less clarity about the monetary policy frameworks. The growth of inflation targeting, which has been very marked in OECD countries, has been less evident in EMCs. Most continue to operate either an exchange rate target (sometimes as extreme as the adoption of the U.S. dollar as their own currency, as in El Salvador and Ecuador), a version of a domestic money target, or a hazardous combination of the two. In fact, of the 172 countries with central banks, around two-thirds report to the IMF that they operate an exchange rate target. Indeed the predominant regime is what is generally known as "managed floating."

The advantages of exchange rate targeting for countries with relatively open economies, a weak record of price stability, and therefore poor credibility are clear. A nominal anchor can be "borrowed" from elsewhere, usually the United States. The policy is easy to describe and it is possible to implement tough domestic measures to maintain the parity. The disadvantages are also powerful. Without strong reserves, the exchange rate targeting country is vulnerable to a loss of market confidence, perhaps supplemented by aggressive positioning by investors. The experience in Europe in the early 1990s, in East Asia later in the decade, and subsequently in Turkey convinced many that only where a country's foreign currency reserves were large enough to resist a sustained speculative attack could a fixed peg safely be maintained— otherwise some flexibility, or indeed a shift to an inflation target, was essential. Asian countries typically adopted the former strategy, which was open to them given their strong balance of payments position driven by high domestic saving and competitive manufacturers. The buildup of reserves by countries like Singapore, South Korea, and Hong Kong has been impressive. Elsewhere, notably in large economies such as South Africa, Chile, and Brazil, inflation targets were introduced, and these have worked tolerably well.

The steep decline in the value of the dollar in 2006–7 put the exchange rate targets under renewed pressure. Combined with high oil and commodity prices, countries pegged to the dollar found themselves importing inflation. Dollar-denominated assets fell in value causing a material welfare loss, especially for countries with large volumes of imports denominated in euros, which is especially true of countries in Africa and the Middle East.

In the short term, a change to the monetary regime in the face of these market pressures can be damaging to credibility. In the case of China, the short-term answer was to allow a more rapid rise in the renminbi, though not rapid enough in 2007–8 to prevent further large inflows of funds. Other countries rebalanced their currency baskets, giving a greater weight to the euro and allowing themselves a little more flexibility as a result. The modest recovery of the U.S. dollar in the summer of 2008 eased these pressures somewhat, but many countries began to ask themselves whether, in the longer term, a regime change would be necessary, with the obvious move being to an inflation target. If IT regimes could work so well for OECD countries that were not members of a currency bloc, and indeed for some larger developing economies, might they not also do service for a wider range of EMCs?

A full-fledged inflation-targeting regime involves more than simply the announcement by the government of a target range for inflation. There is also a need for institutionalized commitment to price stability as the primary goal of monetary policy (with other economic aims being subordinate), for mechanisms to make the central bank accountable for meeting the target, and for increased transparency through public communication about the monetary authority's policies and expectations. A small number of EMCs, like Brazil, Chile, and South Africa, may be regarded as inflation targeters on that definition; a rather larger number have talked of their aims for inflation as a guide to policy but have not yet implemented a fully articulated IT regime.

There is no doubt that inflation targeting is more problematic for EMCs than for large developed economies. Typically, they have weaker fiscal institutions and therefore less ability to maintain fiscal discipline. There are often many administered prices that can reduce the usefulness of an inflation target and give politicians the ability to manipulate the inflation rate. Financial institutions are often less robust and there may be a history of lax supervision and an undercapitalized banking sector. Financial markets themselves are often thin and vulnerable to manipulation. The monetary authorities themselves may lack credibility due to past episodes of high inflation and perhaps also a history of political control. Legislation to make the central bank nominally independent will not cure these problems overnight, and, partly as a result of these weaknesses, the threat is faced that domestic residents may switch to a foreign currency if their confidence in the domestic currency declines. That switch may, in turn, induce domestic banks to offer loans based in a foreign currency (usually dollars), leading to liability dollarization. A further consequence is that the authorities will then be reluctant to allow exchange rate flexibility (inherent in a full inflation-target regime) as they fear the consequences for banks if the value of their foreign currency liabilities rises sharply and suddenly. This phenomenon is usually described as the "fear of floating."[20] Finally, there is evidence that changes in import prices as a consequence of a fall in the exchange rate are passed through to domestic prices more rapidly in EMCs, making inflation more sensitive to parity changes.

These characteristics have led some to argue that inflation targeting is inherently unsuitable for most EMCs. Others, notably Barry Eichengreen and Rick Mishkin, take a different view however. Eichengreen's conclusion, after reviewing the problems described above, is that "none of this is to suggest that inflation targeting is infeasible in open economies, only that it is more complicated to operate."[21] He points out that critics of inflation targeting need to address the problem that no other regime is free of problems:

> Flexible rates tend to fluctuate erratically, especially if abandonment of a peg leaves a country without a nominal anchor, a clear and coherent monetary policy operating strategy, and credibility in the eyes of the markets. Unilateral dollarization limits policy flexibility, gives the country resorting to it no voice in the monetary policy it runs, and sacrifices seigniorage revenues. And ad hoc intervention to limit the variability of the exchange rate in the absence of a credible commitment to a transparent, coherent, and defensible monetary strategy is unlikely to inspire confidence; attempting to prevent the exchange rate from moving beyond set limits under these circumstances can render the central bank and its reserves sitting ducks for speculators.

Martin Wolf[22] argues the same case: "Relatively sophisticated and large countries should consider adopting an inflation target with an independent central bank." He sees a further argument in favor. He is concerned that the buildup of foreign currency reserves on a scale necessary to maintain an exchange rate target has contributed to the buildup of global financial imbalances the unwinding of which is part of the story of the financial crisis.

For countries that cannot generate the level of reserves necessary to maintain a credible currency peg, inflation targeting is certainly an attractive endpoint. There is, theoretically, another option: a currency union. An operating model can be seen on a small scale in former French West Africa. Other countries have given the idea serious consideration. In theory, the countries of the Gulf Cooperation Council (GCC) are committed to a single currency and indeed renewed that commitment in late 2008, with a target date for its launch of 2010, but no serious plans to produce the institutions needed to manage a currency union have been made and it is highly likely that the date will be put back. In May 2009 the UAE unilaterally announced that it was no longer committed to the timetable, following a decision to locate the future GCC central bank in Saudi Arabia. There are even grander ideas for an Islamic dinar, backed by gold, as a unified currency for all Islamic countries, but these look unrealistic at present.[23]

Even more speculatively, the African Union envisages a single currency for Africa by 2020, though again no practical steps have been taken in that direction.

The policy prescription of an independent central bank operating an inflation-targeting regime still looks to be the best option for many EMCs, but there are many important prerequisites. While the legal basis for an independent central bank has been established in many countries, there is much continuing political interference, especially in appointments to senior positions. For example, most governors in Latin America are appointed for terms of at least five years in theory, but in practice each governor only remains in place for two and a half years on average.[7] De Haan and Kooi maintain that it is continuity at the top of the bank, rather than the nominal independence reflected in the statute, that is negatively correlated with inflation.[24] The government must also resist the temptation to use the central bank as a source of short-term financing.

At the same time, to address some of the vulnerabilities of EMCs described above, the prudential supervision of banks needs to be robust.

In particular, supervisors need to pay close attention to the matching of foreign currency assets and liabilities, both directly on the banks' balance sheets and through oversight of loans to corporates who may themselves be unhedged—a feature of the Asian financial crisis of the late 1990s. Restrictions on currency mismatches may reduce a country's vulnerability to exchange rate volatility and there is a prior need for fiscal reforms that provide some protection against spiraling deficits. The Argentina example showed how monetary credibility can quickly disappear when the public sector's fiscal position is perceived to be out of control. The IMF's Financial Sector Assessment Program provides a vehicle for monitoring the progress of reform in countries that decide to set out along this path.

As Mishkin argues,

> inflation targeting can be an effective tool for emerging-market countries to manage their monetary policy. However, to ensure that inflation targeting produces superior macroeconomic outcomes, emerging-market countries would benefit by focusing even more attention on institutional development, while the IMF can provide these countries with better incentives to engage in this development.

It would be unrealistic to expect that a majority of EMCs will quickly be able to make the transition to robust IT regimes in the near future, and the financial crisis has probably set many countries back a number of years. The near-term focus is on rebuilding credibility in the banking system rather than on further institutional reform. But in the longer term an IT regime does offer the best prospect of price stability, especially in a world of highly volatile exchange rates and commodity prices. As Malcolm Knight, former General Manager of the BIS, has argued, emerging market economies with very diverse structures have successfully adopted inflation targeting.[25] More could follow their lead.

FINANCIAL STABILITY

As elsewhere, EMC central banks typically say that their objective is also to promote or maintain financial stability. Few have any formal statutory responsibility to back that objective. Many regard banking supervision as the principal task they perform in its service, and of course in many countries the banks are still by far the dominant financial institutions. In those circumstances it may well be sensible—in spite of the arguments we advance in chapter 5 about the desirability of integrated regulation, with the central bank carrying out a general oversight function—to leave supervision there. The central bank is often the one administrative body with some degree of separation from the party in power and with a reputation for integrity and (relative) independence. Setting up a new regulatory authority, with the ability to take unpopular decisions at arm's length from government, may be difficult in countries with autocratic regimes, weak political infrastructure, and controlled media.

Beyond banking supervision, some EMC central banks have joined the Financial Stability Review bandwagon. Argentina, Brazil, Chile, and Colombia all produce regular FSRs. So do South Africa, where the scale of the financial sector certainly justifies it, Ghana, and Kenya. In Asia, apart from the obvious financial centers of Hong Kong, Japan, and Singapore, other countries like China, Korea, Indonesia, Sri Lanka, and, surprisingly, Macao (where "casino capitalism" has a very precise meaning) all publish FSRs. These reviews suffer from the weaknesses we described earlier in our discussion of financial stability more generally. They are rarely candid or pointed enough to deliver useful warnings to market participants. All of the arguments we advance in chapter 4 about the need for candor and detail in FSRs are even more relevant to EMCs.

ISLAMIC FINANCE

There is one category of EMCs where rather different considerations apply: the countries in which there is a strong political and religious interest in Islamic finance. The growth of Islamic finance poses problems for banking supervisors and, particularly, for central banks in their role as monetary authorities.

The underlying principle of Islamic finance is that it is not permissible to pay or receive interest, known as "riba." The prohibition against interest is sometimes likened to Christian hostility to usury but Islamic scholars describe things rather differently. According to Muhammed Taqi Usmani, a distinguished and influential Pakistani scholar,[26]

> the principle is that the person sending money to another person must decide whether he wishes to help the opposite party or he wants to share in his profits. If he wants to help the borrower, he must resign from any claim to any additional amount...but if he is advancing money to share the profits earned by the other party, he can claim a stipulated proportion of profit actually earned by him, and must share his loss also, if he suffers a loss.

Others argue that this interpretation derives from an over-literal reading of the Koran. Mahmoud El-Gamal, a professor of Islamic economics at Rice University in Houston, maintains that "traditional religious scholarship does not support application of this simplistic view to modern finance." Furthermore, he regards Islamic finance as a worrying development for two reasons:[27]

> It glorifies irrational adherence to outdated medieval jurisprudence, and supports the development of a separatist and boastful Islamic identity. This mixture has proven disastrous in recent years, and Muslims can hardly afford its economic price.

Non-Muslims are wise to be hesitant about entering this debate, but it is clear that the advocates of Islamic finance do see it as a political initiative. Usmani himself notes at the end of the foreword to his book that Muslims "strongly feel that the political and economic dominance of the West during past centuries has deprived them of the divine guidance, especially in the social economic fields." So Islamic finance has a powerful political and religious dimension.

Whether in spite of or because of this religious and political impetus, the market in Islamic instruments has grown rapidly in recent years. The credit crisis in Western institutions gave the market an extra boost. Precise figures are hard to come by, and indeed there are religious and ideological disputes about which instruments may properly be regarded as Islamic and which may not, but most observers would accept that the total capital value of Islamic instruments now exceeds $500 billion and has almost certainly been growing at between 10% and 15% a year for the last decade or more.[28]

To describe all the products now available would go beyond the scope of this volume. There is now a wide range of instruments on both the asset and the liability sides of banks' balance sheets. The market in Sukuk, the equivalent of long-term bonds but with the returns related to a package of real assets, is now large in Southeast Asia, the Gulf, and in London. Sukuk issuance in the Gulf over the period 2000–2008 is estimated at around $42 billion, with the lion's share being in the UAE.[29] Some Western governments, including the United Kingdom's, have begun to explore the issuance of sukuk to take advantage of the demand from Islamic institutions. On the liability side of bank balance sheets there are deposit-type products linked to assets or to bank profitability; there are Islamic mortgages, which are typically constructed as a kind of finance lease (ijara); and there is now Islamic insurance, which is known as taka-ful. Takaful insurers operate effectively as mutuals. The largest, Salama, the Islamic Arab Insurance Company, is based in Dubai.

The market has been sufficiently robust and dynamic to cause a num-ber of financial centers to set out strategies designed to attract mobile Islamic business. While the largest domestic markets in Islamic instru-ments remain in countries like Iran and Saudi Arabia, Malaysia and Singa-pore have set out their stalls to create a regime attractive to Islamic insti-tutions, partly for domestic and partly for international reasons. Several Gulf states, led by Bahrain, have been active in the market, though Gulf Cooperation Council central banks have played more of a reactive than a proactive role.[30] Although Bahrain made a determined attempt to create a regulatory environment appropriate for Islamic institutions, other Gulf centers have lagged behind. More recently, London has become one of the top ten Islamic markets, and the leading Western location for trading and issuing Islamic instruments.[31] The British government was ahead of other European countries in making tax changes to facilitate the devel-opment of the domestic Islamic mortgage market (previously, Islamic mortgages attracted stamp duty twice as the ownership of the property passed first from the seller to the bank and then on from the bank to the buyer). When he was governor of the Bank of England Eddie George took a particular interest in Islamic finance, and the Financial Services Authority was also the first Western regulator to authorize (in 2004) a fully compliant, wholly Islamic retail institution, the Islamic Bank of Britain, followed by several Islamic investment banks. The French and others are now examining ways of catching up. It is surprising, given the large Muslim population in France, much larger than in the United Kingdom, that it was not until July 2008 that the French securities reg-ulator set up a working party to examine the issues. No doubt there are cultural, as well as financial, factors at play here.

Fitting these institutions into a regulatory framework designed for conventional Western financial instruments is not straightforward.[32] A number of complex issues arise. For example, deposits in Western institutions are capital certain, whether they attract interest or not. It is on that basis that they have been incorporated into deposit insur-ance schemes. If the capital value of a deposit varies in relation to the profitability of the bank, then what is the sum insured? Deposit protection schemes do not normally underwrite profit growth, so on that basis they would be excluded. On the other hand, if profit-share deposits are excluded from deposit insurance, Islamic banks are clearly at a competitive disadvantage in the retail market place. The solution found in the case of the Islamic Bank of Britain is that depositors are legally entitled to full repayment of the original sum deposited, to meet FSA requirements, but may choose instead to take part in a profit-sharing arrangement.

Another delicate issue relates to the role of the Shariah Board in an Islamic bank. The role of the Shariah Board is in principle to satisfy itself that the products and services offered by the bank are compliant with Shariah principles, but that role may sometimes cut across the responsibilities of the board of the bank and the senior management to account to the regulator for the proper functioning of specific risk management functions and for other forms of compliance.

In spite of these complexities, and in spite of the fact that the Basel Capital Accords were designed without taking account of the needs of Islamic firms, in London at least it has been possible for the authorities to accommodate Islamic financial institutions with only modest adaptations of the regulatory regime.[33] The Islamic Financial Services Board, based in Kuala Lumpur, has been a helpful interlocutor and has developed its own guidance and codes to facilitate regulatory compliance. The parallel organization responsible for accounting standards and disclosure, the Accounting and Auditing Organization for Islamic Financial Institutions, based in Bahrain, has been similarly constructive. It seems likely that other Western countries will authorize Islamic firms in future, especially where there is a sizable domestic Muslim population with a desire to use Shariah-compliant services. Their success will depend in part on their competitiveness and responsiveness to market needs. While some Muslims will only transact business with an Islamic institution, there are many others who might prefer to do so but are willing to transact conventional business if an attractive Islamic option is not available. This is clear from the small market share taken so far by Islamic mortgages in the United Kingdom.

The IMF has reviewed the financial stability implications of Islamic banking, and particularly the impact on conventional banks in the same jurisdiction.[34] They conclude that there is no significant impact on the soundness of other banks arising from the presence of a substantial competing Islamic sector. As for the Islamic banks themselves, they find that, overall, small banks tend to be financially stronger than either small or large commercial banks but that larger institutions tend to be somewhat weaker than their conventional counterparts. One plausible explanation for this finding is that as banks become larger and more complex the risk management challenge becomes more daunting, even though, in principle, the profit and loss sharing with depositors that is inherent in the model should switch some risk to customers outside the bank. Since many Islamic markets are young and developing, the behavior of the instruments in stressed conditions is more than usually uncertain.

It is observable that in most countries Islamic finance coexists with a conventional capital market. In some cases, as in the Gulf, there are local banks operating on an Islamic basis and others operating in a conventional way, with the use of interest rates. There are also conventional institutions that have opened Islamic "windows" through which they can serve the needs of customers who wish to avoid interest-related products. One of the largest of such institutions is HSBC Amanah, with its own Shariah Board embedded within the HSBC global network.

Other issues arise if a country tries to move to a fully Islamic financial system. While Islamic firms are not supposed to price products by reference to an interest benchmark, the existence of a parallel conventional market can be a helpful check on pricing. Some Islamic scholars dislike it but it is clear that there is more than a coincidental relationship between the returns embedded in Islamic products and interest rates charged on comparable conventional instruments. This problem has come to the surface from time to time and some Shariah scholars have concluded that a number of instruments previously regarded as compliant, such as a proportion of the Sukuk sold in the Gulf, do not meet their more rigorous standards. Holders of these bonds who are obliged to invest only in rigorously compliant instruments have then been forced to sell. Usmani, by contrast, argues that "merely using the interest rate as a benchmark for determining the profit of murabahah does not render the transaction as invalid, haram or prohibited, because the deal itself does not contain interest." (The word murabahah literally means "profit," but refers to the sale of a commodity for its purchase price plus an agreed markup.) This difference of view creates a particular form of regulatory risk that may impede the development of the market if a consensus among Islamic scholars cannot be achieved. Central bank governors and regulators are concerned about these inconsistencies and have called for greater convergence of standards across the Muslim world.[35]

These issues are probably soluble, and it is quite possible to imagine continued peaceful coexistence between Islamic and conventional finance operating in the same market. In most of the countries involved there is a short-term interest rate set by the central bank for monetary policy purposes that can act as a formal or informal benchmark.

As Islamic finance grows, however, and as the political dimension becomes more prominent, this coexistence is coming under threat. Three countries have decided, in principle at least, to move the whole of their financial system onto an Islamic basis: Iran, Sudan, and Pakistan. The Iranian move came as part of the Iranian revolution and is an element in a broader socialization of the economy and withdrawal from many forms of international economic association. Sudan, similarly, has few financial relations with the rest of the world and has an underdeveloped financial sector. It is difficult to regard either of those countries as a model for others. Pakistan is a rather different case, with internationally active banks of its own and relatively sophisticated financial markets. There it is noticeable that the process of Islamicization has proceeded slowly.

Full Islamicization of an economy creates a completely different and far more complex set of issues for central banks from those generated for regulators by the introduction of non-interest-bearing financial instruments. Without access to an interest rate as a means of pricing credit, how does a central bank maintain monetary discipline and control inflation? Monetary policy normally involves the manipulation of short-term financial instruments and the maintenance of very regular influence over liquidity in the financial system. Asset-based or profit-share-based instruments do not lend themselves easily to utilization of that kind, especially where there is no benchmark interest rate.

There are those who argue that there is no theoretical obstacle to controlling the money supply through Islamic instruments.[36] In principle, through the direct control of credit, by varying reserve requirements, and by adjusting the profit-sharing ratios of instruments in issue the central bank can express a view on the tightness of monetary conditions and influence inflation. But as Mahmoud El-Gamal has pointed out, such control relies very heavily on administrative setting of rates of return, in the absence of normal market signals, which places a heavy burden on the central bank. El-Gamal notes that little progress toward a market-based monetary framework has been made in any of the central banks that have tried to operate monetary policy on an Islamic basis so far. In Sudan inflation has remained persistently high and the Sudanese economy is so closed as to offer little in the way of useful experience for the rest of the world. Broadly the same is true in the case of Iran, where the banking system no longer performs the economic functions that would normally be expected of it and credit is to all intents and purposes centrally allocated, with considerable direct control over prices too.

In Pakistan, for the time being, the central bank continues to implement monetary policy through the administration of interest rates. But consistent with a decision in 1991 by the Supreme Court of Pakistan that confirmed the intention of moving to a fully Islamic financial system, the State Bank has published a paper detailing how such a system might operate in practice.[37] That paper, no doubt unintentionally, vividly demonstrates the difficulties inherent in such a course. It argues that the central bank should, for any given year, assess the appropriate demand for money and make an estimate of the elasticity of demand, which will result in a desired rate of monetary expansion. Some of that expansion would be placed in the banking system as central bank deposits "which would be used to advance funds to finance production and commercial activities through the use of Islamic finance." The bank would also issue central deposit certificates to the public that would be deposited and invested through the banking system:

> These certificates would be readily marketable, as they would carry the most diversified and least risky financial investment in the economy. The rate of return on CDCs [central deposit certificates] can, therefore, be used as a benchmark in place of the rate of interest.

The central bank would then conduct open market operations in those certificates.

Whether such a system would work in practice must be open to doubt, and so far the State Bank of Pakistan has not wished to carry out an experiment. It certainly seems to imply an unusual ability on the part of the central bank to determine the needed quantity of money *ex ante*, and also to determine the elasticity of demand—something that has proved impossible to predict with any degree of accuracy elsewhere. The overwhelming implication is that we would then be in a world of central planning and centralized credit allocation, where market signals play very little role. It is hard to see that the system would be compatible with a dynamic free market economy.

It is not surprising that central bank governors in Islamic countries have not been enthusiastic advocates of a move to a comprehensive system of Islamic money and banking. For the moment, in most Muslim countries there is a broadly comfortable coexistence between Islamic and conventional finance, but one which is built on a system of monetary control that incorporates the use of a benchmark interest rate. There are clearly risks, however, of both a political and economic kind that this delicate balance is undone. Indeed the problems of conventional finance in the capital market crisis of 2007 onward have added weight to the views of those who argue that a closer linkage between the real and financial economies, such as is guaranteed by the structure of Islamic finance, is attractive. But that arguable proposition does not lead logically to a fully Islamic system, which would be extremely problematic to introduce. Pressure for complete Islamicization is, therefore, in its most extreme form a potentially serious threat to monetary and financial stability in Muslim countries.

It is not clear at present how these tensions will be resolved. One Islamic central banker observed that it is perfectly possible to offer a wide range of Islamic products to meet the needs of strict Muslims while not putting the whole system on an Islamic basis. This practical view may not satisfy the more rigorous scholars or fundamentalist political movements. The BIS and the IMF might, therefore, usefully undertake some work to try to identify a way in which an Islamic monetary policy might be implemented, in case other countries are pushed in that direction. It is also important that future iterations of the Basel Capital Accord should be developed with the particular characteristics of Islamic institutions in mind from the start. Islamic finance can certainly not be treated by central banks and regulators as an optional extra any longer—to be bolted on to a conventional regime, as has been the case in the past. It is too large and serious to be ignored.

Financial Resources, Costs, and Efficiency

The financial crisis has reminded us that central banking costs money—rather a lot of money if bad decisions are made. It has also reinforced the need for central banks to have the resources to act decisively and quickly when necessary. Of course when solvency support is provided to the banking system, the ultimate guarantor must be the government, and the quality of the government's credit is the decisive element. The Icelandic case illustrated the fact that where the market doubts the tax capacity of the government, the central bank's backing for troubled banks is of little value. The quantitative easing policies implemented in 2009 also depended on government credit.

So does this imply that the central bank's own balance sheet is of no real interest—it is simply a convenient accounting device for the government, and its size and quality are irrelevant?

FINANCIAL RESOURCES

In the extreme conditions of 2008–9 it is certainly arguable that the character of central banks' balance sheets altered very rapidly, as a result of decisions taken by governments. In the fourth quarter of 2008 the assets and liabilities of both the Federal Reserve and the Bank of England more than doubled in size, demonstrating that their "normal" balance sheets were quite inadequate for the task in hand (figure 9.1). But we should not draw from this extreme event the conclusion that the central bank's balance sheet is of no interest. In normal times, and indeed in conditions of moderate market stress, the monetary authority needs the capacity to impose its will on the markets and needs to be able to act to alleviate pressures and failures without going cap in hand to the Ministry of Finance on every occasion. As we argued in chapter 6, financial capacity is a necessary component of effective independence.

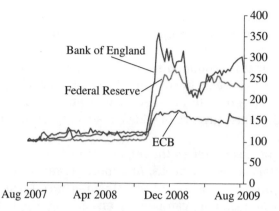

Figure 9.1. Central bank balance sheets (August 2007 = 100). Source: Federal Reserve, ECB, and Bank of England data taken from the Schumpeter Lecture at the Annual Congress of the European Economic Association in Barcelona on August 25, 2009, by Charlie Bean.

It is surprising, therefore, to find that countries have reached remarkably different conclusions about the size of balance sheet an autonomous central bank needs and about how large its own capital base needs to be. A BIS survey of forty-one banks in 2008[1] revealed that capital as a percentage of balance sheet assets ranged from almost 50%, in the case of Switzerland, to −30% in the case of Slovakia. The central banks of Chile, the Czech Republic, Israel, and Mexico also operated with negative capital. In most of these cases negative capital arose either from the financing of bank rescues or from the strengthening of the market value of their own currency liabilities, which generated losses on foreign exchange reserves. While fiscal surpluses or seigniorage income offered the prospect of restoring capital, these deficits did not cause concern, but in general terms there is evidence of a negative relationship between financial strength and inflation. The weaker the central bank's balance sheet, the more likely it is that inflation will rise.

Peter Stella of the IMF found, over a decade ago, that while central banks may not strictly need capital,[2]

> weak central bank balance sheets invariably lead to chronic losses, an abandonment of price stability as a primary policy goal, a decline in central bank operational independence, and the imposition of inefficient restrictions on the financial system in an attempt to suppress inflation.

237

He therefore argues, persuasively, that governments should ensure that their central banks are appropriately capitalized, and that they should recapitalize them when chronic losses are incurred. The BIS agree and point out that it is "common for countries with negatively capitalized central banks to have ineffective monetary and financial policies."[1] This conclusion may prove to be relevant in a number of countries in the future, as the consequences of widespread support for insolvent banks crystallize.

But this conclusion raises the important question of how much capital a monetary authority needs. In a more recent paper[3] Stella argues that "conventional measures of private enterprise financial strength— profitability and capital—can be very misleading when applied to central banks." Governors typically argue that profitability is not a useful performance indicator. The Bank of Canada puts it succinctly:[4]

> Net revenue is not a good indicator of the bank's management performance. The bank deals in financial markets to achieve policy goals, not to maximize its revenues. For this reason the level of operating expenses is a better indicator of the bank's stewardship of public resources.

The Bank of Canada has a good story to tell on the latter measure. As we shall see, many others do not.

But while profitability is not a prime goal, Stella argues that "if credibility is important for the success of monetary policy, the central banks must be financially strong." Others dispute this point. Larry Meyer, when a Fed governor, maintained that "in the abstract, a central bank with the nation's currency finance franchise does not need to hold capital."[5] But central banks do not exist only in the abstract, and in reality the Fed has increased its capital significantly in rescue years: its capital more than doubled between 2001 and 2006. That apparently unnecessary behavior, which has been matched by other central banks in developed countries, may well be justified by the need to maintain operational flexibility. To quote Stella again,[3]

> If institutional independence is desired for the central bank, it is difficult to see how this can be maintained when the central bank relies on the constant goodwill of the Treasury to undertake policy implementation.

"The goodwill of the Treasury" might, indeed, be regarded by many central bankers as an oxymoron.

This unscientific argument does not, however, point to any particular level for the bank's capital, and the BIS data show the extraordinary range of conclusions reached by different countries today. The appropriate level will depend in large part on the type of monetary policy in operation. A currency board regime will depend for its credibility on large reserves of foreign exchange. They do not need to be held in the central bank, but at least a portion of them often is. In those circumstances the balance sheet may be very large. This is very evident in the case of Hong Kong, for example.

The amount required may also be affected by the arrangements in place for the transfer of profits to the government. Where profits are transferred according to a formula, or on a quasi-automatic basis, the bank may need to hold higher reserves; where transfers are more discretionary, the institution is more easily able to accrue capital at short notice, which means that it may safely hold less as a matter of course. But, in general, a central bank should ensure that its net worth is sufficient to ensure that, in the normal course of events, it can procure its financial and operational independence from the Treasury. It is clear that in a number of countries this is not currently the case, and the number of central banks in this position may grow as the consequences of the financial crisis feed through into losses on central bank operations. There are difficult debates ahead between Treasuries and their central banks. In our view governments would be wise to recapitalize their central banks, even if the optics of doing so look politically unattractive in the short term.

OPERATING EFFICIENCY

The concept of efficiency in a central bank is slippery. To capture it we need to distinguish between the different types of output. The most important efficiency is what we might call policy efficiency: the extent to which the bank's decisions on monetary policy (or supervision, where relevant) contribute to economic welfare. There is a great deal of research bearing on this question in different countries, as we have seen, though it is not always possible to isolate the particular contribution made by monetary policy. Measuring the effectiveness of financial stability actions is far more difficult, though the cost of banking crises and the impact on the public purse provide some useful measures. Again, the impact of the actions of the central bank needs to be carefully disentangled, as financial stability is always a shared responsibility.

There is also straightforward operating efficiency, which is the subject of this chapter. How well do central banks manage the resources, both financial and human, at their disposal? The answer ought to be of more interest to policymakers and governors but is a sadly neglected area. Most aspects of the work of central banks have been subject to extensive analysis. The published papers on monetary policy are, not surprisingly, voluminous. In recent years there has been an extravagant flow of research papers devoted to the financial stability function. There is an enormous literature on accountability and transparency. But there is remarkably little work on the costs and efficiency of different central banks.

On the face of it this is a surprising omission, but, on further reflection, perhaps we should not be taken aback. While central banks have become more transparent in their decision-making processes in interest rate setting, many of them are remarkably coy about their own staffing, costs, and remuneration. The reasons are obvious. As researchers at the Swedish Central Bank have pointed out, "central banks tend to have a combination of somewhat vague objectives and soft budget constraints, whilst not being subject to market forces in the usual way."[6] Central banks are, indeed, not normally exposed to competition. There are never two central banks in one jurisdiction. Most of them are funded by top-slicing seigniorage income. No matter how high their costs may be, they are never likely to be more than a small proportion of the total income they generate. In fact this is not quite the case at the Bank of England, where the income and expenditure related to the note issue are passed through a separate account whose surplus goes directly to the government. In our view this is a better model.

This abundance of income, together perhaps with the air of mystique that has been assiduously cultivated by some central bankers, explains why they have been less subject to tough disciplines of cost efficiency than have many other parts of the public sector in recent decades. This relative insulation is not necessarily disadvantageous from an efficiency perspective. As one close observer of the central banking scene has argued: "an optimist might conclude from this that central banks are uniquely able to plan and implement systematic, long term internal change."[7] On the other hand, a pessimist might say that excessive autonomy makes central banks uniquely susceptible to inertia and staff capture. Unfortunately, it would seem that in many countries the pessimist's verdict is more accurate, and that costs are high because there is little incentive to economize. Some central banks behave like workers' cooperatives in their unwillingness to contemplate staff reductions, or even redeployment of staff to new functions.

A recent IMF paper puts the point starkly: "central banks face soft budget constraints that allow the most profitable ones to raise their expenditures."[8] An extensive cross-country analysis shows that income drives expenditure, not the other way round. We can find some further evidence to support this proposition in the work of those few central banks who have taken an interest in operating efficiencies and comparative statistics in recent years. The Swedish Riksbank staged a conference on the subject in 2003 and sought to generate some follow-up activity elsewhere, though so far without conspicuous success. The Bank of Canada has undertaken some useful analysis, as have the central banks of Denmark and New Zealand. The BIS collects useful data to allow cost comparisons of different central bank activities, though most of the material is not in the public domain, and they have promoted debate, at least among a small group of enthusiasts, about governance practices. Together these activities provide some basis, albeit a fragile and imperfect one, to identify leaders and laggards.

Across the world the differences in staffing levels in central banks are very hard to explain. One thing is abundantly clear: central banks vary hugely in their efficiency and cost-effectiveness.[4] Even within the European Union there are remarkable differences in costs and performance based on a simple measure of the number of employees per head of population. The number of staff per million inhabitants varies from 31 in the United Kingdom to 446 in Luxembourg (figure 9.2). If we exclude Luxembourg, on the grounds of its small size and relatively large financial sector, the range is from 31 in the United Kingdom to 279 in Greece. One might expect to find evidence of economies of scale, as there are clearly some substantial fixed costs—the governor's Mercedes, etc.—but it is difficult to detect any hint of such economies in the statistics in figure 9.2, or in other data.

Plotting employees against population produces a scatter diagram with no obvious logic or correlations (figure 9.3).[9] It may be argued that countries with a federal structure carry a natural cost disadvantage. The German federal system required each *Land* to maintain its own "central bank," though the numbers and the functions of these banks have been cut back since reunification and European Monetary Union. But a simple comparison of highly centralized economies like the United Kingdom and France shows that this cannot be the only factor. The Banque de France employs around six times as many people as the Bank of

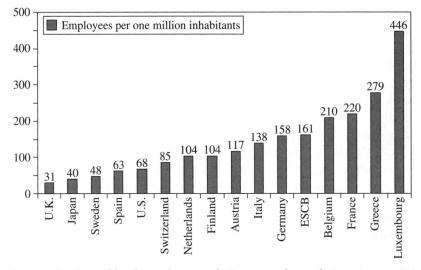

Figure 9.2. Central bank employees relative to total population. Source: BIS.

England, even though it is not now responsible for determining a specifically French monetary policy. It has other functions, of course, but these do not provide a satisfactory answer. In the case of banking supervision they are not sufficiently large employers of people to explain the difference. In the case of the maintenance of local credit registers and bureaux de change, they are functions that could be carried out just as well, and indeed almost certainly more efficiently, in the private sector. In the United Kingdom many of the traditional functions of the Bank of England—notably the provision of basic banking services to the public sector—have been contracted out, allowing the Bank to close its branch network.

When President Chirac visited London on a state visit in 1996 he called at the Bank of England. Impressed by the chandeliers and the gilded salons, he asked how many thousands of people the Bank of England employed to maintain its pomp and circumstance. When he discovered, to his embarrassment, the relativities between the Bank of England and his own central bank, he demanded cuts at home. A program to identify savings, especially in the regional branches, was launched. But the initiative was quickly halted when Banque de France staff went on strike—a vivid demonstration of the difficulty of reforming a sensitive and economically significant part of the public sector.

This demonstrates one significant reason for these differentials: the relative power of the unions in each case, and the restrictiveness or

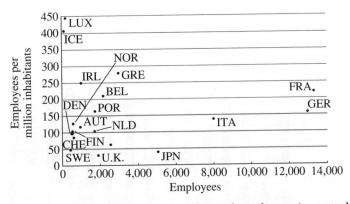

Figure 9.3. The relative and absolute numbers of employees in central banks. Source: central banks' annual accounts and IMF statistics.

otherwise of labor laws. While Bank of England staff could be transferred to the Financial Services Authority at the stroke of a ministerial pen without any disruption or compensation, and may be transferred back again under Conservative party proposals, that option is not open to many other European governments. Several attempts to restructure financial regulation in Europe have foundered on governments' inability to require central bank staff to move to another organization (and indeed by the generous pay and conditions their staff enjoy by comparison with other parts of the public sector). The same is true in the United States, where staff in the Federal Reserve System, particularly those in the New York Fed, are paid more than their counterparts in other regulatory bodies. There is a further complication in the United States, in that the regional Feds, with their semi-private-sector status, pay considerably more than the Federal Reserve Board in Washington for comparable positions.

Staff numbers are, of course, not the only drivers of cost. Basic operating efficiencies and the pay levels of individuals within the central bank are also significant. The Danish central bank has attempted a comparison of total staff costs per employee, expressed in Danish kroner, which shows considerable variation among NCBs, with Austrian costs per employee two and a half times larger than those for Ireland (figure 9.4).[10]

The ECB is an unsurprising outlier given its small complement of senior people. These costs are in part, but by no means entirely, explained by salary differentials from place to place. The Danish researchers have also calculated the staff costs per employee as a ratio of the annual average wage in manufacturing industry in each country to establish a simple measure of pay relativity. One might expect that

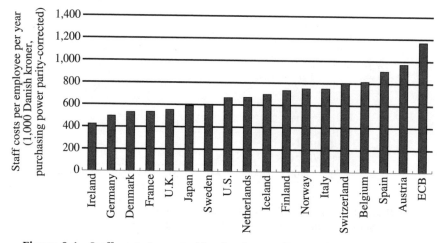

Figure 9.4. Staff costs in central banks. Source: Danmarks Nationalbank.

in places where the financial sector is very strong, and where pay in the financial sector is particularly high, as in the United Kingdom, this differential would be larger. But in fact that is not evident. Although it may be visible in the case of Switzerland, where the ratio is 2.7:1, it is not in the United Kingdom, with a ratio of 1.6:1. Remarkably, Italian central bankers, located in Rome, a city with a very small financial sector, achieve the highest differential on this measure, though when the index is corrected for purchasing power parity the central banks of Austria and Spain look to be, by some distance, the most rewarding places to work.

There are remarkable differences, too, in the pay of governors. Comparisons are not wholly straightforward, as the disclosure practices vary greatly around the world. In Italy, for example, it is impossible to discover how much the governor of the Banca d'Italia is paid. *The Economist* reported in 2003 that Antonio Fazio was paid $700,000—four times as much as Alan Greenspan at the time. That figure has not been confirmed or denied. The search function on the Banca d'Italia website does not recognize the question, "How much is the governor paid?" while in Canada it is easy to find the details of the governor's salary and expenses. The Bank of Canada reveals that it makes a profit on his trips to Basel, as the fees the BIS pays to members of its board more than offset the out-of-pocket cost. The BIS fee in the Canadian case is paid to the Bank of Canada, not to the governor personally. In many European banks these transactions are opaque. We are not told whether they receive the BIS payment personally or not. There are cultural factors at work here, evidently.

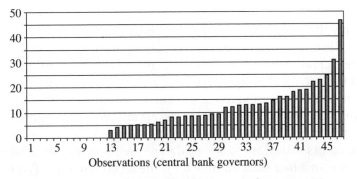

Figure 9.5. Ratio of central bank governors' remuneration to gross national income. Source: Riksbank.

Attempts have been made to assemble such public information as there is on governors' pay. The journal *Central Banking* reported in 2003 that Joseph Yam, the head of the Hong Kong Monetary Authority, topped the list with a salary of $1,120,000 a year. Nout Wellink of the Netherlands was next at $440,000 with Roth of Switzerland, King, and Duisenberg not far behind. Bill McDonough, then at the New York Fed, was on a meager $315,000, but that is still almost twice as much as Alan Greenspan was earning: $172,000.[11] Using a mixture of public and private information, Riksbank researchers have taken a slightly different tack.[12] They have plotted governors' salaries against GDP per head, producing the surprising outcome in figure 9.5.

Of those whose pay is disclosed, the range is from three times GNP per head in the case of Norway to forty-seven times in Hong Kong. These disparities are hard to rationalize, as is the continued reluctance by many banks to even disclose their governor's pay. The ECB has changed tack under Trichet and now discloses individual remuneration rather than the total salary bill for the Executive Board, which is what it did in the past. Unless others follow this example, this will be a continued source of adverse publicity for central banks. Whatever the precise technical status of the institution, in reality public money is involved.

What is the right rate for the job? This is a hard question to answer. The number, and the relativities, may rationally vary from place to place. Perhaps the best approach is to ensure that there is a process in place, with external input, that establishes appropriate benchmarks in each case. This happens in the Bank of England, using nonexecutive members of the Court, who look at pay movements elsewhere in the public and financial sectors, though Mervyn King then typically disregards the recommendation and takes a pay rise of only 2%, the inflation target. (Arguably this is not sustainable in the long run as, unless we think the governor is now substantially overpaid, he or she will not enjoy the gradual rise in real earnings of the rest of the workforce, and differentials within the Bank will be compressed, or may disappear altogether. The problem would be compounded if regulatory staff were transferred into the Bank from the FSA, whose salary levels are generally higher.) The U.S. position is an obvious outlier but reflects the practice in all senior public appointments in the United States of movements in and out of office. The problem with a hair shirt approach for the chairman of the Fed is that it constrains the salaries of more junior staff, where the glory of the office may not compensate for low remuneration. It also encourages former chairmen to compensate for the years of famine when they leave office by speaking and writing extensively on their former responsibilities, for high fees. That is not obviously helpful to the institution or its monetary policy. Former governors of the Bank of England have normally resisted that temptation.

If we look beyond staff costs at operating costs as a whole, then it would seem that the Americans and the Japanese secure the best value from their central banks. In the United States and Japan, costs per billion dollars of GDP are less then half of those in the United Kingdom, and the United Kingdom is by a distance the best performer in Europe on this measure (figure 9.6). If the euro area's central banking costs were the same, as a proportion of GDP, as those of the United States, there could be a saving of $5 billion and staff cuts of around 30,000.

But how valid are these rather blunt comparisons? Do they properly capture different operating efficiencies or are they driven by the range of functions performed by central banks, which, as we have learned, can vary greatly from place to place. It is possible to make some adjustments for these differences of function, and indeed the Danish central bank's researchers argue, surprisingly, that taking banking supervision out of the equation makes little difference to the relativities. It is, of course, also possible to benchmark banking supervision costs, whether they are incurred inside or outside the central bank. We might note that when banking supervision was transferred from the Bank of England to the Financial Services Authority around 450 staff were involved, which would only explain 5% of the difference between the Bank of England and the Banque de France. The IMF paper concludes that the provision of banking supervision services "has only a modest impact on central banks' operating expenditures, increasing them by less than 2 percent."

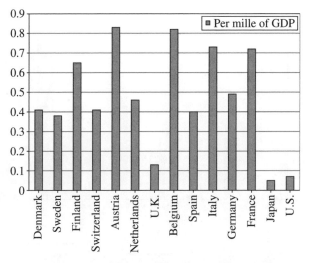

Figure 9.6. Costs of central banks per $1,000 of GDP.
Source: Danmarks Nationalbank.

Most of the rest of the differential is taken up either by the costs of maintaining a large branch network, of doubtful economic value, or by carrying out functions that could be carried out just as well, or better, by private entities. The bureau de change in the Banque de France's Avignon branch says proudly on its front door (or did in the summer of 2005) that "This bureau will close at 12 noon, or earlier if there are too many customers." That is logical, from the point of view of staff keen to be on time for their *kir vin blanc* over lunch, but it is less than ideal from a customer perspective. As the Riksbank's paper argues, "being involved in many non-core activities is also a problem in terms of managerial efficiency and competence."

Many central banks have for this reason chosen to withdraw from the provision of basic banking facilities, which can more effectively be delivered by commercial banks, and have reduced their numbers of branches and staffing levels. Most central banks have made some cuts in the numbers of domestic branches in the last decade, and at least half have implemented a significant reduction. The Bank of England closed all its regional branches in the 1990s but maintains a network of small agencies to collect economic intelligence. Nonetheless, the number of branches per million people still varies by a factor of more then 20:1 in broadly comparable countries (figure 9.7).

It is clear, therefore, that there are opportunities for substantial further cost reductions, especially in the euro area, if governments and

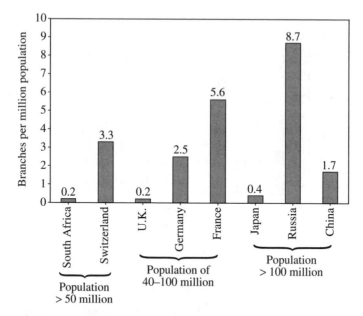

Figure 9.7. Central bank branches per million people.
Source: Danmarks Nationalbank.

central banks are motivated to achieve them. Central banks themselves have some incentive to seek economies, as the move to a low interest rate environment has reduced their income. Such economies are not, however, available without some pain and inconvenience. Where central banks are at the center of the payment system, strong staff unions have a powerful hand to play. In time it is likely that political pressure will mount. In both Germany and France efforts have been made to achieve material savings, with rather more success in the former than the latter. Politicians are increasingly asking themselves why a single financial market, which is supposed to increase competition within Europe in finance, has had so little impact on one area in which functions have been consolidated by law: the conduct of monetary policy.

But beyond this specific case of the euro area, it is hard to avoid the conclusion, which is supported by research from Sweden, Denmark, Canada, and New Zealand, that central banks have been too sheltered from the disciplines of the marketplace, and indeed from the normal disciplines on public spending. Enthusiastic individual central bank governors, like Leszek Balcerowicz at the National Bank of Poland, have made big changes with evident benefits—but such individuals are few and far between. As Karl Brunner argued[13] in a paper on what he called "the art of central banking," written in 1981:

> The protective effect of the mystique lowers public accountability of central bank behavior and offers increased opportunities to exploit monetary powers for political purposes. It also raises the likelihood of mismanagement through sheer ignorance and incompetence. This is particularly serious when we recognize that the world's central bank managers form probably a random collection hardly conducive to systematic selection of competent and knowledgeable personnel. This does not deny the intermittent occurrence of truly outstanding managers of central banks, or of managers with the wisdom and courage to adjust operations rationally to the uncertain knowledge available to us. But these managers remain an exception.

Brunner's conclusion remains valid today.

Some governors argue that monetary policy independence implies full insulation from spending disciplines to protect the integrity of interest rate decisions. But there are many examples of bodies that are independent in respect of their key functions yet still subject to some disciplines on spending and efficiency. This is typically true, for example, of the court systems in democratic countries. And it is particularly important for central banks, whose credibility as policy institutions is grounded at least in part in their successful stewardship of public resources. Unless a central bank demonstrates its commitment to wise stewardship of those resources, both financial and human, it may leave itself vulnerable to the imposition of more damaging controls, especially at a time of economic and financial stress. This conclusion is reinforced by the IMF analysis that shows that there is no clear link between central banks' operating expenditures and macrofinancial outcomes. So the more profligate institutions do not have that defense at their disposal. Indeed, Ize maintains that "higher expenditures appear to be associated with lower inflation volatility and financial volatility, but higher inflation."[8]

If central banks wish to maintain their credibility and legitimacy, they will need to pay more attention to cost efficiency in the future. As Lars Heikensten argues,[14] central banks lack competitive pressure and

> as a result we need to work hard with these issues and invite external evaluation. Cost consciousness is especially important in cases where a central bank determines its own budget, as hard won legitimacy can be quickly lost.

Heikensten argues for more empirical work on efficiency, as does Ize in his IMF paper. Some data are collected, allowing useful comparisons on a few of the basic functions of central banking, such as note circulation or payment systems management, but there are large lacunae. Central banks need to develop a methodology for assessing efficiency of the sort used in private-sector companies and, indeed, in other public-sector bodies. Too many take refuge in the argument that measurement is difficult, which is equally the case for many other public functions. The concept of the "balanced scorecard," whereby an institution uses a range of quantitative and qualitative measures to assess its performance, is little developed in the central bank world. The scorecard should cover all the important areas of the bank's work and use external comparisons where they are available. These comparisons do not need to be restricted to basic staff cost and building cost assessments. There are output measures that be can applied in other areas.

The point is not only relevant to the "nuts and bolts" functions of central banks: it covers the intellectual outputs as well. For example, the Bank of Canada has developed a database on the research output of central banks, using assessment techniques familiar to researchers in universities that measure publication volume, the quality of the outlet in which those publications appear, and the number of times the papers are cited.[15] While academics legitimately complain about formulaic use of these measures, few will deny they have some value in assessing output quality. They produce some surprising and interesting results when applied to central banks internationally. Of course a central bank can choose how much research it wishes to do. (The Bank of England, which scored relatively poorly on these measures a decade ago, has made an explicit decision to increase its research output and is moving rapidly up the table. Some euro area NCBs have done the same.) But it is unarguable that, if a bank is to devote significant resources to research, that research should be demonstrably relevant to the policymaking function, should be of high quality, and should be widely used by other researchers and decision makers. There is little assessment of central bank research along these three dimensions at present (figure 9.8). This is an area of central banking that has remained in its black box for too long.

Governments could make more of an impact. A hands-off approach to monetary policy does not mean that they should pay no attention to the costs incurred by central banks on their behalf. Their expenditure, however formally categorized by statistical offices, is effectively public spending. Ize argues that "periodic reviews of central bank expenditures

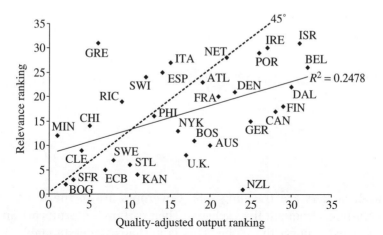

Figure 9.8. Central bank research. Source: Bank of Canada.

by governments...might be a healthy practice." We agree and consider that parliaments have shown too little interest in the subject in the past. In the euro area this role might best be performed by the Economic and Monetary Affairs Committee of the European Parliament rather than by the Council of Ministers.

Whatever the precise accountability mechanism, which will vary from country to country, there is a need to promote more sensitivity on the part of central banks about their costs. This is particularly true at a time when their performance, especially in the financial stability area, is widely viewed as having been very weak. It is likely that many will need to strengthen their staffing in the areas of market operations and financial stability assessment. Central banks around the world will undoubtedly need to strengthen their monitoring of financial market developments and to acquire new skills in areas where expertise is expensive. The price of competent risk managers in the private sector has risen and talent in that area is scarce. To recruit effectively in these new areas central banks will need to pay well, at a time when public expenditure controls will be tight as governments seek to consolidate their fiscal positions. Fortunately, the analysis above suggests that they should be able to make more than adequate savings elsewhere to create headroom for people with these new skills.

International Cooperation

Central bankers are traveling folk. Governors are in the top tiers of every airline's frequent flyer scheme. Their carbon footprints are among the heaviest around the globe. This is perhaps understandable, given the highly mobile character of international finance and the growing interconnectedness of economies and financial markets, though central bankers make far less use of videoconferencing than do private-sector bodies. We want our central bankers, at the very least, to know what is going on in other countries whose markets affect their own and, where necessary, to coordinate their interventions with those of their counterparts elsewhere. Euro area central bankers meet every couple of weeks and the Fed chairman and the ECB president probably see each other at least ten times a year. But is this extensive communication, collaboration, and cooperation as effective as it might be? Have the international networks kept pace with the progress of globalization, or have central banks found themselves overtaken by events? Some commentators argue that they have been sidelined, through an inability to understand the changing shape of international markets.[1] John Gieve, while deputy governor of the Bank of England, said as much in a BBC interview in December 2008.

Governors or their deputies meet regularly in several different contexts. First, they accompany their finance ministers to G7/G8, and now G20, meetings and to the spring and fall sessions of the IMF and World Bank. Governors' hearts do not rise on these occasions: they are cast in the role of junior partners. They carry bags and speak only when spoken to. The same is true at minister–governor meetings in Europe. Discussions on monetary policy are heavily constrained at these events, given the importance that central banks attach to protecting their domestic independence. The presence of a finance minister always has a chilling effect on conversation about monetary policy.

The second collaborative arena, and the one to which central bankers themselves attach the most importance, is in Basel, at the Bank for International Settlements. The third is a new arena that has been opened up in the last decade: the Financial Stability Forum, which was reconstituted by the London summit of April 2009 as the Financial Stability Board.[2] That presents a challenge to the traditional modus operandi of the major central banks, but also an opportunity.

As Lastra notes,[3] an analogy can be found between the role of the central bank at the national level and the role of the IMF at the international level. A central bank is typically entrusted by national law to maintain monetary stability in the domestic jurisdiction. The IMF is the international institution entrusted by international treaty to promote stability in the international monetary order. As we have explained, the cross-border dimension is one of the greatest challenges for central banks, whether in the realm of monetary stability or in the realm of financial stability.

THE INTERNATIONAL MONETARY FUND

The IMF is a useful forum for communication between central banks, especially for those countries with an executive director on its board, and central bank staff are often seconded to the IMF. The Fund issues and checks adherence to a Code of Good Practices in Monetary and Fiscal Policies, while its research department produces a series of valuable papers on central banking issues, though in recent years they have been particularly focused on arrangements in emerging-market countries, reflecting the nature of their clientele. The institution also publishes a *Global Financial Stability Report*, which, as we have seen, was rather less farsighted and penetrating than the BIS equivalent.

Typically, national delegations to the IMF include a senior central banker, often acting as alternate director. Debates within the Fund itself center largely on its own policies and support operations (which have again expanded since the crisis began) rather than on monetary policy. But the so-called Article 4 consultations on the economic conditions and policies of member countries, as well as the discussion of the Fund's *World Economic Outlook*, are often the occasion for debates and disputes on the sustainability of fiscal policy and the effectiveness of policies to promote price stability. And, where the exchange rate is a focus of IMF interest, monetary policy will certainly be part of the debate. For developed countries, however, if they are not borrowing from the Fund, these debates are not normally significant.

The spring and fall meetings, which finance ministers and governors attend, are far more important, though, again, they are more focused on international linkages and exchange rate policies than on the core business of central banking. While global imbalances, and the risks to financial stability that they posed, were certainly extensively discussed in the years before the crisis, it is apparent that no policy decisions were reached that might have corrected them. That may partly be because the IMF, like other international bodies, was slow to extend the membership of its key committees to representatives from the major developing countries that were the source of the savings glut. Nevertheless, the statements made after these meetings are examined minutely for any signs that might point to possible future changes in monetary or exchange rate policies.

The Bank for International Settlements

The BIS—the central bankers' central bank—has a curious history. There were proposals in the late nineteenth century for the creation of an international central bank based in a neutral country. Luigi Luzzatti, responding to the international liquidity crisis of 1907, argued for an institution that could promote lending between international monetary authorities on a regular basis and that would be managed by an international body.[4] He even persuaded the then U.S. Treasury secretary to convene a conference of central banks to work on his proposal.

But no agreement was reached at that time, perhaps because the Bank of England still saw itself as the world's central bank, and indeed the absence of a U.S. central bank—the Federal Reserve was created only in 1913—made it rather unlikely. There was a hiatus in the debate during World War I, but Montagu Norman resurrected the idea of an institution that could formalize cooperation between central banks in the early 1920s. He found a strong fellow advocate in Benjamin Strong of the Federal Reserve Bank of New York. Collectively, however, the Americans were not enthusiastic about an institution that they saw as bound to be dominated by Europeans and it did not loom large in their thinking. Indeed in the first volume of Allan Meltzer's magisterial history of the Federal Reserve,[5] covering the years from 1913 to 1951, the BIS is not mentioned once.

It was not until the late 1920s, and the Baden-Baden conference, that international agreement on a new institution was reached. The stimulus was the decision to restructure German reparation payments. The governments to whom the Germans were required to pay money wanted to receive it as quickly as possible. Commercial bankers could see an investment opportunity in lending to the German government, while the German government in its turn wanted to see some part of the reparations reinvested in German industry. So a scheme for the commercialization of reparation payments was devised, with long-term bonds issued by the German government and a new bank, the BIS, standing at the center of the market and acting as the trustee for the bondholders and providing independent economic and financial information to creditors. The BIS was established in Basel, partly because of Swiss neutrality at a time of continued tension in Europe and partly because Basel sat at the heart of the European rail network and was readily accessible to many governors.

The BIS opened for business on May 17, 1930, with a charter that went well beyond the narrow subject of German debt reparations. Indeed Article 3 of its statute, which remains the basis on which the bank operates, reads[6]

> The objects of the Bank are: to promote the cooperation of central banks and to provide additional facilities for international financial operations; and to act as trustee or agent in regard to international financial settlements entrusted to it under agreements with the parties concerned.

It was fortunate for the staff that these articles were broadly drawn: only a year after the BIS was founded German reparation payments were suspended, so its original narrower raison d'être disappeared.

Montagu Norman was delighted that his project had come to fruition at last, but the first two decades of the BIS's existence were disappointing. It was, of course, quickly overtaken by the great depression—a time when countries, especially the United States, turned in on themselves in economic terms. Borio and Toniolo have produced an index of the overall intensity of central bank cooperation over the last 140 years. That index suggests that the 1930s was a low point. The BIS did attempt to respond to the financial crisis. It organized syndicated loans to assist countries with particular financial difficulties, such as Austria and Hungary, in the aftermath of the default of Creditanstalt. These 1931 loans can be seen as the first multilateral action undertaken in response to a financial crisis. But the BIS actions were not up to the task. As Borio and Toniolo argue in their paper,[7]

> the BIS was too small to make a quantitative difference in international lending. Politics stood in the way of the effectiveness of its coordinating activities. Arguably, adherence to the mainstream economics of the time made the BIS a poor policy advisor even though some of its people on the ground understood the banking structure of central Europe better than banks in London and New York.

Worse was to come. International tensions during the 1930s further limited the BIS's scope for action, and it could do little more than undertake research (albeit under the powerful intellectual leadership of Per Jacobssen, who later went on to head the IMF) and promote the exchange of information. Central bankers continued to meet in Basel and to use the banking services of the BIS for some of their transactions, especially reserve management and exchange rate intervention, but there was no question of coordinated monetary policy action in Europe. (We should note, too, that the United States, at the time of the BIS's formation, declined to take up its proposed shareholding through the Federal Reserve Bank. The Americans regarded the BIS at that time as a predominantly European institution and were suspicious of the notion of any coordination of monetary or economic policy by unelected central bankers. The American stake was then held, as it was for many years, by three commercial banks led by J.P. Morgan.) World War II dented its reputation. It was argued by some that the institution was too close to the Nazi government, though the general manager at the time was a Frenchman, Pierre Quesnay, and the BIS essentially followed the instructions of the governors, including Montagu Norman. (The French managed to hold on to the general manager job until 1981.) Walter Funk, the Nazi minister of economic affairs, and a Gestapo officer called von Schroder remained on the board of the BIS throughout the war, and many believed that it effectively laundered gold seized by the Germans from the governments of occupied countries like Czechoslovakia and Belgium.

The rights and wrongs of these stories are not our concern here (see Toniolo[4] for an assessment of such facts as are available), though it is notable that they remain a matter of debate to this day, with leftist and green parties still promoting websites that see the BIS as the institution at the center of an international conspiracy of unaccountable bankers. The bank's traditional secrecy (significantly amended in recent times) provided fuel for these flames for many years.

More importantly, with its role in the coordination of the gold standard gone and with Keynes having failed to persuade the central banks that, acting in unison at the BIS, they could lower interest rates more than any of them would have done acting alone, the BIS was not seen as a major player. So when the two new Bretton Woods institutions—the IMF and the World Bank—were created in 1945, the future of the BIS was very much in question. The U.S. Administration took the view that it should be abolished, and indeed maintained that position until the end of the 1940s. With some assistance from Keynes, the central banks fought off American attempts to close down their own institution, although it would be hard to point to any notable achievements on its part in the 1940s. A new function for the BIS emerged right at the end of the decade, however, with the Marshall Plan. In the absence of foreign currency convertibility at that time in Europe, some multilateral clearing arrangements were needed to open up regional trade and the BIS acted as the clearing agent for payments between European countries in the late 1940s.[8]

By 1950 the American attitude to the BIS had changed. Szymczak, a Federal Reserve Board governor, concluded that

> from the point of view of finance the arguments for its existence are not so cogent, but as a vehicle for providing monthly gatherings of central bank governors, and others, the arguments for it are overwhelming. The BIS is perhaps the most effective vehicle of cooperation amongst central banks in the world today.

For the next twenty years the Basel Club, as it came to be known, was responsible for many innovations. The gold pool, the sterling area agreements, the IMF General Arrangements to Borrow, the G10 multilateral surveillance exercise, and the preparations for the euro all started in Basel, and the regular discussions among governors were influential in shaping the evolution of the international monetary system. In parallel, Basel was the place where European central bank governors met separately, and indeed did so until the establishment of the European Monetary Institute, the forerunner of the ECB, in the late 1990s. The BIS acted as the agent for the European Payments Union, while within the Bretton Woods currency arrangements, the BIS played a central role. Countries needed to coordinate their exchange rate policies, and to intervene frequently in the foreign exchange markets. The BIS allowed them to meet, and to intervene, discreetly, using the high-class banking and reserve management services it has always provided. Revenue from these services is still the principal source of the BIS's income.

The collapse of the Bretton Woods arrangements in 1973 posed another challenge to the BIS. The banking functions remained intact, and as relevant as before, but there was much less need for the kind of cooperative monetary policy arrangements that had been devised under Bretton Woods. So, while information exchanges and research continued as before, as Borio and Toniolo argue,[7] "the balance of BIS activity shifted towards safeguards against financial instability." At the same time, with the articulation of codes of practice in areas like payments, and indeed banking regulation, the focus of the institution's activities altered in geographical terms as well. From being essentially a European operation, it became a global one.

What turned out to be the most significant development in the longer term, though it would have been hard to identify it as such at the time, was the establishment by the G10 governors in December 1974 of the Basel Committee on Banking Supervision, which was originally known as the Committee on Banking Regulations and Supervisory Practices. The stimulus for setting up the Committee were the failures of Bankhaus Herstatt and Franklin National Bank of New York during that year. The initial idea was simply to exchange information on the condition of internationally active banks, which at the time were not required to produce consolidated accounts. The prime mover in the establishment of the new committee was the Bank of England, not surprisingly perhaps, as London, home to the international activities of many foreign banks, was particularly vulnerable to failures of institutions not supervised there. (That remains true, as the Lehman Brothers collapse in the fall of 2008 demonstrated once again.) The Committee began to build the basis for closer collaboration between the different supervisors of cross-border banks. It has throughout its life been chaired by a central banker, most recently Nout Wellinck, the president of the Dutch central bank.

Six years later the G10 governors also set up a group of experts on payment systems, which subsequently became the Committee on Payment and Settlement Systems (CPSS). In 2009 this was chaired by Bill Dudley of the New York Fed. The third key committee in Basel is the Committee on the Global Financial System (CGFS), which grew out of the Euro Currency Standing Committee (ECSC), which had been in existence since 1971. Since 2006 the CGFS has been chaired by Don Kohn of the Federal Reserve Board. Its principal role is to identify emerging risks in financial markets and to suggest responses to them. In January 2006,

Table 10.1. BIS performance criteria.[11]

Criterion	Performance
1. Meeting the initial mandate: central bank cooperation	Positive
2. Meeting new goals, e.g., Basel Accord	Positive
3. Performance as a supplier of banking services to central banks	Satisfactory (but lack of transparency)
4. Cost–benefit: value for money	Positive (but restricted)
5. Performance relative to Bretton Woods organizations: IMF and World Banks	Very positive
6. Transparency	Room for improvement

operational aspects of central bank interventions in the financial markets), all have a dotted line to the BIS secretariat under its general manager. In addition, the BIS hosts the secretariat of the Financial Stability Board, the International Association of Insurance Supervisors, and the International Association of Deposit Insurers. These last two organizations were set up by the relevant supervisors in individual countries, but they chose to collocate them at the BIS so that their small secretariats could benefit from proximity to the other staff and resources of the BIS.

How effective have these international cooperative arrangements been in the past, and how well suited are they to coping with the challenges of the future?

The first question leads to another: what might we reasonably expect from collaboration? Fratianni and Pattison suggest six performance criteria and these are set out in table 10.1.[11] Their view is that the BIS has certainly met its key objective as set out in Article 3 of its statute. It has been adaptable and has been ready to redefine its role as circumstances have changed. They evidence the shift to a greater interest in financial regulation and financial stability as proof of this adaptability. They acknowledge that it is hard to assess the BIS's performance as a service provider but note that central banks continue to use it, which suggests that the customers are broadly satisfied. They find it difficult to assess the performance of the BIS on a cost–benefit basis (a problem that applies to all central banks, as we have seen) but note that governors do spend a lot of time there. And they believe that the BIS, by comparison with the Bretton Woods institutions, has remained more tightly focused on its key objectives and less vulnerable to political interference. They do note, however, that transparency has not, in the past, been a distinguishing characteristic of the BIS, perhaps reflecting the traditional preference of its members for doing good by stealth.

An assessment carried out by the BIS's own staff[7] is, interestingly, more nuanced. They note that there are a priori reasons to think that the establishment of some neutral territory for cooperation is likely to be beneficial and that the regular meetings have generated continuity and depth that has facilitated consensus building and strong interpersonal relationships. But they say bluntly that it is "hard to find uncontroversial evidence for the usefulness of the BIS," outside the specific occasions when it has been invited to carry out clearing or trustee functions or to organize specific support operations. They do, however, also acknowledge that the institution has been resilient and has reinvented itself at several points in its history.

These look realistic long-term assessments, but the more interesting question is whether the current architecture of the BIS is adequate to guarantee it a continuing useful role in the new environment. Has not the financial crisis highlighted deficiencies in its functioning? If we accept that central banks did miss, or turn a blind eye to, growing financial imbalances, was that not a sign that their international surveillance, in which the BIS is supposed to play a central role, was inadequate? Might one not also regard the establishment of the Financial Stability Board as an implied criticism of the failings of the BIS itself? If the BIS had taken a more imaginative approach to changing financial markets it might not have been necessary to invent the FSB. Arguably, the BIS, and especially the G10 governors, did not react quickly enough to changes in the global balance of financial power.

It is also certainly arguable that the G10 governors did not exercise sufficiently strong discipline over the Basel Committee. The Committee reports to them, yet many took little interest in what it was doing. Why did Basel II take over a decade to develop and introduce? Why, when it *was* implemented, did it still have procyclical elements, to which many critics had drawn attention? If it is true that, as one senior central banker has put it to us, the radar was disconnected from the missile shield, is that not in effect a charge to be laid at the door of the governors? They have both monetary and financial stability objectives, whether statutory or self-generated.

We do not see the FSB as posing a challenge to the viability of the BIS itself. As we have explained, the original purpose of the Financial Stability Forum was to bring central banks together with finance ministries and non-central bank supervisors of various kinds—a function that could not be performed by the BIS on its own. But its introduction does represent an acknowledgment that the G10 governors failed in their oversight role, were too slow to integrate regulatory considerations into their view of the world, and were too slow to expand their membership to include important developing economies. The G10 governors will therefore no longer occupy as central a position in the global architectures and further changes to the governance and structure of the BIS are needed if it is to perform as useful a role as it could do in the future.

First, the process of "democratization" of the BIS's governance structure, and the outreach to newly important financial centers, has gone too slowly. As we pointed out in *Global Financial Regulation: The Essential Guide*,[12] before the G20 summits the Basel Committee remained seriously unbalanced, with no place on it yet for China or India, or any Islamic banking center. The first G20 summit, in November 2008, decreed that "the other major standard setting bodies should review their membership."[13] The Basel Committee membership has now been very substantially adjusted to add the countries engaged in the Financial Stability Board. But if the Committee is to retain its legitimacy, and its role at the center of banking regulation, its working practices will also need to adapt. The same is true of the board of governors of the BIS itself, which has been changed only rather slowly in the light of altered market circumstances. The case for further broadening of the board to include representatives of rapidly growing large financial markets is compelling. Similarly, the other important Basel Committees will need to be refashioned.

Second, if the BIS focus is to remain on financial stability, which seems more appropriate than ever in the light of recent events, then its structures will need to reflect the changing landscape of banking supervision and other financial regulation better. Of the membership of the Basel Committee up to 2009, around a half were non-central bank supervisors. Of the new members, in many cases a non-central bank agency is in charge. The non-central bank supervisors have, for many years, been included as full members of the Committee, but the governance of the Committee remains inappropriate. The BIS argues that it now reports to a group of central bank governors and heads of financial supervision. It is true that that group, convened at the initiative of Governor George in the teeth of opposition from some other European governors, meets once a year at Basel but it has not, in practice, been the effective oversight mechanism for the Committee. It does not, for example, choose the Committee chair, and the governors have so far insisted that it is always chaired by a central banker. Successive general managers at the BIS, alert to the possibilities for the BIS to establish a more central role for itself in financial regulation, have attempted to make changes along these lines, but they have been resisted by some of the governors on the board.

The potential prize for the BIS if it can reform its governance structures appropriately is that it could become even more central to the regulatory system than it has been hitherto. It has managed to attract the secretariats of two relatively new associations: those of insurance supervisors and deposit protection authorities. But, so far, IOSCO, which would benefit from being located alongside the Basel Committee and the International Association of Insurance Supervisors, has resisted efforts by some of its members to move its secretariat to Basel. (The International Forum of Independent Audit Regulators still needs to find a permanent home.) The argument advanced by opponents has been that the Basel Committee is too much dominated by central bankers and that securities supervisors are seen as "second class citizens." There is some truth to this observation, as when other non-central bank regulators have been invited to meetings in Basel they have typically been sent off to a restaurant in town for dinner while the governors go upstairs to their dining room. This "upstairs–downstairs" approach is not likely to build confidence among other types of regulator, which is necessary if they are to throw in their lot with the BIS. And there would be considerable advantages if they were to do so. Collocation of all the key secretariats, while not in itself a guarantee of effective collaboration, would certainly send a powerful signal to the effect, first, that regulators need to look at financial market developments in the round, as well as to the wider economic environment, and, second, that they need to work in an integrated fashion rather than on a sectoral basis that no longer reflects the reality of intermediation and credit creation.

Third, it needs to review its own committee structure and ensure that strong linkages are in place between the different groups. One central banker, sympathetic to the strengthening of the BIS, argues that the three main committees "exist in parallel universes," with too little cross-fertilization of membership, though this may as much reflect lack of adequate collaboration at national level. Looking back at the period leading up to the crisis one can identify many warnings from all these committees. The analytical record was good, with attention drawn to the risks created by narrowing risk spreads, credit creation outside the banking sector, and even to the conflicts of interest within the credit rating agencies. But these warnings were not structured so as to generate responses.

The committees tended to produce thoughtful papers, consider them at lengthy meetings, and then move on. The CGFS, whose title might suggest that it is the key observatory for financial stability, publishes too little of practical policy use in the outside world, perhaps so as to avoid challenging the strongly held views of some central bank governors. Its private analysis is excellent, but it needs to be prepared to take risks by publishing more and suggesting the practical actions that should follow on from its analyses. The BIS cannot be blamed for the Fed's unwillingness to accept that the U.S. housing market was out of control, but a closer link between the CGFS and the Basel Committee might have produced an earlier, fuller, and more persuasive argument for some form of countercyclical prudential regulation. The question of whether monetary policy should have been adapted in the face of financial imbalances could also have been addressed.

The language in the public CGFS reports has been deliberately understated, partly because the innovations that have created risks also generated some benefits. This has meant that readers have had to sift through the details of these carefully reasoned and extensively documented reports diligently in order to extract any kind of policy message, in the absence of strong or unqualified warnings in the summaries. Intelligent observers are expected to draw their own conclusions. The CGFS reports have also had a low public profile against the background of the proliferation of financial stability reviews referred to earlier. This needs to change, and there is now the opportunity for this to happen since the BIS has been put in charge of the vulnerabilities assessment process for the Financial Stability Board.

There is, perhaps, no particular logic in the construction of the BIS as the nerve center of global financial regulation. Basel is not in itself a financial center of any very great significance. And the recent record, while analytically good, demonstrates a lack of credibility and clout, and a curious lack of engagement by central banks themselves. But the BIS has the inestimable advantages of existing and of having its own financial resources, so it makes sense to give it more to do. There is a concentration of open-minded financial-market and macroeconomic expertise. The culture of the BIS, promoted strongly by general managers Crockett and Knight rather than by the governors themselves, encourages its staff to see the links between national markets, to adopt a global perspective, and, crucially, to understand the interactions between monetary policy and financial stability. The new general manager, Jaime Caruana, who was previously governor of the Bank of Spain and chairman of the Basel

Committee and who then took charge of what is effectively the financial stability area of the IMF, is well-placed to continue that tradition. It is potentially a huge asset to the global financial authorities, therefore, and one that is currently not fully exploited.

THE FINANCIAL STABILITY BOARD

The Financial Stability Forum was set up in 1999, after the Asian financial crisis of the two previous years. Its origins lay in the perception that the international financial institutions—the IMF and the World Bank—had paid less attention to the quality of financial regulation in member countries than to their monetary and fiscal policies, while regulatory gaps or shortcomings could be a source of tension and disruption, as the crisis had demonstrated. Finance ministers noted that there was no forum in which finance ministries, central banks, regulators, and the international financial institutions came together. So, following an initiative by Gordon Brown, Hans Tietmeyer, a recently retired president of the Bundesbank, was asked to produce a proposal to fill this gap. The eventual outcome was disappointing to some, in that the decision was to establish only a forum, with a small secretariat and no enforcement mechanism of its own. At the outset there were many doubts about the utility of the forum, with the Americans, in particular, skeptical of its added value. An early burst of work, with initiatives on highly leveraged institutions, offshore centers, and capital flows, was followed by a lengthy pause, during which the FSF encouraged other groups to address issues and limited itself to producing private "vulnerabilities" papers for its members, which in some senses duplicated financial stability reviews produced elsewhere, though in retrospect their forecasting record looks quite good. But the crisis of 2007–9 gave an added boost to the FSF and it was charged by the G7 finance ministers with producing a coordinated set of recommendations for responses to the crisis by international financial institutions and others. Their reports became important in setting the agenda for a wide range of actors—especially the regulatory groups that had not previously been subject to any central oversight.

In our book on global financial regulation[12] in 2008 we argued that it was time to give the FSF more explicit authority, to rename it the Financial Stability Council, to adjust its membership to include countries of growing importance like China, and to reemphasize its centrality in the management of financial stability. These changes have now been made, following the G20 summits on the credit crisis in 2008–9.

The first G20 financial summit reinforced the central position of the FSF in the global regulatory architecture. Heads of government recommended that it should expand "to a broader membership of emerging economies" and instructed the IMF to work "in close coordination" with the FSF in drawing lessons from the crisis.[13] The summit correctly distinguished between the roles of the IMF "with its focus on surveillance" and the FSF "with its focus on standard-setting." An exchange of letters between Dominique Strauss-Kahn, managing director of the IMF, and Mario Draghi, the chairman of the FSF (as it then still was), sought to clarify the respective roles of the two.

Nonetheless, in the run-up to the second London summit there was a resurgence of the turf war between them. Some governments wanted the IMF to become the central coordinator of financial regulation around the world and also to be the principal "early warning" mechanism. Others opposed these plans, on persuasive grounds. First, the IMF is not, and never has been, a financial regulator. It performs a useful quasi-enforcement function through its financial stability assessment programs, which check whether countries are complying with global standards and codes, but it does not set regulatory requirements itself and has not been a member of the key bodies that do so, like those in Basel. Second, its record in identifying risks in the run-up to the crisis was clearly inferior to that of the BIS. That may in part be because its board, made up of representatives of finance ministries and central banks from member countries, found it difficult to be overtly critical of the state of their own financial systems. But, whatever the reason, in retrospect the IMF's assessments look complacent. For example, its *Global Financial Stability Report* of April 2006, summed up the staff view as follows:[14]

> There is a growing recognition that the dispersion of credit risk by banks to a broader and more diverse group of investors, rather than warehousing such risk on their balance sheets, has helped make the banking and overall financial system more resilient. The improved resilience may be seen in fewer bank failures and more consistent credit provision. Consequently the commercial banks may be less vulnerable today to credit or economic shocks.

Influenced by these arguments, the summit conclusion was that the FSF should be given a more central role in regulation and oversight and that the IMF should concentrate on its traditional roles, which have indeed become more important in the light of the crisis. Heads of government agreed that the FSF should be renamed. It became a Board.

(Arguably, the designation as a board carries a stronger message of authority than the word council, though it still has no formal, treaty-based powers.) In addition, the membership was expanded to include all members of the G20. While we agree that the membership needed to be wider, and indeed recommended as much in 2008, it is now probably too large. There are countries in the G20, like Argentina, whose financial systems are not internationally important. The original rationale for membership of bodies like the Basel Committee and the FSF—that the members should be countries that are home to globally significant banks or financial markets—has now been lost.

It is too early to be certain about how the FSB's work will evolve, but after a lengthy period in which it relied exclusively on the work of other bodies, it now has a demanding agenda of its own, dictated by the G20 heads of government. The summits reestablished it as a decision-making body, and gave it a form of oversight of the standard-setters. The members committed themselves not only to implementing international financial standards but also to submitting themselves to peer review.

From the perspective of central banks, the original creation of the FSF brought some advantages—and posed some threats. One obvious advantage was that the central banks are well-placed to make a major contribution to its work. One potential problem was that it could devalue the BIS, which is much more closely and effectively controlled by central banks themselves. The early central bank response was astute. Andrew Crockett was advanced as the favored candidate to be the first chair of the FSF—a post he held in a personal capacity in conjunction with his role as general manager of the BIS. While central banks failed to establish this as an ex officio role (a move that was resisted by finance ministries), they nonetheless secured another of their own, Roger Ferguson, then vice chairman of the Federal Reserve Board, as his successor and then a third in the form of Mario Draghi, governor of the Banca d'Italia, who took over in 2007. The BIS also successfully offered to host the secretariat. Since there was no obvious source of funding for the FSF at the outset this offer was gratefully accepted by finance ministers. (It may seem surprising that relatively small sums of money can have an effect on the location and ownership of crucial international agencies, but it is certainly the case.) Until 2007, the FSF agenda was in effect controlled by central banks. Nonetheless, other signals have shown that they have not yet come to regard it as an entity of the highest importance. The chairman of the Fed, the president of the ECB, and the governor of the Bank of England do not attend in person, delegating the responsibility to deputies, while regulators are required to attend at chairman level, thus preserving the "class" distinctions to which central bankers attach great importance. They have remained ambivalent about its value, while at the same time trying to exert as much control over its agenda as possible. In our view, central banks would be well-advised to make a more whole-hearted commitment to the upgraded FSB. It is the one grouping that brings together all the authorities that are needed to deliver an effective global response to a global financial crisis and it is undoubtedly on an upward trajectory. Its expanded secretariat continues to sit in Basel and is a useful window for the central banks onto parts of the financial system with which they are less familiar.

The G10 governors have lost much of the authority they used to have, certainly in the regulatory arena. The FSB is the new game in town; central bankers will need to learn how to play it better.

Leadership

Central bankers often congratulate each other at their frequent international gatherings on how remarkably well they get on together by comparison, say, with their finance ministry colleagues or even their friends in the supervisory world. They believe they think the same way and have the same reactions in the face of a rather hostile, uncomprehending non-central banker world. There is a distinct sense of a central bankers' club, bound together by a common psyche that seems to transcend differences in history, functions, degrees of independence, size, or importance.

THE CENTRAL BANKER'S PSYCHE

This attitude has a number of characteristics, which can be seen to bring both advantages and handicaps. They include secrecy, a belief in quasi-papal infallibility, caution, over-analysis, and "constructive ambiguity."

Central bankers have traditionally been secretive and not averse to cultivating a sense of mystery. Of course, as bankers with customers and the associated fiduciary and custodial responsibilities, they are subject to some of the same constraints as their purely commercial colleagues. In the case of central banks, however, the customers may well be foreign governments and central banks whose foreign assets they are managing and protecting, so the secrecy of their actions and intentions must be fiercely guarded, even perhaps in relation to the central bank's own government. Although it is widely believed that the vaults under the Bank of England contain one of the largest concentrations of gold on Earth, no one outside the Bank, and very few within it, knows how much there is or to whom it belongs, other than that very little of it belongs to the U.K. government or to the Bank itself.

The ability of central banks to preserve absolute secrecy about the business of their customers, particularly foreign ones, is one of the indispensable elements in preserving trust in the financial system. They also need to be able to preserve absolute secrecy because leaks about their own intentions or those of others, whether in respect to domestic or foreign exchange operations, can be enormously damaging. The central banker must be totally immune from even the hint that loose talk might have facilitated market abuse, still less caused instability in markets.

The imperative of secrecy has been modified in recent years by the increasing belief, supported by academic work, that the deliberate management of inflation expectations can itself make for better policy outcomes. However, even the process of generating public statements for this purpose needs to remain highly disciplined and requires sticking to an unvarying public script until it is next modified. For a central banker there is a positive virtue in being repetitive to the point of tedium.

The need for secrecy about acts or intentions leads to inbuilt inhibition about saying or doing anything that gives away any information or thinking that could damage trust. This preoccupation with secrecy is intensified when the central bank is also the prudential supervisor and is in possession of information that, if made public, could have consequences not just for markets but also for individual firms.

Caution about saying anything with decisive content is, however, also driven by a desire to keep options open. This is because the world in which central banks work is extraordinarily fluid. In the ECB's description setting out the rationale for the exhaustive analysis undertaken in formulating policy[1] they describe in some detail the many factors that, taken together, generate "an environment of considerable uncertainty." The list is long and starts with the partial predictability of economic outcomes and of shocks to individual variables that themselves cannot be predicted in advance. The ECB goes on to highlight

> other, arguably more profound, forms of uncertainty which include the inevitably imperfect measurement, interpretation and understanding of the available information, of economic behaviour and, in particular, of the way in which the economy functions.

This inherent and unavoidable uncertainty naturally carries implications for the behavior of those charged, nevertheless, with making decisions about what action to take, if any at all. They also need to persuade others, including the markets, that their decisions are appropriate, without any hint or appearance of uncertainty, which of itself could have damaging consequences. There is thus a considerable premium on decisions, once made, or advice, once given, not being questioned. The promotion of a belief in infallibility arises from these driving forces.

Although it could be regarded as an exaggerated or false parallel, an analogy with the concept of infallibility in the religious context may not be entirely far-fetched. The need to support both the inspiration of total confidence and the conviction that what the central bank says is right is also manifested in the physical architecture. Central bankers often inhabit buildings that not only inspire confidence in their soundness and stability but also seek to impress the visitor, so that they are inclined to follow what is said to them with less challenge and enquiry than might otherwise be the case. Some central bankers quite openly acknowledge that their offices are stage machinery designed to increase the probability, against a background of real uncertainty, that a desired outcome will be reached more quickly. The mere prospect of a summons to the central bank can influence the frame of mind, especially if reinforced by a cup of tea in an impressive, historic parlor, as in England, or a gilded gallery, as in France.

The admission of past mistakes would therefore undermine the confidence in current decisions in a world where objective certainty is not available. So central bankers typically present a change in tack as being caused by the arrival of new information and not by the realization that mistakes were made earlier.

The desire not to appear to make mistakes at all is a considerable driver of behavior and it can lead both to caution or inaction and to endless, often unproductive, analysis. In general, central bankers are to be found at one end of the scale in arguing that something should not be done because its effects are uncertain. They are, of course, entirely right that effects will be uncertain in a world where manipulation of a central bank balance sheet is a very blunt instrument against the vast range of other factors at play. Nevertheless, a monetary policy act will certainly have consequences and can come too late, through waiting for sufficient certainty that may only itself come too late. This may be as good an explanation as any for the slow reaction, certainly in Europe, to the galloping recession of 2008 onward.

The constant search for sufficient certainty leads to demand for potentially infinite amounts of analysis, which non-central bankers may find quite disproportionate to the relative straightforwardness of the decision: quite often simply whether to change interest rates or not and, if so, by how much. Governors of the Bank of England from the private sector have been shocked at the depth, length, and intensity of analysis devoted to issues that seemed to them susceptible of straightforward, commonsense solutions.

The ECB again explains one reason for this insatiable demand for analysis:[1]

> A reflection of the uncertainties about, and the imperfect understanding of, the economy is the large range of models proposed in economics literature, which incorporate a multiplicity of views on the structure of monetary economics and the transmission mechanism of monetary policy within them. Many of these models capture important elements of reality, but none of them appears to be able to describe reality in its entirety. Therefore, any single model is necessarily incomplete... the set of plausible models is very broad... moreover, these sets of models are undergoing continuous evolution as new empirical and analytical tools are developed.

Against this background, no amount of analysis is ever quite enough, whether in relation to the modeling of economic behavior or to deciding just what kind of central bank communication behavior might be optimum.

This environment contributes to a tendency to opacity in public statements. The need to avoid saying something that could turn out to be wrong, given all the uncertainties involved, causes central bank statements to be crafted with the most intense care so that ambiguity can be seen almost as a virtue, and obscurantist drafting skills can command every bit as high a premium as analytical expertise or market knowledge.

In the LOLR context, central bankers have taken the concept a stage further by, for a time at least, holding out as a virtue something called "constructive ambiguity," and they have tended to hint at the circumstances in which support might be given in such a way as to seek to influence market behavior without giving any clarity of commitment about the central bank's own future behavior if a bank runs into trouble.

The above description of the central banker's psyche starts to point toward the mix of qualities that might be needed at senior levels, including in a monetary policy committee or in the single person of a governor. Extreme discretion and the ability to say precisely what one intends to say, neither more nor less, are mandatory qualities. So is the ability to marshal a massive array of economic and financial evidence and analyze it with a sufficiently open mind to be able to dismiss a model that seems no longer to explain the behavior of markets or the economy.

The most critical element is to know how much analysis is enough and when to reach a conclusion and act on it. Implementing a decision then requires skills of personal diplomacy so as to influence in a discreet way those who need to go along with the decision, all along preserving the trust and confidence that are vital when dealing with a financial system that at times can be exceedingly fragile.

Within the central bank as a whole, straightforward operational and management skills are also needed. Clearly not all the members of a senior management team or monetary policy committee need to be generalists possessing every one of these skills, but the team needs to cover all these bases and balance is therefore important. This will usually be achieved through informal means. The process for choosing Federal Reserve governors seems to incorporate consideration of a mix of skills, as well as the political considerations more often focused on by the press. This also involves having a team-player criterion too, not least in order to make sure that the nuts and bolts of day-to-day workings are in order. Insiders say that, in the Fed at least, there can be tensions if, say, academic economists with a major public profile turn out not to be very keen on also helping run a medium-sized business.

Sometimes the mix can work out surprisingly: for example, although William Miller was felt to fall well below the policymaking skills normally expected of a Fed chairman, the Fed nevertheless functioned extremely well internally from an organizational point of view while he was chairman. This was often not the case when more effective policymakers were in charge.

THE GOVERNORS

Clearly, however, whatever the mix of skills below the top, so much of what a central bank does is undertaken personally by the governor. In a commercial company, what is ultimately important is the final output of products to the customer. In a central bank, it is usually what the governor says and does. In spite of the trend toward collective decision making, and the introduction of oversight boards, three-quarters of those boards (seventy-four out of ninety-eight) are chaired by the governor.[2] And the growth of public communication by the central bank, and of accountability mechanisms, have all contributed to the increasing identification of the institution with its head.

Though central banks have existed since the late seventeenth century the personalities of their leaders became far more important in the twentieth century, partly because their powers grew but also because the typical length of appointment was extended. For the first two centuries of its existence most Bank of England governors served only one or two years in post—hardly long enough to make a distinctive mark on policy or practice. Many men served on the Court (Board) of the Bank for decades, but the chairmanship role typically rotated among the members. Other central banks operated in the same way.

In London that practice changed decisively with the appointment of Montagu Norman in 1920. Norman served as governor until illness forced him to retire in 1944, and his personality, and strong views, molded the institution at a crucial time.[3] In the United States, contemporaneously, Benjamin Strong was president of the New York Fed for fourteen years until his early death in 1928, and he exerted a major influence on the status and functions of the Federal Reserve System, which came into being only in 1913. At the Reichsbank in Germany Hjalmar Schacht, a complex individual with ambiguous links to Adolf Hitler and the Nazi party, established the German tradition of strong and visible central bank leadership, which was maintained in the Bundesbank in the very different circumstances of postwar economic reconstruction by Karl-Otto Pöhl, Helmut Schlesinger, and Hans Tietmeyer. In the United States, the personalities of Paul Volcker and Alan Greenspan dominated the scene for many years.

Looking across a broader range of countries, the most common term of appointment is five years, which applies to over sixty central banks at present, but twenty or so have shorter terms and over forty have terms of up to eight years. A further twenty-five appoint governors on a variable basis or with an infinite term, which in many cases may amount to the same thing. There is often a marked difference between theory and practice in the matter of appointments, and in quite a large number of countries supposedly independent governors, with a fixed term, are expected or perhaps required to leave office when the government changes. So, without careful interpretation of the context, these data on terms of appointment can be misleading. Between a quarter and a third of governors leave office before the end of their term. In the postwar era the average tenure of governors of the Banca d'Italia is about eleven years, while in Argentina it is only just over twelve months.

But whatever the formal position, the dominance of the governor is strong almost everywhere. This growing personalization of the function makes it important to know who these Titans are. From whence do they spring?

One obvious point is that these Titans are nearly always men. There is little sign in the world of central banking of the move toward greater balance that is being seen in other parts of the economy and the public sector. Of the 160 or so governors (or chairmen/presidents) in 2008 only

10 were women (and that figure includes the governors of the Pakistani and Malaysian central banks) and there are few indications among the rising stars in the roles below governor that the proportion will increase substantially in the near future. It is true that banking, overall, remains a male-dominated profession, and the same is true of economics. Central banks reflect the environments in which they work, but governments could nonetheless make more effort to achieve greater diversity.

The first chairman of the Fed was Charles Hamlin, a Boston lawyer who at the time was an assistant secretary in the U.S. Treasury. The *Biographical Dictionary of the Board of Governors of the Federal Reserve System* describes him as organized and conciliatory, but also as a "weak leader" who was too responsive to the requests of the Treasury secretary.[4] His deputy, Frederic Delano, was a railway boss from Chicago; his successor, Harding, was a Birmingham (Alabama) banker. There was an economist on the first board, well before the Bank of England considered importing such an exotic creature, in the form of Adolph Miller, but he did not become chairman. The dominant personality in the early years of the system was Benjamin Strong, the first head of the New York Fed (with the title at that time of "governor" rather than the current "president").[5] Meltzer characterizes him as

> a sophisticated banker, with little formal training, who had gained enough understanding of the functioning of the domestic and international payments mechanisms to be ahead of most of his contemporaries.... His prewar policies can be described succinctly as an attempt to recreate Lombard Street on Wall Street, with the Federal Reserve System, particularly the New York bank, playing the role of the Bank of England. He regarded the twelve reserve banks as eleven too many. The appropriate number was one.

His relationship with Montagu Norman was crucial. They sustained close personal ties, largely through the medium of regular transatlantic letters. Like Strong, Norman was a banker first and foremost. Indeed his formal education was modest. He went from Eton to Trinity College, Cambridge to read history, but declined to follow the syllabus recommended by his tutor, read a few books on comparative religion, a subject that interested him at the time, and left after a few months without taking a degree. The third colossus of the interwar years, Schacht, was an economist by formation, though also a politician—a combination more common in Germany even today than it is in the United States, the United Kingdom, or France.[6] German central bankers still have a political affiliation.

The contrast with today is striking. Of the last five chairmen of the Federal Reserve Board, four—Arthur Burns, Paul Volcker, Alan Greenspan, and Ben Bernanke—have been economists, though both Volcker and Greenspan of a more practical, policy-oriented kind than Burns or Bernanke. During this period only Miller, not a conspicuous success overall and who lasted only fifteen months before being translated to the Treasury, was a banker. Successive U.S. presidents have reached the view that they should appoint economists, which may be especially appropriate where the bank exercises independence in interest rate determination. While the Fed has a role in financial stability and in banking supervision, indeed one that has expanded as a result of the credit crisis, other agencies carry out most of the frontline institutional supervision in the United States—and would do all of it if the Paulson plan, or something like it, were implemented. Also, the New York Fed, whose presidents are formally appointed by market representatives, is the Federal Reserve System's lead participant in financial market oversight.

For two decades Alan Greenspan bestrode the financial world like a colossus. But Bernanke was as well-placed as anyone to take up the challenge of succeeding him. His academic interests were wholly apt; the *New York Times* dubbed him the man who "knew more about central banking than any economist alive." He had also served as a Fed governor for three years and been chairman of the President's Council of Economic Advisers. Furthermore, he is the leading authority on the great depression of the 1930s. In an oration on Milton Friedman's ninetieth birthday, speaking for the Fed, he said, "You're right, we did it. We're very sorry. But, thanks to you, we won't do it again." This background well explains the aggressive easing he engineered in response to the credit crisis beginning in the summer of 2007.

As an academic he is also associated with two other propositions. First, he believes that monetary policy should not seek to respond to asset price bubbles. We discuss the merits of that argument elsewhere. Second, he had argued, before he took up office at the Fed, that inflation targeting is the preferred monetary regime—preferred mainly because of its impact on expectations. In office, while the Fed's communications have begun to emphasize a longer horizon, he has not made the change that some might have expected in the light of his previously declared views. He knows that it would be hard to explain a shift, which would appear to downgrade the Fed's employment objective, during a downturn.

His financial markets experience is more limited, and his views in this field less firmly formed. In 2006 he offered conventional Fed views on the importance of carrying out (some) banking supervision but he now seems attracted to a system that would give the Fed a broader financial stability objective at the expense of its hands-on role.

In private conversation he can give the impression of shyness. Small talk is not his forte. He has the alarming habit of pausing before he answers a difficult question. Has he misheard? Is the question itself absurd? But the reason for the pause is that, unlike many of us, he tends to think before he speaks. It is usually worth the wait. This character-istic, allied to natural intellectual curiosity, has led him to a different method of managing the FOMC. He has listened to colleagues more and developed a more collegial style, rather than giving an early indication of his own views, as his predecessor did.

Some have argued that at a time of crisis a more decisive and com-manding approach would have paid dividends. Others point to his abil-ity to hold the Committee together at a difficult time. His approach is also arguably more in line with the sprit of the legislation. He has not insisted on unanimity where there were genuine differences of view. But if we are only now beginning to see Greenspan's regime in proper per-spective, it is too soon to produce a considered verdict on Bernanke's management style or his economic record. In the early phases of the cri-sis Tim Geithner of the New York Fed, subsequently President Obama's Treasury secretary, was the crisis manager, but Bernanke remained in the lead on monetary policy. In 2009 he launched an initiative to explain the Fed's policies to a wider constituency, with public meetings and a far broader range of communications than in the past. Perhaps this new, more open approach, in the face of pressure from some in Congress for more formal accountability mechanisms for the Fed, helped to persuade President Obama to nominate him for a second term, which he did in August 2009.

At the Bank of England, which was the United Kingdom's exclusive banking supervisor until 1997 but is not any longer, practice has been different. Following Montagu Norman most governors were merchant bankers. Leslie O'Brien was the first Bank "lifer," Gordon Richardson was again a merchant banker (though with a legal background too), and Robin Leigh-Pemberton was the first commercial banker to be appointed. None would have considered themselves to be professional economists and none had any formal economic training. In the tradition of British pub-lic service they prided themselves on having "a good mind" and, in the latter two cases, the ability to take a brief. Eddie George, appointed in 1993, spent forty-two years in the Bank and came to have an unrivaled understanding of the dynamics of the U.K. economy and financial system. His initial academic formation was a combination of economics and Russian.

His successor Mervyn King's career has been a vivid illustration of the rise of the academic governor. Until his early forties he was pursuing a conventional, if brilliant, academic career, most prominently as a professor of economics at the London School of Economics, where he founded the School's Financial Markets Group. Brought into the Bank of England initially as a nonexecutive director, he became full-time chief economist in 1991.

He was in that role when the central pillar of the then Conservative government's economic policy, ERM membership, collapsed in September 1992 and he played a decisive role in the redefinition of policy that ensued. King was the strongest advocate within the official sector of a regime built on an inflation target and he also actively influenced the design of the new regime of Bank independence that the Labour government introduced in 1997.

King had long been in favor of hiving off responsibility for banking supervision, so the establishment of the FSA to handle most of the Bank's market oversight responsibilities delighted King, and the creation of a new Deputy Governor for Monetary Policy gave him an ideal new role in the Bank. It also made him the obvious choice to succeed Eddie George as governor in 2003.

King is not, perhaps, a natural manager. Critics accuse him of disregarding the capabilities of people whom he regards as not "good economists." He was not a natural public performer, either, but has become very adept at the presentation of policy at his *Inflation Report* press conferences in particular. He has assiduously cultivated the economic commentators in the media and has been careful to treat the Treasury Committee with respect. Over time he has developed a very artful, and often very witty, turn of phrase, which has softened his owlish image.

Internationally, he is less widely appreciated. In Washington he is seen as too inclined to dismiss others' views and to plough an idiosyncratic furrow on important issues like the reform of the IMF. Initially a reluctant traveler to Basel he now makes some effort to pull his weight there, but he makes only rare appearances at the ECB in Frankfurt, finding the agendas of the General Council, on which he sits, resistible. European colleagues notice his absence, nonetheless, and also know that he has always been hostile to British membership of the single currency. This aloofness was seen as particularly unfortunate in the early phase of the credit crisis, given the interconnectedness of Europe's financial markets.

His reluctance to support Northern Rock, and his insistence on the moral hazard created by central bank liquidity provision, led to much criticism in the press, the City, and in Parliament. Decisions he had made earlier to downplay the Bank of England's financial stability role and to reduce his own interactions with banks were seen as having damaged the Bank's understanding of markets.

Criticism of his rigorous and single-minded approach to the delivery of the inflation target also resurfaced in the fall of 2008. The Bank seemed slow to appreciate the speed with which the recession struck the British economy. An out-of-phase 50 basis point cut in early October followed by a sudden 150 basis point reduction at the next meeting demonstrated that the MPC had fallen behind the curve. But he had not been alone in continuing to focus on the inflationary risks of high oil and commodity prices during the summer. And as the crisis developed, King proved able to adopt unconventional approaches as necessary. This growing flexibility contributed to some recovery in his personal stock. He discovered a new interest in financial regulation and, having strongly advocated the transfer of responsibility for banking supervision from the Bank to the FSA in 1997, by the summer of 2009 he was arguing for more powers for the Bank to intervene in the banking system—a position that aligned him with evolving thinking in the Conservative party.

Elsewhere in Europe, and outside it, the practice has varied. At the Bundesbank Hans Tietmeyer was an economist, but he was also a politician of sorts. His successor, Ernst Welteke, was first and foremost a politician. He left under a cloud after a hospitality scandal. Carlo Ciampi, the most distinguished governor of the Banca d'Italia in recent decades, was educated in Italian literature. Wim Duisenberg, governor of De Nederlandsche Bank and first president of the ECB, was an IMF economist who also became a finance minister in his earlier life, while his successor Jean-Claude Trichet might best be described as a technocrat in the French tradition. Before joining the French Treasury and moving on to be governor of the Banque de France he was educated at the École des Mines, Sciences Po, and the École Nationale d'Administration, though it is not clear at which of those seats of learning he acquired his love of poetry.

It would be idle to pretend that Trichet has achieved Greenspan's global profile, but at the end of 2007 the *Financial Times* chose him as their Person of the Year for his decisive role in responding to the credit crisis. The presidency of the ECB is the job for which his whole career has been carefully designed. The French have long adopted a strategic approach to securing top positions in international finance.

At the ECB he has been far more popular outside France than within it. Indeed in Paris it is a fashionable cross-party sport to attack him. If the euro rises, hurting French exports, it is his fault. If interest rates rise, he is deliberately strangling the economy. Both Chirac and Sarkozy have been free with their public advice to him and have sometimes descended to overt abuse. His cause was not helped when he declared to the European Parliament, "I am not a Frenchman." The sentiment, that he had to be seen to act in the interests of Europe as a whole, might have been understood—the fact that he said it in English was not.

Trichet accepts the brickbats with good grace. His critics are maddened by his quiet modesty, his unfailing, rather old-fashioned courtesy, and his refusal to be provoked. When attacked he has a well-developed instinct for survival, retreating into central bank speak, with ritual intonations of the litany of price stability, which governors learn at their mothers' knees.

He is a highly cultured man, and very Parisian—most at home in the apartment in the Palais Royal that comes with the Banque de France job. It is hard to imagine him outside the Boulevard Peripherique, though he ran the ECB's market operations during the crisis of 2007 by Blackberry from St. Malo.

He never, though, takes refuge in the comforting critique of New York and London that comes easily to many in central banks and regulatory authorities in continental Europe. We asked Trichet in the summer of 2008 whether the crisis had, in his view, revealed fundamental weaknesses in the liberalized markets across the English Channel and the Atlantic. His reply was characteristically oblique, but revealing:

> When I joined the Banque de France in 1993 I decided to spend some time in the archives. The Bank is proud of its history and I thought it wise to show some respect for its traditions. As I read through the history of the early years, in the 1820s, I was struck by the number of references to the lack of prudence of the Bank of England. The French were regularly lending gold to London, to help its London counterpart out of a short-term problem. This gave successive governors great satisfaction. Not for them the booms and busts of London.

We wondered where this digression would lead. Was this a worrying "senior moment" on the part of a man who held the financial fortunes of 400 million Europeans in the palm of his hand?

We should not have been concerned:

> At no time did it occur to the Banque de France that Britain was in the throes of an industrial revolution, its economy leaping suddenly ahead of France by a couple of generations. It was not a surprise that the financial system was under strain. They were the problems of economic success, not of failure. Since then, I have been reluctant to write off the inventiveness of American and British capital markets.

The euro, and the ECB, are fortunate to have him in charge at a formative stage for EMU. His calmness under fire in the very trying conditions of 2007–9 was a source of strength for the ECB.

If we look more broadly at the G10 governors, the trend toward the economics profession is clear. Beth Simmons of Harvard has analyzed their backgrounds over the previous fifteen years.[7] She notes a marked increase in the homogeneity of their backgrounds over this relatively short period, but the most interesting phenomenon is that the increase in economic literacy has been accompanied by a sharp decline in the number of governors with a background in industry or private finance. Twenty years ago a third of governors had experience in a private-sector firm: usually a bank. Now none of them have worked in banks. Did that prove to be a disadvantage in the credit crisis? It is arguable that it did—and the central banks were both taken by surprise and found it difficult to understand the dynamics of the debt markets whose malfunctions they were trying to correct.

Simmons sees only benefits arising from this change. An economist herself, she believes the sharp and persistent rise in academic experience disposes the governors to take a cooperative approach to monetary and financial problems. As she puts it, "G10 governors are increasingly likely to be academics, interested in learning and persuasion; possibly more open than others to the power of evidence and reasoned argument." To anyone who has been involved in academic management, this seems a remarkably starry-eyed view of the professoriate—though not as congenitally disputatious as historians, economists are not always famous for their open-mindedness to divergent views.

Christopher Adolph has taken a slightly different approach to measuring changes in the backgrounds of leading central bankers.[8] His sample is much broader and his time period begins a little earlier. Covering twenty developed countries over a fifty-year period, from 1950 to 2000, he plots the career profiles of 600 monetary policy decision makers, including governors and their deputies, together with members of monetary policy boards and committees. Once again, he notes the steady growth in economics as a preparation for these roles. But with this sample the striking points are first the waning and then the waxing of private financial-sector experience in their backgrounds, and second the decline in the proportion of their careers spent elsewhere in the public sector. As a proportion of the total career experience of central bankers, the financial sector accounted for 17% in the early 1950s; the figure fell to 7% in the 1970s but is now back at around 17%. Public-sector experience rapidly receded after 1980, with no sign of resurgence.

So while governors themselves are now far more frequently economists than they were before, they have been balanced to some extent, on boards and committees, with financial-sector people. The extent to which these outsiders offset the economics bias is moot, in our view. Indeed, where outsiders have decisive roles, such as on the MPC in London, they are invariably economists. The bankers and industrialists on the Court (as the board of the Bank of England is called) have no material influence on policy. Following the post-crisis legislative changes there will be fewer of them. That will make no difference to the way the Bank runs.

Should we regard this growing dominance of the economics profession as an unalloyed benefit: a Pareto-optimal move, if we can put it that way?

The primacy of the monetary policy responsibility of a central bank today does argue that economic competence is now the key requirement for a successful governor, even though some amateurs have done well. As Eddie George was wont to say, you do not have to be an academic economist to work in a central bank but "economics is the language of the Bank of England." However, an exclusive focus on the macroeconomy and on retail price inflation can be dangerous. The credit crisis showed that a central bank must be more than a monetary policy institute or the economics department of a university. To forget that a central bank is a bank can be a huge mistake.

Governors, therefore, do need an understanding of national and global financial markets, both in a technical sense and also in terms of the psychology of market participants. They need to understand the changing nature of financial intermediation and credit creation. Governors who emerge from within the institution are likely to have acquired that knowledge, as long as they have been rotated through different departments of the Bank. This may argue for a bias toward internal appointments, or at least for a career structure that develops internal candidates for the most senior jobs.

But three other characteristics are important. We have argued that independence for the central bank in its monetary policy task is crucial.

Independence is not simply a matter of statute but is also one of personality. A governor with no record of achievement outside the central bank may find it harder to assert himself or herself in a confrontation with a Treasury or finance minister, facing an imminent election, pressing him or her to loosen policy.

Second, the task of explaining and defending policy decisions is now increasingly important, both in the formal setting of Congress or Parliament and in public forums and the media. Alan Greenspan gave no media interviews during his time at the Federal Reserve but his lectures were famously pedagogical, and his Humphrey–Hawkins testimonies before Congress were carefully crafted and highly persuasive—perhaps even more persuasive than the content justified. Mervyn King, similarly, puts great effort into his presentations of the *Inflation Report* and into his appearances before the Treasury Committee. His repertoire of intellectual jokes has given him a cult following in parts of the British media. Wim Duisenberg, by contrast, was unpersuasive in public. Trichet has greatly improved the ECB's performance in that respect.

The third key area is chairmanship, especially where interest rate decisions are made collectively. Good chairmanship is an art not a science, but the structure of meetings can help to ensure that all members have the opportunity to put their points of view. In that respect the MPC procedures look preferable to those in operation at the Fed or the ECB. The Fed is vulnerable to the whims of an autocratic chairman—and succumbed for a period early in this century. The ECB is opaque, and vulnerable to management by an inner clique, if not an individual. But in each case the way the system operates owes as much to the character and skills of the governor as it does to the black letter of the legislation.

Today's ideal governor is therefore a first-rank macroeconomist who also understands financial markets, albeit one open-minded enough to listen to dissenting views, who has experience of chairing meetings, and who has a stubborn streak, yet also a silver tongue. Such individuals are hard to find.

An Agenda for Change

The events of the recent past have brought a sharp reminder of just how much a well-functioning economy is dependent on a stable financial infrastructure and of just how delicate and fragile the financial infrastructure can be. Its stability depends on the preservation of confidence in its different elements, in the internal and external value of the currency, and in the reliability of payment and settlement mechanisms, and on the ability of financial firms to provide, without disruption, intermediation between borrowers and lenders at costs that reasonably reflect risk.

The authorities, whether central banks or other parts of government, need to have regard to all these requirements simultaneously and continuously. This has not always been the case, though, as a consequence of excessive focus on one or other objective at the expense of the others.

The tools available to a central bank are inherently limited yet several objectives ideally need to be fulfilled. There has therefore been a tendency to shift objectives quite abruptly to focus on addressing whatever was perceived to be the most recent shortcoming. To take just one example, over the last three decades there have been shifts of focus in the United Kingdom from credit to money, then to the exchange rate, then to consumer price inflation, and then, in 2009, back to money and credit again.

Pursuit of a single philosophy, while apparently effective for a period, may mean that other critical aspects of the system will be neglected. The achievement of apparent stability in some subset of prices at the same time as credit growth has far outstripped long-term debt-servicing capacity may not be an optimal or even least-worst outcome.

Monetary policymakers need to recall that monetary policy only takes effect through the financial system and that without well-functioning financial markets and intermediaries neither price- nor quantity-driven policies can achieve predictable results. Equally, supervisory policy needs to remember that financial activity is affected by what is happening in the economy. Supervisors need explicitly to have regard to the way the economic environment affects the behavior of financial intermediaries and their customers and be ready to adjust the supervisory regime in the light of the changing risks.

Our underlying theme has been that the credit crisis revealed flaws in the way central banks have been operating. They need to rebalance, and return to their roots as banks operating within and through the financial system. Some had become close to being Monetary Policy Institutes, led and staffed by economic technocrats, with a narrow focus on retail price inflation and too little attention to financial markets. They had also lost sight of the global context and its impact on their own markets—as some have explicitly acknowledged. They paid little attention to credit creation, or the indebtedness that is its counterpart, and disregarded the importance of asset price moves.

This narrowing of focus left on one side the tools central banks have used in the past to influence conditions in financial institutions and markets. As the crisis began they were either unavailable or were rusty through lack of use. So even those who recognized the risks to financial stability lacked the ability to respond effectively.

We advocate a range of reforms that we believe will help to refurbish and reinforce central banking for the twenty-first century. The combination of changes required will be different from country to country, as the starting points differ. Many are taking steps already: strengthening their staffing, enhancing their understanding of banks' balance sheets and of nontraditional credit markets, and in some cases acquiring new powers. So we are taking aim at a moving target. But here we summarize what we see as the principal conclusions to emerge from the analysis above and from recent academic work. Adrian and Shin of Princeton University put our central point succinctly: "We conclude... that the time is now ripe to redress the balance and bring financial institutions back into the heart of monetary economics."[1] Charlie Bean of the Bank of England now agrees: "we need to put credit back into macroeconomics in a meaningful way."[2]

STRUCTURE AND STATUS

Where monetary policy is conducted through domestic instruments (rather than an exchange rate link), the arguments for central bank independence in setting interest rates and managing its own balance sheet remain strong. Governments will always be tempted to take risks with inflation for short-term advantage. De facto independence is as important as it is de jure. It means little if governors are routinely removed after elections, or if they must have a particular political affiliation, or if the government manages interest rate policy behind the scenes. So the arrangements for the appointment of governors and other senior decision makers are important. We argue for terms longer than the political cycle. The arrangements for appointments should meet best practices elsewhere in the public sector, with advertisement and transparent processes. Reappointment may be possible, but these reappointments should not be indefinite, to avoid the "overmighty citizen" problem.

But in democratic societies independence needs to be buttressed by robust accountability procedures, to ensure that the central bank explains itself well and conducts effective stewardship of its resources. There is therefore a key role for an oversight board: to act as a buffer between government and the governor. The board should take responsibility for financial independence, staffing, and efficiency—a neglected area in central banks—but it cannot substitute for direct accountability to the legislature for monetary policy. Accountability is enhanced where the bank's objectives and performance criteria are clearly set out in legislation.

MONETARY POLICY

Despite the risks we describe, and the weaknesses revealed by the crisis, some form of inflation targeting still looks to be the most robust policy framework for a large developed economy. Confidence in the internal value of the currency is a sine qua non for a well-functioning economy, and we see a case for more emerging markets to move in that direction too. We prefer a regime in which the target is set by the government, with the central bank responsible for implementation. That puts accountability in the right places and clarifies the public debate. But the target needs to be set in the context of other objectives, not just for economic growth but also for financial stability, so that both may be seen as legitimate grounds for deviation from the target for a period. Doing so will give the central bank more flexibility to respond rapidly to deteriorating economic conditions or to the buildup of imbalances within the financial system. Of course, the potential risk to inflationary expectations of divergence from longer-term targets must be carefully managed, but it is crucial that the monetary authority has the flexibility to adjust the target horizon to allow it to respond to shocks to the price level—on both the upside and the downside. It is important, finally, that the target is symmetrical, with a range above and below the central objective. This all points to the need for further refinement of inflation-targeting regimes.

Where inflation targets are not yet possible, perhaps because the authorities lack the necessary credibility, a currency bloc may be attractive, or an exchange rate target related to a trade-weighted basket of currencies.

Especially at times of crisis, monetary policy, fiscal policy, and financial-sector policies interact. There is therefore a need for a clear decision-making framework within which the necessary coordination can take place. Where the monetary and regulatory bodies are separate, some form of tripartite coordination is required. The U.K. tripartite paradigm is an attempt to create an institutional framework that reflects the interdependence between the monetary, fiscal, and supervisory functions and it has been widely adopted elsewhere. This approach is now more effectively in place globally, through the Financial Stability Board. Regional and domestic arrangements should work in parallel. In the EU, while the European Systemic Risk Council could be a useful step forward, more still needs to be done to promote coordination between the monetary, regulatory, and fiscal authorities.

It is quite reasonable, in our view, for central bankers to offer opinions, both privately and, in the limit, publicly, on regulatory policy and indeed on fiscal policy. The bank also needs systematic input to debt-management policy, even if that is carried out by a separate agency.

Committee decision making looks to generate superior monetary policy decisions, but the committee needs to be collegial, not autocratically run. Appointments to it need to be made in an open and transparent manner. Published minutes and individual votes provide an effective guarantee of collegiality. But in a federal system, where individuals represent geographical areas and may therefore be vulnerable to pressure from regional interests, the drawbacks may outweigh the advantages. In those circumstances a system of independent audit of the committee's procedures and practices may be a useful check.

Inflation-targeting regimes need, however, to take more account of the external position, which may reveal the buildup of imbalances the unwinding of which may threaten stability—and they need to take more account of credit growth and asset prices too. Housing costs need to be incorporated into the target index where they are not already. We explain that internal imbalances can be built into the monetary policy framework and into an assessment of financial stability.

FINANCIAL STABILITY

In recent years monetary and financial stability have drifted apart in ways that make them seem independent of each other. The dichotomy has been used as a basis for institutional organization, which is a mistake, as it suggests that the two stabilities can be separately assessed and that the tools used to implement one are not related to the other. There has been a further imbalance in that central banks have typically had a formal statutory responsibility for monetary stability but only an informal "oversight" of financial stability.

A statutory duty, as has now been introduced in the United Kingdom, and the recent restatement in the United States of the responsibilities of the Federal Reserve in both monetary and financial stability should help to correct that imbalance. But there is continued uncertainty about what such a duty might mean and what tools are available to deliver it: a central bank with two potentially conflicting, albeit interdependent, statutory objectives and only one tool—its own balance sheet—available to deliver them can sometimes find itself in an uncomfortable position.

We set out in chapter 3 what we see as the minimum key components of a comprehensive financial stability function in a modern central bank and the way in which that function should interact with other parts of the institution and with other authorities with relevant powers.

We argue in particular that there is an urgent need for better metrics of financial stability and for far better understanding of the interlinkage with monetary policy. As the ECB has suggested, this area needs the kind of sustained intellectual investment, on a global scale, that has helped to improve the conduct of monetary policy. Ideas like a "stress index," advocated by the Swiss National Bank, look promising, but these are at an early stage of development. Deeper links with academic institutions, which are patchy at present, would help to push this work forward. Stronger staffing in the financial stability area will be needed too. Central banks will need even closer links with financial institutions and markets, and not simply with banks. Stronger international networks will be required, and ones that go beyond the G10 club that has been the mainstay for too long. The central banks will need a greater willingness to assert their views and question market or even social assumptions. Bland financial stability reviews that report that all is for the best in the best of all possible worlds are worse than useless. Central banks will need to take more risks themselves, in drawing attention to emerging risks, imbalances, and asset price bubbles, and they will need to provoke debate on how these should be addressed. FSRs should always include recommendations, whether for firms, regulators, the monetary authority itself, or the government. Where the central bank and the regulator are separate, as they often are, they should produce a joint FSR. Regulators should follow up these recommendations with systemically significant firms.

If the "financial stability" role is to be meaningful, central banks need to be prepared to use interest rates to influence credit growth when appropriate, but they may also need another tool at their disposal. The most promising candidate is the so-called macroprudential mechanism: that is, adjusting prudential requirements for macro reasons. This could be done where overall market conditions appear to be pointing to an enhanced risk of a disorderly unwinding of imbalances or a sharp asset price adjustment. There remain many unresolved issues as to how such add-ons to existing capital ratios should be devised. The mechanisms need to be developed carefully at a global level, involving central banks and supervisors jointly, though they will need to be implemented differentially market by market. It is to be hoped that this work is done more expeditiously than was the development of Basel II, which took over a decade from conception to delivery.

But it is important to recognize that this mechanism, which is being presented as an aspect of prudential regulation, will have an impact on the economy as a whole. If banks are required to hold more capital, their cost of lending will rise and effective interest rates for some, perhaps all, borrowers will increase. So this is in effect the use of a form of monetary policy to influence credit conditions. It needs to be considered alongside the alternative of an across-the-board increase in interest rates.

There is a danger that this debate focuses on regulatory structure, as it has done in both the United States and the United Kingdom. In the former the need for reform is obvious, as by international standards the pre-crisis U.S. system was balkanized and hopelessly complex. A regulatory system built around the different legal forms firms take does not match the needs of financial markets in the twenty-first century. But elsewhere it is impossible to draw firm structural conclusions from the performance of different countries in the crisis. Some regulatory systems built around central banks performed well; some performed very badly indeed.

In our view central banks do not need to be hands-on supervisors, but equally there is no conclusive case against their being so. The crisis has, however, emphasized the advantages of integrated supervision, particularly in relation to capital, with one institution overseeing the prudential soundness of the whole of the financial sector—a role that many central banks are reluctant to take on, with good reason. They are concerned about the distraction from monetary policy. Others may reasonably worry about excessive concentration of power. As we have seen, there is also some evidence that nonsupervisory central banks have been more candid in their market assessments, though the arguments are not decisive in either direction. But central banks that are not frontline regulators do need closer links with those regulators in their jurisdictions than they have had in some countries in the past, with a defined structure for joint decision making and a planned program of cross-secondments. They should also maintain a direct relationship with systemic firms, at least, for liquidity management purposes and to understand significant changes in financial intermediation that may have implications for the monetary policy transmission mechanism and for emerging risks to financial stability. This may create some overlap in areas where the statutory supervisor is not the central bank but that is a price worth paying—and it can be managed, as it already is in some jurisdictions.

They also need stronger institutionalized links with their finance ministries. In some circumstances, for example when the central bank engages in quantitative easing, the respective responsibilities overlap and, of course, fiscal policy and monetary policy both affect the economy more widely as well as just the banking system. The challenge will be, as John Gieve has said, "to preserve the advantages of nonpolitical decision making in central banking and regulation"[3] while strengthening policy coordination.

MARKET OPERATIONS AND FINANCIAL INFRASTRUCTURE

The management of its own balance sheet is the core substantive tool at the central bank's disposal. All the major central banks found their techniques for injecting liquidity at times of stress wanting in a crisis. Some have already implemented reforms that should reduce the stigma effect of accepting official liquidity support. (After the events of the last two years that stigma risk will in fact be reduced for some time: all banks have been obliged to accept assistance of some kind.) But satisfactory and enduring arrangements need to be put in place in all jurisdictions.

It is likely that, for some time to come, central banks will have to continue to accept a far wider range of collateral for liquidity management purposes than they did in the past. But they should withdraw as soon as possible from the role of central counterparty to the banking system, and still more rapidly from acting as commercial lenders or market-makers of last resort.

The crisis has also demonstrated the importance of a strong balance sheet. Countries should ensure that their monetary authorities are strong enough to act decisively, with the confidence of their counterparties. Relying on the finance ministry for support at times of urgent need is not satisfactory.

Payment and settlement system oversight is a crucial function. Central banks have often relied on only informal powers in that area. Where they do not have statutory authority they ought to be granted it.

OTHER FUNCTIONS

Many central banks have accreted to themselves other responsibilities over time—some of them with little relationship to their core functions. Some, like the management of personal bankruptcies, raise no points of principle. Others, like a promotional role in relation to the domestic financial sector, or national financial center, do. Foreign firms may fear bias against them, reducing their willingness to participate in local markets, and, on the other side of the account, there may be pressure to admit institutions with doubtful solvency and poor business practices. The BIS has developed a useful taxonomy of "good and bad bedfellows" that will help to decide when a function is creating a potential conflict of interest.

EUROPE

Most of the arguments above apply pari passu to the euro area, but there are other particular issues relating to the unusual structure of the ECB and the European System of Central Banks that need to be addressed.

The ECB has done well, so far, in both its monetary and financial stability roles. But the economic context in which it has been operating has been relatively benign and the system now faces its first serious test, with the prospect of divergent growth rates and fiscal deficits leading to dilemmas over the right course of action for the euro area as a whole.

The Bank's decision-making process will require further attention as the zone expands. Otherwise, as we explain, there is a risk that interest rate policy becomes excessively influenced by smaller countries. The European "misrepresentation index" is high and should not be allowed to increase.

The ECB's relationships with the NCBs also need to evolve further: they are only half reformed at present. The NCBs need to acknowledge their subservient role in monetary policy and market operations and to reduce unnecessary duplication. They need to continue to shrink considerably: the costs of central banking in the euro area are remarkably high and they risk damaging the credibility of the system, where political accountability is already a live issue. There is a role for the NCBs in research (especially in relation to the financial systems of their own countries), but it is hard to escape the conclusion that there is much redundancy in the assessment of economic conditions in the euro area at present. The single interest rate cannot be refined to respond to different regional conditions, in any event. NCBs should come to be seen as ECB branches, not as "full-service" independent central banks, as they currently prefer to present themselves.

Some NCBs retain banking supervision responsibilities. If integrated supervision is not an option (and in some cases it seems impossible to transfer staff out of the central bank), the Dutch solution—of building a cross-sectoral prudential supervisor within the central bank—can be an attractive route to take. But we believe that, in the long run, if the goal of a truly integrated single European market in financial services is to survive (and we hope it will), the European Economic Area needs a pan-European regulator to sit alongside the ECB, and one with access to solvency assistance for banks if necessary. The useful reforms proposed in the de Larosière report, especially the upgrading of the Lamfalussy committees into authorities and the introduction of a European Systemic Risk Board, are moves in that direction, but they do not go far enough. Further moves toward consolidated oversight of European financial markets will pose a challenge to future U.K. governments, in particular. If the United Kingdom wishes to maintain a position of influence in Europe commensurate with the size of its markets, it will need to be prepared to engage more wholeheartedly with its partners.

EMERGING MARKETS

Many of the general points we have made apply to central banks in emerging economies as well, even though, as we have noted, many still use an exchange rate target, whether fixed or adjustable, as their price stability anchor. Unfortunately, some have learnt the lessons of the Asian crisis too well. Their buildup of reserves to support currency pegs has contributed to the global imbalances that played a part in generating the crisis. The larger EMCs should run more flexible exchange rate regimes, which will require them to adopt fresh approaches to domestic monetary management.

Often, as we have shown, central bank independence is more nominal than real, as senior appointments change with political regimes, and the institutions often lack the financial independence they need to exercise authority. There is also continued evidence of a highly politicized approach to senior appointments. The IMF and the FSB should now address these points more forcefully within the enhanced role given by the G20 in the enforcement of the "Compendium of Standards" that are internationally accepted as important for sound, stable, and well-functioning financial systems.

On the other hand, some of the arguments about the appropriate functions for central banks may present themselves rather differently in EMCs. It may be difficult to create new independent institutions and this argues for the use of the central bank for regulatory and other tasks if its independence and authority are reasonably secure.

There are particular challenges to be addressed in regimes based on Islamic finance. Islamic products and services can exist harmoniously alongside conventional finance, but fully Islamic regimes, without a benchmark interest rate, pose an unusually difficult challenge. It is hard to see how a central bank can maintain control of monetary and financial conditions without an interest rate tool.

EFFICIENCY

The range of costs incurred by central banks, whether in relation to the size of the economy or the financial sector they oversee, is remarkable. The differences are hard to justify on any measure of output or performance. Many seem to have interpreted policy independence as excluding them from normal disciplines on the use of what is essentially public money.

More transparency and accountability in the use of resources is required. Central banks have been reluctant to submit themselves to scrutiny. No central bank, whether as regulator or as monetary authority, has published anything approaching the FSA's internal audit reports on regulatory failures. Reports of that kind, though painful in the short term, allow an organization to learn and improve. Accountability should be seen as a safeguard of independence, not something that is in conflict with it. This is especially true for euro area NCBs. We outline a framework, involving an oversight board with independent appointees, that should help.

Many central banks will need to invest in additional staff in the financial stability area, where suitably qualified and experienced individuals are not easy to find and are certainly not cheap in the current circumstances. This does not need to result in increased expenditure overall as many banks have the ability to redeploy resources from elsewhere, as long as they are able to manage their budgets and staffing more flexibly. Rigid labor agreements, especially in Europe, make that difficult, so reform is needed there also.

INTERNATIONAL COLLABORATION

Central banks need to strengthen and broaden their networks of international collaboration, which, in spite of all the efforts of the BIS in particular, have been found wanting. Although many insightful papers were prepared on global imbalances, risk, credit bubbles, and so on in the buildup to the crisis, the important messages were not always easy to find and few relevant actions followed. In the early stages of the meltdown there was also the unfortunate appearance of a lack of coordination and cooperation.

The G20 has now become the key political grouping, with the Financial Stability Board below it. Central banks will need to adapt their collaborative arrangements, including through the BIS, in response to that new reality. Greater contact with finance ministries and other regulators may bring them unexpected advantages.

The committee structure of the BIS also needs to be overhauled to take account of the new working groups established by the FSB. The BIS structures need to take a more forthcoming approach to key non-central bank supervisors, who should be included in more of the committees as full members. If that can be done, and progress is already visible, then we see the BIS as the best location for all the networks of regulators (many are already there) and as the key global financial stability observatory. It is the place, for example, where the new financial stability tools that are needed, such as a countercyclical macroprudential mechanism, can best be engineered. The test will be whether the enhanced role for the

BIS in assessing system "vulnerabilities" leads to an effective and timely response.

CULTURE AND LEADERSHIP

Central banks are in cultural transition. The past model—a secretive institution little inclined to explain itself and maintaining an air of mystery, cloaked in constructive ambiguity, and led by a philosopher king—has run its course. The new model central bank will be more accountable, transparent, and frank about the limitations of its powers. It will be led by an individual who is skilled in chairmanship and communication and one who has a deep understanding of the financial sector and the wider economy, on a global scale. Taciturn autocrats need no longer apply.

Afterword

The world of central banking does not stand still. Aftershocks following the earthquake continue to strike and the ground is not yet again stable.

In two respects the debates we outline above have moved on since we completed our draft in summer 2009. There is a growing, though still by no means universal, acceptance that central banks should seek to promote financial stability as well as price stability, and furthermore that there is room for an explicit role for asset prices in a sophisticated monetary policy framework.

Signs of a shift in the center of gravity of central bank opinion could be seen at the Federal Reserve Bank of Kansas's Jackson Hole Conference in August 2009.[1] Mark Carney, the governor of the Bank of Canada, referred to "an emerging consensus that price stability does not guarantee financial stability and is, in fact, often associated with excess credit growth and emerging asset bubbles." He may have been somewhat anticipatory in identifying such a consensus, but he is correct in spotting the trend. He also described the challenges of integrating financial stability into a price stability framework. His argument for doing so was cogent. The regulatory response to the crisis, which is likely to include stronger and more countercyclical capital requirements, "will change the transmission mechanism and, consequently, the implementation of monetary policy."

In a subsequent speech to the Frankfurt European Banking Congress on November 20, 2009, Jean-Claude Trichet, president of the European Central Bank, provided further evidence of the growing appeal of "leaning against the wind" policies.[2] "Recent experience", he said "has demonstrated the limitations of a wait and see approach." He argued for

> a symmetric approach: one that leans against the emergence of asset price booms as well as dealing with the consequences of asset price busts. By encouraging more responsible behaviour on the part of investors, such an approach should make cycles of boom and bust less likely.

We agree. We also agree with Trichet when he says that "substantial practical questions remain" on how to integrate financial and price stability. We describe above the attempts to produce metrics of financial stability that would allow it to take its place alongside the beguiling simplicities of inflation targeting, and we note that there has been sporadic discussion about "macroprudential" approaches for thirty years. So we recognize, as now does Trichet, that far more work is necessary to produce a working model.

Both Carney and Trichet see macroprudential regulation as potentially the first line of defense against bubbles and financial instability. But they acknowledge that monetary policy must also play a role, as we strongly argue above. The Bank of England have characterized macroprudential policy as a "missing ingredient from the current policy framework," but have so far been less willing to accept that the approach to monetary policy must consequently also be at issue.[3] Indeed, the formulation of monetary policy objectives in general is still to be revisited after the wholesale adoption of unconventional measures in so many jurisdictions.

The second area in which events have moved the debate along concerns the appropriate role for central banks themselves, whether in banking supervision specifically or financial regulation more generally. Here it would be even more ambitious to claim an emerging consensus, but there have certainly been signs of change. In Europe the European Systemic Risk Board, chaired by the president of the ECB, will attempt to produce early warnings of instability so as to prevent a renewed buildup of excessive risk in the financial system as a whole. This is undoubtedly a core function for central banks. But how far does that need to translate into a role in operational institutional supervision?

In the United Kingdom, the Conservative opposition now argues for a transfer of much direct supervisory responsibility from the FSA to the Bank of England. The new coalition government in Germany similarly intends to move functions from the BaFin to the Bundesbank. The Belgian government propose an enhanced role for their central bank too.

But in the United States the position remains unclear. As we write, there are competing proposals from the Administration as well as from both Houses of Congress in relation to the role of the Federal Reserve. The Obama Administration proposes that the Federal Reserve should be the prime overseer of financial stability, and also a supervisor of individual institutions, as it currently (partially) is. Others, concerned about conflicts of interest and concentration of power, argue for a separate institution, or indeed for a Financial Stability Council, and for a new integrated banking supervisor to take over functions previously exercised by the Fed. At the time of writing there is no sign of agreement on this essential point, which leaves the U.S. system of financial regulation still in a state of uncertainty, which can only be regarded as deeply unsatisfactory. Even the urgent need to reform a clearly malfunctioning system in the aftermath of a deep crisis has not overcome deep political and institutional fault lines.

At the global level central banks must now work in new, broader-based forums based around the G20 grouping. It is too early to say how effective those new structures will be. There are already signs of tensions between the Financial Stability Board and the IMF. These new arrangements will certainly be tested in what continue to be challenging conditions in the global economy and in financial markets.

Notes

INTRODUCTION

1. Roach, S. 2007. The great failure of central banking. *Fortune Magazine*, August 16.

2. Taylor, J. B. 2008. The financial crisis and the policy responses: an empirical analysis of what went wrong. Paper (available at www.stanford.edu/~johntayl).

3. Gieve, J. 2009. Central banks need to avoid fighting the last war. *Financial Times* (May 11; available at www.ft.com).

CHAPTER ONE: WHAT IS CENTRAL BANKING AND WHY IS IT IMPORTANT?

1. Dowd, K. 1995. *Private Money.* London: Institute of Economic Affairs.

2. Capie, F., C. Goodhart, S. Fischer, and N. Schnadt. 1994. The development of central banking. In *The Future of Central Banking.* Cambridge University Press.

3. Rochet, J. 2008. *Why Are There So Many Banking Crises? The Politics and Policy of Bank Regulation.* Princeton University Press.

4. BIS. 2009. *Issues in the Governance of Central Banks.* Basel: Bank for International Settlements.

5. Thornton, H. 1802. *An Enquiry into the Nature and Effects of Paper Credit in the United Kingdom.* London: Hatchard.

6. Morgan Stanley. 2008. *Central Bank Directory.* London: Central Banking Publications.

7. Friseld, L., K. Roszbach, and G. Spagnolo. 2006. *Governing the Governors: A Clinical Study of Central Banks.* Stockholm: Swedish Riksbank.

8. Pringle, R. (ed.). 2007. *How Countries Supervise their Banks, Insurers and Securities Markets, 2007.* London: Central Banking Publications.

9. Collyns, C. 1983. *Alternatives to the Central Bank in the Developing World.* Washington, DC: International Monetary Fund.

10. Lastra, R. M. 1996. Appendix. In *Central Banking and Banking Regulation*, pp. 249–86. Financial Markets Group, London School of Economics and Political Science.

11. Corrigan, G. 1995. Quoted in M. Deane and R. Pringle's *The Central Banks.* London: Viking.

12. Buiter, W. 2006. Rethinking inflation targeting and central bank independence. Lecture given at the London School of Economics, October 26.

CHAPTER TWO: MONETARY STABILITY

1. Lastra, R. M. 2006. *Legal Foundations of International Monetary Stability.* Oxford University Press.

2. Tucker, P. 2009. The repertoire of official sector interventions in the financial system: last resort lending, market-making and capital. Speech at the Bank of Japan International Conference, May 27-28 (available at www.bankofengland.co.uk).

3. Capie, F., C. Goodhart, S. Fischer, and N. Schnadt. 1994. The development of central banking. In *The Future of Central Banking*. Cambridge University Press.

4. Blinder, A. S. 2008. Keynesian economics. In *The Concise Encyclopedia of Economics* (available at www.econlib.org/library/enc/keynesianeconomics.html).

5. Friedman, M., and A. Schwarz. 1971. *Monetary History of the United States, 1867–1960*. Princeton University Press.

6. Meltzer, A. H. 2002. Monetarism. In *The Concise Encyclopedia of Economics* (available at www.econlib.org/library/enc/monetarism.html).

7. Mishkin, F. S. 2007. *Monetary Policy Strategy*. Cambridge, MA: MIT Press.

8. Goodhart, C. A. E. 2005. The future of central banking. Special Paper 162, Financial Markets Group, London School of Economics.

9. Tucker, P. 2006. Reflections on operating inflation targeting. *Bank of England Quarterly Bulletin, Summer 2006*, pp. 212–24. London: Bank of England.

10. Hammond, G. 2009. *State of the Art of Inflation Targeting*. Centre for Central Banking Studies Handbook, no. 29. London: Bank of England.

11. Petersson, T. G. 2004. Formulation of inflation targeting around the world. In *Monetary Bulletin*. Reykjavik: Bank of Iceland.

12. Bernanke, B., and F. Mishkin. 1997. Inflation targeting: a new framework for monetary policy? *Journal of Economic Perspectives* 11(2):97–116.

13. BIS. 1986. Recent innovations in international banking (Cross Report). Report prepared by a study group established by the central banks of the Group of Ten Countries.

14. ECB. 2000. The two pillars of the ECB's monetary policy strategy. In *ECB Monthly Bulletin, November 2000*, pp. 37–48. Frankfurt: European Central Bank.

15. White, W. 2006 Is price stability enough? Working Paper 205, BIS (April).

16. Borio, C., C. Furfine, and P. Lowe. 2001. Procyclicality of the financial system and financial stability issues and policy options. BIS Papers No. 1 (part 1; March).

17. King, M. 2009. Speech at the Lord Mayor's Banquet (June 17; available at www.bankofengland.co.uk).

18. Roger, S., and M. Stone. 2005. On target? The international experience with achieving inflation targets. Working Paper WP/05/163, IMF.

19. Department of the Treasury/Federal Reserve. 2009. The role of the Federal Reserve in preserving financial and monetary stability. Joint Statement by the Department of the Treasury and the Federal Reserve (March 23; available at www.federalreserve.com).

20. Adrian, T., and H. Shin. 2009. Financial intermediaries, financial stability and monetary policy. *Maintaining Stability in a Changing Financial System*. Federal Reserve Bank of Kansas City.

21. Bernanke, B. 2002. Deflation: making sure "it" doesn't happen here. Speech to the National Economists Club, Washington, DC, November 21.

22. Spiegel, M. 2006. Did quantitative easing by the Bank of Japan "work"? Economic Letter 2006.28, Federal Reserve Bank of San Francisco (October 20).

23. Bernanke, B. 2009. The crisis and the policy response. Speech at the London School of Economics (January 13; available at www.lse.ac.uk).

24. Trichet, J.-C. 2009. Introductory statement (May 7; available at www.ecb.int).

25. Bank of England. 2009. Monetary policy and asset purchases. Statement (March 5; available at www.bankofengland.co.uk).

26. Bank of England. 2009. Minutes of the Monetary Policy Committee meeting (March 5; available at www.bankofengland.co.uk).

27. Dale, S. 2009. Tough times, unconventional measures. Speech to the Association of British Insurers by the Bank of England's chief economist (March 27; available at www.bankofengland.co.uk).

28. Bernanke, B. 2009. Monetary policy report to the Congress (July 21).

29. Latter, A. 1996. The choice of exchange rate regime. In *Handbooks in Central Banking*, volume 2. London: Centre for Central Banking Studies, Bank of England.

30. Rey, H., and H. Hace. 2004. Can portfolio rebalancing explain the dynamics of equity flows and exchange rates? *American Economic Review* 94(2):126–33.

31. De Grauwe, P. 2008. The bank must act to end the euro's rise. *Financial Times* (September 5; available at www.ft.com).

CHAPTER THREE: FINANCIAL STABILITY

1. Caprio, G., and D. Klingebiel. 2003. Episodes of systemic and borderline financial crises. World Bank report (available at www.worldbank.org).

2. Davies, H. 2005. Two cheers for financial stability. William Taylor Memorial Lecture, number 9 (available at www.group30.org).

3. Padoa-Schioppa, T. 2004. Central banks and financial stability. In *Regulatory Finance*, chapter 8. Oxford University Press.

4. Allen, W., and G. Wood. 2005. Defining and achieving financial stability. Paper 160, Financial Market Group, Cass Business School, LSE (April).

5. Greenspan, A. 1996. Global risk management. William Taylor Memorial Lecture, number 3 (available at www.group30.org).

6. Goodhart, C. 2004. Some new directions for financial stability. Per Jacobsson Lecture (available at www.bis.org).

7. de Haan, J., and S. Oosterloo. 2006. Transparency and accountability of central banks in their role of financial stability supervisor in OECD countries. *European Journal of Law and Economics* 22:255–71.

8. Heikensten, L. 2004. Speech at the Risk Management Conference, Swedish Riksbank, Stockholm (November 16; available at www.riksbank.com).

9. ECB. 2005. *Financial Stability Review* (December; available at www.ecb.int).

10. Aspachs, O., C. Goodhart, M. Segoviano, D. Tsomocos, and L. Zicchino. 2006. Searching for a metric for financial stability. Special Paper 167, Financial Markets Group, London School of Economics.

11. ECB. 2008. Preface. In *Financial Stability Review* (June; available at www.ecb.int).

12. Swiss National Bank. 2005. Introduction to the financial stability review (available at www.snb.ch).

13. King, M. 2008. Oral evidence by the Governor of the Bank of England to the House of Commons Treasury Committee (July 22).

14. Crockett, A. 2003. Financial Stability and International Financial Regulation Lecture (February 5; available at www.iea.org.uk).

15. Central Bank of Iceland. 2006. *Financial Stability Review* (available at www.sedlabanki.is).

16. Buiter, W., and A. Sibert. 2008. The Icelandic banking crisis and what to do about it: the lender of last resort theory of optimal currency areas. Policy Insight Paper 26, Centre for Economic Policy Research.

17. Mishkin, F. 1991. Anatomy of financial crisis. Working Paper 3934, National Bureau of Economics Research.

18. Foot, M. 2003. Protecting financial stability—how good are we at it? Speech given at the University of Birmingham (June 6; available at www.fsa.gov.uk).

19. Bagehot, W. 1873. *Lombard Street: A Description of the Money Market.* London: Henry S. King.

20. Davis, P., and D. Karim. Forthcoming. Research and policy for financial stability—what have we learnt? In *New Frontiers in the Regulation and Oversight of the Financial System* (ed. D. Mayes and R. Pringle). London: Central Banking Publications.

21. Goodhart, C., and D. Tsomocos. 2007. Analysis of financial stability. Special Paper 173, Financial Markets Group, London School of Economics.

22. Fell, J., and G. Schinasi. 2005. Assessing financial stability—exploring the boundaries of analysis. *National Institute Economic Review* 192:70–85.

23. Department of the Treasury and the Federal Reserve (joint statement). 2009. The role of the Federal Reserve in preserving financial and monetary stability (March 23).

24. Das, U., M. Quinty, and K. Chenard. 2004. Does regulatory governance matter for financial system stability? Working Paper WP/04/89, IMF.

25. HM Treasury. 1997. Letter from Chancellor of the Exchequer Gordon Brown to Governor Eddie George (May 20; available at www.hm-treasury.gov.uk).

26. HM Treasury. 2008. Letter from Chancellor of the Exchequer Alistair Darling to Rt. Hon John McFall MP, Chairman of the Treasury Committee (June 19; available at www.hm-treasury.gov.uk).

27. King, M. 2009. Speech at the Lord Mayor's Banquet (June 17; available at www.bankofengland.co.uk).

28. Cihak, M. 2006. Central banks and financial stability: a survey of financial stability reports. Speech given at a seminar on "Current developments in monetary and financial law" in Washington DC (October; available at www.imf.org).

29. Oosterloo, S., J. de Haan, and R. Jong-A-Pin. 2007. Financial stability reviews: a first empirical analysis. *Journal of Financial Stability* 2(4):337–55.

30. Bowen, A., M. O'Brien, and E. Steigum. 2003. Norges Bank's financial stability report: a review (available at www.norges-bank.no).

31. King, M. 2006. Reform of the International Monetary Fund. Speech delivered in New Delhi (February 20; available at www.bankofengland.co.uk).

32. IMF. 2006. *Global FSR* (April; available at www.imf.org).

33. Capie, F., C. Goodhart, S. Fischer, and N. Schnadt. 1994. The development of central banking. In *The Future of Central Banking.* Cambridge University Press.

34. Davies, H., and D. Green. 2008. *Global Financial Regulation: The Essential Guide.* Chichester, U.K.: Polity Press.

35. Peek, J., E. Rosengren, and G. Tootell. 1997. Is bank supervision central to central banking? Study prepared for "After the Fall: Re-evaluating Supervisory, Regulatory and Monetary Policy, 54th Economic Conference of the Federal Reserve Bank of Boston" (available at www.bos.frb.org).

36. Bernanke, B. 2007. Central banking and bank supervision in the United States. Speech given at the Allied Social Science Association annual meeting, Chicago, IL (January 5; available at www.federalreserve.gov).

37. Briault, C. 1999. The rationale for a single national regulator. Occasional Paper 2, Financial Services Authority (available at www.fsa.gov.uk).

38. Briault, C. 2000. FSA revisited, and some issues for European securities regulation. Paper presented at the European University Institute (December 15; available at www.fsa.gov.uk).

39. Cihak, M., and C. Podpiera. 2006. Is one watchdog better than three? International experience with integrated financial sector supervision. Working Paper WP/06/57, IMF (March; available at www.imf.org).

40. Buiter, W. 2009. Central banks and financial crises. In *Maintaining Stability in a Changing Financial System*, pp. 495–633. Federal Reserve Bank of Kansas City.

41. McKinsey & Company. 2007. Sustaining New York's and the US's global financial services leadership. Report prepared for Mayor Bloomberg and Senator Schumer (January 22; available at www.nyc.gov).

42. FSA. 2008. The FSA's internal audit review of its supervision of Northern Rock and the FSA management response (March 26; available at www.fsa.gov.uk).

43. National Audit Office. 2009. HM Treasury: the nationalisation of Northern Rock. Report (available at www.nao.org.uk).

44. House of Commons Treasury Committee. 2008. The run on the Rock: government response to the Committee's fifth report of session 2007–08. Eleventh Special Report of Session 2007–08 (available at www.parliament.the-stationery-office.co.uk).

45. Buiter, W. 2008. Lessons from Northern Rock: how to handle failure. *VoxEU* column (March 5; available at www.voxeu.org).

46. HM Treasury. 2008. Letter from Chancellor of the Exchequer Alistair Darling to Rt. Hon John McFall MP, Chairman of the Treasury Committee (June 19; available at www.hm-treasury.gov.uk).

47. Turner, A. 2009. *The Turner Review: A Regulatory Response to the Global Banking Crisis.* Financial Services Authority (available at www.fsa.gov.uk).

48. Sassoon, J. 2009. The tripartite review: a review of the UK's tripartite system of financial regulation in relation to financial stability. Preliminary Report (February; available at www.tripartitereview.co.uk).

49. U.S. Treasury. 2008. Blueprint for regulatory reform (available at www.ustreas.gov).

50. Cox, C. 2008. Remarks on the MOU with the Federal Reserve (July; available at www.sec.gov).

51. Tett, G. 2009. *Fool's Gold: How Unrestrained Greed Corrupted a Dream, Shattered Global Markets and Unleashed a Catastrophe.* London: Little, Brown.

52. Jackson, H. 2008. A pragmatic approach to the phased consolidation of financial regulation in the United States. Special Paper 184, Financial Markets Group, London School of Economics (available at www.lse.ac.uk).

53. Committee on Capital Markets Regulation. 2009. The global financial crisis: a plan for regulatory reform. Report (available at www.capmktsreg.org).

54. Geithner, T. (U.S. Treasury secretary). 2009. Written testimony to the House Financial Services Committee (March 26; available at www.ustreas.gov).

55. U.S. Treasury. 2009. *Financial Regulatory Reform: A New Foundation* (available at www.financialstability.gov).

56. *Financial Times.* 2009. The conundrum of financial stability. Editorial (June 20; available at www.ft.com).

CHAPTER FOUR: FINANCIAL INFRASTRUCTURE

1. Turner, P. 2009. Central banks, liquidity and the banking crisis. In *Time for a Visible Hand: Lessons from the World Financial Crisis* (ed. S. Griffith-Jones and J. E. Stiglitz). Oxford University Press.

2. BIS. 2008. *78th Annual Report, 2007–8* (June 30; available at www.bis.org).

3. Bank of England. 2009. *Financial Stability Review* (available at www.bankofengland.co.uk).

4. King, M. 2007. Turmoil in financial markets: what can central banks do? Paper submitted by the governor of the Bank of England to the Treasury Committee (September 12).

5. Summers, L. 2007. Beware moral hazard fundamentalists. *Financial Times* (September 23; available at www.ft.com).

6. George, E. 1993. Speech at the London School of Economics by the governor of the Bank of England (available at www.bankofengland.co.uk).

7. Roubini, N. 2007. Coordinated central banks liquidity injections: too little too late to address the fundamental problems of the financial system. In Nouriel Roubini's *Global EconoMonitor* (December 12; available at www.rgemonitor.com).

8. Geithner, T. 2008. Actions by the New York Fed in response to liquidity pressures in financial markets. Testimony before the U.S. Senate Committee on Banking, Housing and Urban Affairs, Washington, DC (April 3; available at www.newyorkfed.org).

9. Buiter, W. 2008. The Greenspan Fed: a tragedy of errors. *Financial Times* (April 12; available at www.ft.com).

10. Summers, L. 2008. A long way from the 1970s. *Newsweek* (April 7; available at www.newsweek.com).

11. *The Economist.* 2008. Litterbin of last resort. Editorial (June 12; available at www.economist.com).

12. Bank of England. 2008. Special liquidity scheme. News release (April 21; available at www.bankofengland.co.uk).

13. Tucker, P. 2009. The repertoire of official sector interventions in the financial system: last resort lending, market-making and capital. Speech at the Bank of Japan International Conference (May 27–28).

14. Senior Supervisors Group. 2008. Senior Supervisors Group's report on observations on risk management practices during the recent market turbulence (March 6; available at www.financialstabilityboard.org).

15. Institute of International Finance. 2008. Final report of the Committee on Market Best Practices (available at www.iif.com).

16. Gonzales-Eiras, M. 2004. Banks' liquidity demand and the presence of the lender of last resort. Working Paper 61, Universidad de San Andres, Buenos Aires (May 20).

17. Aspachs, O., E. Nier, and M. Tiesset. 2005. Liquidity, banking regulation and the macroeconomy: evidence on bank liquidity holdings from a panel of U.K. resident banks. Mimeo, London School of Economics Financial Markets Group (February; available at www.bis.org).

18. Diamond, D., and R. Rajan. 2009. The credit crisis: conjectures about causes and remedies. Working Paper 14739, National Bureau of Economic Research.

19. Tucker, P. 2008. The new financial frontiers. Remarks by Tucker, executive director of the Bank of England, at Chatham House, London (April 29).

20. Goodhart, C. 2007. Liquidity risk management. Special Paper 175, Financial Markets Group, London School of Economics (October; available at www.lse.ac.uk).

21. Congdon, T. 2007. Quoted in Goodhart's "Liquidity risk management."[20]

22. FSF. 2008. Report on enhancing market and institutional resilience (April; available at www.fsf.org).

23. Basel Committee on Banking Supervision. 2008. Principles for sound liquidity risk management and supervision (available at www.bis.org).

24. FSA. 2007. Review of the liquidity requirements for banks and building societies. Discussion Paper 07/7 (December; available at www.fsa.gov.uk).

25. Foot, M. 2008. Comments on FSA Discussion Paper 07/7, Promontory Group UK Ltd (March).

26. Bank of England. 2008. The development of the Bank of England's market operations. Consultation Paper (October; available at www.bankofengland.co.uk).

27. FSA. 2008. Strengthening liquidity standards. Consultation Paper 08/22 (available at www.fsa.gov.uk).

28. Turner, A. 2009. *The Turner Review: A Regulatory Response to the Global Banking Crisis.* Financial Services Authority (available at www.fsa.gov.uk).

29. King, M. 2008. Banking and the Bank of England. Speech to the British Bankers Association (June 10; available at www.bankofengland.co.uk).

30. Goodhart, C. 2008. Liquidity and money market operations: a proposal. Special Paper 179, Financial Markets Group, London School of Economics (available at www.lse.ac.uk).

31. Bank of England. 2000. Oversight of payment systems. Report (available at www. bankofengland.co.uk).

32. Committee on Payment and Settlements Systems. 2000. Core principles for systemically important payment systems: report of the task force on payment system principles and practices (available at www.bis.org).

33. Khiaonarong, T. 2003. Payment systems efficiency, policy approaches, and the role of the central bank. Discussion Paper 1/2003, Bank of Finland (available at www.bof.fi).

34. Green, E., and R. Todd. 2001. Thoughts on the Fed's role in the payments system. *Federal Reserve Bank of Minneapolis Quarterly Review* 25(1):12–27.

35. Green, E. 2005. The role of the central bank in payment systems. Paper presented at the Bank of England Conference on the Future of Payments Systems (available at www. bankofengland.co.uk).

36. Lowe, P., and I. Macfarlane. 2005. Payments system reform: the Australian experience. Speech given at the Reserve Bank of Australia (available at www.rba.gov.au).

37. BIS. 2005. Central bank oversight of payments and settlement systems. Report, Committee on Payments and Settlements Systems (available at www.bis.org).

38. Cruikshank, D. 2000. Competition in U.K. banking. Report (August; available at www.hm-treasury.gov.uk).

39. King, M. 2007. Speech at the Lord Mayor's Banquet (June 20; available at www. bankofengland.co.uk).

40. Federal Reserve Board. 2006. Policy on payment system risk. Policy statement (available at www.federalreserve.gov).

41. Geithner, T. (U.S. Treasury secretary). 2009. Written testimony to the House Financial Services Committee (March 26; available at www.ustreas.gov).

42. BIS. 2009. Improving the safety of financial markets. In *Annual Report 2008-9*, pp. 127–28 (available at www.bis.org).

43. Currie, E., J.-J. Dethier, and E. Togo. 2003. Institutional arrangements for public debt management. Policy Research Paper 3021, World Bank (available at www.worldbank. org).

44. Archer, D. 2009. Roles and objectives of modern central banks. In *Issues in the Governance of Central Banks*. Basel: Bank for International Settlements.

45. Treasury Committee. 2000. Government's cash and debt management. HC 154 (May 25; available at www.publications.parliament.uk).

46. Blejer, M. 1999. Public debt management and monetary policy: macroeconomic and institutional interactions. In *European Union Accession: The Challenge for Public Liability Management in Central Europe*. European Commission.

47. Horgan, M. 1999. The building blocks of effective government debt management. Document 8, UNITAR (December; available at www.unitar.org).

48. Wolswijk, G., and J. de Haan. 2005. Government debt management in the euro area—recent theoretical developments and changes in practice. Occasional Paper 25, European Central Bank (available at www.ecb.org).

49. Jensen, H. F. (Danmarks Nationalbank). 2002. The central bank's role in reserve and debt management: the Danish experience. Paper presented to an IMF Conference on Challenges to Central Banking from Globalized Financial Systems (December 16–17; available at www.imf.org).

50. Reddell, M. (Reserve Bank of New Zealand). 2002. Discussant's comments on Jensen's paper.[49]

51. Goodhart, C. 2009. Evidence to the Treasury Committee (January 13).

52. Congdon, T. 2009. Quoted in "Pressure on Debt Management Office as gilt issues hit record levels" by Philip Aldrick. *Daily Telegraph* (March 26; available at www.telegraph.co.uk/finance).

CHAPTER FIVE: ASSET PRICES

1. Roach, S. 2007. The great failure of central banking. *Fortune Magazine* (August).

2. Lyons, G. (chief economist, Standard Chartered Bank). 2008. BBC radio interview (July).

3. Taylor, J. 2008. The financial crisis and the policy responses: an empirical analysis of what went wrong. Paper (November; available at www.stanford.edu/~johntayl).

4. Wadhwani, S. 2008. Should monetary policy respond to asset price bubbles? Revisiting the debate. Paper presented at the SUERF Colloquium, Munich (June 12).

5. Buiter, W. 2009. The unfortunate uselessness of most "state of the art" academic monetary economics. *Financial Times* (April 5; available at www.ft.com/maverecon).

6. Shiller, R. 2008. *The Sub-Prime Crisis.* Princeton University Press.

7. White, W. 2006. Is price stability enough? Working Paper 205, BIS (April).

8. Crockett, A. 2003. International standard setting in financial supervision. Sixth Institute of Economic Affairs Discussion Paper (Cass Business School, London; February 5).

9. Bean, C. 2003. Asset prices, financial imbalances and monetary policy: are inflation targets enough? Working Paper 140, BIS.

10. Greenspan, A. 2008. A response to my critics. *Financial Times* (April 6; available at www.ft.com).

11. Cecchetti, S., H. Genberg, and S. Wadhwani. 2002. Asset prices in a flexible inflation targeting framework. In *Asset Price Bubbles: The Implications for Monetary, Regulatory and International Policies* (ed. W. C. Hunter, G. G. Kaufman, and M. Pomerleano). Cambridge, MA: MIT Press.

12. Goodhart, C. 2001. What weight should be given to asset prices in the measurement of inflation? *The Economic Journal* 111:F335–56.

13. Alchian, A., and B. Klein. 1973. On a correct measure of inflation. *Journal of Money Credit and Banking* 5(1):173–91.

14. Vickers, J. 1999. Monetary policy and asset prices. Lecture at the Money, Macro and Finance Group 31st Annual Conference, Oxford University (September 23).

15. King, M. 2008. Evidence to the House of Commons Treasury Committee (July).

16. Cecchetti, S. 2006. The brave new world of central banking: policy challenges posed by asset price booms and busts. *National Institute Economic Review* 2006:107–19.

17. Bernanke, B., and M. Gertler. 2000. Monetary policy and asset price volatility. Working Paper 7559, National Bureau of Economic Research (February).

18. Keynes, J. M. 1936. *The General Theory of Employment, Interest and Money.* Cambridge University Press.

19. Heikensten, L. 2008. More to it than just "leaning against the wind." *Financial Times* (May 28; available at www.ft.com).

20. Greenspan, A. 2007. *The Age of Turbulence: Adventures in a New World.* London: Allen Lane.

21. King, M. 2009. Speech at the Lord Mayor's Banquet (June 17; available at www.bankofengland.co.uk).

22. IMF. 2003. *World Economic Outlook.*

23. Ahrend, R., B. Cournede, and R. Price. 2008. Monetary policy, market excesses and financial turmoil. Working Paper 2008/5, OECD (available at www.oecd.org).

24. Bean, C. 2009. The great moderation, the great panic and the great contraction. Schumpeter Lecture at the Annual Congress of the European Economic Association, Barcelona (August 25).

25. BIS. 2009. *BIS Annual Report 2008/09.*

26. White, W. 2009. Should monetary policy "lean or clean": that is the question? Working Paper 34, Federal Reserve Bank of Dallas Globalization and Monetary Policy Institute.

27. IMF Research Department (approved by O. Blanchard). 2009. Lessons of the global crisis for macroeconomic policy. Report, International Monetary Fund (February 19; available at www.imf.org).

28. Mishkin, F. 2008. How should we respond to asset price bubbles? Speech at the Wharton Annual Financial Institutions Center and Oliver Wyman Institute's Financial Risk Roundtable, Philadelphia, PA (May 15; available at www.federalreserve.gov).

29. Turner, A. 2009. *The Turner Review: A Regulatory Response to the Global Banking Crisis.* Financial Services Authority (available at www.fsa.gov.uk).

30. BIS. 1986. Recent innovations in international banking. Report, G10 Study Group (available at www.bis.org).

31. Goodhart, C., and A. Persaud. 2008. How to avoid the next crash. *Financial Times* (January 30; available at www.ft.com).

32. Brunnermeier, M., A. Crockett, C. Goodhart, A. Persaud, and H. Shin. 2009. The fundamental principles of financial regulation. In *Geneva Report on the World Economy 11.* Geneva: International Centre for Monetary and Banking Studies.

33. Dewatripont, M., *et al.* (eds). 2009. Macroeconomic stability and financial regulation: key issues for the G20. Report, Centre for Economic Policy Research.

34. Group of Twenty. 2009. *Global Plan Annex: Declaration on Strengthening the Financial System* (available at www.G20.org).

35. Swiss Federal Banking Commission. 2008. SFBC and large banks agree to set higher capital adequacy targets and introduce a leverage ratio. Media Release (December 4; available at www.sfbc.ch).

36. Bank of England. 2008. *Financial Stability Review* (October; available at www.bankofengland.co.uk).

CHAPTER SIX: STRUCTURE, STATUS, AND ACCOUNTABILITY

1. Cukierman, A. 2005. Central bank independence and monetary policymaking institutions—past present and future. Lecture at the Annual Meeting of the Chilean Economic Society, Vina del Mar, Chile.

2. Fry, M., D. Julius, S. Roger, L. Mahadeva, and G. Sterne. 2000. Key issues in the choice of monetary policy framework. In *Monetary Policy Frameworks in a Global Context.* Routledge.

3. Lastra, R. M. 2006. Institutional developments to promote monetary stability. In *Legal Foundations of International Monetary Stability.* Oxford University Press.

4. Buiter, W. 2007. How robust is the conventional wisdom in monetary policy. Report, National Bureau of Economic Research (available at www.nber.org).

5. Artus, P. 2007. *Les Incendiaires: Les Banques Centrales Depassées par la Globalisation.* Paris: Perrin.

6. Moreau, E. 1954. *Souvenirs d'un Gouverneur de la Banque de France.* Paris: Librairie de Medicis. (As quoted in *Montagu Norman* by Andrew Boyle (1967). London: Cassell.)

7. Blinder, A. 1998. *Central Banking in Theory and Practice.* Cambridge, MA: MIT Press.

8. Buiter, W., and A. Sibert. 2000. Designing a monetary authority. In *Challenges for Central Banking* (ed. A. Santomero, S. Viotti, and A. Vredin), pp. 173–85. Boston, MA: Kluwer.

9. Jacome, L., and F. Vazquez. 2005. Any link between legal central bank independence and inflation? Evidence from Latin America and the Caribbean. Working Paper 05/75, IMF.

10. Cukierman, A., and N. Liviatan. 1992. Measuring the independence of central banks and its effect on policy outcomes. *World Bank Economic Review* 6:353–98.

11. Eijffinger, J., and A. De Haan. 1996. The political economy of central bank independence. Special Papers in International Economics, no. 19, International Finance Section, Department of Economics, Princeton University.

12. Rogoff, K. 1985. The optimal degree of commitment to an intermediate monetary target. *Quarterly Journal of Economics* 110:1,168–90.

13. Fischer, S. 1994. Modern central banking. In *The Future of Central Banking* (ed. F. Capie, C. Goodhart, S. Fischer, and N. Schnadt). Cambridge University Press.

14. De Haan, A., and J. Eijffinger. 2000. The democratic accountability of the European Central Bank: a comment on two fairy-tales. *Journal of Common Market Studies* 38(3): 393–407.

15. Meltzer, A. 2003. *A History of the Federal Reserve: Volume 1, 1913–1951.* University of Chicago Press.

16. Chang, K. 2003. *Appointing Central Bankers: The Politics of Monetary Policy in the United States and the European Monetary Union.* Cambridge University Press.

17. Hix, S., B. Hoyland, and N. Vivyan. 2007. From doves to hawks: a spatial analysis of voting in the Monetary Policy Committee of the Bank of England during Gordon Brown's chancellorship. Report, London School of Economics.

18. Brunner, K. 1981. The art of central banking. Working Paper GPB 81-6, Centre for Research in Government Policy and Business, University of Rochester Graduate School of Management.

19. Buiter, W. 1999. Six months in the life of the euro. What have we learnt? Remarks at a seminar on EMU, Utrecht (June 25; available at www.nber.org).

20. Dincer, N., and B. Eichengreen. 2007. Central bank transparency: where, why and with what effects? Working Paper 13003, National Bureau of Economic Research.

21. Poole, W., R. Rasche, and D. Thornton. 2001. Market anticipations of monetary policy actions. Mimeo, Federal Reserve Bank of St. Louis.

22. Meyer, L. 2001. Inflation targets and inflation targeting. Speech delivered to the University of California at San Diego (July 17).

23. Mishkin, F. 2004. Can central bank transparency go too far? Working Paper 10829, National Bureau of Economic Research.

24. Goodhart, C. 2001. Monetary transmission lags and the formulation of the policy decision on interest rates. *Federal Reserve Bank of St Louis Review* 83(4):165–81.

25. Chortareas, G., D. Stasavage, and G. Sterne. 2002. Does it pay to be transparent? International evidence from central bank forecasts. *Federal Reserve Bank of St. Louis Review* 84(4):99–117.

26. Geraats, P. 2006. Transparency of monetary policy: theory and practice. *CESifo Economic Studies* 52(1):111–52.

27. Kohn, D., and B. Sack. 2003. Central bank talk: does it matter and why? Finance and Economics Discussion Series 2003-55. Staff Working Paper, Board of Governors of the Federal Reserve System.

28. Connolly, E., and M. Kohler. 2004. News and interest rate expectations: a study of six central banks. Paper presented at the Reserve Bank of Australia Conference on the Future of Inflation Targeting (August).

29. Blinder, A. 2007. Monetary policy by committee: why and how? *European Journal of Political Economy* 23:106–23.

30. Lybeck, T., and J. Morris. 2004. Central bank governance: a survey of boards and management. Working Paper WP/04/226, IMF.

31. Pollard, P. 2004. Monetary policymaking around the world: different approaches to different central banks. PowerPoint presentation, Federal Reserve Bank of St. Louis (available at www.stlouisfed.org).

32. Central Bank Governance Group (BIS). 2009. Issues in the governance of central banks. Report, Bank for International Settlements (May).

33. Blinder, A., and J. Morgan. 2000. Are two heads better than one? An experimental analysis of group vs. individual decision-making. Working Paper 7909, National Bureau of Economic Research.

34. Gerlach-Kristen, P. 2006. Monetary policy committees and interest rate setting. *European Economic Review* 50(2):487–507.

35. Berger, H., V. Nitsch, and T. Lybeck. 2007. Central bank boards around the world: why does membership size differ? Working Paper 1897, CESifo.

36. Sibert, A. 2006. Central banking by committee. *International Finance* 9(2):145–68.

37. Tumpel-Gugerell, G. 2008. Speech given in Brussels (May 6; available at www.ecb.europa.eu).

38. Blinder, A. 2004. *The Quiet Revolution: Central Banking Goes Modern.* Yale University Press.

39. Chappell, H., R. McGregor, and T. Vermilyea. 2005. *Committee Decisions on Monetary Policy: Evidence from Historical Records of the Federal Open Market Committee.* Cambridge, MA: MIT Press.

40. Meade, E., and D. Stasavage. 2008. Publicity of debate and the incentive to dissent: evidence from the Federal Reserve. *Economic Journal* 118(528):695–717.

41. Marsh, D. 2009. *The Euro: The Politics of the New Global Currency.* Yale University Press.

CHAPTER SEVEN: EUROPE: A SPECIAL CASE

1. Marsh, D. 2009. *The Euro: The Politics of the New Global Currency.* Yale University Press.

2. Treaty on the European Union. 1992. Article 105 (available at www.ec.europa.eu).

3. Padoa-Schioppa, T. 1999. EMU and banking supervision. *International Finance* 2(2): 295–308.

4. Enderlein, H. 2006. Adjustment to EMU: the impact of supranational monetary policy on domestic fiscal and wage-setting institutions. *European Union Politics* 7(1):51–76.

5. Werner, P. 1970. Report to the Council and the Commission on the realisation by stages of economic and monetary union in the Community. Report (available at www.ec.europa.eu).

6. Greenspan, A. 2006. Comments to Goldman Sachs Partners' Conference 2006. As quoted in Marsh.[1]

7. MacDougall, D. 1977. The role of public finance in European integration. Report (available at www.ec.europa.eu).

8. Delors, J. 1989. Report on economic and monetary union. Report (available at www.ec.europa.eu).

9. Major, J. 1993. Quoted in *The Economist* (September 25).

10. Bank of England. 1996–2002. *Practical Issues Arising from the Introduction of the Euro,* issues 1–16 (available at www.bankofengland.co.uk).

11. European Commission. 2008. EMU@10: successes and challenges after 10 years of economic and monetary union. Report (available at www.ec.europa.eu).

12. De Grauwe, P. 2002. Challenges for monetary policy in Euroland. *Journal of Common Market Studies* 40(4):693-718.

13. Mayer, T. 2008. Quoted in "The euro at ten. A decade in the sun." *The Economist* (June 7).

14. Morris, R., H. Ongena, and L. Schuknecht. 2006. The reform and implementation of the stability and growth pact. Occasional Paper 47, European Central Bank.

15. Duisenberg, W. 2002. Some remarks on the euro in a U.S. context. Speech to the Council of Foreign Relations, New York (April 19).

16. Heinemann F., and F. Huefner. 2004. Is the view from the Eurotower purely European? National divergence and ECB interest rate policy. *Scottish Journal of Political Economy* 51(4):544-58.

17. Berger, H. 2006. Optimal central bank design: benchmarks for the ECB. *Review of International Organisations* 1:202-35.

18. Meade, E., and N. Sheets. 2002. Regional influences on U.S. monetary policy: some implications for Europe. International Finance Discussion Paper 721, Board of Governors of the Federal Reserve.

19. Berger, H., J. de Haan, and R. Inklaar. 2004. Restructuring the ECB. In *Managing European Union Enlargement* (ed. H. Berger and T. Moutos). Cambridge, MA: MIT Press.

20. Waisman, G. 2003. Decision-making in the ECB's Governing Council. Should minutes and forecasts be published? Royal Economic Society Annual Conference, Paper 214.

21. Buiter, W. 2008. Central banks and financial crises. Discussion Paper 619, London School of Economics Financial Markets Group.

22. ECB. 2008. The Eurosystem's open market operations during the recent period of financial market volatility. *ECB Monthly Bulletin* (May). Frankfurt: European Central Bank.

23. Dermine, J. 2006. European banking integration: don't put the cart before the horse. *Financial Markets, Institutions and Instruments* 15(2):57-106.

24. Amato, G. 2008. La crisi dei mercate. *Il Sole 24 Ore* (October 11).

25. ECB. 2001. The role of central banks in prudential supervision. Report (available at www.ecb.eu).

26. Goodhart, C., and D. Schoenmaker. 2006. Burden-sharing in a banking crisis in Europe. Special Paper 164, London School of Economics Financial Markets Group.

27. Mayes, D., M. Nieto, and L. Wall. 2007. Multiple safety net regulators and agency problems in the EU: is prompt corrective action partly the solution? *Journal of Financial Stability* 4(3):232-57.

28. Centre for European Policy Studies. 2008. Concrete steps towards more integrated financial oversight: the EU's response to the crisis. Task Force Report (December; available at www.ceps.eu).

29. de Larosière, J. 2009. Report of the high-level group on financial supervision in the EU (February 25; available at www.ec.europa.eu).

30. House of Lords. 2009. The future of European financial regulation and supervision. Fourteenth Report of Session 2008-09.

31. Lamfalussy, A. 2001. Final report of the committee of wise men on the regulation of European securities markets. Report (available at www.ec.europa.eu).

32. Almunia, J. 2008. Statement at the "Euro at 10" conference at the Peterson Institute for International Economics, Washington (October 10).

33. Jones, E. 2009. European fiscal policy co-ordination and the persistent myth of stabilization. In *The Future of EMU* (ed. L. S. Talani). Basingstoke, U.K.: Palgrave Macmillan.

34. Eichengreen, B. 1992. Designing a central bank for Europe: a cautionary tale from the early years of the Federal Reserve System. In *Establishing a Central Bank: Issues in Europe and Lessons from the U.S.* (ed. M. B. Canzoneri, V. Grilli, and P. R. Masson). Cambridge University Press.

CHAPTER EIGHT: CENTRAL BANKING IN EMERGING MARKET COUNTRIES

1. Calvo, G. A. 2006. Monetary policy challenges in emerging markets: sudden stop, liability dollarization, and Lender of Last Resort. Working Paper 596, Inter-American Development Bank and National Bureau of Economic Research.

2. Schuler, K. 1996. *Should Developing Countries Have Central Banking?* Institute of Economic Affairs Research Monograph 52. London: Institute of Economic Affairs.

3. Fry, M., D. Julius, S. Roger, and G. Sterne. 2000. Key issues in the choice of monetary policy framework. In *Monetary Policy Frameworks in a Global Context* (ed. L. Mahadeva and G. Sterne). London: Routledge.

4. Grilli, V., D. Masciandro, and G. Tabellini. 1991. Political and monetary institutions and public financial policies in the industrial countries. *Economic Policy* 13:341–92.

5. Anone, M., B. J. Lorens, and J.-F. Segalotto. 2006. Measures of central bank autonomy: empirical evidence for OECD, developing, and emerging market economies. Working Paper WP/06/228, International Monetary Fund (available at www.imf.org).

6. Cukierman, A., G. P. Miller, and B. Neyapti. 2002. Central bank reform, liberalization and inflation in transition economies—an international perspective. *Journal of Monetary Economics* 49:237–64.

7. Carstens, A., and L. I. Jacome. 2005. Latin American central bank reform: progress and challenges. Working Paper WP/05/114, International Monetary Fund.

8. Jacome, L. I., and F. F. Vazquez. 2005. Any link between legal central bank independence and inflation? Evidence from Latin America and the Caribbean. Working Paper WP/05/75, International Monetary Fund.

9. BIS. 2006. Central banks and the challenge of development. Report (available from www.bis.org).

10. Mboweni, T. 2004. The global economy and central banking in Africa. Report, National Bank of Belgium, Brussels (November 9).

11. Dibeh, G. 2009. The political economy of central banking in the MENA region with special reference to Lebanon. In *Monetary Policy and Central Banking in the Middle East and North Africa* (ed. D. Cobham and G. Dibeh). London: Routledge.

12. Gisolo, E. 2009. The degree of legal central bank influence in MENA countries: international comparisons and macroeconomic implications. In *Monetary Policy and Central Banking in the Middle East and North Africa* (ed. D. Cobham and G. Dibeh). London: Routledge.

13. Xiaochuan, Z. 2009. Reform the international monetary system. Speech, People's Bank of China (March 23; available at www.pbc.gov.cn).

14. He, D., and L. Pauwels. 2008. What prompts the People's Bank of China to change its monetary policy stance? Evidence from a discrete choice model. Working Paper 06/2008, Hong Kong Monetary Authority.

15. Goodfriend, M., and E. Prasad. 2006. A framework for independent monetary policy in China. Working Paper WP/06/111, International Monetary Fund (available at www.imf.org).

16. Reddy, Y. V. 2008. The Indian economy and the Reserve Bank of India—random thoughts. Speech by the governor of the Reserve Bank of India at the Indian Institute of Public Administration, Mumbai (March 31).

17. Reserve Bank of India. 2000. Report of the Advisory Group on Transparency in Monetary and Financial Policies.

18. Cavioloi, A., and R. Rajan. 2008. Should emerging economies like India adopt inflation targeting arrangements? *Asia EconoMonitor* (June 3; available at www.rgemonitor. com).

19. Rajan, R. 2008. Report of the Committee on Financial Sector Reforms in India.

20. Mishkin, F. 2004. Can inflation targeting work in emerging market countries? Working Paper 10646, National Bureau of Economic Research.

21. Eichengreen, B. 2002. Can emerging markets float? Should they inflation target? Working Paper, Banco Central do Brasil (available at www.bcb.gov.br).

22. Wolf, M. 2009. *Fixing Global Finance: How to Curb Financial Crises in the 21st Century.* Yale University Press.

23. Divana, J. A. 2006. *Understanding Islamic Banking: The Value Proposition that Transcends Cultures.* London: Leonardo and Francis Press.

24. De Haan, J., and W. Kooi. 2000. Does central bank independence really matter? New evidence for developing countries using a new indicator. *Journal of Banking and Finance* 24:643–64.

25. Knight, M. 2007. Inflation targeting in emerging market economies. Speech at the Bank of Morocco (April 4; available at www.bis.org).

26. Usmani, M. T. 2001. *An Introduction to Islamic Finance.* Washington, DC: CQ Press.

27. El-Gamal, M. 2007. Incoherent pietism and Sharia arbitrage. *Financial Times* (May 23; available at www.ft.com).

28. International Financial Services London. 2008. Islamic finance. Report (available at www.ifsl.org.uk).

29. Islamic Finance Information Service (London). 2008. Available at www.securities. com/products/ifis.html.

30. Wilson, R. 2008. Islamic finance: can the GCC states provide global leadership? Report, Kuwait Research Programme, London School of Economics.

31. Wilson, R. 2007. Islamic finance in Europe. RSCAS Paper 2007/02, European University Institute, Florence.

32. Archer, S., and R. A. Abdel Karim (eds). 2007. *Islamic Finance: The Regulatory Challenge.* Wiley Finance.

33. Ainley, M., A. Mashayekhi, R. Hicks, A. Rahman, and A. Ravalia. 2007. Islamic finance in the U.K.: regulation and challenges. Paper, Financial Services Authority (November; available at www.fsa.gov.uk).

34. Cihak, M., and H. Hesse. 2008. Islamic banks and financial stability: an empirical analysis. Working Paper WP/08/16, International Monetary Fund (available at www. imf.org).

35. Akhtar, S. 2008. Financial globalization and the Islamic financial services industry. Report, State Bank of Pakistan (available at www.sbp.org.pk).

36. Zaher, T. S., and M. K. Hassan. 2001. A comparative literature survey of Islamic finance and banking. *Financial Markets Institutions and Instruments* 10(4):155–99.

37. Ayub, M. 2002. Islamic banking and finance in theory and practice. Report, State Bank of Pakistan.

CHAPTER NINE: FINANCIAL RESOURCES, COSTS, AND EFFICIENCY

1. BIS. 2009. Issues in the governance of central banks. Report, Central Bank Governance Group (available at www.bis.org).

2. Stella, P. 1997. Do central banks need capital? Working Paper 97/83, IMF (available at www.imf.org).

3. Stella, P. 2008. Central bank governance structures, policy constraints and inflation. Working Paper 08/49, IMF (available at www.imf.org).

4. Bank of Canada. 2005. *Annual Report* (available at www.bankofcanada.ca).

5. Meyer, L. 2000. Testimony before the Committee on Banking and Financial Services, U.S. House of Representatives.

6. Blix, M., S. Daltung, and L. Heikensten. 2003. On central bank efficiency. Swedish Riksbank Economic Review 3/2003 (available at www.riksbank.com).

7. McKinley, V., and K. Banaian. 2005. Central bank operational efficiency: meaning and measurement. In *Central Bank Modernisation* (ed. N. Courtis and P. Nicholl). London: Central Banking Publications.

8. Ize, A. 2006. Spending seigniorage: do central banks have a governance problem? Working Paper WP/06/58, IMF (available at www.imf.org).

9. Pringle, R. (ed.). 2005. *Central Bank Directory.* London: Central Banking Publications.

10. Pedersen, E. H. 2006. Denmark's National Bank's operating costs and number of employees in an international comparison. Working Paper 2006.35, Danmarks National-bank.

11. Central Banking Publications. 2003. *Newsmakers* (August 26; available at www.centralbanking.co.uk).

12. Frisell, L., K. Roszback, and G. Spagnolo. 2006. Governing the governors: a clinical study of central banks. Report, Swedish Riksbank (available at www.riksbank.com).

13. Brunner, K. 1981. The art of central banking. Working Paper GBP 81/6, Center for Research in Government Policy and Business, University of Rochester Graduate School of Management.

14. Heikensten, L. 2003. How to promote and measure central bank efficiency. Speech, Swedish Riksbank (available at www.riksbank.com).

15. St-Amont, P., G. Tkacz, A. Guerrard-Langlois, and L. Morel. 2005. Quantity, quality and relevance: central bank research, 1990–2003. Working Paper 37, Bank of Canada (available at www.bankofcanada.ca).

CHAPTER TEN: INTERNATIONAL COOPERATION

1. Artus, P. 2007. *Les Incendiaires: Les Banques Centrales Depassées par la Globalisation.* Paris: Perrin.

2. Group of Twenty. 2009. Communiqué from the G20 financial summit, London (April 3).

3. Lastra, R. M. 2006. History of international monetary cooperation. In *Legal Foundations of International Monetary Stability*, chapter 12. Oxford University Press.

4. Toniolo, G. 2005. *Central Bank Cooperation at the Bank for International Settlements: 1930–1973.* Cambridge University Press.

5. Meltzer, A. 2003. *A History of the Federal Reserve: Volume 1, 1913–1951.* University of Chicago Press.

6. BIS. 1930. Statute (available at www.bis.org).

7. Borio, C., and G. Toniolo. 2006. One hundred and thirty years of central bank cooperation: a BIS perspective. Working Paper 197, BIS (February; available at www.bis.org).

8. Deane, M., and R. Pringle. 1995. *The Central Banks.* London: Viking/Penguin.

9. Committee on the Global Financial System. 2006. Housing finance in the global financial market. CGFS Publication 26 (available at www.bis.org).

10. Ahamed, L. 2009. *Lords of Finance: 1929, the Great Depression, and the Bankers Who Broke the World.* London: William Heinemann.

315

11. Fratianni, M., and J. Pattison. 2001. The Bank for International Settlements: an assessment of its role in international monetary and financial policy coordination. *Open Economics Review* 12:197–222.

12. Davies, H., and D. Green. 2008. *Global Financial Regulation: The Essential Guide.* Cambridge, U.K.: Polity Press.

13. Group of Twenty. 2008. Communiqué from the G20 Financial Summit, Washington (November).

14. IMF. 2006. *Global Financial Stability Report* (April; available at www.imf.org).

Chapter Eleven: Leadership

1. ECB. 2000. The two pillars of the ECB's monetary policy strategy. *ECB Monetary Bulletin* (November).

2. Lybeck, T., and J. A. Morris. 2004. Central bank governance: a survey of boards and arrangements. Working Paper 04/226, IMF.

3. Boyle, A. 1967. *Montagu Norman.* London: Cassell.

4. Katz, B. (ed.). 1992. *Biographical Dictionary of the Board of Governors of the Federal Reserve System.* New York: Greenwood.

5. Meltzer, A. 2003. *A History of the Federal Reserve: Volume 1, 1913–1951.* University of Chicago Press.

6. Weitz, J. 1967. *Hitler's Banker: Hjalmar Horace Greeley Schacht.* London: Little, Brown.

7. Simmons, B. 2006 The future of central bank cooperation. Working Paper 200, BIS.

8. Adolph, C. 2003. Paper autonomy, private ambition: theory and evidence linking central bankers' careers and economic performance. Speech delivered to the Annual Meeting of the American Political Science Association.

Chapter Twelve: An Agenda for Change

1. Adrian, T., and H. Shin. 2009. Financial intermediaries, financial stability and monetary policy. *Maintaining Stability in a Changing Financial System.* Federal Reserve Bank of Kansas City.

2. Bean, C. 2009. The great moderation, the great panic and the great contraction. Schumpeter Lecture at the Annual Congress of the European Economic Association, Barcelona (August 25).

3. Gieve, J. 2009. Central banks need to avoid fighting the last war. *Financial Times* (May 11; available at www.ft.com).

Afterword

1. Carney, M. 2009. Remarks to a symposium sponsored by the Federal Reserve Bank of Kansas City, Jackson Hole, Wyoming (August 22; available at www.bank-banque.canada.ca).

2. Trichet, J.-C. 2009. Today's financial institutions and tomorrow's monetary order. Speech at the 19th Frankfurt European Banking Congress (November 20; available at www.ecb.int).

3. Bank of England. 2009. The role of macroprudential policy. Discussion Paper (November 21; available at www.bankofengland.co.uk).

Index

Italic page numbers refer to tables and figures